D1143249

Laws of Our Fathers

Laws of Our Fathers:
Popular Culture and the U.S. Constitution

Ray B. Browne
Glenn J. Browne

880320

Bowling Green State University
Bowling Green, Ohio 43403

Dedicated
With Deepest Appreciation and Love
To
Russel B. Nye
Friend and Companion Through the Years

CONTENTS

Preamble

Ray B. Browne and Glenn J. Browne

The popular culture—the everyday, vernacular life styles and activities and arts of the people—of the United States is both directly and indirectly controlled by the laws, and thus the Constitution, of the land. Because life in a civilized country is dictated by law and order, the Constitution has been for the past 200 years both a guarantor of the well-being and yet an inhibition to the development of the country's popular culture and the channels in which it develops. Now at the celebration of the Bicentennial of that Constitution, it is proper that we see how this magnificent instrument, which has often been called the greatest political document ever written, has affected the everyday lives of the ordinary citizens.

Popular culture has a wide political range. In general the popular culture outside the arts, which may in fact be only remotely influenced by the arts, at times seems to be politically and culturally neutral or conservative, inclined to go along with ways of life that already exist and have existed, leaving things as they are. At times it seems that popular culture percolates down from and is a kind of detritus of the elite culture. This observation, however, is less valid than it seems. Throughout life's activities, the popular culture constantly pushes out the frontier of elite culture, by demands and innovation, by necessity and choice. Architect Frank Lloyd Wright's adoption of his Prairie style homes is only one example; in this thrust an age-old, tradition-bound style of house-building revolutionized the elite architecture of a nation. In the popular arts the ferment of creativity is even more demanding and innovating.

In America the capitalistic, entrepreneurial political system has encouraged the individual statements and actions of *all* people. The result has been what one would expect: that everybody has felt free to contribute to the culture and the arts in his or her own individual way. In this development historically the elite culture has been most obvious; in the past it has been, with some major exceptions, the elite culture which has been apparently predominant. Elite culture, however, has been a growth which obviously could not dominate forever in a democracy; so the popular culture, the *vox populi*, has increasingly through the years pushed its head to the forefront. Both cultures have followed patterns; the elite has been more individualistic, more "creative" in unconventional senses, than the popular culture. To that extent elite culture may have been more radical, more insistent on change, at least in the past.

To a certain extent popular culture, and the popular arts, recapitulated the yesterdays of a nation. Russel B. Nye has properly felt that "The popular artist corroborates (occasionally with great skill and intensity) values and attitudes already familiar to his audience; his aim is less to provide a new experience than to validate an older one. Predictability is important to the effectiveness of popular art, the fulfillment of expectation, the pleasant shock of recognition of the known, verification of an experience already familiar." Yet in many other ways, popular culture, and especially the popular arts, is artistically, politically and culturally both evolutionary and revolutionary. It is evolutionary in demonstrating through the years the patterns set for it; sometimes these patterns have been set by the elite culture, sometimes by the folk culture, but more frequently by the popular culture itself. Popular culture is like all other aspects of life and nature which move inexorably forward; once a genie is released, there is no forcing it back into the bottle of the past. So the popular arts are in fact quite obviously revolutionary in concept and development.

Popular art is driven by many thoughtful and creative people whose works strongly influence and are taken into the fold by the elite world; specifically think of the remarkable radical influence of such literary works as *Uncle Tom's Cabin* and *Gone With The Wind*, the political and social flurry caused by individual stars (especially in popular music—Elvis Presley or the Beatles, for example) and the motion picture and television. At first the motion picture was the peep show and next the nickelodeon, the domain of the ethnic groups who had nothing else to do with their time than watch them and nothing better to watch, but they were culture bombs waiting to explode. At first television was despised by the elite as something small and impractical. Both, however, have widened and deepened democracy and given vast new areas for development. Perhaps popular culture, and the arts, is most revolutionary in its demonstration that in a democracy culture and the arts vote by dollars. As the culture of the middle-class, ethnic and color groups, and youth, continues to assert itself, it will become even more the dominant culture, eventually making irrelevant the minority culture which in the past ruled over society. Though the popular arts tend at times to be formulaic and conventional, to follow well-established genres and types, they still pulsate with the energy of change and with a newness and timelessness which tends to overthrow elite art both in the assertiveness of the material, the power of the practitioners, and the replacement of elite art with popular art. Elite culture has always had a skill to expand its horizons and definitions to accommodate the powerful popular individuals who threatened its hegemony, but increasingly the popular individuals have turned their backs on their elite superiors and have not wanted to be taken into their fold.

The popular arts are revolutionary in yet another way. Elite arts generally have been designed not to earn large sums of money—prestige and glory and exclusivity, yes, but not money. Popular arts, on the contrary, are designed to earn money, the more the better. Therefore in our capitalistic society, the popular arts tend to follow financial returns, and in so doing to create, for better or worse, a cash-culture, though there are many types of popular culture which are indifferent to the lure of money. It is a mistake to think that all popular arts prostitute esthetic accomplishment for financial returns; "prostitute" is the wrong concept.

Since American popular culture's purpose is to reflect, speak to and for democracy and capitalism, it generally asserts itself strongly. Because its permission to assert itself is guaranteed by the Constitution, especially the First Amendment, popular culture quite properly thinks that anything not forbidden by the Constitution is fair game for development. In pornography, for example, the Supreme Court has decided that it cannot give a definition and is therefore reluctant to make laws against it, lest those laws abridge the First Amendment. Therefore popular culture consistently tests the range of tolerance. Certain other areas of culture—such as drinking of alcohol, using drugs, driving automobiles, etc.—create fuzzy areas into which the Supreme Court moves with considerable self-consciousness and reluctance. As a matter of fact, members of the Supreme Court, the lawyers who interpret the laws, and the authorities who enforce them, being generally uncreative and therefore suspicious of the arts, have been notoriously nervous among and therefore inclined to be repressive of things creative. This tendency has been very self-consciously inhibited. There has therefore resulted a healthy tension between the creators and practitioners of popular culture and the restrictions which hold it back in its extremes.

Whereas most forms of popular culture merely live *in* the Constitution, some concern themselves directly with the information contained in the document. Utopian fiction, for example, by the very nature of its purpose in creating the ideal society, has had to worry about the forms of government in those societies. Science fiction, being a vision of the future, although it ought to grapple with new and perfect societies has contented itself generally with a continuation of present-day society in a world that is technologically-dominated and studies less the potential perfect society than the problem of how people who have not improved their attitudes or society can survive.

Detective and mystery fiction, on the contrary, has had to deal with the guarantees of the First Amendment on a more immediate and earthly level.

Through the years the authors of these kinds of works have dealt with the question in several ways. In the 1920s and 1930s, for example, the question of law and order and violence, in the world of gangsters and outlaws, authors of detective fiction saturated their works, especially in pulp fiction, with a strong reaction. It was a fiction of violence: crooks were violent, police were violent; the vigilante cop cared very little for the guarantees of the First Amendment that suspects were to be treated as innocent until proven guilty—though there was a considerable literature of lawyers who fought for the rights of individuals and for law and order.

Detective fiction through the years has developed through several ways. Much aware of the *Miranda vs. Arizona* decision (1966) nowadays—that suspects are to be informed of their rights and cannot be forced to testify against themselves without the presence of counsel—American detective fiction, some agreeing with the decision, some flouting it—is still violent, still filled with vigilante cops, with heroes who are fighting for mankind and for heroic acts. But generally crime fighters—whether private detectives or police officers—work within the law for the good of society; they may at times test the outer limits of the law and protest against it, but there are not many like James Bond, "007," who envision themselves superior to the nation's laws and therefore determined to flout them.

Generally, on the contrary, authors go to great lengths to observe the realism of their writings by outlining the *Miranda* decision in detail, as in Martha G. Webb's *Even Cops' Daughters* (1986), in which the act of informing the suspect before interrogation is explicit, as in this scene inside a police station:

> Just listen to me, would you? See this card? Read it. What it means is, you don't have to answer any questions if you don't want to and you can call a lawyer if you want one, and if you can't afford one, tell me and I'll call the judge and he'll get you one for free. And if you do start talking to me, you can stop any time you want to (p. 23).

There are, however, other fringe groups which question the authority of the Constitution in every act—the Ku Klux Klan, for instance—and many others, especially religious groups which are in full flower in the United States in 1986, that, though curbed by the worldly Constitution would actually like to heed only a higher one. "The Bible is actually the Constitution of the United States," evangelist Jimmy Swaggart, one of televangelism's superstars, asserts. "The Bible is really the unsung, hidden Constitution." These groups work constantly to erode the line separating church and state, currently with the assistance of the President of the United States, trying to slip into accepted practice prayer, or at least a moment of silence, into the public schools.

Deliberately kept dissociated from any connection with Divine power or association, the Constitution is nevertheless essentially an elitist document, written *by* legal minds *for* legal minds. Through the years the elite in control have resisted change, just as they resisted inclusion of the Bill of Rights and subsequent Amendments, claiming that the Constitution is a sacred document, an icon, incorporating all the wisdom of the "founding fathers" and therefore complete in itself. Changes if needed at all should be slow in coming and carefully planned—reacting to a present and dire need rather than anticipating one. Yet, through the years, twenty six Amendments have been made, modifying and modernizing the Constitution as times and political and social conditions have dictated. The Amendments that are most important to the people at large have been forced into acceptance by the people who benefit most from them.

Still, the elite of the country, those in control, especially the lawyers and people directing the government, are chary of letting the people ruled by the Constitution have much voice in how it should be modified. The Constitution is not to be construed as a popular document (that is, to be assumed to belong to the people who are controlled by it). Thus there is the reluctance of the elite now in 1986 to call a Constitutional Convention to take up a single item (like an Amendment legalizing school prayer or the question of abortion), though there is considerable talk about it, for fear that various pressure groups will be able to rewrite the whole Constitution, a thought generally felt by all to be something of a potential national disaster. Yet, perhaps the Convention would not be as dangerous as some people fear. Perhaps it might even be desirable. The sanctity of the Constitution as an instrument of government seems to have grown through the years, especially with the rise of anti-democratic governments throughout the world. Yet people increasingly feel that the Constitution should be dynamic and living, not static and unresponsive to needs. Thomas Jefferson looked upon it as a transitory thing, which might have to be changed every generation. Newspaperman David Broder attended a mock Constitutional Convention in Virginia in 1985 dedicated to "reacquaint today's citizens with the issues embedded in the Constitution" and discovered that the people there were not all conservative radicals who wanted to destroy the whole Constitution but were instead individuals interested only in improving it. Broder reported that more than 700 letters and calls resulted in the first two weeks after his newspaper column appeared. He reported that "Plans for celebrating the living legacy of the Constitution are under way in a majority of the states" (*Toledo Blade*, Dec. 29, 1985).

Obviously, however, most people agree that an instrument which has stabilized the political process in a country that is so mixed with ethnic, color and financial groups as the United States should not be tinkered with unnecessarily. Sometimes the price of liberty is stability.

Yet this stability rests on an elite culture that has some dangerous potential. Now at the Bicentennial Celebration of the Constitution, the single document that controls everybody's public life, the politicians in control of that celebration are narrow-visioned and short-sighted. It is bound to be a *celebration* rather than an *examination* of the true dynamics of the document. The "Newsletter of the Commission on the Bicentennial of the United States Constitution" (vol. 2, No. 1, January 1986) made that clear. In outlining projects that might be approved for this celebration, the demands are explicit: "In general, the criteria for Commission recognition are that a project must be: regional, national or international in scope; of substantial educational or historical value; directed by people with a record of successful work in the field; and organized and funded so that the likelihood of success is high." The buzz words are obviously "a record of successful work in the field," that is, conventional workers in the conventional approach to the Constitution. Excluded therefore is the approach which includes popular culture. In fact, one of the editors of this volume of papers approached the National Endowment for the Humanities with a plan to hold a national conference on the Constitution and popular culture and was told that this was not the kind of thing people in the NEH and the Commission would be interested in: Funded projects would be controlled by Constitutional lawyers and political scientists— generally only the priests touch the sacred icons! Yet the popular culture is that most deeply affected by the Constitution.

The popular culture is the most visible culture of a nation, that of the majority of the people, and is therefore easily recognized and identified, and often condemned and feared, and since it moves with so much muscle and such a loud voice is not at all easily controlled. Somewhat less visible is the folk culture, which constitutes one segment of the popular culture, but which because it is more individualistic, less committed to print or electronic media and is a minority voice, is of less concern to the protectors of the Constitution. All in all, however, the popular culture in all its manifestations is the life blood of a society and therefore of the Constitution. The hope of democracy, the popular culture chips away at the Constitution and modifies it gradually but inevitably. The inevitably of this change makes study of the relationship between the Constitution and the popular culture imperative.

Because the Constitution touches all aspects of American culture in one way or another and to one degree or another, and because popular culture is omnipresent, any collection that purports to be a survey of the Constitution and popular culture should include studies of all aspects of that culture. Such a study, however, would be far too large to be manageable. The following collection, though incomplete, attempts to be representative, to take up issues that are obvious and issues that are less than obvious. The purpose of this selection has been to demonstrate the need to study the popular culture vis a vis the Constitution, and to encourage other studies along the same line.

*   *   *

The U.S. Constitution has long been analyzed as a legal document. As the source of all legislative, executive, and judicial power in this country, the interpretations of its requirements have shaped American political, economic and legal history. But while its legal-political demands command constant scrutiny, its socio-cultural aspects have received little academic attention. To what extent has American cultural development been influenced by Constitutional guarantees and restrictions? It is the aim of this book to explore, generally and specifically, the role of the Constitution in this cultural development.

The Constitutional Convention in Philadelphia was attended by 55 white males, most of whom were lawyers. The document they produced was the most ambitious of its kind in history, guaranteeing rights to the people, and restricting the power of goverment. As Diana Raymond points out, the Constitution has been generally sanctified by historians, and new normative interpretations of the document are necessary. But as Alan Gordon shows, a mythology soon grew up around the Constitution, producing satiric as well as sanctimonious political cartoons.

The early interpretations of the Constitution invigorated the document and ensured the survival of the fledgling nation. Chiefly responsible for these interpretations was Chief Justice John Marshall, whose opinions in *Marbury v. Madison, Martin v. Hunter's Lessee, McCulloch v. Maryland* and *Gibbons v. Ogden* established judicial review of Congressional, Executive, and State court actions, federal supremacy and the Commerce Power.[1] These principles established the relationship between the federal government and the states and provided the necessary stability and security for the emergence and expansion of culture.

The human need for expression takes many forms, including the need for public discussion of ideas, the need for worship and the need for artistic endeavor. Despite the fact that the Constitution was, as Raymond and Robert Schneider point out, an essentially elitist document, the framers recognized the basic need for expression and included those types of expression they thought most important in the First Amendment. Hence freedom of speech, of the press, and freedom of religion are expressly guaranteed. The penumbra of freedom of speech and press has long been construed to include freedom of expression in many forms, including literature, art and music.

One requirement of freedom of expression is that the government remain "content-neutral" toward subject matter. This requirement is designed to protect expression which is not in the mainstream of popular American thought. Thus in a case of libel, for example, an article in the *National Enquirer* merits as much constitutional protection as an editorial in the *New York Times*. As Nathan Rosenberg points out, however, the popular media have traditionally been given less protection than so-called "serious" works.[2]

Another problem occurs in the application of First Amendment protection toward various types of media. While regulation of the "press" is expressly forbidden by the First Amendment, broadcasters in this country have always been regulated based on the "scarcity of channel" rationale. Under the current laissez-faire attitude of the Federal Communications Commission, some regulations are being removed, but there is no clearly consistent treatment of media. We live in an age of rapidly expanding media technology. As Linda Fuller points out, cable and other new technologies present perplexing legal dilemmas, and seem to suggest the need for a uniform Constitutional treatment of print, broadcast and cable media.

A related issue involves the so-called "Fairness Doctrine," the legal requirement that broadcasters air differing viewpoints on issues of public concern. As Richard Knecht points out, critics of the Fairness Doctrine claim that the rule disregards the right of broadcasters to determine the editorial content of material presented (newspaper editors are protected), and may actually inhibit speech by discouraging broadcasters from presenting any view-points at all. However, as Rep. Timothy Wirth (D-Colo.) has recently stated, the Fairness Doctrine may invigorate freedom of speech because it causes more speech, requiring broadcasters to air differing views.[3] Because broadcasting is the most popular of the popular arts, the resolution of the Fairness Doctrine dilemma is of concern to popular culture scholars.

Another collision between interpretations of the First Amendment and popular culture occurs in the area of pornography. Attempts to regulate pornography have been made since the dawn of civilization. Under the First Amendment, however, pornographic works have recently been afforded considerable protection unless, taken as a whole, they lack "serious literary, artistic, political, or scientific value."[4] During the past several years, pornography has come under attack by some feminists as humiliating and degrading to women. Despite the logical and evidentiary problems with this argument, several cities have recently enacted ordinances attempting to create a cause of action for women against authors and distributors of pornography.[5] As William Brigman points out in his exhaustive essay on Pornography and the Constitution, liberal feminists and traditional conservatives make strange bedfellows in this current battle against pornography.

A related problem also currently in the news is the attempt by a group of Washington, D.C. women, most of them wives of U.S. Congressmen or Senators, to force the enactment of legislation regulating the lyrics of rock music. The proponents would like a rating system warning parents of sexually-explicit, violent or drug or alcohol related lyrics, similar to the Motion Picture Association of America's film rating system. As Jack Santino points out in his article, this attempt by the "Washington Wives" is probably an undue intrusion into the First Amendment rights of rock singers. The chief problem is not a rating system per se; if the system were created voluntarily by a non-governmental organization it would not have the force of the state behind it. But when the government becomes involved, the state has lost its "content-neutrality" and is essentially defining what is "explicit" and what is not. Under the Supreme Court's interpretation of the First Amendment, government regulation of speech may occur only when a work is adjudged "obscene."[6] A governmental regulation of rock lyrics based on explicitness or lack thereof would therefore seem impermissible.

An older argument with the public over admissible and inadmissible content—something of the granddaddy of all such questions in the popular arts—arose in the question of what could or should be included in or out of the movies, since the movies were so powerful in society. According to Garth Jowett, in his article, the 1915 Supreme Court unanimous decision in *Mutual Film Corporation v. Industrial Commission of Ohio*, which abrogated the guarantee of freedom of speech to the motion picture industry, was a "momentous decision which would affect the course of the motion picture industry for the next thirty-five years, and have a profound effect on the nature of the content which this new medium of communication would be allowed to explore."

A final article on freedom of expression concerns not what the First Amendment specifically permits, but rather what it generally allows. In his article on the Constitution and architecture, Dennis Mann argues that the freedom which the First Amendment allows is in large part responsible for the variety of architecture, and indeed art, in this country. The lack of any degree of architectural homogeneity is the result of nearly unfettered creativity among American architects. The chief regulation imposed on architecture in this country is in the form of zoning laws, and these laws are neither theoretical nor universal. The point is that because of the political and social freedoms we enjoy, art has been able to flourish.

As mentioned earlier, the First Amendment forbids the establishment of any religion by the government and guarantees citizens the right to the free exercise of religious beliefs. As Marshall Fishwick points out in his article on religion in America, religion has always been a part of American life. But, he argues, American history does not reflect prominence by any particular religions, but rather a general collective religiousness which he terms "civil religion." This civil religion has included myths, symbols and rituals which have contributed heavily to the history of popular culture in America. Particularly recently, American religion has become quite commecialized, with television evangelists, religious pop tunes and the transformation of Christmas into a retailer's dream.

A related theme is explored in David Bromley's article on cults and the Constitution. Bromley argues that there is a public morality in the U.S., a group of generally accepted values and principles. Violation of these principles on a collective level results in what the popular media term "cults." Periodically "scares" occur in American because of fears of the actions of some group or groups. The First Amendment proscribes laws made against the exercise of religion. However, Bromley argues, fear of unusual collective behavior sometimes allows society to "override the constraints on state intervention into religious practice," despite the fact that the cult may not have violated any laws. And if thwarted on Constitutional grounds from continuing criminal proceedings, individuals may sue cults in civil court. As Bromley points out, in civil suits against cults, testimony has often involved debates over the propriety of religious beliefs, something the First Amendment appears to forbid.

The federal government is one of enumerated powers, i.e., any power not specifically given to the federal government was reserved for the states through the Tenth Amendment. The responsibility of education, although left to the states, was considered very important by the framers of the Constitution and the nation's early leaders. As Ross Pudaloff points out, the early leaders deemed education important to the political process and also as a tool for achieving cultural homogeneity (which some leaders assumed necessary for the ultimate success of the new republic). The family unit was generally considered an obstacle to education, and insofar as education sought cultural homogeneity, this was certainly the case because the family unit, with the country's considerable ethnic diversity, prevented any glimpse of cultural homogeneity. Pudaloff argues, in essence, that although education did not create a homogeneous culture, it did indeed mark the boundaries of culture.

Concern with the Constitution still plays an important role in everyday American life, as newspaper columnist David Broder points out in his article, in which he recounts a trip he took to Virginia to attend a mock Constitutional Convention to investigate the depth and power of the Constitution.

The history of the United States is largely a history of popular movements and popular myths. As Robert Schneider points out, American history is replete with popular themes, including the Agrarian myth, status anxieties, prejudice, the Abolitionist Movement, the New Deal and many more. And as W. Russell Gray shows, abolitionist John Brown is a perfect example of popular mythology in U.S. history. From the lines in *The Battle Hymn of the Republic* to Stephen Vincent Benet's Pulitzer winning poem, Brown was and remains a mythical and heroic figure in American popular culture. Myth also plays an important part in some literary works and their predictions. This was particularly true in the case of the novel *1984* with its gloomy prediction of dire convulsions that were to shake society at that date in the calendar, as Gray points out in his story of the book.

A related theme is explored by Phillip Seitz in his article on comics and contemporary society. Seitz contends that seemingly undemocratic eras in U.S. history (e.g., McCarthyism in the 1950s) have usually been justified because of the fear of attack on American values or the entire American way of life. Comics, he insists, like most other popular literature, are reflections of the society from which they are created. Cold War paranoia is the result of fear, conservatism and other insecurities; all of these issues are addressed and conquered in the comics. Comics, like any fantasy world, allow us to explore and develop principles and actions which we may not dare or be allowed to believe or practice in real life. Comics, therefore, are a release for fears of attack and other repressed anxieties.

The opposite of anxieties is self-confident and bold statements of a nation's political beliefs, which can be made in various ways. They are particularly important when made in the form of decorations on government buildings, for there they make bold statements of the government in particularly visible and impressive ways. They say what the government wants to say in a way that makes the statement support and perpetuate the government's statements. As Aileen Goodman points out in her article, the air in a nation's capital (as in Washington, D.C.) can be heavy with these statements.

In the most basic sense, laws or rules in a society are what permit culture to exist. The constraints on anarchy and chaos, and the security of living in a stable society, allow time for the creation of cultural artifacts. Law seeks to maximize stability and predictability while allowing for as much irregularity, diversity and change as possible. In this sense, law as an organizational tool is akin to the theoretical aims of all information transmission; that is, to impose only those limits necessary to insure accuracy, without unnecessarily inhibiting the range of possibilities or the potential for richness and complexity. In a democratic society, law seeks to put limits on behavior which is dangerous to society at large or which violates the rights of specific others. The history of U.S. Constitutional law is a history of the tension between the rights of individuals to behave and the right of the state to control behavior. The compromise, the continual ebb and flow between these two competing needs, determines the diversity and complexity of popular culture.

Notes

[1]Marbury v. Madison, 1 Cranch 137, 2 L.Ed. 60 (1803), Martin v. Hunter's Lessee, 1 Wheat, 304 (1816), McCulloch v. Maryland, 4 Wheat. 316, 4 L.Ed. 579 (1819), Gibbons v. Ogden, 9 Wheat 1, 6 L.Ed. 23 (1924).

[2]This problem is akin to the Supreme Court's attitude toward "commercial speech," e.g., advertising, which is certainly popular culture. Commercial speech has traditionally been accorded less protection than "pure" or "political" speech. *See Central Hudson Gas & Electric Corp. v. Public Service Comm'n of New York*, 447 U.S. 557, 65 L.Ed.2d 341,349 (1980).

[3]*Broadcasting*, Vol. 110, No. 7, Feb. 17, 1986, p. 70.

[4]Miller v. California, 413 U.S. 15, 37 L.Ed.2d 419 (1973).

[5]In the most recent decision to date, the Supreme court upheld lower court rulings that an Indianapolis law violated the First Amendment. The law had created a cause of action for women against pornography distributors under a sex discrimination rationale. The federal court of appeals had rejected the law as an attempt toward "thought control." Hudnut v. *American Booksellers Association, Inc.*, 89 L.Ed.2d 291 (1986).

[6]Miller v. California, 413 U.S. 15, 37 L.Ed.2d 419 (1973). Nor may the government use the "time, place and manner" argument. That is not part of the issue here.

Philosophical Reflections on the Constitution
Diane Raymond

MOST TREATMENTS OF THE CONSTITUTION tend to dwell almost rhapsodically on the merits of that document and the unflagging courage and selflessness of its creators. From newspaper editorials to political science texts to supposedly cold-blooded historical analyses—everywhere we hear of the almost limitless potential for resolving conflict and preserving order of that "living document." And, though we are often treated to discussions of the history of the formulation of the Constitution, we are seldom invited to explore the ways in which that treatise is historically bound. We are encouraged to view the "founding fathers" as operating with what amounts to almost divine inspiration; Catherine Drinker Bower's lengthy study of the Constitutional Convention, to cite just one example, is entitled *Miracle at Philadelphia.*[1] Though this is not to suggest that there is a complete absence of critical treatments of that period in American history,[2] it does seem that popular culture remains largely untouched by most of it. It is usually quite simple to silence a critic by deeming his/her position "unconstitutional"; and it is not uncommon to hear that same accusation flung by opponents on some issue from both sides of the fence, as we have witnessed on questions like gun control, pornography, capital punishment and the Equal Rights Amendment.

Most of us learned that the Constitution evolved as a result of the conflict between advocates of states' rights and those who favored a strong central government. Teachers (at almost any grade level) emphasize that the Constitution limits political authority and checks abuses of power, that it protects the rights of minorities in this country, that it reflects a basic pluralism which leads to input from all constituents so that, ultimately, every group has a say and no one group dominates, and that, despite whatever defects it may possess, the Constitution is the guarantor of our democratic tradition. And, so most commentators argue, the final product reflects an almost sacred balance among compromises—between liberty and protection, between a strong executive and a popular voice, between change and stability, between the interests of large states and those of smaller ones, between rich and poor—that each of us has a duty to preserve. Historian George Bancroft, for example, leaves little room for a critical investigation of the Constitution:

The Constitution establishes nothing that interferes with equality and individuality. It knows nothing of differences by descent, or opinions, of favored classes, or legalized religion, or the political power of property. It leaves the individual alongside of the individual. As the sea is made up of drops, American society is composed of separate, free, and constantly moving atoms, ever in reciprocal action... so that the institutions and laws of the country rise out of the masses of individual thought which, like the waters of the ocean, are rolling evermore.[3]

It is no wonder that most of us lack the temerity to challenge such sweeping assumptions!

In this essay I want to suggest an approach to the Constitution which I have found helpful in teaching philosophy classes. I defend this strategy for two reasons, one perhaps more obvious than the other. First, it seems to me that our almost visceral reluctance to subject the Constitution to a critical investigation is the very reason to do so. It is sometimes said that even the Devil can quote the Bible for his own purposes. And, like the Bible, the Constitution is cited in innumerable contexts, often to defend competing positions. It is interpreted and reinterpreted, used to vilify one's intellectual adversaries as well as to glorify one's own moral posture. Yet the document itself is seldom subjected to normative analysis. It seems fitting, then, in the long-standing tradition of the philosopher as Socratic gadfly that one probe more deeply, not only in an attempt to assess some of the implications of that document, but also to understand more clearly some of the key philosophical assumptions which served to guide its creators. If we agree with the ancient dictum that "the unexamined life is not worth living," then surely we must examine the philosophical underpinnings of the Constitution, for it has had and continues to have profound implications for our shared social and political life.

Second, moral philosophers casually refer to distinctions between facts and values, between description and prescription. Philosophy, we tell our students, focuses on the world of values—of "oughts"—and not simply on what is (or even could be) the case; and we tend to assume, I think, that this distinction is an obvious one. Yet, the "popular mind" frequently conflates the two, viewing the rightness or wrongness of actions as reducible to legal codes or social approval or empirical studies of custom and belief. To do so, however, is to rob philosophy of its normative underpinnings and to reduce the discipline to sociological inquiry. Students, for example, when asked to grapple with a moral dilemma—for example, should a lesbian be allowed to teach in a public school system? should pornography be allowed? should marijuana be legalized? should capital punishment be permitted for certain crimes? should a person be disconnected from a life-support system? should there be public funding for abortion?—frequently want to know what popular codes proscribe. So, they might want to hear about legal precedents, or Biblical injunctions, or the American Medical Association's Code of Ethics, or the Constitution. In part, this is a kind of ethical "laziness" which seeks out easy answers to moral questions as if it were only a question of finding the right rule book; but, in addition, it is a product of a lack of practice at formulating values and thinking critically about institutions and ideas. Students may even abandon a position if they are told that it is forbidden by the Bible or circumscribed by some article in the Constitution. Similarly, in the popular media, such codes are often seen as arbiters between competing views; if such were the case, then it would be sufficient simply to "discover" the correct interpretation of the document in question, and to apply it to the situation at hand. I want to argue that it is neither sufficient nor necessary to do so, and that exploring what this means with students is a way of illuminating philosophy and its connection to values and their justification; in addition, this strategy makes clear the futility of using cultural codes as courts of appeal in moral disputes, forcing students to think critically for themselves. Though here I choose to focus most of my attention on the Constitution, any code of ethics—religious, political or professional—would serve this purpose.

Ironically, though the disagreements and competing interests of the members of the Constitutional Convention are often cited by historians, what is more striking is just how similar those interests actually were. Of the 55 men who gathered at Philadelphia in 1787 to draw up the Constitution, the majority were lawyers, most were wealthy, 40 held government bonds, at least 15 held slaves, and at least half had money loaned out at interest. Almost all, then, had a direct interest in creating a strong federal government, from manufacturers who needed protective tariffs; to moneylenders who wanted to stop the use of paper money to pay off debts; to land speculators who wanted protection as they invaded Indian territories; to slave owners who wanted security against rebellion and runaways. And the memory of Shays' rebellion of "desperate debtors" haunted the delegates in Philadelphia; the rebellion was quelled, but many argued that its occurrence pointed to the "excesses" of democracy and cried out for a stronger government. As Hamilton noted, "the people are turbulent and changing; they seldom judge or determine right."[4] Another participant, clergyman Jeremy Belknap, put it: "Let the people be taught ... that they are not able to govern themselves."[5]

There is even some question among scholars as to how much popular support there was for this new proposal. Of the 13 states, initially 7 were against, 3 were for, and 3 were uncertain. As one historian notes, "the drive for ratification was managed by a small group of men who owned a disproportionate amount of power and prestige."[6] These supporters were able to win ratification largely because of their wealth, because they could count on the appeal of national heroes like Franklin and Washington, because they could control the media (reporting, for example, that Patrick Henry favored the new program, when in fact he was radically opposed), and even in some cases, because of bribery and threats of economic pressure (like calling in notes). This was a case of, according to one prominent

Massachusetts supporter of the Constitution, "bad measures in support of a good cause."[7]

The Constitutional Convention was not, then, a debate between the "haves" and the "have-nots," but rather between different "haves" with different interests; in fact, consensus on the issue of a strong national government was quickly reached once the smaller states were given equal representation in the Senate. This is not to suggest that the delegates were unprincipled, but rather that they did not doubt that their class interests went hand in hand with the interests of the "higher" good of society. Or as John Jay noted, "the people who own the country ought to govern it." What this should make clear is that codes—political or professional— embody the cultural and historical assumptions of their times as well as the interests of the dominant group. This is no less true for the Constitution than the Bible or the Hippocratic Oath. And the normative principles that such codes enforce will also reflect the limitations of their times. Hippocrates, for example, abjured surgery in favor of herbal and dietary remedies; in its historical context, prior to knowledge of physiology and antisepsis, such a "value" makes sense.

But codes are not simply bound by historical realities, but rather can also serve as a means to perpetuate and reinforce certain kinds of values. If we think of politics as "who gets what, when, and how,"[8] then we must look beyond the wording of the Constitution with its classic opening "we the people" to the numbers of people who were excluded from that process, including women, blacks and Native Americans. The Constitution forbids neither slavery nor the importation of slaves, but allows states to count non-free persons as "three-fifths of all other persons" for representation. In addition, as of 1787, property qualifications for voting left perhaps as many as a third of the white male population disenfrachised. Debtor jails were common; in one county jail in Massachusetts in 1785, 86 of the 103 prisoners were debtors and 6 had failed to pay their taxes. Property qualifications for holding office were so steep as to prevent most voters from qualifying as candidates. In South Carolina, for example, to be a State Senator, one had to possess estates worth at least 7000 pounds, clear of debt—the equivalent of almost 6 million dollars today. As Josiah Quincy asked

Who do they represent? The laborer, the mechanic, the tradesman, the farmer, the husbandman or yeoman? No, the representatives are almost if not wholly rich planters.[9]

Seen in this light, then, the Constitution becomes a tool by which the ruling elite maintain control. Indeed, as one reads carefully through the Constitution, one is struck by its focus on commerce and preserving stability, unlike its predecessor, the Articles of Confederation. And the Bill of Rights, it is important to note, does not open the document, but rather was added only after ratification looked doubtful. Though today it is popular to interpret the Constitution as providing for minority protection, to its formulators, the minorities to be protected were the wealthy and the propertied. And the so-called "checks and balances" we hear glorified in our civics classes actually serve to prevent a popular majority from gaining control of the government. The document is extremely difficult to amend (thus, for example, though national polls indicate that a substantial majority of Americans support the Equal Rights Amendment, it has failed to be ratified); the members of the Supreme Court hold life tenures and are appointed to the bench by the President rather than elected; the electoral college elects the President; and it was only in 1913, with the adoption of the 17th amendment, that senators were chosen through election. The "passions" of the majority, then, had to be kept in check. Indeed, Hamilton referred frequently to the "imprudence of democracy" and the "ordinary depravity of human nature."[10] Another delegate, Gouverneur Morris, argued against giving voting rights to workers:

Children do not vote. Why? Because they want prudence, because they have no will of their own. The ignorant and dependent can be as little trusted with the public interest.[11]

And, in this case, the "dependent" meant anyone who "received their bread from their employers"!

Like all other codes, the Constitution reflects certain normative assumptions about human nature itself. And the picture we glean from statements of its creators on the subject is a fairly grim one. From Federalist Paper No. 34:

To judge from the history of mankind, we shall be compelled to conclude, that the fiery and destructive passions of war, reign in the human breast with much more powerful sway, than the mild and beneficial sentiments of peace; and that to model our political systems upon speculations of lasting tranquility, would be to calculate on the weaker springs of the human character.[12]

To justify a life term for the nine Supreme Court justices, Hamilton maintains that it would otherwise be impossible to persuade candidates to leave lucrative law practices. Madison refers repeatedly to the "contradiction" between liberty and stability:

The genius of republican liberty seems to demand on one side, not only that all power should be derived from the people, but that those entrusted with it should be kept in dependence on the people, by a short duration of their appointments; and that even during this short period, the trust should be placed not in a few, but in a number of hands. Stability, on the contrary, requires that the hands, in which the power is lodged, should continue for a length of time the same, and the energy of government requires not only a certain duration of power, but the execution of it by a single hand.[13]

This tension remains largely unresolved in the liberal tradition.

In addition, codes, because they are meant to embody generalizable principles, are often so open-ended that they are highly vague and hence lend themselves to a variety of conflicting interpretations. Take, for example, the fifth commandment: Thou shalt not kill. Pacifists, just war theorists, defenders of capital punishments, and advocates of vegetarianism all may claim that they have adopted that moral principle. Who is right? Clearly not all can be, but how does one determine the normative implications of this value-claim? Some translations of the Bible new reformulate the commandment as "Thou shalt not murder," but all that maneuver accomplishes is to trap us in a hopeless circularity. The Constitution is no less problematic. Does the 8th Amendment forbidding "cruel and unusual punishment" thereby proscribe capital punishment? Does the first amendment protect all forms of speech, including, for example, pornography and political dissent? This is hardly a new issue. No more than seven years after Congress passed the first amendment, the Sedition Act made it a crime to write anything "false, scandalous, and malicious" against the government. Today, we get equally heated arguments for and against censorship of obscene materials, both positions citing the Constitution for support. "Very unpopular causes may be as freely advocated under our Constitution as those in popular favor,"[14] says one author. Contrast that with the following:

Some speech content—speech utterly without redeeming social value—is not and ought not to be protected by the first amendment.[15]

Some commentators profess to base their interpretations of the Constitution on an alleged knowledge of the inner workings of the minds of the founding fathers.

Unfortunately,this [argument against censorship] rests on a misreasding of the First Amendment. As every schoolboy used to know, the Bill of Rights was a limitation on the new Federal Government. Hence it begins, "Congress shall make no law . . . ." That merely ensured that central power would not be used in such a way as to abridge—what? Not a vague "freedom of expression," but THE "freedom of speech, or of the press"—that is, freedoms already existent, and in the forms in which they were already known, including the limitations already defining them. [This freedom] was far from absolute.[16]

In 1973 in the classic case Roe v. Wade which legalized abortion the majority view held that a concept of privacy implicit in the Constitution entailed a woman's right to an abortion; Justic White, in his dissenting view, maintained that the Court "simply fashions and announces a new Constitutional right for pregnant mothers."

Even amendments that might seem, at first glance, more clear-cut and straightforward, have lent themselves to some surprising judicial interpretations. In the landmark 1896 case Plessy v. Ferguson, the court ruled that the 14th Amendment which appeared to grant full equality to all racial minorities, could permit segregated facilities for blacks and whites:

The object of the amendment was undoubtedly to enforce the absolute equality of the two races before the law, but in the nature of things it could not have been intended to abolish distinctions based upon color, or to enforce social, as distinguished from political equality, or a commingling of the two races upon terms unsatisfactory to either.

"Individual invasion of individual rights is not the subject matter of the amendment," the court declared. Even odder, though, the Supreme Court used the 14th Amendment as protection for corporations; in 1896 alone, the Court did away with 230 state laws that had been passed to regulate corporations. Striking unions, on the other hand, were construed as acting in restraint of trade. Between 1890 and 1910, of all the 14th Amendment cases brought before the Supreme Court, 19 dealt with civil rights issues and 288 with corporations.

Though second-guessing the "real" intentions behind social codes may be interesting historically, it offers little of philosophical value. Not only is the Constitution value-laden, but so are the interpretations of that document. It is not simply a matter of determining whether some law or practice squares with a constitutional mandate. As Chief Justice Hughes once said, "We are under a Constitution, but the Constitution is what the judges say it is."[17]

Finally, most codes serve only to raise deeper, more problematic normative questions. The Hippocratic Oath, for example, instructs physicians to swear to the following:

I will follow that method of treatment which, according to my ability and judgment, I consider for the benefit of my patients, and abstain from whatever is deleterious and mischievous.

Yet this oath is an ethical tautology, demanding only that physicians do what is, in their judgment, morally right. It puts the onus on each practitioner to assess the rightness or wrongness of some course of action, based on some other indeterminate ethical standard. Even the American Medical Association's Code of Ethics, when dealing with the issue of confidentiality, reminds physicans to report such information when required by law or when in the physician's judgment to do so would be beneficial to the welfare of society. But what justifies the law in these cases? And by what standards do we judge harm and benefit?

When one considers the richness of human experience and the fallibility of the human intellect, it is no wonder that a single set of guidelines, however sophisticated, must inevitably fail to respond neatly to all of our ethical demands. In addition, no code can anticipate all of the changes wrought by contemporary technology. The Constitution has shown amazing historic resiliency and flexibility; yet each amendment, any departure in interpretation, poses new sets of normative questions.

Further, whenever one adopts some particular maxim from a code of ethics, logical consistency demands that we commit ourselves to a complete package. Those who, in support of some position they espouse, cite the Bible, for example, may wish to ignore other passages in that text which might not be so supportive or might threaten other beliefs they hold. But notice what happens when the argument is articulated:

> The Bible says adultery is wrong.
> Therefore adultery is wrong.

It should be apparent here that a crucial normative premise is missing in this syllogism, and that the complete formulation of the argument is as follows:

> The Bible says adultery is wrong.
> Whatever the Bible says is wrong, is wrong.
> Therefore adultery is wrong.

So, to be consistent, committing oneself to the argument above commits one not only to condemning adultery but also eating shellfish, wearing red, and cutting one's hair. Similarly, if one accepts the Constitution as one's personal code, one might argue, for example:

> The Constitution prohibits excessive bail.
> Therefore excessive bail is wrong.

Once again, though, implicit in this argument is the premise "whatever the Constitution says is wrong, is wrong." This would not only require that one consistently support every precept of the Constitution (assuming that one knew how to interpret and apply it properly), but it would also make questioning or changing it impossible, for what rational basis could there be for seeking to modify that is already justified? These comments make clear how important philosophical analysis is, not only in terms of conceptual clarification but also in aiding in the formulation of values.[18]

The Constitution is in many ways a progressive document: it limits the terms individuals can hold office; it assigns salaries for officeholders, and requires no religious test for holding office; and it, through the Bill of Rights, protects certain fundamental personal liberties. But the creators of the Constitution never questioned the normative assumptions of the developing liberalism of their time. In particular, they accepted inequalities in property and power which would mitigate against any genuine possibility for individual liberty. Indeed, they saw the preservation of those inequalities as coextensive with the preservation of society. Since it was "inevitable" that these inequalities would exist, it was also "inevitable" that jealousies would occur among differing fashions. The delegates to the Constitutional Convention were persuaded that strong central government coupled with the expanding geographical borders of the new nation would provide sufficient safeguards against a majority suffering from, as they put it, "popular distempers." This tension between protection of property and individual liberty is pervasive throughout *The Federalist Papers,* and it continues to plague contemporary liberalism on a multitude of issues including abortion funding, school bussing, and paternalism, to name just a few. I do not urge these points to dishearten, but only to suggest that resolving these ethical dilemmas requires much more than a careful reading of the Constitution. Indeed, it may require that we question some of the assumptions underlying it, and, ultimately, a more radical restructuring of social relations.

Mere (blind) adherence to codes without a ground in normative analysis ultimately commits one to a profound relativism in which the creation of values is simply a matter of discovering social norms. We must not be intimidated by Hamilton's insistence that this is "one of those rare instances in which a political truth can be brought to the test of mathematical demonstration."[19] To be critical of codes is to commit oneself to exploring the ideas and assumptions which underpin our shared social life. To argue that these guidelines are neither divinely inspired nor absolute is to insist on a contextual analysis of values. One will surely win no popularity contests if one pushes for a critical exploration of the Constitution. But philosophers should be wary of the temptation toward popular opinions. At least until they bring on the hemlock.

Notes

[1]Catherine Drinker Bower, *Miracle at Philadelphia* (Boston: Little, Brown, 1966).

[2]See, for example, Charles Beard's classic *An Economic Interpretation of the Constitution of the United States* (New York: Macmillan, 1913); and Howard Zinn, *A People's History of the United States* (New York: Harper Colophon Books, 1980).

[3]George Bancroft, quoted in Zinn, p. 89.

[4]Alexander Hamilton, quoted in *Records of the Federal Convention,* ed. Max Ferrand (New Haven: Yale Univ. Press, 1927), Vol. 1, passim.

[5]Jeremy Belknap, quoted in Edward S. Greenberg, *The American Political System: A Radical Approach* (Boston: Little, Brown, 1983), p. 60.

[6]Clinton Rossiter, *1797: The Grand Convention* (New York: Macmillan, 1966), p. 277.

[7]George Richards Minot, quoted in Jackson Turner Main, *The Anti-Federalists* (Chapel Hill: Univ. of North Carolina Press, 1961).

[8]Harold Laswell, *Politics: Who Gets What, When, How* (New York: McGraw-Hill, 1936).

[9]Josiah Quincy, quoted in Sidney H. Aronson, *Status and Kinship in the Higher Civil Service* (Cambrige: Harvard Univ. Press, 1964), p. 49.

[10]Alexander Hamilton, John Jay and James Madison, *The Federalist Papers* (New York: Washington Square Press, 1964), p. 149.

[11]Farrand, Vol. 2, pp. 200ff.

[12]*The Federalist Papers,* p. 73.

[13]*The Federalist Papers,* p. 85.

[14]Carl Cohen, "Skokie: The Extreme Test," in *The First Amendment in a Free Society,*

ed. Jonathan Bartlett (New York: Wilson, 1979), p. 142.

[15]Chaplinsky v. New Hampshire, 315 U.S. 568, at 572, 1942.

[16]M.J. Sobran, Jr. "I Say Lock 'Em Up," *National Review* 29, June 24, 1977, pp. 712-713.

[17]Hughes quoted in Dexter Perkins, *Charles Evans Hughes* (Boston: Little, Brown, 1956), p. 16.

[18]And these remarks hold true even if one rejects my analysis above.

[19]*The Federalist Papers*, p. 166.

Diane Raymond is on the faculty of Simmons College, Boston.

Education and the Constitution: Instituting American Culture

Ross J. Pudaloff

Minds are formed by the character of language, not language by the minds of those who speak it.

Vico *New Science*

A greater degree of civil freedom appears advantageous to the freedom of mind of the people, and yet it places inescapable limitations upon it; a lower degree of civil freedom, on the contrary, provides the mind with room for each man to extend himself to his full capacity.

Kant, "What is Enlightenment?"

THE TRANSFORMATION OF THE CONSTITUTION from political document to cultural icon has tended to obscure both the legitimacy of the opposition to its ratification and, more important, its limitations in the eyes of supporters and opponents alike. Ironically, it was the very essence of the Constitution—the federal system and the famous checks and balances used to sell it to a somewhat reluctant public—that concerned many eighteenth-century Americans. As members of what Henry May has labelled the Moderate Enlightenment, it would seem that the framers shared "the belief that *everything* can be settled by compromise."[1] The limitations of compromise, however, inhere in the strengths of the Constitution. James Madison's argument in "Federalist No. 10" that the Constitution would inhibit the power, if not the existence, of factions indicates this boundary by noting what the Constitution would not accomplish: to bring into existence the uniform culture assumed necessary for a successful polity.[2]

Whether as ideological statement, political reality or cultural guide, the Constitution could not, by its very nature as a compromise, provide a basis for a functioning social order. Even and especially after ratification and Washington's inauguration, many Americans expressed the need to create cultural uniformity for the new republic. They continued to respond to the premise underlying Montesquieu's assertion that republics could succeed only if they were geographically small: i.e., political success in a republic was a function of restriction of diversity in the population.[3] The American republic, however, was too large; its political existence acknowledged that diversity. Thus the problem confronting the theorists of culture and education was that "these United States" remained plural culturally as it did linguistically.

The arguments for a system of national education made in the last two decades of the eighteenth century emerge in context of the desire for a uniform culture to support a federal polity. Put in other terms, the interest in national education in late eighteenth-century America was a response to a situation in which the ideal of a uniform culture confronted a weakening of traditional authority.[4] This statement may seem banal both because we are always being told there is a crisis in authority and because that particular crisis has long since been evident to observers and historians. While historians have not resolved whether to consider the American Revolution a social as well as political upheaval, the central assumption of their studies has been the existence of fundamental intellectual and ideological changes throughout the eighteenth century. These changes mark the transfer of authority from persons to institutions. Education was a means of the reinsertion of authority through its imposition of a culture which all shared. The power of authority was no longer manifest in its possessor but rather in its objects. Through the familiar Enlightenment processes of division and classification, the child, the criminal and the student became the objects of power and knowledge. Cultural authority no longer called attention to itself; instead, it could be measured and proved efficacious insofar as it illuminated its products.

Traditional authority combined the visibility of the figure embodying that authority with an ideal of unity through relationship to that figure. For Americans, the most familiar example was that of Great Britain where church and state were united in the person of the king. Thus political independence was articulated in the Declaration of Independence through the series of evils "He"—i.e., the monarch—had visited upon Americans. Separation from Great Britain had repudiated this model of authority and left Americans with the problem of how to provide for a uniform culture in its absence. The Constitution, although in many respects a conservative counterweight to the Declaration, did not remedy this perceived lack especially because it abandoned the theory of virtual representation in favor of a system of representation by state and population. The other traditional source of authority, the church, was hopelessly fragmented even before the Revolution and greatly weakened, in the various states, after it. Furthermore, the Constitution detached religion from the state by omitting any religious test for citizenship and political participation.

Diversity could not be denied and only a few, including Madison, were willing to accept factions as facts of American culture as well as politics. When the first census was being debated, Madison proposed that it classify citizens by occupation. But, as Patricia Cline Cohen has recently pointed out, "the very idea conflicted with the traditional principles of a common good that embraced the entire community.''[5] Much to the dismay of later social historians, the Census did not group by occupation. The common good was not the sum of individual interests: Rousseau's General Will, however resistant it has been to complete analysis, exemplifies a conventional distinction in eighteenth-century thought between the total of individual desires and a common center to politics and culture greater than and independent of those desires. The common good was the source of identity and meaning, not the reflection of individual and group interests. Madison believed that the government and thus the society would succeed insofar as they were knowledgeable about the interests that made up society. His opponents, by far the more numerous and powerful, felt that it was the task of society to "impress," a term they took from Locke and others, the structure of the General Will upon the citizenry.

Insofar as education was to be a means of articulating the common good, theories of education should be seen as constitutive of an American culture, not as reflections of an existing reality. To summarize the contents of educational plans then current ignores their intended role as material and productive. We need, as Richard J. Storr has argued, to reconsider "the kind of questions that we put to our material."[6] So, in considering some of the concepts associated with education and their link to culture and the Constitution, I am not seeking in the usual sense to interpret these ideas, to read through or beyond them to what they cannot or will not say. Rather I am analyzing a discourse of power and identity in late eighteenth-century America in which education played a central role and thus following Michel Foucault's advice to "weigh" that "which characterizes their [statements] place, their capacity for circulation and exchange, their possibility of transformations,...."[7] I wish, that is, not to point out the truth or truths concealed within or beyond various educational schemes. Instead, I describe the logic of signification at work in terms of the goal of a uniform culture.

Nor do I desire to arraign once more a series of oppositions—federalist vs antifederalist, elite vs mass education, English vs Latin language instruction, public vs private schooling, agrarian vs commercial society, rural vs urban life, Locke vs the Common Sense philosophers, etc.— which have dominated the study of thought and politics of late eighteenth-century America.[8] This is not to say that the explication of these positions and their oppositions is or has been unimportant. It is, however, to investigate how they could exist as oppositions, to describe the logic which generated them as oppositions.

The following analysis of American culture has three aspects. First, it makes visible the relationships among education, justice and the family as parallel disciplinary institutions with the same system of signification by tracing education's rise as a master discourse. Second, it follows the strategic reformulation of power granted to education as power becomes invisible and is dispersed in culture while its objects—student, criminal, child—are instituted within their disciplines. Finally, I argue that the effort to establish an American culture of uniformity not only failed but produced those differences it intended to exclude.

*   *   *

The Constitution seems to have placed a specific obstacle in the way of any system of national education: the Tenth Amendment which reserved all powers to the states not enumerated elsewhere. Moreover, when James Madison and Charles Pinckney proposed that the Constitution include a provision for a national university, they were defeated with four states voting yes, six no, and one divided.[9] Despite this apparent legal barrier, however, both Samuel Knox and Samuel Harrison Smith, co-winners of the prize for the best system of national education offered by the American Philosophical Society in 1797, included such a university as the acme of their respective schemes.[10] Neither they nor the Society made any mention of a constitutional prohibition against the university. What was to become a staple of American politics, that education is reserved primarily if not exclusively to the states, was not obvious to the Founding Fathers. George Washington, for example, left $25,000 in stock in the Potomac River Company for the purpose of supporting a national university.[11] He did so, in large part, because the university could assist in the creation of that uniform culture by eliminating "those jealousies and prejudices which one part of the union had inbibed against another part."[12] The supporters of a national university, as did the supporters of a national system of education, ranged from arch-federalists such as John Fenno to arch-democrats such as Joel Barlow. The American political elite was, at least through the administration of John Quincy Adams, committed to a national university because they believed a uniform culture was necessary for the country to survive.[13] Local control of education, like the party system, was neither designed by nor desirable to the Founding Fathers and their peers.

Although these efforts to found a university and a system failed, the failure should not cause us to overlook the role education was designed to play in the new republic.[14] Regardless of their stances on the formal structure of education, these Americans agreed, following Montesquieu in particular and the tenor of the Enlightenment in general, that education was central to political success in and of a republic. Although differences about the form and content of education are not to be slighted, one must first note the meaning Americans assigned to education. This was that education, because of its overriding importance in the absence of and in opposition to king and church, must be reorganized. The success of Rousseau's *Emile* suggests this broader interest. For Americans, we might say that even those who disagreed with Rousseau's prescriptions agreed about the centrality of education and assented to its removal from parental control.

Education, that is, had become integral to politics. Schools were conceived as primary disciplinary intitutions with responsibilities that went far beyond the inculcation of literacy. In fact, any division between the educational and disciplinary roles was inconceivable to American thinkers. All the reformers were in agreement on the crucial point: the localism and particularity of American education was just what was wrong not only with education but with the country itself. Education could provide the cure; no issue was too small. From the exhortations to reform spelling to the movement for a national university, education was perceived as the means to American success. All agreed with Benjamin Rush's opening statements in "Thoughts Upon the Mode of Education Proper in a Republic" (1786): "The business of education has acquired a new complexion by the independence of our country. The form of government we have assumed has created a new class of duties to every American."[15] Clearly Rush is invoking republican virtue as the touchstone of the republic. Just as clearly, he envisions education as the means of transforming the people although by "every American" he means only while males. Such a transformation, according to federalists and antifederalists alike, could only occur if there were an all-embracing system of education. By all-embracing, of course, was meant not the inclusion of everyone but the total inclusion of those selected to receive and be altered by education. Only then could Americans become, in Rush's now infamous phrase, "republican machines."[16] His language is critical. It asserts that uniform identity had to be created among the citizens if it were to be established in the nation.

By a necessary definition, a republican education was a mass education, the model for which the former colonists found in what the British called an "English education."[17] This term had originally designated a curriculum which deviated from the traditional liberal education through its omission of Latin and Greek. Instead, it was an education conducted in English and concerned with the study of the English language. An "English education" was directed toward groups who were excluded by reasons of birth, wealth or religion from the system of schooling established for the genteel, Anglican upper class male. Thus historically an "English education" was shaped by the distribution of power within Great Britain although one might argue that it represented some erosion of that distribution. Still, knowledge was not power; the middle class and the Dissenters did not come to political power in Great Britain despite their rising rate of literacy.

The commercial revolution, fostered in large part by the confluence of mercantilist economic thought and the growth of the British empire, meant that an increasing number of people must be literate and numerate. Hence the proliferation of English language grammars and dictionaries in the eighteenth century as the language was standardized. This standardization certainly made access to literacy easier and did so in the interests of commerce and trade. These grammars often included readings whose praise of trade as "so noble a Master"[18] made explicit the link between economic demands and educational expansion. A rising literacy rate was not, however, necessarily associated with the spread of liberal values and democratic politics. While some, like the seventeenth-century colonial governor of Virginia, William Berkeley, equated schooling with sedition, the evidence about literacy and politics suggests that literacy was as compatible with reaction as it was with revolution, if not more so. Outside what was to become the United States, the two most literate countries in western Europe were Scotland and Sweden. In both countries, close to universal male literacy was achieved by intense educational labor of the national church and, according to Kenneth Lockridge, served "to reaffirm traditional values in a time of social transition."[19]

The schoolbooks of the newly literate never failed to remind the students of their place in the scheme of things. Thomas Dilworth's *A New Guide to the English Tongue* (originally 1740) provides a typical example by conjoining its acceptance of its place below a liberal education with calls for deference on the part of its students. Part III of Dilworth's grammar was intended for those "as have the Advantage only of an English education."[20] For those students the message remained what the rest of society told them: "Enquire not into the Secrets of God, but be content to learn your Duty according to the Quality of your Person or Employment."[21] Dilworth's text was quite popular in America; there were nearly forty editions between 1747 and 1840, including one used by Abraham Lincoln.[22] Its longevity suggests that one must look at other elements of the text and of language study to explain the politics of language study in the early United States.

Those politics are present in the concept of the English language displayed in the majority of eighteenth-century grammars, one which differed from Dilworth's assumption that the grammar of Latin provided a model for that of English. These grammars asserted that English grammar differed from that of Latin, further attacking the notion that the study of classical language was the necessary preliminary to competence in English. For example, Robert Lowth's *A Short Introduction to English Grammar* (originally 1762), more popular than Dilworth's text in America, denied the existence of the ablative case in English.[23] The separation of the two grammars made it possible to grant the study of English a higher value than heretofore. Lowth himself was the Bishop of London and certainly had no social or even intellectual revolution in mind. His patriotism meshed with the turn against general grammar which was itself an index of rising nationalism in the latter half of the eighteenth century. Insofar as Lowth suggested an equality of national grammars, he did so precisely because the extension of literacy posed new problems for social control in an era when access to literacy and access to power were becoming distinct. Lowth's argument for a unique and perfect English grammar, one adopted by Americans, established a hierarchy between the language and its ordinary use: "It is not the language, but the practice that is in fault."[24] That is, language was already conceptualized in Great Britain what it needed to become, even more so, in America: a disciplinary institution whose function was to produce a stable and unequal society.

An "English education" was the education for the middle class and, regardless of the demographic truth of the assertion, everyone agreed that the United States was the middle class if only by virtue of the extensive economic opportunities available. Everyone also agreed that a successful republican government absolutely depended upon universal white male literacy. At this point, what was not said by the theorists and reformers is crucial to an understanding of education's function in the republic. In the flurry of proposals about education, which can be divided into those concerned with the English language and those proposing systems of education in English, there were never any claims that the citizens were illiterate. It was easy enough to scoff at the ways in which Americans received their educations. John Davis, teacher, traveller and writer, quoted the competition: "*Anthony Macdonald* teaches boys and girls their grammar tongue; also Geography terrestrial and celestial.—Old hats made good as new."[25] Davis' sarcasm should not obscure the central fact about literacy. While it is true that literacy rates are notoriously hard to determine, both contemporary and modern observers have agreed that eighteenth-century Americans had one of the highest literacy rates in the world. Kenneth Lockridge states flatly that by 1760 literacy was "the basic condition of men in New England" and that male literacy "rose to the two-thirds level by the early eighteenth century, then stagnated there for the rest of the colonial era" in Pennsylvania and Virginia.[26] If anything, Lockridge's conclusions about the areas outside New England may be low. Even the most isolated areas of the republic had achieved very high literacy rates by the eighteenth century. According to Richard Beale Davis, male white settlers in frontier South Carolina at this time had a literacy rate between eighty and ninety percent.[27] At least in the narrow sense of the term, literacy had been achieved when the republic came into being.

The educational mechanisms of colonial America, reinforced in some cases by religiously inspired laws, had produced a level of literacy unparalleled except, as Lockridge points out, in Scotland and Sweden where centralized national efforts achieved the same result. The combination of private tutoring, dame schools, district schools, intinerant teachers and, most important, the family had combined to raise the literacy rate in a mostly rural country. It would seem that institutionalized national education was neither necessary nor feasible. Furthermore, the failure to establish uniform systems of education after the Revolution did not apparently hinder access to schooling and literacy. Despite the lack of a common school system, teacher certification, a uniform curriculum and pedagogy, and a secure funding basis, the patchwork system worked at least as well after the Revolution as it had before. New York City, for example, saw a steady and dramatic rise in school enrollment between 1750 and 1825. At the earlier date, 37% of children under twenty attended school; by the later date, 60% of that group did so.[28] And what was true for New York held for the rest of the country: the "proportion of children attending school each year was rising, particularly among girls and particularly in the Northwest."[29]

What mattered, then, was not so much the achievement of literacy as control of the conditions under which literacy was inculcated and through which a literate population would appear. The movements to standardize American English and to establish a national system of education were assertions of the culture's power to legitimate knowledge and identity. An "English education" in America claimed the power to institute norms of language and behavior, norms from which any deviation would be severely punished, as will be demonstrated.

*   *   *

American education would make American politics possible by setting the rules for and marking the boundaries of the culture. Typically, recommendations for a national system of education were embedded within rhetorical relationships that describe the culture destined to emerge. These relationships were precise, seldom varied, and central to educational achievement. The student and the bodies of knowledge were the effects of education, not its cause. That is, the discourse of education in late eighteenth-century America was united in the minds of its theorists and practitioners with issues now peripheral to education. Education did not just promise more social benefits; it presented the schoolbook and the classroom as the sites from which the culture would appear. The republic rested on the virtue of its citizens; their virtue could be guaranteed only by the machinery which produced them and it.

Two of the most frequently invoked of these related discourses were those of justice and criminality and the state and family. They were binary discourses. In each, the first term represented a universal truth and good, while the second was particular and dangerous. Each pairing is a hierarchy, an appropriation of the narrower concept by the more extensive one. Each second term is a point of resistance which must be accommodated as it is controlled. Each hierarchy was delicately balanced; subversion of one imperiled the other. The wonder is not that education could not deliver on its promises of ending criminality and restructuring the relationships between state and family and between individual and state. The wonder was that eighteenth-century Americans believed that these tasks were possible. The irony is that failure valorized those institutions and beliefs which had been perceived as defects.

Although writers often differed in their specific recommendations, they all participated in the discursive logic which linked education with justice and the family. Sometimes, indeed, education was not the announced topic of discussion and appeared in a treatise ostensibly devoted to other topics. I do not wish to minimize the practical relationships at work; obviously a commercial country needs a significantly larger number of literate individuals than a peasant society. Yet the very success of American education before and after the Revolution, combined with the failure of educational planners to mention illiteracy as a pressing social problem, suggests that practical reasons do not account for these rhetorical and political relationships.

These relationships and their dependence upon a uniform culture are nowhere more evident than in Thomas Jefferson's *Notes on the State of Virginia*. Although it predates the Constitution, *Notes* shares with later texts the desire to create that uniform culture from which a national identity could emerge. Written as a series of responses to queries from the secretary of the French Legation at Philadelphia during the Revolutionary War, *Notes* may appear episodic and unstructured. Yet Jefferson's text does possess thematic and structural coherence: the ideal of cultural uniformity gives rise to the logic which connects Jefferson's discussion of education, justice, race and agrarianism. *Notes* is well-known for its defense of the American environment against Buffon and Raynal's thesis that all forms of life degenerate in the new world. That is, it engages the materialism of the Enlightenment on its own ground. Yet, in doing so, Jefferson included culture as a material factor in the production of social stability. His educational reforms cannot be evaluated apart from his understanding of culture as a system of production. The failure to observe this link has led to the discovery of a seeming contradiction between Jefferson's democratic egalitarianism expressed in the extension of free education to all and his characterization of ordinary people in that discussion: "the best geniuses will be raked with the rubbish annually."[30] The contradiction is only apparent, the product not of the logic Jefferson used but rather of an abstraction called Jeffersonianism which did not appear until well into the nineteenth century.

His logic establishes the relationships between the categories as well as the categories themselves. Jefferson's discussion of education gains its meaning from its place in the text. It appears in Query XIV on the "administration of justice and the description of the laws," rather than in the chapters on the "progress of human knowledge" or "the colleges and public establishments,...." Query XIV is best known for its discussion of slavery and race in which Jefferson urged emancipation coupled with removal of the freed blacks from America. This combination has presented the same problem of reconciliation as has his proposal on education with its characterization of ordinary people. Although justice demanded emancipation, nature, according to Jefferson, obliged emigration: "To these objections [to having blacks stay], which are political, may be added others, which are physical and moral."[31] Jefferson's reasoning on race derives from a premise with which almost all agreed, although many quarrelled with its application in this case. No republican state could tolerate natural differences in its population; insofar as he believed that blacks were not members of the same species as whites, there could be no place for them in Virginia. His racism did not contradict his republicanism; it was a logical, if not necessary, accompaniment.

The sequence of this chapter—description of the laws, advocacy of emancipation and removal, proposals for reform in the system of legal punishments, and the creation of a state system of education—derives from the perceived necessity that a uniform citizenry was essential for the success of a republic in the new world. Only with visible and uniform subjects— where the term refers both to the citizen and the one who is subject to authority—does it become possible for Jefferson to construct the graded classification schemes for education and punishment while urging removal of the blacks because they cannot be made identical to the rest of the people. We can recognize the democratic implications of Jefferson's educational ideas: "we hope to avail the State of those talents which nature has sown so liberally among the poor as the rich."[32] As well, we ought to recognize that education is more than just a counterweight to criminality. Justice and education, the courtroom and the schoolroom, are disciplinary institutions whose function is judgment, evaluation and grading.

A republican culture could succeed only by treating everyone alike. To do that, it first needed to insure that everyone was the same. "Nature" was Jefferson's code for this guarantee. His attack on cities and commercialism and his apostrophe of farmers as "the chosen people of God"[33] contrast a society in which differences are mediated but retained by exchange with the vision of a social order in which all are the same. Republican virtue demanded a uniform citizenry which, in turn, education promised to produce. Samuel Harrison Smith stated the proposition most explicitly: "for the more men think, the more they resemble each other, and the more they resemble each other, the stronger all their mutal attachment be."[34] Education, that is, could not overcome natural differences. However, within the boundaries of this restriction, education guaranteed virtue through homogeneity.

Other writers were more optimistic about the power of education to inculcate virtue, so much so that they omitted the logic of the inverse relationship between education and criminality. For Benjamin Rush, this was self-evident. When he urged the state of Pennsylvania to establish a public school system in 1785, Rush thought it enough to point out that the "German Lutherans in Pennsylvania take uncommon pains in the education of their youth."[35] It was conclusive evidence of the benefit of education that "not one of this society has submitted to the ignominy of a legal punishment, of any kind, in the course of the last 17 years."[36] The idea of education, like the idea of justice, was inseparable from its institutional nexus. Almost certainy, when Rush referred to "ignominy," he did not have prison in mind. Rather, as is the case in Jefferson's proposed criminal punishments, Rush was thinking of sentences that were public in nature such as the stocks, mutilation, or hanging. Thus it is no surprise that Rush, who was the great advocate of the school, also participated in the movement to transform the treatment of criminals from public display to private incarceration. In "An Inquiry into the Effects of Public Punishments upon criminals and upon society," he drew the parallel between prison and school to argue for the penitentiary as the mode of punishment: "If crimes were expiated by private discipline, and succeeded by reformation, criminals would probably suffer no more in character from them, than men suffer in their reputation or usefulness from the punishments they have undergone when boys at school."[37] Rush's optimism about reformation and about education derives from placing the individual within an environment that controls him completely.

Thus the two disciplinary institutions, the school and the prison, appeared at the same moment in American history. The American Philosophical Society had culminated two decades of debate about an American education with its 1797 call for essays on the best system. Between 1796 and 1800, New York, New Jersey, Virginia, Kentucky and Massachusetts either appropriated funds for or completed the construction of state prisons.[38] School and penitentiary isolated the individual from the community, putting him instead in relationship to a totalitarian power whose goal was to remake the individual in the image of the institution. An effective school—which is to say one part of a national system—would make the penitentiary unnecessary by doing earlier what the prison did later. Robert Coram, the most "democratic" of the writers on education, came close to promising the abolition of crime when he argued that "A SYSTEM OF EQUAL EDUCATION"[39] could eradicate the social evils occasioned by the unequal distribution of property. Samuel Smith, although inclined to defend the rights of property, agreed, at least about the inverse relationship between education and crime: "The moment, however, which marks the universal diffusion of science, by withdrawing the temptation to, as well as the means of, injury, will restore knowledge to its original purity and lustre.''[40] If Smith was more cautious about the sequence of events, he shared with Coram and Rush the certitude that knowledge could be restored and crime eliminated only through the institutionalization of a national system of education.

The agreement on the necessity of a national system transformed the British debate on the relative merits of a private education, one within the family, versus those of a public education, one at school. In the United States, this became an argument whether education should take place in the midst of society or withdrawn from it. Both sides shared two values. First, they agreed that the appropriate environment for a school was one in which the student was under the greatest possible control, was, we might say, visible at all times and places. Education would succeed insofar as it placed the student in a world from which he could not imagine escaping. Enlightenment was not merely the description of the extension of knowledge. It was as well the trope of power. So Samuel Knox argued that an urban education was preferable because it made any withdrawal into privacy and vice more difficult: "But it requires no very elaborate proof to manifest that most dangerous temptations to vice more effectively succeed in the private and retired shades of bad example, and domestic indulgence, than in the social scene, bustling crowd or public assembly.''[41] That is, despite the dangers of the city, of which Knox was certainly aware, its great advantage was the opportunity to keep the student under observation at all times.

The second shared value is also present in Knox's statement. Vice could be controlled only if the school were clearly dominant over the family. "Domestic indulgence" was perhaps the most dangerous and certainly the most common form of interference with education. Thus the family, itself the prime and most efficient educator, came under attack as the locus of error and an impediment to reform. Often this attack was couched in the rhetoric of the Whig ideology. For example, Benjamin Rush balanced the relative merits of the family and state through education: the pupil should "be taught to love his family, but let him be taught at the same time that he must forsake and even forget them when the welfare of his country requires it.''[42] The best indication of the power assumed to be inherent in a national system of education is not the ranking of state over family. Rather it is present in Rush's assumption that any student will "be taught to love his family" at school rather than at home.

To some extent, of course, this revision of the power of the family reiterates the rhetoric of the Revolution which had asserted that the colonies were grown children who should no longer be kept in a childish dependence upon Great Britain. That rhetoric is central to Thomas Paine's *Common Sense*, to pick only the most famous example. Furthermore, as Jay Fliegelman has recently demonstrated, its political use was only a part of a larger cultural ideology which Americans had derived from their readings of such books as *Robinson Crusoe* and *Clarissa*, readings which stressed the potential for tyranny in parental power.[43] In politics and literature, late eighteenth-century Americans never got very far from an awareness of this tyranny. *The American Museum* printed "Maxims for republics" from Algernon Sidney and included among them his advice about the relative merit of state and family: "A good citizen is the highest character for a man in a republic. The first duty we owe is to God— the second to our country—and the third is to our families. The man who inverts the gradation of these duties, breaks in upon the order of nature, established by God for the happiness and freedom of the world."[44] ·A republic could not tolerate the existence of institutions with competing claims on individuals. The family thus became the object of attack as an institution, not just because certain types of families might be tyrannical.

The family was local and particular; a republican education was universal and thus at odds with the family.[45] Inevitably, then, educational theory tended to view social divisions, even the time-honored one of the rich and poor, with suspicion. Education began and ended with keeping students "in a state of subordination without respect to persons."[46] Those children who were indulged and spoiled were at the greatest risk: "the rod is often necessary in school; especially after the children have been accustomed to disobedience and licentious behavior at home."[47] At particular issue here were children raised in what Phillip Greven has denominated the "genteel mode." They were, according to Greven, members of families which "cherished and fostered a sense of domesticity and intimacy within the family group."[48] These, not surprisingly, were the children most likely to receive a private education from a tutor and/or be sent off to boarding school—in either case, missing a public education. It is a good measure of the importance granted to education's role in the production of culture that these writers believed it necessary to include upper-class children in a national system. It is, as well, an important indication that the family, especially the best families, was regarded as an impediment to the success of the United States. To the extent children were removed from state control, not only they but the entire society were damaged. The issue was, as always, the establishment of authority. As a "Letter on education," probably written by President Witherspoon of Princeton, put it: "to establish, as soon as possible, an entire and absolute authority over them."[49] Authority, like the culture of the United States, was indivisible.

The concern about upper-class families resulted from the realization that they, unlike the rest of society, possessed educational alternatives. It did not mean that discipline should not be imposed upon the children of the middle and lower classes. The planners silently assumed that these either would welcome the discipline or could do nothing about it.[50] Educational theory denigrated the idea of the family as anything other than a reflection of the culture. The actual family and its educational role represented points of resistance which must be overcome. Samuel Harrison Smith's treatise returns time and again to the dangers of the family. According to Smith, the "one principle" essential for the success of his national system was the inclusion of "all children."[51] Smith attacked the family's authority from a variety of eighteenth-century points of view. He worried about the "negligence" of parents, asserted youthful innocence by citing the "attachment to truth which is the property of the unperverted," noted, like a good American revolutionary, the dangers of "an entire dependence onto parents," and linked "independent reflection and conduct" with freedom "from rigid parental authority."[52] Smith's catalogue is comprehensive. He was not listing particular defects of families in order to arrive at remedies to assist the family. The problems were, rather, the inevitable consequences of the family's strength, its capacity to resist the culture. With the possible exception of "negligence," the other concerns testify to the family's success in childrearing and identity-formation as the calls for a national education system acknowledged the family's efficacy in inculcating literacy.

The Whig tradition, as the maxim from Sidney states, had ranked the state higher than the family. However, by making deviation from this order a sin, it had implied that resolution was individual rather than cultural. Given the task of creating a wholly republican culture, Americans transformed the relationship of state and family into an institutional conflict with a social solution. Smith concluded his discussion of the family by quoting Cambaccres: "It is proper to remind parents, that their children belong to the state, and, that in their education, they ought to conform to the rule which it prescribes."[53] The family had to be weakened, parental authority had to become a permeable membrane, so that republican virtue could be extended to the next generation. That is, as the one universal institution in American society, education attacked the family because the latter was not universal. When Americans began to call Washington the "Father" of their country, they were doing more than honoring his achievements. One "Father" meant one country. The ascription of paternity subverted the claims of all other fathers.

The Enlightenment critiqued the family at the point where, in the nineteenth century, the family was to derive its strength: as a mediating institution between private and public realms of experience and as a structure which protected domestic, emotional and religious values from the onslaught of an unfriendly outside world. No such need occurred to most late eighteenth-century Americans. The rebellion against parental tyranny, not the dangers of cultural hegemony, occupied their attention. The irony may be that the comprehensive assault on familial tyranny itself could have had a significant role in the creation of the most valued aspect of Americanism: individualism. The assault did that in two steps. First, it subordinated all sources of values to the standard of whether they contributed to the identity of the individual and the culture. Second, culture was defined as an abstraction which necessarily differed from actuality. In a democratic culture, Tocqueville pointed out, men were more willing to "sacrifice themselves for mankind" than to "sacrifice themselves for other men."[54] The attempt to create a uniform citizenry led to a situation in which each citizen looked inside himself for guidance.

*   *   *

Only God remained uncriticized. However, the writers on education attempted to insert education where theology had been. Education was, according to Robert Coram, *"the rock on which you must build your political salvation."*[55] Coram's own religious beliefs are not at issue here. Rather, it is education's role as the text which would write American culture. An equation of education and religion marks almost all the plans. Even if Coram were to be dismissed as a wild radical, Samuel Harrison Smith and Samuel Knox, the authors of the prize-winning essays, were certainly not so regarded by the American Philosophical Society. Smith's rhetoric was as dramatic as Coram's, though perhaps less startling to a people brought up hearing about the errand into the wilderness. The promise of education was that of the Lord of Sinai: "For the era is at hand when America may hold the tables of justice in her hand, and proclaim them to the unresisting observances of the civilized world."[56] The concept of universal truth found a new home in the schoolroom.

These writers sought less to eliminate religion than they did to appropriate it. When Noah Webster, for example, argued against the use of the Bible as a schoolbook, he did so in the name of religion: "In ours [country], it is as common as a newspaper, and in schools, is read with nearly the same degree of respect."[57] Despite a sincere respect for religion, Webster and the other writers were redefining its place as private. Education would take on its mantle of authority and as the means of providing unity and uniformity. Samuel Knox described his vision of the national university as the generative center of American life: "Considered in this point of view, and the different seminaries connected with it, it would resemble that great source and centre of light to the Natural world, which, together with the primary and secondary bodies enlightened and preserved by its influence, form that wonderful, that harmonious system, which just excites our adoration of him, who is the great source of all knowledge."[58] Education was the central figure of a new trinity which, as it enlightens, gives this world and its inhabitants their life.

The schoolroom was a world in which institutional power produced the student through the relationships that shaped it and him. Samuel Knox, for instance, urged that students sit in "pews somewhat similar to those common in churches"[59] undoubtedly to remind the students of education's cultural place. But Knox's parallel of church and school was not exact. He also proposed that the pews in the classroom rise in order that the teacher could be seen by all."[60] In church the believer looks up and ultimately beyond the building to what it imperfectly represents; in school the student is enclosed within a self-sufficient and totalized world of which he is the representation. The teacher is not so much an actual person as he is a necessary figure who gives order by his place in the world. Knox's teacher was the necessary center to the universe of the schoolroom, as education was to the republic, and as America was to the world.

We may admire the glory of this vision or recoil from its grandiosity. We recognize that no national system ever existed outside the minds of the writers. But we must also recognize that the discourse of education, justice and the family sought to produce an American culture free of conflict and faction because it was composed of a uniform citizenry. Indeed this desire for unity and uniformity may be the Enlightenment's legacy to us. If so, to conclude with this desire would imply that this discourse succeeded at least in its claim to represent totally the world. But as discursive unities must suppress in order to appropriate, I conclude with that suppression necessary for this gesture of appropriation: the exclusion of women. The attempt to inculcate republican virtue and to insure identity depended upon the exclusion of women from the school and thus from the world. Male republican freedom and female servitude appear together in America. In the *Memoirs of Carwin*, Charles Brockden Brown makes explicit what the other writers silently omitted: that participation in the much-desired "empire of reason" is possible only through a sexualized distribution of power. Ludloe tells his pupil Carwin that his freedom, his citizenship in the "empire of reason" must come at the expense of another's liberty: "This relation is *sexual*. Your slave is a woman; and the bond, which transfers her property and person to you, is ... marriage."[61] Free citizens were produced by totalitarian schools, free men by unfree women.

Aiming for all, the discourse of education constituted the feminine realm as one which had no voice and no existence. Restricted from the public world, women found a privatized, interior life, ironically liberated from the political demands of American culture and its imposition of uniform identity. Women thus came to speak the language of those feelings omitted from the regimen of education, a language which bears the mark of its genesis as it articulates a criticism of republican virtue.

Notes

[1]Henry F. May, *The Enlightenment in America* (New York: Oxford, 1976), p. 99. May does not address the issue of cultural uniformity and hence, I argue, may overemphasize the differences among his four-part classification: the Moderate, Skeptical, Revolutionary and Didactic Enlightenments. It is true that such men as John Adams and James Madison were

skeptical about the possibility of establishing a uniform culture. But more of their contemporaries than heretofore observed shared the desire and belief. In any event, "everything" could not be resolved by compromise for compromise in politics made uniformity elsewhere more necessary.

[2]Thus Madison constructed his argument for the containment of factions by first arguing that the causes of faction could not be removed. His argument was acceptable insofar as it was confined to politics.

[3]Montesquieu's statement is found in Book 4 of his *The Spirit of the Laws*. It is a text central to the American Whig tradition, often cited and seldom controverted.

[4]A persuasive recent example of the response of literary intellectuals to the crisis in their authority is Emory Elliott, *Revolutionary Writers: Literature and Authority in the New Republic* (New York and Oxford: Oxford Univ. Press, 1982). Elliott's text is particularly useful because it considers the work of Timothy Dwight, Joel Barlow, Philip Freneau, Hugh Henry Brackenridge, and Charles Brockden Brown as articulating a series of strategies to this crisis. He traces the common ground of their writing rather than, as is traditional, summarizing their ideas in order to measure the political and literary differences among them. I would disagree, however, with Elliott's statement that "outmoded literary principles ... limited their possibilities and stifled true originality" (p. 49). Here Elliott seems to ignore his own premise that continuity within a period depends upon discontinuities between periods and instead suggests that there is a linear, progressive development of literature, defined as a body of writing set aside from cultural influences, culminating in the American Renaissance.

[5]Patricia Cline Cohen, *A Calculating People: The Spread of Numeracy in Early America* (Chicago: Univ. of Chicago Press, 1982), p. 163. Not until the census of 1820 was "the common good ... broken into constituent parts" (p. 164), a fact which suggests the power of the earlier concept as well as the impact of what is too-narrowly called the Jacksonian Revolution.

[6]Richard J. Storr, "Commentary: An Historian of Education Looks at the Newagen Study," in Alexandra Oleson and Sanborn C. Brown, eds., *The Pursuit of Knowledge in the Early American Republic: American Scientific and Learned Societies from Colonial Times to the Civil War* (Baltimore: Johns Hopkins Univ. Press, 1976), p. 342. Storr continues to suggest that educational institutions illustrate "shifting American attitudes toward the responsibilities of the family and the state" (p. 342), although he seems to imply that the family's loss of educational tasks was a new idea in nineteenth-century America.

[7]Michel Foucault, *The Archeology of Knowledge*, trans. by A.M. Sheridan Smith (New York: Harper & Row, 1972), p. 120. In addition to *The Archeology*, I am also drawing upon Foucault's *Discipline and Punish: The Birth of the Prison*, trans. by A.M. Sheridan Smith (New York: Vintage, 1979) for its account of the transformation of authority at the end of the eighteenth century and for the rise of institutions which functioned to produce their subjects for treatment, education and reform. In a more general sense, I am also indebted to Foucault's *The Order of Things: An Archeology of the Human Sciences* (New York: Vintage, 1973) for its description of what Foucault labels the "classical *episteme*." Despite the American publication dates, *The Archeology* was written after *The Order* and modifies its argument somewhat. *The Archeology* offers a more complex concept of representation, one which better accounts for contradictions in a period by stressing what endures over long periods of time.

[8]In *Federalists in Dissent: Imagery and Ideology in Jeffersonian America* (Ithaca, N.Y.: Cornell Univ. Press, 1970), Linda Kerber argues "that what united members of the post-Revolutionary generation on matters of educational theory was quite as significant as what divided them" (p. 96). For obvious reasons, however, historical and scholarly attention has been fixed on the differences as Kerber's title makes clear.

[9]David Madsen, *The National University: Enduring Dream of the USA* (Detroit: Wayne State Univ. Press, 1966), pp. 21-26. Despite its title, Madsen's own evidence makes clear that the "dream" was episodic rather than enduring.

[10]The full titles of these two essays are: Samuel Knox, *An Essay on the Best System of Liberal Education, Adapted to the Genius of the Government of the United States. Comprehending Also, an Uniform, General PLAN for Instituting and Conducting PUBLIC SCHOOLS, in this Country, on Principles of the Most Extensive Utility* (Baltimore: Warner

and Hanna, 1799); and Samuel Harrison Smith, *Remarks on Eduation: Illustrating the Close Connection Between Virtue and Wisdom: To Which is Annexed, A System of Liberal Education* (Philadelphia, 1797).

[11]David Madsen, *Early National Education: 1776-1830* (New York: Wiley, 1974), p. 9.

[12]Quoted in Madsen, *National University*, p. 30.

[13]Madsen, *National University*, pp. 21, 44.

[14]A parallel to the national university was the suggestion from John Adams and others to form a national language academy, an idea which bore no institutional fruit. Such suggestions are summarized in Shirley Brice Heath, "A National Language Academy? Debate in the New Nation," *Linguistics* 189 (1977), 9-43. Heath argues that the failure to establish an academy illustrated that it "could not be reconciled with the democratic political theories of the United States" (10), asserting rather that a tolerance for pluralism characterized the new republic. But she makes two significant errors. First, she asserts the existence of "widespread illiteracy" (9) as a social problem Americans recognized and sought to solve without a national standard for language. Such was not the case (see below). Second Heath's argument depends on an unsupported distinction between language as a "pragmatic tool" and language as "ideal or ideological symbol" (11). This distinction collapses the moment one reads any grammar or speller from the era.

[15]Benjamin Rush, "Thoughts Upon the Mode of Education Proper in a Republic," in Frederick Rudolph, ed., *Essays on Education in the Early Republic* (Cambridge: Belknap Press of Harvard Univ. Press, 1965), p. 9. I draw heavily upon this collection. It also includes the Knox and Smith essays although my references are to the microfilm editions published in the *Early American Imprints* series.

[16]Rush, "Thoughts," p. 17.

[17]For a survey of eighteenth-century American interest in language, see Raoul N. Smith, "The Interest in Language and Languages in Colonial and Federal America," *Proceedings of the American Philosophical Society* 123 (1979), 29-46, esp. 36-42 on English language spellers and grammars. In this section, Smith reviews the issue whether English grammar differed from that of Latin.

[18]Thomas Dilworth, *A New Guide to the English Tongue* (Philadelphia, 1793. Reprinted Delmar, N.Y.: Scholars' Facsimiles and Reprints, vol. 322, 1978, intro. by Charlotte Downey, R.S.M.)p. 133.

[19]Kenneth Lockridge, *Literacy in Colonial New England: An Enquiry into the Social Context of Literacy in the Early Modern West* (New York: Norton, 1974), p. 101. Despite his recognition that literacy and democracy are not necessary partners, Lockridge appears to distinguish between the literate modern age and traditional folk beliefs. David D. Hall has contested this distinction in America, arguing that the culture of literacy was pervasive by late seventeenth-century America: "the colonists lived easily in a world of print." He argues against the division made by social historians "between 'high' culture and that which is usually described as 'popular'; between books and collective belief" ("The World of Print and Collective Mentality in Seventeenth-Century New England," in John Higham and Paul K. Conkin, eds. *New Directions in American Intellectual History* (Baltimore: Johns Hopkins Univ. Press, 1979), pp. 173, 166.

[20]Dilworth, p. 1.

[21]Dilworth, p.131.

[22]Dilworth, pp. vi, xiv.

[23]Robert Lowth, *A Short Introduction to English Grammar* (Philadelphia, 1775). Reprinted Delmar, N.Y.: Scholars' Facsimiles and Reprints, 1979), p. 79, n. 9.

[24]Lowth, p. vi.

[25]John Davis, *Travels of Four Years and A Half in the United States of America; During 1798, 1799, 1801, and 1802* (London, 1803. Reprinted with intro. by A.J. Morrison. New York: Holt, 1909), p. 364.

[26]Lockridge, pp. 27, 73.

[27]Richard Beale Davis, *Intellectual Life in the Colonial South, 1585-1763*, 3 vols. (Knoxville: Univ. of Tenn. Press, 1978), I, 270.

[28]Carl F. Kaestle, *Pillars of the Republic: Common Schools and American Society, 1780-1860* (New York: Hill and Wang, 1983), p. 24.

[29]Kaestle, p. 25.

[30]Thomas Jefferson, *Notes on the State of Virginia*, intro. Thomas Perkins Abernathy (New York: Harper & Row, 1964), p. 142.

[31]Jefferson, p. 133.

[32]Jefferson, p. 142.

[33]Jefferson, p. 157.

[RS]Smith, *Remarks*, p. 83.

[35]Rush, "Thoughts," p. 7.

[36]Rush, "Thoughts," p. 7.

[37]Benjamin Rush, "An Inquiry into the Effects of Public Punishments upon criminals and upon society," *The American Museum* 2, 2 (August 1787), 150. See also Nathanial Chipman, *Sketches of the Principles of Government* (Rutland, VT.: J. Lyon, 1793) who argues that executions ought to be private in order to "cultivate a sentimental attachment to the government" (p. 164).

[38]David J. Rothman, *The Discovery of the Asylum: Social Order and Disorder in the New Republic* (Boston: Little, Brown, 1971), p. 61.

[39]Robert Coram, "Political Inquiries to Which is Added, A Plan for the General Establishment of Schools Throughout the United States," in Rudolph, *Essays*, p. 111.

[40]Smith, *Remarks*, p. 40.

[41]Knox, *An Essay*, p. 64.

[42]Rush, "Thoughts," p. 14.

[43]Jay Fliegelman, *Prodigals and Pilgrims: The American revolution against Patriarchal Authority, 1750-1800* (Cambridge: Cambridge Univ. Press, 1982). The abridgements of *Clarissa* published in America, according to Fliegelman, "virtually 'rewrite' the novel in such a way as to render it an unadulaterated polemic against parental authority" (p. 86).

[44]*The American Museum* 2, 1 (July 1787), 82.

[45]The theorists were, so to speak, inventing what they inveighed against. They were not confronting an autonomous and private family but rather seeking to prevent its development. In its actual existence as opposed to its private possibility, "the family was not coterminous with some 'private' sphere" at this time (Mary P. Ryan, *Cradle of the Middle Class: The Family in Oneida County, New York, 1790-1865*. [Cambridge: Cambridge Univ. Press, 1981], pp. 41-2). According to Bernard Farber, "As late as the early 1800s, parents considered separation from children to be beneficial to socialization" (*Guardians of Virtue: Salem Families in 1800* [New York: Basic Books, 1972], p. 161).

[46]Coram, "Political Inquiries," p. 139.

[47]"Education," *The American Magazine*, 4 (March 1788), 210.

[48]Philip Greven, *The Protestant Temperament: Patterns of Child-Rearing, Religious Experience, and the Self in Early America* (New York: Knopf, 1977), p. 266. Greven connects the "genteel mode" with the assertion of the self, a likely enough relationship and one which suggests why the educational writers sought to include this group in the national system.

[49]"Letter on education," *The American Museum* 4, 2 (August 1788), 110.

[50]When schooling was not under local and/or parental control, its disciplinary function became most evident. Urban charity schools were "designed to intervene between parents and children, to introduce children to a culture different from that of their parents" (Kaestle, *Pillars*, p. 39).

[51]Smith, *Remarks*, p. 39.

[52]Smith, pp. 39, 55, 61, 63.

[53]Smith, p. 88.

[54]Alexis de Toqueville, *Democracy in America*, 2 vols. (New York: Schocken Books, 1961), 2, 119.

[55]Coram, "Political Inquiries," p. 127.

[56]Smith, *Remarks*, p. 80.

[57]Noah Webster, "Education," *The American Magazine* 2 (January 1788), 81.

[58]Knox, *An Essay*, p. 149.

[59]Knox, p. 95.

[60]Knox, p. 96.

[61]Charles Brockden Brown, *Wieland or the Transformation: An American Tale* and *Memoirs of Carvin, the Biloquist*, Bicentennial edition (Kent, Ohio: Kent State University Press, 1977), pp. 277, 289

"A Capacity for Evil":
The 1915 Supreme Court *Mutual* Decision

Garth S. Jowett

Congress shall make no law ... abridging the freedom of speech, or of the press...
Amendment I, The Bill of Rights, Constitution of the United States

Today the moving picture machine cannot be overlooked as an effective protagonist of democracy. For through it the drama, always a big factor in the lives of the people at the top, is now becoming a big fact in the lives of the people at the bottom.
Joseph Medill Patterson, "Nickelodeons,' Saturday Evening Post, November 23, 1907, p. 10.

On February 23, 1915, the Supreme Court of the United States handed down a unanimous decision in *Mutual Film Corporation v. Industrial Commission of Ohio* which denied the motion picture the constitutional guarantees of freedom of speech and press.[1] Although not widely recognized as such at the time, this was a momentous decision which would affect the course of the motion picture industry for the next thirty-five years, and have a profound effect on the nature of the content which this new medium of communication would be allowed to explore. From our historical vantage point, the Mutual Decision can be seen as the culmination of the eighteen year struggle, caused by the increasing popularity and socializing power of this new entertainment medium in conflict with the desires of those who wished to curb its influence, and to make it more responsive to a variety of social and legal control mechanisms.

The motion picture controversy was much more than a fight between reformers and a morally suspect group of filmmakers. For the long-dominant Protestant segment, the new entertainment medium was, in reality, a dramatic and highly visible symbol of those social and political changes in turn of the century America which they seemed powerless to prevent, and which threatened to inexorably alter the face of the nation they had striven to build. For most of its history the United States had been a Protestant nation, but at the beginning of the twentieth century this was changing. As late as 1927 Andre Siegfried noted: "the civilization of the United States is essentially Protestant. Those who prefer other systems, such as Catholicism, for example, are considered bad Americans and are sure to be frowned upon by the purists. Protestantism is the only national religion, and to ignore that fact is to view the country from a false angle."[2]

The fact that America had essentially been created as a Protestant nation, despite the legal fiction of separation of church and state contained in the Constitution, had led to an ingrained belief that only through Protestantism could one be a true "Christian" and an American. David Reimers, in his thoughtful essay on the subject, has pointed out that at the turn of the twentieth century, American Protestants accepted this contention, and often used the word "Christian" as a synonym for "Protestant," and that, "Protestants also claimed that America was a Protestant nation in the sense that the political, moral, and social norms of American life were derived from Protestantism. Basically the churches were identifying Americanism with Protestantism."[3] It was firmly believed that America had achieved its high level of industrial and material civilization because of the inherent superiority of Protestantism and its underlying moral code, which stressed hard work, and adherence to a simple God-fearing, evangelic faith.

It was against the background of this unerring belief in the positive role of Protestantism in American society that we must view the reaction to the introduction of the motion picture in the late 1890s. By the end of the nineteenth century, the security of Protestantism's position in American life was being threatened by a variety of powerful changes. The combined forces of industrialization, urbanization and immigration represented a demographic, religious and political threat to the dominance of the rural-based, Protestant hegemony. Leaders of the Protestant church indicated their concern about the growing influence of these forces, aiming most of their wrath at the place where the changes were most obvious—the city. The Reverend Josiah Strong, in his widely-read book *Our Country: Its Possible Future and Its Present Crisis* (1885), attacked the city as the source of all the greatest evil in American society: "The city has become a serious menace to our civilization .... Because our cities are so largely foreign, Romanism finds in them its chief strength .... The city, where the forces of evil are massed, and where the need of Christian influence is peculiarly great, is from one-third to one-fifth as well supplied with churches as the nation at large."[4] It was also in the cities where the most visible aspects of the recreation revolution were taking place, and by 1907, the movie house was a common sight throughout working class districts, and just beginning to emerge as a popular middle-class entertainment.[5]

The increasing number of non-Protestant immigrants during these years, as well as the large number of migrants from the rural areas served to swell the cities with a working-class population which eagerly sought out new, inexpensive forms of entertainment as diversion from the tedium of their long working hours.[6] The emergence of dance-halls, professional sports, dime museums, beer-gardens, bowling alleys, saloons and even trolley rides were all in response to the need for recreation by the new urbanites of every class. In particular, the institutionalization of vaudeville, and its racier cousin burlesque in the late nineteenth century foreshadowed the emergence of the true "democratic" theater, and the most widely attended of all the new entertainment forms—the movies. Each of these entertainments had its own particular role to play, but they often served as potent socializing agents for "explaining" the American way of life to newcomers.[7] It was precisely this obvious but little-understood ability to be both a diversion and a disseminator of information which aroused deep suspicion about all of these popular theatrical entertainment forms, but nowhere was this concern more concentrated, or more clearly articulated than in the attack against the motion picture.

Protestantism, Progressivism and the Movies

By 1907, one journalist estimated that there were more than 500 movie houses in New York, which had a daily attendance of more than 200,000.[8] There were similar statistics in other urban centers, and the ubiquitous nickelodeon was already a familiar sight in smaller cities and towns across the nation.[9] The age of the nickelodeon was, in fact, short-lived as most theater operators, seeking to capture more of the middle-class trade, turned their attention to improving their operations, and moving to larger theaters, which often featured a mixture of vaudeville and movies. We know that in New York City and Boston this did indeed succeed in creating a wider audience; however, it is difficult to generalize about the exact nature of the early motion picture audience across the country.[10]

What can be established with some certainty is the initial reaction to the growth of the movies as a social and cultural force as the medium soon became the largest commercial entertainment in the nation. Almost from its first appearance in penny arcades, and then later in projected form in storefront nickelodeons and larger theaters, the medium found itself under intense scrutiny from social workers, teachers and members of the clergy, as well as those interested in the welfare of children or the general moral state of the public. These were the "progressives"—the newly emerged professional middle-class who would "form the bulwark of those men and women who dedicated themselves to replacing the decaying system of the nineteenth century."[11] It is ironic that while their training and urban orientation provided them with the insight to recognize that the old ways and old values could no longer meet the demands of the new urbanized society, they forged their urban ideals in the crucible of the traditional rural-based value system. While they were obsessed with the development of viable bureaucracies, they also indicated a concern for the individual which tended to continue the domination of traditional village and "Protestant" values. The Progressives undoubtedly contributed to solving the problems created by the wrenching experience of urbanization and industrialization, however they often did so with a Protestant-based perspective. While not all social reformers were motivated by religious fervor, the desire to create a "Christian" i.e., "Protestant" nation was a deep concern for many, and this was evidenced by the emergence of such evangelical activities as the social gospel movement in the late nineteenth century, with its emphasis on individual renewal and revivalism, and a belief that the teachings of Jesus Christ could be applied to industrial and urban America.[12]

The Progressives placed a great deal of faith in "science" and the use of rational, scientific reasoning as the answer to many of the social ills of the day. In particular, the emerging social sciences of psychology and sociology were lauded as a means of gaining greater understanding of the behavior of mankind as a collectivity, while economics and political science also received academic and public acceptance.

Educational theory also became more scientific in approach, and this resulted in a major reorientation of the American school system toward a pragmatic form of "learning by doing" which adapted the subject matter to the everyday world and the needs of the child. The school was now perceived as never before as a lever of social change, and the educator a social reformer.[13] Because of the difficulty in legislating against technology, the school also became the ideal place to give instruction on how to cope with these changes, and to instill the proper form of Christian morality at an early age. This ideological shift was of significance in the subsequent attitude toward the movies, because when it became obvious that these seemingly innocent diversions could also inform as well as entertain, educators took a vital interest in the issue of "the evils of the movies." The motion picture soon proved itself to be a potent competitor to the formal instruction of the classroom, and many a teacher was heard to complain about the unfair nature of the competition.

It is little wonder that faced with the perspective of the destruction of the traditional American society they revered so much, Protestant leaders responded by attempting to legislate not only against change but also the carriers of change. Clearly the long fight for the prohibition of alcohol can be seen as an attempt to legislate a peculiarly Protestant form of morality (Catholics have never had any objection to the appropriate consumption of alcohol), intensified in the face of "unAmerican" cultures which increasingly consumed beer and wine in public places such as parks and restaurants with obvious enjoyment.[14]

In its response to the changes around it, the Protestant church demonstrated its awareness of the threat to its dominant status, and taking a firm legislative stand where this was possible, it succeeded in introducing a significant amount of moral legislation. Ultimately this would have far-reaching implications for the motion picture industry which became a prime target upon which to vent the frustrations brought about by "a loss of status."[15]

Why all this fuss about the motion picture? Surely there were other more pressing issues in society, and certainly there were more obvious vices which deserved the attention of the reformers and social workers. In fact, a great deal of attention and effort was devoted to combating prostitution, child labor, unsanitary housing conditions, alcoholism, tuberculosis, and a myriad of other social ills. Viewed from this wider perspective, the attack on the motion picture was only one of a series of reactions to the convulsive changes then shaking the roots of American society. However, there are several reasons why this particular issue is of historical significance. First, the intensity of the attack was so unexpected, in that initially the nickelodeons were considered to be a mere passing diversion for the immigrant working classes; however, once the medium gained in popularity, and began to attract the patronage of the middle-classes, it became more symbolic of the loss of control over the socialization of the child being experienced by the Protestant hegemony. As a form of communication the motion picture established direct contact with its audience, at least a third of whom were under the age of sixteen, thereby circumventing the traditional socializing role of home, church and school in imparting information. As alarmed reports filtered back about children learning crime and sex techniques directly from the movies, this confirmed the fears that outside agencies were now replacing these bastions of Protestant America.[16]

Second, the movie houses were highly visible and permanent targets, easily identified, and unlike many other social ills, subject to direct pressure from authorities in the form of legislation and licensing, even though it took several years for specific legislation to be passed which dealt adequately with problems such as lighting, ventilation, fire regulation and sanitary conditions.[17] The filmmakers were less subject to direct pressure because they were widely scattered throughout the nation in the early period, besides which, their product was distributed by regional (usually state-based) organizations, and these could be subjected to state regulations.

Third, there was a great deal of suspicion concerning the ethnic origins of some of the filmmakers, especially after the first decade of the industry. Robert Sklar has pointed out that "before 1910 the movies were as completely in the hands of respectable, established Anglo-Saxon Protestant Americans as they were ever to be."[18] However, after 1911, a new breed of immigrant, mostly Jewish entrepreneurs rose from their storefront theaters to become the heads of the giant film studios, which eventually controlled the industry. While the vestiges of Victorian decorum prevented outright articulation of anti-semitic sentiments, the issue of "foreign" control of the motion picture industry was never very far from the surface, and undoubtedly was an important motivation in the continued desire to control the medium. These concerns underscore the clash between the established Protestant power and the threat of new alien cultural influences in American society.

Finally, the motion picture represents a significant anomaly in American legal history. It has the distinction of being the only medium of communication ever subjected to systematic legal prior-restraint in the history of the United States. So great was the fear of the perceived power of the motion picture, and so persistent were the reformers in their zeal, that the motion picture industry was eventually denied the right of protection of "freedom of speech" guaranteed by the First Amendment to the U. S. Constitution. As such, the history of this legal decision stands as a monument to what can be accomplished by a group in the last throes of a "loss of status." Together with the creation of prohibition by the passing of the Eighteenth Amendment and the Volstead Act in 1919, the control of the motion picture represented a hollow triumph for the forces of Protestant conservatism faced with the immense changes in their "Christian" environment.

The Introduction of Censorship

No sooner had the first peep show machines been introduced in 1894 than the spectre of censorship loomed over the entertainment. The first recorded court case involving a movie was *People v. Doris* in 1897, in which the presiding New York judge ruled that a pantomime of a bride's wedding night was "an outrage upon public decency."[19] Throughout this early period of the motion picture industry's development there were official attempts to control the new entertainment by the imposition of various licensing-laws, which were often the same laws used to control circuses and other forms of travelling side-shows and carnivals.[20] While these regulations were often nuisance laws as much as attempts to bring legitimate municipal order, they failed to control the content of films, and this lead to continued pressure for a more systematic method to deal with what many saw as an increasing social menace.

On November 4, 1907, after continued pressure from reformers, and the press, the Chicago City Council passed a movie censorship ordinance to be effective November 19th of that year. The ordinance empowered the General Superintendent of Police to issue permits for the exhibition of motion pictures, with the right of appeal to the Mayor, whose final decision was binding. Permits could be refused if in the Superintendent's judgment a film was "immoral or obscene, or portrays depravity, criminality or lack of virtue of a class of citizens of any race, color, creed or religion and exposes them to contempt, derision or obloquy, or tends to produce a breach of the peace or riots, or purports to represent any hanging, lynching or burning of a human being."[21] This was the first movie censorship ordinance ever passed in the United States, and with occasional amendments, was in force until 1961. The violation of this provision lead to a fine of not less than fifty dollars, nor more than one hundred dollars for each offense, but each day's showing was to constitute a separate violation. For practical reasons, the Superintendent delegated his power to deputies, who levied a fee of three dollars for every one thousand feet of film inspected. The ordinance also contained the first age classification scheme ever used to control the attendance of patrons at movie houses, providing for a special permit for movies which could only be seen by those over twenty-one years of age.[22]

This ordinance raised the ire of the movie makers, the distributors, and especially the exhibitors, and was immediately tested in the courts. The resulting case, *Block v. Chicago* (1909) stands as a landmark because it was the first movie censorship case to be tried in the U.S. Courts.[23] The Superintendent refused to issue permits for the films *The James Boys* and *Night Riders* because they were deemed to be immoral. The exhibitor of these films argued before the Supreme Court of Illinois that the ordinance was discriminatory because it did not apply to the legitimate theater, that it constituted a delegation of legislative power to the Superintendent of Police, and that it deprived him of his property without due process. All of these arguments were swept aside because according to the court the purpose of the ordinance was to secure decency and morality in the motion picture business, "and that purpose falls within the police power," unless constitutional rights were transgressed. Further, the standards of "immoral" and "obscene" were quite adequate, since "the average person of healthy and wholesome mind" knew what these terms meant. The court specifically examined the films, as well as the constitutional questions, and noted that one of the films did depict the lives of the James brothers which was a part of American history; however, movies that attempt to document such happenings "necessarily portray exhibitions of crime ... [and] ... can represent nothing but malicious mischief, arson and murder. They are both immoral, and their exhibition would necessarily be attended with evil effects on youthful spectators ...." The court forcefully pointed out that the issue relevant to the due process clause of the Fourteenth Amendment was not applicable, because of the plaintiff could have no legitimate property rights in immoral or obscene commodities.[24]

This case also represents the first time that we can find a clear legal articulation that movies were potentially dangerous because they were considered to be a lower-class activity, and therefore needed to be carefully controlled. Chief Justice James H. Cartwright, speaking for the court, noted that the ordinance applied to the "five and ten cent theaters," which "on account of the low price of admission, are frequented and patronized by a large number of children, as well as by those of limited means who do not attend the productions of plays and dramas given in the regular theaters. The audiences include those classes whose age, education and situation in life specially entitle them to protection against an evil influence of obscene and immoral representations.''[25] As De Grazia and Newman have pointed out, all of *Block*'s constitutional arguments would probably prevail today, but in 1909 a different set of political, religious and moral conditions determined the attitude toward the motion picture.

Another historically significant event took place in New York on December 24, 1908, when Mayor George B. McClellan issued an order to close down all of the movie houses in that city, following a clamorous public meeting the previous day which discussed the general conditions of movie theaters. Earlier, in June 1907 the Mayor had received a report from his police commissioner, which recommended the cancellation of all licenses for nickelodeons and penny arcades. The issue then lay smoldering for eighteen months before the Mayor decided to take action. The reasons for this drastic decision were not really clear, but it was claimed that he was influenced by a group of reformers, headed by Canon William Sheafe Chase of Christ Church, Brooklyn, who had charged at the public hearing that the exhibitors "had no moral scruples whatever. They are simply in the business for the money there is in it."[26] For the next twenty years Canon Chase would devote a large part of his life to the cause of cleaning up the movies, and he was a prominent leader in the drive to establish federal control over the content of the medium.

As a result of this action, the movie house owners obtained an injunction against the mayor's decision, which was granted by Justice Gaynor on Saturday, December 26. This was the last serious attempt to close down all the city's movie theaters, and it underscored the seriousness with which this issue was viewed by the parties involved. The main outcome of this New York incident was the establishment of the National Board of Censorship in March 1909, under the auspices of the People's Institute, a local civic organization which had previously conducted a lengthy investigation of the conditions of motion picture exhibition. The National Board of Censorship (an unfortunate choice of name, because it never really *censored* films), acted as an advisory board between the film producers and the general public, basing its power not on legal authority but rather on "moral coercion" of the film industry.[27]

John Collier, the executive secretary of the People's Institute, who had been one of the earliest social workers to recognize the importance of the motion picture as an integral part of the lives of the working class, became the architect of this attempt to make the motion picture industry more responsive and sensitive to its social and cultural obligations. Collier felt that if the motion picture was to exist, then it had to recognize the need to conform to prevailing moral norms. He also stressed that the exhibitors had to put pressure on the film manufacturers and demand better films, and to demonstrate the good intentions of the industry, Collier proposed a form of censorship which would be enforced by the exhibitors, with control vested in the hands of civic bodies representing the public interest. It was essentially this model which was put into operation in March 1909; however, the plan to inspect films in the theaters was soon abandoned, and the more practical approach of reviewing films at their source—the manufacturer—was adopted. Thus films could be modified, if necessary, prior to their exhibition in the nation's theaters. After some hesitation all of the major film manufacturers, including the powerful Motion Picture Patents Company, agreed to have their films reviewed and certified by the National Board. The film manufacturers' willingness to voluntarily submit their product was based upon the knowledge that without a certificate of approval they ran the risk of having their films refused by the important Association of Exhibitors of New York, which commanded enormous audiences.

The Board was only partially successful in its attempt to quell the rising tide of criticism about the content of motion pictures. While it was able to censor about eighty-five percent of the films exhibited in the U.S., it could not exert control over the exhibition of "special release" or wildcat productions which circulated the theatrical circuit. Having set itself up as the agency to mediate between movie content and public morality, the National Board became a ready target for the whole variety of complaints about the state of the motion picture industry. Also, because it depended upon the financial support of the motion picture industry in the form of licensing fees, it was always under suspicion for being a dupe of the film makers. The industry initially supported the Board, even though it was generally opposed to censorship of any sort on constitutional grounds, because it preferred to have to obtain just one form of approval rather than have to face a variety of censorship boards at all legislative levels, with widely differing standards. (For this reason, some motion picture industry leaders flirted with the notion of a Federal Censorship Commission in 1914 and 1916, which they quickly backed away from when the National Board pointed out that even if federal censorship was instituted, few states would be willing to give up their power to Washington).[28] Recognizing that the word "censorship" was a misleading indication of its real function, it became the National Board of *Review* in 1916.

In the long run the National Board of Censorship (Review) not only failed to prevent the clamor for the reform of the movies, it also served to underscore for many convinced reformers that only officially legislated prior-restraint could bring about a morally-responsible film industry. Staffed by well-meaning social reformers, the Board represented a compromise between complete freedom from legal censorship and the various forms of local, state or possibly federal censorship by politically appointed commissions. There was no disagreement by the various camps of social reformers that the movies were in desperate need of controlling.

The conflict was essentially between those who wished to see the establishment of viable self-regulatory mechanisms, which fell within the guidelines of the First Amendment guarantee of "free speech," and those who were unwilling and afraid to concede that the movies were indeed legitimate forms of "speech" or "free press."

The Movies and the Supreme Court

The Case of *Block v. Chicago* was based upon a local city or ordinance, but by the time it was decided, several states were already considering the introduction of state-wide movie censorship laws. Pennsylvania was the first to legislate official censorship of motion pictures in 1911, with Ohio following in 1913, Kansas in 1914, Maryland in 1916 and New York and Virginia in 1922. Operating under various provisions, these states set up censorship boards to review and license films that met vague and often arbitrary standards of morality and decency. It was a protest against state censorship which formed the basis of the landmark case in motion picture history considered by the U.S. Supreme Court in 1915.

The only way to make any sense of the decision in *Mutual Film Corporation v. Industrial Commission of Ohio* is to consider both the legal and social conditions which were prevailing upon the deliberations of the Justices of the Supreme Court. The facts of the case were these: Ohio had passed in 1913 a statute which provided for the creation of a motion picture censorship board whose duty it was to examine, in advance, all film that was to be shown publicly for profit in any part of the state. Section 4 of the act stated that "only such films as are in the judgement and discretion of the board of censors of a moral, educational or amusing and harmless character shall be passed and approved ...." Section 3 required a mandatory inspection fee from those submitting films to the censorship agency.[29]

The film industry was obviously concerned that state laws such as this would inflict serious financial damage to their business, and the large interstate film exchange conglomerate, Mutual Film Corporation, decided to challenge the constitutionality of the Ohio censorship law in court. Mutual shipped films into Ohio from their base in Detroit, and because movie house owners would not rent uncensored films for fear of prosecution, Mutual was forced to pay for the state inspection. The film distributor sought an injunction to restrain the enforcement of the law, claiming that the statute imposed an unfair burden on interstate commerce, that it was an invalid delegation of legislative powers to the board of censors because it failed to set up precise standards by which films were to be approved or rejected, and that it violated the free speech guarantees of the Ohio Constitution and the First Amendment. The request for the injunction met with failure and the case was appealed to the Supreme Court.

In their appeal before the Supreme Court, the attorneys for Mutual assumed that the justices knew little about the workings of the film industry, and they therefore prepared an elaborate background paper describing the role of Mutual as a film distributor and the industry as a whole. As the Court pointed out, "The bill is quite voluminous."[30] In particular, Mutual tried to show that motion pictures were similar to the press, in that:

They depict dramatizations of standard novels, exhibiting many subjects of scientific interest, the properties of matter, the growth of the various forms of animal and plant life, and explorations and travels; also events of historical and current interest—the same events which are described in words and by photographs in newspapers, weekly periodicals, magazines and other publications, of which photographs are promptly secured a few days after the events which they depict happen; thus regularly furnishing and publishing news through the medium of motion pictures under the name of "Mutual Weekly." Nothing is depicted of a harmful or immoral character.[31]

The Mutual lawyers were obviously aiming directly at the heart of the issue, trying to demonstrate that by 1915, the movies had clearly become transmittors of information on a wide range of issues, and were therefore comparable to other news media.

The Supreme Court heard the case on January 6 and 7, and reported its findings on February 23, 1915. The unanimous Court, speaking through Justice McKenna, ignored the federal free speech claims and rejected the other complaints. Although the list of justices who heard the case included such legal luminaries as Oliver Wendell Holmes, Jr. and Charles Evan Hughes, there was to be no freedom from prior-restraint for the motion picture at this time. A close analysis of the decision reveals the somewhat tortured reasoning of the justices to justify their decision. In rejecting the claim that the law placed an unfair burden on interstate commerce, Justice McKenna noted that: "The censorship ... is only of films intended for exhibition in Ohio, and we can immediately put aside the contention that it imposes a burden on interstate commerce." Once the films were in Ohio they were "mingled as much from their nature as they can be with other property of the State," and at this time they were subject to regulation by the State.[32]

In rejecting the delegation-of-power issue, the Court decided that the Ohio statute did not suffer from "arbitrary judgment, whim and caprice ... resulting 'in unjust discrimination against some propagandist film,' while others might be approved without question." The justices felt that the law could be fairly enforced because, "its terms ... get precision from the sense and experience of men and become certain and useful guides in reasoning and conduct."[33] The statute could not be specified with any greater clarity because the law relied upon the ascertainment of the facts of the individual case, based upon which the policies would be applied with this "sense and experience." The question of the precise definitions of such terms as "immoral" and "obscene" was to plague the film industry throughout its history, and even today, courts are forced to deal with the various interpretations arrived at by individual judges and juries.

It was the decision on the question of whether movies fell within the free-speech guarantees of the Ohio State Constitution that was to make *Mutual* such an historically significant case. Despite the evidence provided by the appellant, the justices were not prepared to accept the parallel between the motion picture and the press. First, the Court noted that under the statute films of a "moral, educational or amusing and harmless character shall be passed and approved," and therefore "however missionary of opinion films are or may become, however educational or entertaining, there is no impediment to their value or effect in the Ohio statute."[34] This reasoning, of course, did not deal with the constitutionality of prior-restraint, for no matter that films meeting these standards "would be passed" the real issue was why they needed to be examined and licensed *before* their public exhibition. The answer to this question is found in Justice McKenna's description of motion pictures for, despite their educational or entertaining value, motion pictures were to be treated differently because:

... they may be used for evil, and against that possibility the statute was enacted. Their power of amusement and, it may be, education, the audiences they assemble, not of women alone nor of men alone, but together, not of adults only, but of children, make them the more insidious in corruption by a pretense of worthy purpose or if they should degenerate from worthy purpose .... They take their attraction from the general interest, however eager and wholesome it may be, in their subjects, but a prurient interest may be excited and appealed to. Besides, there are some things which should not have pictorial representation in public places and to all audiences .... We would have to shut our eyes to the facts of the world to regard the precaution unreasonable or the legislation to effect it a mere wanton interference with personal liberty.[35]

The Court considered Mutual's arguments that motion pictures were a "means of making or announcing publicly something that otherwise might have remained private or unknown," and therefore within the protection of the Ohio Constitution; however, this argument was rejected, even though the justices conceded that motion pictures were "mediums of thought," but then so were many other things, such as "the theater, the circus and all other shows and spectacles." The Court held that "the argument is wrong or strained which extends the guarantees of free opinion and speech to the multitudinous shows which are advertised on the bill-boards of our cities and towns."[36] Further, there was a long history of legal precedent for extending police power over such forms of entertainment.

In trying to gauge what was on the minds of the justices as they considered what to do with this new medium of information, there is little doubt that they were unwilling to leave the general public unprotected from what they saw as a powerful, unregulated social force. It is here that we see the clear articulation of the problem that the motion picture symbolized. The telling phrase was Justice McKenna's declaration that:

It cannot be put out of view that the exhibition of moving pictures is a business pure and simple, originated and conducted for profit, like other spectacles, not to be regarded, nor intended to be regarded by the Ohio constitution, we think, as part of the press of the country or as organs of public opinion. They are mere representations of events, of ideas and sentiments published and known, vivid, useful and entertaining no doubt, but, as we have said, capable of evil, having power for it, the greater because of the attractiveness and manner of exhibition.[37]

Thus the movies were capable of disseminating ideas, but the fear of the court was that they *could* be used for "evil" purposes by those seeking merely to make a profit, and that this danger was only increased by the enormous inherent attraction the medium held for the public, especially those classes who were more susceptible to outside influences. In the face of this further threat to the power of the traditional (i.e., "Christian/American") socializing agencies, the concerns of the Protestant hegemonists were perfectly echoed in the words of the Supreme Court.

The decision of the Supreme Court in the *Mutual* case can be faulted in three specific ways. First, the reasoning that the motion picture was to be excluded from First Amendment protection because it was "a business pure and simple, originated and conducted for profit," has been rightly condemned for being constitutionally unsound.[38] Newspapers and magazines had long been operated for private profit, and this had never lead to their disqualification from protection. There was certainly no precedent in law for the blanket condemnation of a form of communication because it made money.

Second, the classification of the movies in the same category as circuses and other sideshow spectacles reflected the traditional judicial suspicion of the theater and the arts, expressed in the dichotomy between entertainment and ideas. The belief that because motion pictures were entertainment they therefore could not convey ideas was clearly false, for by 1915 they had amply demonstrated their ability to inform, and even influence. Throughout history there had been a fear of the theater as a medium for conveying ideas, and both the English and American courts had long held the legitimate stage to be subject to arbitrary restraint. For many years plays were forbidden altogether in Massachusetts, and in 1915 the drama was not considered as a medium under the protection of the First Amendment.[39] There was, however, no systematic legal censorship of plays in the United States at this time, although theaters themselves were licensed. The courts were clearly reluctant to extend the protection of the First Amendment to new and potentially dangerous forms of expression, and it was not until *Hannegan v. Esquire* in 1946 that the Supreme Court actually held that materials which were characteristically entertainment were protected free speech.[39]

The third criticism of the *Mutual* decision is in the characterization of the motion pictures as having a greater "capacity for evil" than other forms of mass communication, and therefore subject to prior-restraint. As the *Yale Law Journal* pointed out: "Such a capacity has certainly affected the type and amount of community control, but has never meant that all expression within a medium will be restricted from the outset. It has meant only that when a particular act of expression is sought to be restrained, the community's need for protection against the evil must be weighed against the value of the expression."[40] The acceptance of this view of the motion picture was clearly the major motivation for the decision to allow the continuation of censorship, although, as Ira Carmen has noted, this finding "was unnecessary to establish the fact that the medium itself was not protected by the free speech clause of the Ohio Constitution."[42]

Once the Court had found that the motion picture was not speech, it was unnecessary to consider the claim of protection under the First Amendment; in any case, in 1915 it had not yet been settled as to whether the First Amendment was binding on the states. Only in 1925, in the case of *Gitlow v. New York* did the Supreme Court (including four of the justices who had decided the *Mutual* case) decide that the states must be mindful of the guarantees of free speech and press set forth in the Constitution.[43] While this equally significant decision did not immediately remove state and local censorship of motion pictures, it did leave open the issue of when a state could properly censor speech, and ultimately provided one of the legal precedents upon which the downfall of censorship was based.

The Mutual *Decision: The Evaluation and the Effects*

In his evaluation of the *Mutual* decision, the founder of the National Board of Censorship, John Collier, pointed out that the Court had chosen to use a narrow interpretation of the Constitution to justify its decision, and the justices' use of legal precedent was faulty, for while *playhouses* were traditionally licensed, individual *plays* themselves were never licensed, until now. In a series of articles under the general title "The Lantern Bearers—A Series of Essays Exploring Some Thoroughfares of the People's Leisure" appearing in the social work journal, *The Survey* in late 1915, he traced the history of legal restraint of expressions of opinion in the theater and the motion picture. While these well-researched and articulate essays can be seen as an attempt to intellectually justify the function of the National Board of Censorship as the ideal form of social control, Collier was one of the few individuals at this time who was astute enough to recognize what the motion picture really symbolized for the reformers. He pointed out that: "It is clear that the court was swayed by what it believed about public opinion and public necessity; that its grounds for decision were psychological, not primarily legal, and were the consequences of its lack of first-hand experience with motion pictures...."[44]

Collier was also concerned that this decision would lead to legal censorship being applied to other forms of expression, particularly to the theater itself, and "it would involve no radical extension of the motion-picture decision to validate constitutionally a form of censorship of comic supplements and even of illustrations in general." Even political censorship, or the censorship of opinion which the Supreme Court seemed so confident could not take place under the Ohio statute, was possible, for "there are always reasons to spare for every censoring act, and the inner heart cannot be placed in evidence." Subsequent history has demonstrated that Collier had every reason to be apprehensive about the encroaching power of legally-protected censors, for many films were censored or attacked for their political or social ideas.[45] Collier was at his most perceptive about the *Mutual* decision when he suggested that it was the result of the "manifold influences" which were at work in extending the power of censorship, and that "They have concentrated on motion-pictures for the moment because these are ubiquitous, disturbingly potent, and new, and because their producers are as yet hopelessly unorganized to defend themselves .... A vastly extended censorship is the aim of many of those who have been in sympathy with this beginning."[46]

Nowhere can these "manifold influences" be better observed at work than in the two Hearings held before the U.S. House of Representatives Committee on Education, on the Bills to Establish a Federal Motion Picture Commission in 1914, and again in 1916.[47] These two Hearings, on essentially the same Bill, but in different congressional sessions, neatly frame the period of the *Mutual* decision, and provide insight into and confirmation of the Protestant reformers' position.

In 1914, Congressman Dudley M. Hughes of Georgia was prevailed upon by the Rev. Wilber Crafts, Superintendent of the International Reform Bureau, to introduce a Bill (H.R. 14805) which would have established a Federal Motion Picture Commission, composed of five commissioners appointed by the President to "license every film submitted to it and intended for entrance into interstate commerce, unless it finds that such a film is obscene, indecent, immoral, or depicts a bull fight or a prize fight, or is of such a character that its exhibition would tend to corrupt the morals of children or adults or incite to crime." The penalty for violating this act was "a fine of not more than $500, or imprisonment not more than one year, or both ...."[48] The Rev. Crafts, in his opening testimony in favor of this Bill, went to great pains to establish the right of the federal government to censor films based upon the interstate nature of film commerce. He claimed that the National Board of Censorship ("the unofficial board of censors in New York") had failed to do an adequate job, so that "State and local boards have turned down a great many of the pictures which they have passed." He also suggested that he had firm evidence that "the moving-picture men desire one censorship that will take the place of the vexatious State and local censorships."[49]

The real issue for Crafts was that motion picture theaters were teaching lessons in morality as well as entertaining, and so, he pointed out, it was only natural that movies should be supervised by a division of the Bureau of Education. He reasoned:

The public would recognize the fact that the pictures to be presented would be of real educational force, and it would incline, in my opinion, a great many more of the thoughtful mothers to take their children to moving-picture shows. They would feel, if the business was under the board of education, that it was a safe place for them and their children to attend, and the moving-picture men would themselves gain dignity in the business. They would gain patronage from among the solid class of citizens which would more than offset any loss there might be from the riffraff who might have attended a salacious picture that had been cut out. *At any rate, they recognize that censorship of some sort, or licensing of pictures, which is the preferable way to do it, is a coming event.*[50]

In the period just before the *Mutual* decision, Crafts, and other reformers favoring this bill, always went to some lengths to claim that they were advocating the "licensing" of films, and that this was different from censorship, because it merely utilized the federal authority to license interstate commerce. Technically, under this bill, a film produced and confined within the geographic boundaries of a state would not be subject to examination. Of course, as the industry always pointed out, the economic structure of film production and distribution was such that this meant that in practice all films would be censored by the federal commission.

The major speaker for the reformers was the Rev. William Sheafe Chase, Rector of Christ Church, Bedford Avenue, Brooklyn; head of the Social Service Commission of the Diocese of Long Island, and also vice president of the New York Society for the Prevention of Crime, and very well-known in Protestant reform circles. The Rev. Chase read into the record a series of debates he had precipitated in *Motion Picture Story Magazine* in 1914 with Frank L. Dyer, President of General Film Co. which neatly outlined the differences toward censorship between the industry and the advocates of legal control. Chase clearly subscribed to the notion that the motion picture was a potentially dangerous weapon, because "a bad motion picture does ten times as much harm among children as a bad book. An evil book injures only those that can read and have some power of imagination. But the evil motion picture carries its influence to the youngest and most ignorant." Further, "This form of amusement makes no demand of punctuality, or patience, or of intelligence. Those who can not understand the English language and those who can not read at all are attracted." In referring to the impending *Mutual* decision, he noted that even if the court found the Ohio statute to be unconstitutional, "it will not affect my contention, for the Ohio law is more sweeping in its provisions than any moderate and reasonable restriction ... and is much more open to the charge of improperly restraining the freedom of the press."[51] However, just twenty months later, after the *Mutual* decision, which affirmed the state's right to legally censor films, Chase and others were only too eager to praise the court's denial of First Amendment protection to the motion picture.[52]

Despite a unanimous Education Committee report in favor of establishing a Federal Motion Picture Commission, the first Hughes bill did not make it through Congress, so in 1916, the same bill was reintroduced, this time with the weight of the *Mutual* decision behind it. Dr. Crafts introduced the findings of the Supreme Court at the start of the January 1916 hearings with the statement that: "The same principles are involved in the Federal censorship proposed in this bill as in the Ohio ... case, and the same constitutional objects were urged there as have been urged here; ... the Supreme Court denies that there is any analogy between the press and miscellaneous pictures exhibited for amusement and financial profit."[53] In his testimony, Crafts offered a unique insight into how he perceived his achievements as a long-time advocate of social and movie reform, as well as providing a glimpse of his personal philosophies. In referring to another Supreme Court ruling[54] which condoned the barring of prize fight films, specifically the Willard-Johnson heavyweight title fight, he explained his own role in this case:

The initiatory work on this law was my first work in restraining motion-picture films. *I would be content if I had initiated only this one of the 16 acts of Congress introduced at my request,* and had no other definite civic accomplishment to my credit for my whole life. It would have been worth while to have lived if only to save the country from being flooded with pictures of a negro indicted for white slavery and a white man voluntarily standing on the same brutal level, which, but for that law, would have been shown all over the country as a brace of heroes.[55]

While Crafts could not be called an outright racist, he was reflecting the commonly held viewpoint that motion pictures could widely disseminate such antisocial information, which was so antithetical to the accepted values of middle-class Protestant America.

The same parade of reformers and industry witnesses appeared before the education committee, as in the 1914 hearings, but this time the industry was much more on the defensive, while the reformers exhibited a confidence resulting from the affirmation of their task provided by the *Mutual* decision. Given that decision, the reformers wondered why the committee even bothered to hold hearings, for as Crafts told them, "I hope the committee will hold the other side down to using their time in the presentation of new matter that has not been outlawed by the Supreme

Court.''[56] Much to Crafts' and the Rev. Chase's consternation, the industry continued to insist that motion pictures were being unfairly singled out, and that censorship was unconstititional, despite what the Supreme Court may have said.

The industry's position, as described by William Marston Seabury, the general counsel to the motion picture people, was in opposition to the bill, and censorship in general. Seabury, who would become one of the most articulate proponents of a "free" use of motion pictures in society, came straight to the point: "We are opposed to what we call prepublication censorship. We say it is vicious, un-American, and unfair in every principle."[57] The industry claimed that *Mutual* only dealt with the censorship of a film within its borders by a state, and that this did not sanction federal censorship. Throughout these hearings the industry also produced a parade of witnesses who tried to make the case that movies were analogous to other forms of speech, while the reformers constantly cited *Mutual* as a refutation of this claim. Clearly the Supreme Court's decision was now a major weapon in the reformer's arsenal against the motion picture industry.

Not all Protestant clergymen were fearful of the motion picture in the way that Crafts and Chase were, and those who worked in poorer working-class districts were more inclined to be sympathetic to the need for such diversions in the lives of their neighbors. In opposing the bill, the Reverend Cyrus Townsend Brady, of Yonkers, the author of some sixty-five books, made this clear:

it is a discriminating measure; it is a measure which discriminates against the poor man, for the moving play is the poor man's grand opera. It is the poor man's motor car; it is the poor man's trip to Europe; it is the poor man's golf club; it is his only recreation .... I know the lack of amusement, I know the monotony—the life of loneliness in these communities—and it can scarcely be imagined .... The Church is back of this desire for censorship .... And there is no more pernicious tendency in American institutions than the tendency of the church as an organization to come up and demand the passage of laws to do what the church ought to do itself .... If the church can not compete with the moving pictures, it is a sign that it is not using its influence in the right way .... We can not make men righteous by law.[58]

Brady's testimony before this committee elicited one of the few recorded instances of applause from segments of the audience, no doubt the representatives of the industry, and their friends, when he said, "if there is another thing beside the greatest amount of personal liberty consistent with the rights of man for which this country stands without regard for special privilege, it is disassociation of church and state."[59]

The reformers, however, saw it in a different light. They were not about to give up their privileges without a fight against those forces which they saw as a threat to their position as the moral arbiters of Americanism.

In this regard they felt that they were representing the fundamental will of the majority of Americans. Rev. Chase made this quite clear when he said:

Now, this Smith-Hughes law is progressive. It is not reactionary. *New occasions make new duties* . . . . We must have new laws to meet new conditions . . . . Here is a new condition with reference to the childhood of our country, a new danger that confronts them, and we come, representing the will of the whole people, and ask you to appoint a few good men to carry out the will of the whole people in order that the good of the whole people may be secured . . . . Who are going to be the people, if this bill is not enacted, who will educate the children of our lands? A few motion-picture manufacturers, whose principle motive is making money."[60]

These 1916 hearings represented a unique forum for airing the debate about the concept of separation of church and state in deciding who should take responsibility for shaping the moral direction of the United States. The Protestants were adamant that only they could provide the guidance needed to ensure the correct path, for, as Rev. Chase put it, "We have to prepare this country for the future. Preparedness is what we are talking about here today, and the preparedness of soul and spirit is of tremendous importance. The education of our children is of supreme importance in national preparedness. Have we not a right to insist that the morality of the theater-going public shall be raised to the standard of the general morality of the people?"[61] This was answered by John D. Bradley, president of the Washington (D.C.) Secular League, who claimed that the commission established by this bill would have as its main function "to censor not the food of the body, but the food of the mind, to say what shall and what shall not be given expression from the minds and to the minds by means of this great instrumentality for the expression and communication of thought—the motion picture." Attacking the reference to members of the education committee as "representatives of God" made by Rev. Chase the night before, Bradley called attention to the fact that, "the Constitution of this secular Republic knows neither gods nor devils; that it knows no source of political power but that of the people and recognizes no divine prerogative or representation in the representatives of the people."[62]

After six evenings of testimony, the committee on education voted 11 to 5 to send the bill forward; but it too died in Congress. Both in 1923 and in 1926 there were other serious attempts to establish a Federal motion picture commission. In 1926 once again there were lengthy hearings held to discuss the issue. Rev. Chase had by this time been promoted to *Canon* Chase, but he was there, voicing the same concerns, leading the charge. However, by 1926 the film industry had become much more organized under the leadership of former Postmaster-General Will H. Hays who had become president of the Motion Picture Producers and Distributors of America in 1922. Under Hays' direction the industry had managed to stave off several state censorship bills, most notably in crushing a censorship referendum in Massachusetts in 1922.[63] In fact, the high-pressure tactics used to defeat this referendum by the politically astute Hays, who had previously managed Warren G. Harding's election campaign, was the subject of much debate at these hearings.[64] It was no happy coincidence that Hays was a prominent member of the Presbyterian General Assembly at the time that he was selected to provide the film industry with a veneer of public respectability.[65]

At these 1926 hearings it was clear that the concerns about film content were now widening beyond the original Protestant reformer group to include a variety of social organizations, particularly women's clubs. The public relations efforts of the Hays Office (known as the "Open Door Policy") was also very evident in the number of civic and special interest groups represented who opposed the bill, including many citizen's "Better Films" committees from all over the U.S.; the International Federation of Catholic Alumni; the National Catholic Welfare Conference; the American Federation of Labor; and the Women's Cooperative Alliance.[66] Speaking in favor of the bill were such groups as the Women's Christian Temperance Union; the Citizens League of Maryland for Better Motion Pictures; and the Department of Moral Welfare of the Presbyterian Church of the United States of America.[67] The official presentations on behalf of the film industry were all made by representatives from the Hays Office, who provided details about the cooperative efforts they were mounting to improve the relationship between the industry and the general public by providing a forum for public input through a series of conferences and representative committees.

But it was precisely the failure of the industry to appease the ardent reformers which had brought about the introduction of this bill in 1926. Despite the *Mutual* decision eleven years before, which had legally sanctioned the establishment of a substantial number of state and local censorship boards (especially in the largest states and cities), the Protestant reformers would only be satisfied with censorship at the federal level, much like they had achieved with prohibition and the passing of the Volstead act in 1919. The comparison was even clearly articulated by Charles A. McMahon, representing the National Catholic Welfare Conference, when he told the committee that: "Personally I can not help but think that these proposals represent the most pessimistic appraisal of the character and the moral fiber of the American people ever made, as well as the most reckless intrusion upon their rights and upon their personal liberties that has been submitted to Congress since the passage of the Volstead act."[68] To which the sponsor of the bill, Representative Upshaw of Georgia, replied, "I will only ask you to remember that the Volstead Act was made mandatory by the eighteenth amendment ... the law was passed, after generations of education and agitation by both branches of Congress ... and we stand by it."[69]

It was, however, Canon Chase who summed up the frustration that the reformers felt about the motion picture industry, and why they had thought it necessary to fight for federal censorship since 1914:

> The producers have centralized their business and fortified it by engaging a political manipulator of wide experience and influence to whom it has entrusted czarlike power ... [Will H. Hays]. To expect to meet this incorporated, highly financed, national evil by local or State laws or by the vague and academic process of education is puerile ... whenever any business is so great and so intricate in its control and influence over the life and morals of the people, that business should be regulated by the United States Government or it should be regulated by some power big enough to regulate it—big enough to control it.[70]

It was only an ironic accident of history that during the same period the film industry had become a major social influence in American life, the traditional power of the Protestant majority had declined. Despite repeated attempts to seize control of this ubiquitous and very tangible symbol of their increasing loss of status in American society, the best the Protestants could achieve was their victory in the *Mutual* decision. This was not an unimportant triumph, for it provided the legal platform to sustain film censorship for a period of more than thirty-seven years, between 1915 and 1952. However, the *Mutual* decision by itself was unable to bring about the desired result of making the content of motion pictures more responsive to the pure version of what Protestant Americanism stood for. Yet American movies did, on the whole, represent the basic American virtues; but these were no longer exclusively Protestant in origin or outlook. Also, while the motion picture was singled out for attention, there were other vast social and cultural forces at work in America at this time which contributed to undermining the Protestant hegemony.

The true measure of Protestant decline was made obvious in the early 1930s, when after decades of complacency, the Roman Catholic Church, angered and alarmed by the increasing "anti-Catholic" nature of the content of the new "talkies," which featured sophisticated and often suggestive dialogue, divorce and birth control, decided to take up the cause of "cleaning up the movies." In three short years, through the efforts of the Catholic Legion of Decency, the power of the pulpit and the reluctant backing of the Hays Office, the Catholic Church was able to achieve in 1933 a viable form of social control through the acceptance of the famous "Code."[71] The Protestant could debate control and introduce legislation, but the organized power to authorize morality and achieve effective control now lay with the Catholic Church.

Notes

* I would like to acknowledge the help of Allan Stegman, who, following a suggestion of mine, wrote a graduate essay on "The Mutual Film Corporation Versus the Industrial Commission of Ohio: A Critical Review." Mr. Stegman's thorough analysis of the case was

extremely useful in my own research. The concept of the Protestant response is entirely my own.

[1]*Mutual Film Corporation v. Ohio Industrial Commission.* 236 U.S. 230 U.S. Supreme Court, 1915 (hereafter cited as *Mutual*).

[2]Andre Siegfriend, *America Comes of Age* (New York: Harcourt, Brace and World, 1927), p. 33.

[3]David Riemers, "Protestantism's Response to Social Change: 1890-1930," in Frederic Cople Jaher, ed., *The Age of Industrialism in America* (New York: Free Press, 1968), pp. 364-365.

[4]Josiah Strong, "Perils of the City," in Anselm Strauss, ed., *The American City: A Sourcebook of Urban Imagery* (Chicago: Aldine Publishing Co., 1968), pp 127-129.

[5]For a detailed discussion of the history of the recreation revolution and the emergence of the nickelodeon see Garth Jowett, *Film: The Democratic Art* (Boston: Little, Brown, 1976), pp. 11-50; and Russell Merritt, "Nickelodeon Theaters 1905-1914: Building an Audience for the Movies," in Tino Balio, ed., *The American Film Industry* (Madison: Univ. of Wisconsin Press, 1976), pp. 59-79.

[6]The history of urban amusements is dealt with in Foster Rhea Dulles, *America Learns to Play* (New York: Appleton-Century-Crofts, 1965), pp. 211-229.

[7]For the importance of vaudeville as a socializing agent, see Albert F. McLean, *American Vaudeville as Ritual* (Lexington: Univ. of Kentucky Press, 1965).

[8]Barton W. Currie, "The Nickel Madness," *Harper's Weekly*, August 24, 1907, pp. 1246-1247.

[9]For a discussion of motion picture exhibition in small towns, see David O. Thomas, "From Page to Screen in Small Town America," *UFA Journal*, vol. 32, no. 3 (Summer, 1981), pp. 3-13.

[10]The history of nickelodeons and the difficulties in trying to analyze the compositions of audiences is dealt with in an elegant manner in Robert C. Allen, "Motion Picture Exhibition in Manhattan, 1906-1912: Beyond the Nickelodeon," in Gorham Kindem, ed., *The American Movie Industry* (Carbondale: Southern Illinois Univ. Press, 1982), pp. 12-24; and for Boston, see Merritt, "Nickelodeon Theateres, 1905-1914," *op. cit.*

[11]Robert H. Wiebe, *The Search for Order* (New York: Hill and Wang, 1967), p. 129. This book is an excellent introduction to the emergence of the "progressive" movement.

[12]See Charles Hopkins, *The Rise of the Social Gospel in American Protestantism, 1865-1915* (New Haven: Yale Univ. Press, 1940); and Henry May, *Protestant Churches and Industrial America* (New York: Harper and Row, 1949).

[13]For information on the shift in educational ideology, see Lawrence A. Cremin, *The Transformation of the School* (New York: Random House, Vintage Books, 1964).

[14]The Protestant role in prohibition is discussed in Joseph R. Gusfield, *Symbolic Crusade: Status Politics and the American Temperance Movement* (Urbana: Univ. of Illinois Press, 1963); and Andrew Sinclair, *Era of Excess* (New York: Harper Colophon Books, 1962).

[15]The results of the decline in status for groups is discussed in detail in Richard Hofstadter, *The Age of Reform* (New York: Vintage Books, 1960).

[16]The issue of socialization and the reformist response is discussed at length in Jowett, pp. 74-107; and Robert Sklar, *Movie-Made America* (New York: Random House, 1975), pp. 122-140.

[17]It was not until 1913 that the New York City Council was able to pass a comprehensive law dealing with motion picture theaters. See Sonya Levien, "New York City's Motion Picture Law," *American City*, October, 1913, pp. 319-321.

[18]Sklar, p. 33.

[19]14 App. Div. 117, 43 N.Y.S. 571 (1st. Dept. 1897).

[20]The history and legal issues of film censorship are discussed in the following books: Ira H. Carmen, *Movies, Censorship and the Law* (Ann Arbor: Univ. of Michigan Press, 1966); and Richard S. Randall, *Censorship of the Movies* (Madison: Univ. of Wisconsin Press, 1968).

[21]Quoted in *Block v. Chicago*, 239 Ill. 251, 87 N.E. 1011 (1909).

[22]Carmen, pp. 186-189.

[23]239 Ill. 251, 87 N.E. 1011 (1909).

[24]Carmen, p. 188; Randall, p. 12.

[25]Edward de Grazia and Roger K. Newman, *Banned Films* (New York: R.R. Bowker, 1982), p. 178.

[26]*New York Times*, Dec. 24, 1908, p. 1.

[27]The best description of the history and function of this organization is found in Charles M. Feldman, *The National Board of Censorship (Review) of Motion Pictures, 1909-1922* (New York: Arno Press, 1975).

[28]For details of the motion picture industry's attitude toward all levels of censorship see Jowett, 108-138.

[29]Carmen, p. 11; Jowett, pp. 119-120; and Randall, p. 18.

[30]*Mutual*, p. 231.

[31]*Ibid.*, p. 232.   [32]*Ibid.*, p. 241.   [33]*Ibid.*, pp. 245-246.   [34]*Ibid.*, pp. 241-242.   [35]*Ibid.*, p. 242.   [36]*Ibid.*, p. 244.   [37]*Ibid.*

[38]For a useful analysis of this case see "Motion Pictures and the First Amendment," *Yale Law Journal*, vol. 60 (1951), pp. 701-705.

[39]*Hennegan v. Esquire*, 327 U.S. 146 (1946).

[40]*Ibid.*, p. 703.

[41]Carmen, p. 14.

[42]Carmen, p. 14.

[43]*Gitlow v. New York*, 268 U.S. 652 (1925).

[44]John Collier, "The Learned Judges and the Films," *The Survey*, Sept., 14, 1915, p. 516.

[45]See Carmen; De Grazi and Newman; Morris Ernst and Pare Lorentz, *Censored: The Private Life of the Movie* (New York: Jonathan Cape and Harrison Smith, 1930); and Randall all outline this long history of film censorship for political and other social reasons.

[46]Collier, p. 516.

[47]These two hearings have been conveniently made available in reprint editions. They are *U.S. House of Representatives, Committee on Education, Motion Picutre Commission Hearings, 1914;* and *U.S. House of Representatives, Committee on Education, Motion Picture Hearings, 1916* (New York: Arno Press, 1978). Hereafter they are cited as *Hearings, 1914* and *Hearings, 1916*.

[48]*Hearings, 1914*, pp. 3-4.

[49]*Ibid.*, p. 6.   [50]*Ibid., pp.* 21-22.   [51]*Ibid.*, pp. 21-22.

[52]Chase insisted on having the full record of *Mutual* inserted into the record. See *Hearings, 1916*, p. 151.

[53]*Ibid.*, p. 8.

[54]*Weber v. Freed*, 224 F. 355 (1915), which dealt with the banning of the film of the boxing match between Willard and Johnson. See De Grazia and Newman, pp. 185-186 for a complete description of this case.

[55]*Hearings, 1916*, pp. 8-9 (italics added).

[56]*Ibid.*, p. 12.

[57]*Ibid.*, p. 28. Seabury later wrote two important books, *The Public and the Motion Picture Industry* (New York: Macmillan, 1926); and *Motion Picture Problems: The Cinema and the League of Nations* (New York: Avondale Press, 1929).

[58]*Ibid.*, pp. 119-121.   [59]*Ibid.*, p. 121.   [60]*Ibid.*, p. 155 (italics added).   [61]*Ibid.*, pp. 169-170.   [62]*Ibid.*, pp. 209-211.

[63]For details of this see Jowett, pp. 167-169.

[64]U.S. Congress, House of Representatives, Committee on Education, *Hearings, Proposed Federal Motion Picture Commission*, 69th Congress, 1st session, 1926, pp. 200-204.

[65]For his important role in the National Presbyterian hierarchy, see Will H. Hays, *Memoirs of Will S. Hays* (New York: Doubleday, 1955), pp. 559-568.

[66]The public relations activities of the Hays Office was always a point of great contention during this period. For more details on this issue, see Herbert Shenton, *The Public Relations of the Motion Picture Industry*, for the Federal Council of Churches, 1931 (reprinted, New York: Jerome S. Ozer, 1971).

[67]At these hearings, Miss Maude M. Aldrich, National Director of Motion Pictures, Woman's Christian Temperance Union, read into the record a motion passed by the W.C.T.U. at the National Convention in 1925. It said, in part, "we work for Federal, State, and local regulation of motion pictures of such a nature that each may supplement the other and all may seek to preserve American ideals at home and guarantee a right interpretation of

American life to the nations of the world." *Hearings, 1926*, p. 117.

[68]*Ibid.*, p. 240.   [69]*Ibid.*, p. 241.   [70]*Ibid.*, p. 139.

[71]There are surprisingly few comprehensive works on the history and structure of the Catholic Legion on Decency. The best are Paul W. Facey, *The Legion of Decency: A Sociological Analysis of the Emergence and Development of a Pressure Group* (New York: Arno Press, 1974); and John M. Phelan, S.J., "The National Catholic Office for Motion Pictures: An Investigation of the Policy and Practice of Film Classificatin" (Unpublished Ph.D. dissertation, New York University, 1968). See also Jowett, pp. 246-256.

Mythical Animals and the Living Constitution: Interpreting Tradition

Ailene S. Goodman

Actually [The American Constitution] was largely an evolutionary product.
[Nevins and Commager]

THE IDEA OF A CONNECTION between the history and strength of the Constitution and mythical animals occurred to me one day when I was standing in front of the National Archives, a historic fifty-year old building in Washington, D.C.

Built to preserve records of legal and historic importance, the Archives "enshrine for posterity" some 900,000 cubic feet of permanently valuable records for the Federal Government. Three documents (on view in its Exhibition Hall) that serve as charters of our democracy—are the real, original Declaration of Independence, Constitution of the United States and Bill of Rights.

The classical architecture of the building itself helps "define a nation and a people." From its massive Corinthian columns to its neoclassical sculptured art carvings, it is a "temple of our history" where "written words endure."

Etched in marble on the pedestals of four solid statues at the entrances outside the building are these words: "Eternal vigilance is the price of liberty." "The heritage of the past is the seed that brings forth the harvest of the future." "Survey the past." And (from Shakespeare's *The Tempest*) "What is past is prologue."

The U.S. Constitution which it houses belongs to a nation that is at once very new and very old. "Oldest of the 'new' nations—the first one to be made out of an Old World colony," writes historian Henry Steele Commager, "[the United States] has the oldest written constitution, the oldest continuous federal system and the oldest practice of self-government of any nation."

The word "constitution" itself is interesting, because from its early linguistic origins it seems to have had the two meanings it has now—that is, physical, a metaphor of the human body, as well as mental, a sense of government. The same is true of the word "state," meaning "condition." One's constitution is one's physical and vital powers, and the personality traits one is composed of. The person is made up of, composed of, or *constituted* of, body and mind, the ruled and the ruler, nature and the will, force and law, acting upon each other, neither part to dominate the other, and each to limit the excesses of the other. Applied to modern government, this, in its Graeco-Roman origins, suggests the philosophy of John Locke, to which (with Montesquieu) our own written statement of government owes much. Both words ("state" and "constitution") take the human mode or condition of *being* as a metaphor of government—what it is capable of, its characteristics, and the natural laws that limit its powers.

Language, like our understanding of what is "human nature," is not static. It changes with changing customs. The so-called Bill of Rights to the Constitution and subsequent amendments recognize change. Words, architecture and even principles—moral and physical—adjust to what are perceived as the needs of the times. Interpreting tradition takes values of the past to instruct the unforeseeable future.

The images of metaphor and symbolic language, of classical motifs and of literature, reflect their contemporary interpretations of customs and traditions. On the public buildings of our dynamic society, the use of mythical animals and allegorical fantasies is a reminder of values once felt worth saving and considered by later generations at least worth remembering. Such dream-like expressions are a profound, sometimes whimsical, memory of the universal creative impulse that binds the twentieth century to the history of civilization and to the ideas of modern medical-mental/emotional/behavioral (psychiatric) science. For one thing, the responses and reactions of the combined imaginary creations of fantasy and biological creatures of nature, in many respects, help us understand our own responses and reactions. In addition, wishful thinking, conscious and unconscious—what we are and what we would like to be—governs our self-image and the mold we create for theirs.

Does the artistic expression create or does it rather interpret? In some 2,000 years, since the beginning of our era no one has been able to answer that question. But among classical mood makers are many who re-invented the natural behavior of fabulous animals. The ancient Aesop of Aesop's *Fables* is one, and another is his early-modern follower in the royal court of the Sun King—the Baroque era Frenchman, La Fontaine. Other great writers and artists both named and anonymous created political commentary and social satire using talking animals who think and act like human beings.

Symbolism, of course, can be over-interpreted. While it is true that moderns may be able to "read" images in the same way as their originators intended, it is also true that an object (or an animal) in itself can be found worthy of interest and enjoyment and respect simply in terms of itself, outside of any consideration of spiritual or moral ideas.

It is appropriate that the massive United States National Archives building, where the Constitution is preserved, has a symbolic face. If there is anything symbolic about the Constitution, it is as a representation of the people who drafted it, and their faith in the people it would govern. As a place for "the preservation of federal records," it has 72 columns with Corinthean capitals, each column 53 feet tall, 5 feet 8 inches in diameter, weighing 95 tons apiece, and adorned with four 12-foot neoclassical figures. This sturdy beautiful building, planned and completed during the presidencies of Herbert Hoover and then of Franklin Delano Roosevelt, answers the "goal of permanence [for the] records from which history is written." As much as for what they say, the living documents it conserves are symbols in themselves.

To a visitor seeking symbols, it is appropriate that the solid footings of constitutional government are made ageless by design. The various government and non-government architects and designers of the nation's capital over the years have adorned many of its marble halls and facades with imaginary beings that lend an airy dimension to the solid marble and limestone and granite in which they are carved. At the National Museum of American History of the Smithsonian Institution, George Washington, President of the Constitutional Convention of 1787, sits Roman toga-clad and sandal-footed in marble an Olympian eleven feet high. This giant of history is sculpted, comfortably bare-chested for the heat of summer in the sub-tropical climate of the city that memorializes his name. The hand of George Washington's statue raises forefinger and thumb as if to point out the direction in a symbolic gesture befitting the President who is inscribed "first in the hearts of his countrymen." But even the great Revolutionary hero now and then is subjected to today's awelessness. (Exercise-minded Washington wags, perhaps apologizing for their own scanty costume, affectionately look at his showerbath-style toga and his sandals and upward pointing gesture, and they interpret that the dignified gentleman is thinking: "Yes, indeed, my heart is up there with my countrymen but I left my clothes in the gym locker room.")

Up on Capitol Hill at the east end of the Mall between Constitution and Independence Avenues, The Library of Congress (edifying memorial to Thomas Jefferson—President George Washington's Secretary of State, principal author of the Declaration of Independence, and a principal prodder of his friend James Madison to add a Bill of Rights to the Constitution), is ornamented with creatures from timeless mythology and unbounded regions. Halfway down the Hill, the Rayburn Building (the House Office Building) is guarded by a most extraordinary double pair of

Pegasus-like creatures. Between the Smithsonian Mall and the Hill, the National Archives, where the original "Charters of Freedom" of American history are on permanent display, wears a crowning frieze on each of two sides, of mythic animals and imaginary men and women.

Washington, Adams, Jefferson and Madison are monumentalized by the living documents of government, in a city that constructs its monuments both architecturally and philosophically.

Sculptured, painted, etched, embossed, carved in marble, granite, sandstone, limestone, oils, copper, bronze, brass and bright gold are various mythical animals, adding charm, delight, solidity, controversy, profundity, absurdity, the weight of tradition, exuberance to the exteriors and interiors of various Capitol Hill public buildings. Craning one's neck to see them (though they can often be seen only with the aid of field glasses), or bending down to peer in amazement at some imaginary creature one has just irreverently stepped on, one is aware of how deep in our popular culture is the conservation of the rights of the people—or what one historian of the science of government, Charles Howard McIlwain, calls "the retention of 'ancient' liberties." Conserving the limitation of government by means of the law is (he writes), if not the most important, the most ancient part of our constitutionalism.

ii

The universality of the motifs on the buildings is striking, for they come from many diverse sources; the originality of their treatment imparts interest, beauty, continuity and a certain sense of daring.

They are symbols, subject to interpretation, at once new and old.

Probably no building is as rich in animal symbolism as the matchless national library whose very founding is James Madison's, John Adams' and (principally) Thomas Jefferson's legacy to the nation. On many levels the grand old federal building complex is symbolic—a treasury of books themselves and a trove of ideas. From the Neptune Fountain outside it; to the seahorses and mermaids and allegorical, or winged, babies within, to the centaur and smiling sun of a zodiac that includes a wise scorpion, a fertile fish, a prosperous crab and a fierce bull in bronze; to the bird-headed figure over the door of the satellite John Adams Building, what does it mean? Why have the architects and designers of some of the government buildings located in the nation's capital seen fit to let flights of imagination adorn reality?

What are these designs on the temples of constitutional government? As symbolic of enlightenment as the Constitution itself, what do the mythical creatures mean to convey?

The national institutions some of whose decorations the reader will find pictured with this essay are: The National Archives (housing the Constitution); and (principally) The Library of Congress on Capitol Hill, occasional reference to [in order of subsequent mention] the Jefferson and the Lincoln Memorials, the Capitol itself, the Washington Monument, an emblem and an exhibit visible among part of the Smithsonian Institution's family of museums, the Rayburn Building, the Supreme Court, and the Folger Shakespeare Library.) The Library of Congress complex includes three buildings which are named for the United States' presidents John Adams, Thomas Jefferson and James Madison. The architecture of each of these tasteful buildings differs, reflecting the period in which each was constructed. (The Thomas Jefferson was completed in 1897; the John Adams opened in 1939; and the James Madison was dedicated in 1980). Together they comprise a "three-building multi-media encyclopedia."

The Library of Congress was designed as a temple of learning, and it is to preserve and disseminate learning that its collections exist. Jefferson's personal library was the core of the original Library of Congress collections, which he offered to Congress in 1814 to replace the small library in the Capitol burned by the British. Adams, first vice president and second president, who signed the bill that removed the seat of government to the new capital city of Washington in 1800 (and in so doing created a Congressional reference library), was one of the leaders of the American Revolution, and a key person in expounding the principles of government by checks and balances. Madison, fourth president, is often called "the father of the Constitution." (Coincidentally, as early as 1783 Madison had proposed that a collection of books for "a library of Congress" be assembled.)

The James Madison Memorial Building is comparatively stark, modern, but beautiful and expressive. Dedicated only within the past few years, the Madison Building is decorated with massive bronze books superimposed upon its austere white marble structure. This exterior "Falling Books" sculpture is evocatively carved with abstract forms which I view as patterns of prehistoric life. But it is not until one stands almost directly under the sculpture that the designs seem (to me) recognizably paleoecological.

Both the Adams Building exterior, and the copper-domed Jefferson Building abound with classical decorations. Jefferson's epithet, "architect of the American republic," is significant (given Jefferson's architectural bent). The Jefferson Building is dominated by a massive cupola, its classical circular dome is akin to Jefferson's plan for the rotunda of the University of Virginia and to the rounded, low Jefferson Memorial that— with the Lincoln Memorial—graces the manmade Potomac River Park. At the Library of Congress' Jefferson Building, mermaids, stylized seahorses, Neptune's watery court, Pegasus the "flying horse," unicorns, the Zodiac signs, and countless other mythic or dream-like creatures, surprise and delight the observer.

Metaphor, as we have said, and the use of language to symbolize the human condition has been the essence of some of the greatest of animal stories. One seldom thinks of Aesop's delightful fables as metaphoric of the political scene, but of course this is probably how they developed from ancient Greece and Rome. Aesop's animals dramatize all human behavior, talking and acting like people. The French fabulist La Fontaine (1621-1695) adapted ancient Aesop's style and content to the writing of his own early modern social satire. As if in prophecy (unlikely) of the First Amendment of the United States Constitution's Bill of Rights, La Fontaine, declaring his fables to be servants of the truth, wrote, "Tout parle en mon ouvrage, et meme les poissons." ("Everything in my work speaks, even the fish," says the Baroque writer in the court of King Louis XIV.)

Customs and traditions are often clothed in fables about fabulous or mythical creatures. This has been a technique of parable down through the ages from (for example) ... the Bible, to Aristophanes, to Aesop, to "The Arabian Nights," to Shakespeare, to La Fontaine, to Lewis Carroll, to George Orwell, to ....

One person who figured in the evolution of the United States as a nation, who loved to use anecdotes for pleasurable teaching and did it beautifully, was perhaps the most genial (if controversial) genius this country ever had—Benjamin Franklin, born in 1706—a generation after La Fontaine. The early history of the United States is fastened by its umbilical cord to that epoch of about one hundred and fifty years which art-history and musicology loosely call by the descriptive term "Baroque"—a period to which, of course, La Fontaine belonged—and the Baroque in turn was fascinated by and deeply rooted in the whole history of thought, both ancient and modern. The lifetime of the sculptor Bernini, the core of John Locke's political philosophy, the education of Benjamin Franklin, place easily within that age in England and on the Continent which is now called Baroque. When Jefferson was in France (as Washington's minister) the reaction against Baroque architectural excess was already well advanced in much of Europe, and so-called *Palladian* architecture was a focus of the movement toward a purist revival of classicism. The buildings and publications of Andrea Palladio (1508-1580), one of the most influential designers in the development of European architecture, attracted the admiration and study of Thomas Jefferson, whose own architectural interest and skill are expressed by the designs he carried out for his Monticello home as well as plans for other residential and official building designs submitted by him, sometimes anonymously (such as his plan for The White House—whose architectural selection committee at the time rejected it). The architect historian Sidney Fiske Kimball, writing in 1939 observes that "[Jefferson], in wanting to make an artistic declaration of independence from England as well as a political one, turned to the Greeks and Romans whose republics, 'in the freshness of modern republicanism,' seemed very near."

The purist "temple front" pedimented porticoes (current examples are our National Archives, National Gallery of Art, Supreme Court, Capitol ...) and rounded or semi-rounded projection (examples: The White House, The Octagon...) or circular dome (examples: The Jefferson Building of The Library of Congress and the Jefferson Memorial ...) pleased Palladio's influential seventeenth-century architect-follower Inigo Jones, as they pleased Europeans and the American minister to France, Jefferson, in the eighteenth century. These symbolic ideas, expressed both philosophically and artistically through architectural design, arrived in the Washington capital region largely because of Jefferson's European experience.

Other ideas travelled to the young nation with the highly symbolic arrival after some twenty years of congenial diplomacy in England and France, of a person who sometimes got the left handed compliment of being called by Europeans "the first civilized American."

As [President] Washington's ambassador to France, Jefferson replaced the ebullient and resourceful Benjamin Franklin. The very popular Franklin, "renowned" (says the current *Encyclopaedia Britannica*) "for his skillful furtherance of the welfare of the British colonies which became the United States of America," was 79 when he began his last journey home.

Benjamin Franklin once referred to humankind as a species of "a tool-making animal." That venerable inventor, scientist, philosopher and statesman, was 81 when the Constitutional Convention met in 1787. Frankin had tried to bring the American colonies into a confederation within King George III's British empire, was principal author of the Albany Plan of Union in 1754, signed the Declaration in 1776, and eleven years later he joyfully put his name to the new Constitution.

Historians have given such titles to the Constitutional Convention as "Miracle in Philadelphia," "The Great Rehearsal," "The Grand Convention." What the momentous event represented was the combined wisdom of some very great public servants based on their backgrounds of experience and what they knew of other republics. Their success was remarkable. The living Constitution they created continues to function well. This is amazing because the United States has changed from an agricultural society to a predominantly industrial society that is only 7% agricultural, but the Constitution still works.

The delegates were chosen by their state legislatures to go to Philadelphia—were (in Shakespeare's timeless phrase) "the choice and master spirits of the age." Or, as John F. Kennedy remarked once, at a dinner at which Nobel Prize winners were present, "I think this is the most extraordinary collection of talent, of human knowledge, that has ever been gathered together at the White House, with the possible exception of when Thomas Jefferson dined alone."

Not symbol but substance was the delegates' objective and their goal. By the time the Constitutional Convention was adjourned, however, a certain curious symbol had emerged. The venerable old philosopher and scientist, Ben Franklin, at 81 already a legend of inspiration, advising the meeting of far younger men throughout the long days and weeks and months, got up to praise its members. Franklin was well liked, old age increased the respect his colleagues already felt for his knowledge, and they enjoyed his sense of humor. They did not expect the wonderful sally he told them, but it has become a classic.

The story begins on the second Monday in May 1787, when commissioners began the long process of considering the situation of the United States. Their purpose was, to "devise such further provisions as shall seem to them necessary to render the Constitution of the Federal government adequate to the exigencies of the Union."

That evening Benjamin Franklin gave a dinner party for the delegates straggling into town. James Madison and George Washington were among the guests. Not delegates to the Convention were Thomas Jefferson, because he was in Europe serving as Washington's minister to France, and John Adams, who was also away as minister to England. But Jefferson's teacher of law—who also taught law to Madison—was at the dinner table.

Five months after Franklin's memorable dinner (historians Allan Nevins and Henry Steel Commager relate), the Convention held its last meeting. Most of the members were delighted by what had been achieved; only three refused to sign. The aged Franklin said that while there were parts of the Constitution he did not approve of, he was astonished to find it so nearly perfect. For the sake of unanimity he begged those delegates who may not like some of its features not to consider themselves infallible but to accept the document. Similarly, Alexander Hamilton declared that although he had wanted a more centralized form of government, he asked how could a true patriot prefer anarchy and convulsion over order and progress. Convinced, though perhaps reluctant, and seeming oppressed by the solemnity of the occasion, delegates from 12 states came forward to sign. George Washington, as he often had done, sat silently in grave meditation.

James Madison, in his published notes about the historic event, reports the suspenseful story. Madison writes, it was at that point that 81-year-old Benjamin Franklin came forward to relieve the tension in the air with his characteristic good humor. Looking towards the half sun painted in brilliant gold on the back of Washington's chair, Franklin remarked that artists had always found it difficult to distinguish between a rising and a setting sun: "I have often and often, in the course of the session, and the vicissitudes of my hopes and fears as to its issue, looked at that behind the President, without being able to tell whether it was rising or setting; but now, at length, I have the happiness to know that it is a rising, and not a setting, sun."

As I read Madison's account of the symbol, moved by the immediacy of history, I recalled that since the legendary days of the Greek god Apollo, and his forerunners in medical prehistory, the sun has been a welcome sign of warmth and healing. I thought of how, emblazoned as a Smithsonian Institution colophon I had seen a lovely identifying image of a golden sun. And I thought how at the Jefferson Building of the Library of Congress, a wonderful happy sunball radiates its pleasure in golden bronze all around the great marble red and white floor of that marvelous center for the book; and how the visitor entering the National Archives steps first across a bronzed golden sun surrounded by winged imaginary human figures, allegories of Legislation, Justice, History, and War and Defense.

iii

To depict the detail of the art work against a backdrop of living history is to recognize its classical origins as these have been interpreted and re-expressed down through the years.

A Congressional Library 1901 handbook description of the original Jefferson Building is prefaced to the effect that:

> ...Commissions were given to nearly fifty sculptors and painters—all Americans. Both inside and out, the Library of Congress is mainly in the style of Italian Renaissance—derived, that is to say, from the architecture of buildings erected in Italy during the period roughly fifteenth century or earlier, when elements of classical art were revived and recombined in a renascence or new birth, of the long-neglected models of Greece and Rome.
>
> The building reflects through sculpture and murals our cultural ancestry, and the disciplines on which our civilization is based. Man's great achievements and intellectual conquests in such areas as medicine, law, physics, mathematics, theology, architecture and zoology are portrayed through various forms of art often expressed allegorically and with an uplifting significance.

I have tried to project the classical art work as it once appeared and as it has come down to us interpreted through literature, behavioral and medical sciences, fine art, caricature, social history and just plain fun.

My research on "Mythical Animals and the Living Constitution: Interpreting Tradition" finds mythical creatures on American public buildings, and explores their stabilizing symbolism in the rapid development of a new country, its culture and its Constitution. It cannot be overemphasized that among the various functions the symbols served one of the most important was the stabilizing projection of the past to the present and into the future. Tradition, no matter how it is pictured, by tying the present with the past, guarantees stability of the future.

The mythical animals and legendary creatures that decorate the marble halls and painted ceilings are intended to remind the viewer that civilized traditions rest upon eons of human history.

Across the street from the Library of Congress, close by the United States Capitol, and almost across East Capitol Street next to the Supreme

Court, at the Folger Shakespeare Library, a fairy Puck grins gracefully over a fountain and says, in Shakespeare's words—"What fools these mortals be."

Down the street, however, we find the bard again. For, as Shakespeare (and the marble inscription at the National Archives repository of the original U.S. Constitution documents) reminds us: "What is past is prologue."

iv

Library of Congress Great Hall (mermaids, ceiling). Two winged figures holding a cartouche with a lamp and a book. The blue of the cove is flecked with stars.

Beginning with a figure of a stork at the bottom, the ornamental staircase figures each represent a portion of the earth's surface on the globe. "America," a native American [Indian] with Wampum necklace, headdress, bow and arrow, shades eyes, gazes intently into distance. The eight allegorical "babies" represent music, literature, and architecture.

Bust of George Washington is below, in a niche.

U.S. Capitol seen from the Library of Congress. Its architecture reflected renascence of long-neglected models of Greece and Rome. Topped by Freedom (19½ feet high). The dome was designed from motifs of three European cathedrals—St. Peter's (Rome); St. Paul's (London); St. Isaac's (St. Petersburg).

Zodiac centaur (bronze inlay in marble floor), Jefferson Building

Zodiac sun photographed from above.

Jefferson Building Entrance to Great Hall with its grand staircase; nearby is a sculpted Minerva of peace with globe signifying learning. Note scroll. Minerva of war holds the torch of learning.

Relief doorhead shows seahorses with medallion seal of the United States with the torch of learning. Jefferson Building, outside Main Reading Room.

A Phoenix design, between main reading room and the photocopy and computer search room. The symbol of the fiery nest reminds one of Prometheus' fire. The Phoenix is fabled by ancients to live 500 years, then repair to the desert, build a pyre, be consumed in flames, and rise again.

Jefferson Building, Great Hall. Mosaic of Apollo with lyre upon Pegasus. Inventor of music (lyric) and poetry.

This is the ornate and beautiful Neptune fountain outside the Jefferson Building. It also has a nymph and sea horse (with a fish's tail), and (sculpted from real life) giant Florida turtles.

Across the second floor corridor (Thomas Jefferson Building) from Lincoln memorabilia decorated with mythic eagles, is this beautiful mosaic "Minerva" at landing of stairs leading to Visitor's gallery of Rotunda Reading Room. It is inscribed with the words "Nil Invita Minerva quae monumentum aere perennius exegit." (Not unwilling Minerva raises a monument more lasting than brass" [from Horace, *Ars Poetica*]) 15½ feet by 9 feet wide. She is the Minerva of peace. The border shows twisting serpents and a head of Medusa. The scroll represents law, statistics, sociology, botany, bibliography, mechanics, philosophy, zoology, i.e., the various branches of learning, science and art.

A bas relief sculpture on the large bronze doors of the John Adams Building depicts Thoth, one of many legendary or historic figures credited with giving the art of writing to their people.

Mythical lion, exterior wall, John Adams Building.

"Falling Books" sculpture of bronze and slate.
(James Madison Building.)

A rhyton decorates the Rayburn House Office Building. The Rhyton was modelled after an ancient Greek drinking horn with mythical chimaera on bended knee. The cornucopia is a classic symbol of abundance and plenty. The Rhytons rest on a calyx of water leaves. Note Ram's horn, symbolic of wisdom and power, strength of purpose, defender of the right. The horn is of marble, weighs 12 1/2 tons. Date: 1964.

National Archives Building, showing pediment, Constitution Avenue entrance. The central figure of a dignified elderly man, represents the recorder of the Archives. He is seated on an architectural throne, which rests on recumbent rams; they are symbols of parchment. Above the rams is a frieze based on the papyrus plant. These two mediums—papyrus and parchment—make possible the housing of documents of a great nation in a single building. The attendant figures stand in front of Pegasus—classical symbol of aspiration. The dogs at the ends of the pediments symbolize guardianship.

U.S. Archives, mural painting showing the twenty-five delegates to the Constitutional Convention. 19 signed (#1,6,9,11,20,22 did not.) (Both Madison and Washington are of the state of Virginia.) The painting shows Madison submitting the Constitution to George Washington and the Constitutional Convention.

National Archives. Four winged figures in bronze on the floor symbolize Legislation, Justice, History, and War and Defense.

The Myth of the Constitution: 19th Century Constitutional Iconography

Alan Ira Gordon

THE MYTH OF THE CONSTITUTION, evident from the time of the ratification itself, represents an American tradition that transcends generations. Regarding any tradition, the majority of the population of most societies are the recipients of tradition as a result of the tradition-recommending initiative of some of their contemporaries.[1] Such contemporaries as intellectuals, writers and artists (including political cartoonists) initiate the form that tradition, or myth, will take. Concerning the Constitution, political cartoonists in each generation analyzed, interpreted and re-shaped the myth, making each period interpretation of the Constitution unique. As such, the myth of the Constitution was in flux between generations.

This study focuses upon three periods of American history in which iconographical interpretations of the Constitution were numerous in political cartoons—the period of the early Republic (1787-early 1800s), the Jacksonian era (1830s-1840s) and the Civil War (1861-1865). Reinterpretations of the Constitution in these periods may be regarded as the result of 19th century nation-building. As immigration increased and America expanded economically and geographically, political cartoonists strove to depict symbols of heritage common to the American experience. In the absence of other traditional sources of common imagery, the Constitution came to be relied upon as a mythic source of solidarity.

An overall view of the three periods reveals an ongoing intensification of the myth of the Constitution among the periods. Veneration and respect for the Constitution deepened as political cartoonists depicted the Constitution in symbols that increasingly intensified the sacredness of the document. The iconographical evolution of the Constitution's sacredness is supported by historical assumptions concerning the role of tradition in society. Tradition-seeking persons exhibit an intense and active sensitivity to elements of the sacred contained in monuments, documents or texts which have come down from the past.[2] In the process of sanctification the original myth or interpretation surrounding an article or event may become distorted beyond all recognition of its original purpose or meaning. As will be seen, this process of traditional sanction is evident among 19th century political cartoon interpretations of the Constitution.

Many political cartoons from the early Republic are revealing of the myth of the Constitution at that time. An untitled engraving that dealt with the recently-ratified Constitution appeared in the Spring 1788 issue of *Columbia Magazine*. The setting of the cartoon is a scene from Greek mythology. In the background is a Greek temple with the phrase "E Pluribus Unum" on the dome and the words "Sacred to Liberty, Justice, and Peace" on the triangular arch above the pillars. Beyond the temple, a ship sails upon a sea into the sunset, while a farmer leans upon his hoe.

In the foreground are three figures—Clio, Columbia, and Concord, depicted as a cherub with wings. Clio kneels on the ground with open book and quill ready. Columbia stands, holding a bowl in her outstretched hand. Concord points to the temple with his left hand, while holding in his right hand a half-unrolled scroll, labelled "Constitution." The caption of the cartoon is a poem, that reads:

> Behold! a Fabric now to Freedom rear'd,
> Approv'd by friends, and ev'n by Foes rever'd,
> Where JUSTICE, too, and Peace, by us ador'd,
> Shall heal each wrong, and keep unsheath'd the sword,
> Approach then, Concord, fair Columbia's Son:
> And faithful Clio, write that 'WE ARE ONE.'"[3]

An analysis of the cartoon's iconographical symbols reveals two clear perceptions of the Constitution. First, by affiliating it with Clio, the Greek muse of history, and the Greek Temple, the artist depicted the document as derived from the heritage of Greek democratic principles. The interpretation of an object as representing an inheritance from the past is a common myth-making device. Initiators of tradition often think that the past had more wisdom than the present and that what has come down to us is sounder and more correct than that which has been devised more recently.[4] Secondly, the Constitution is stressed as the foundation of justice, peace and prosperity for the country. The farmer leaning upon his hoe was a common early Republic iconographical symbol of prosperity.[5] The caption emphasizes the benevolent nature of the Constitution, by characterizing the document as representing freedom, justice and peace.

Another political cartoon dealing with the Constitution was printed on the cover of *Bickerstaff's Boston Almanack, or Federal Calandar for 1788* (see figure 1). The explanatory note inside the calendar described the cartoon as depicting "the heroick Washington holding in his hand the grand Fabrick of American Independence, the Federal Constitution, offering it with paternal affection to his freeborn brethren the Sons of Columbia. The Goddess of Fame, flying with a trumpet in her hand, spreading the glad Tidings of Union through the States, sounds a peal to the immortal honour of the 39 members of the late Federal Convention who framed the present Constitution. The Sun, entirely clear of the Horizon, shines resplendently on the American Federal Union.⁶"

Again, the Constitution was depicted by an early Republic cartoonist as being approved by a representative of the heritage of Greek democracy—in this instance, the Goddess of Fame. By depicting the sun as resplendently shining down upon the unified country, the artist symbolized the Constitution as an instrument of benevolence and unification.

A well-known political cartoon dealing with the Constitution entitled "The Providential Detection" was published independently in 1800 (see figure 2). Jefferson is depicted on bended knee before the flaming altar of Gallic Despotism, upon which the works of Godwin, Paine, Voltaire and Rousseau are burning. He is about to cast the Constitution into the flames, but is halted by the American eagle, which seizes the document with one of his claws and threatens Jefferson with the other. In the right upper hand corner of the cartoon hovers an eye keeping watch over the eagle, as depicted by vision lines beaming down from the eye to the eagle.⁷

Although the emphasis within "The Providential Detection" is upon the anti-Jeffersonian theme, various iconographical symbols reflect a positive view of the Constitution. The Constitution is represented as a vital document that must not be desecrated and which the nation itself, represented by the American eagle, must protect. Protecting its validity is stressed as a positive virtue, approved by "the gods" or "those above" as represented by the eye watching over the eagle.

While the Constitution was interpreted by some early Republic cartoonists as representing a heritage from past democratic principles, other cartoonists saw the Constitution as a source of strength or durability, that would help the country weather present circumstances. An example of this type of iconography is a cartoon drawn in 1798, entitled "Cong-ss Embark'd on board the Ship Constitution of America bound to Conogocheque by way of Philadelphia (see figure 3). The topic of the cartoon concerns the removal of the seat of the Federal government from New York to Philadelphia. The Constitution, represented as a ship, is about to shift course toward the rocks in the river and fall before reaching Philadelphia.

The fact that the Constitution is represented as the ship of state emphasizes the perception of the document as central in importance to the structure of the Federal government. That "structure," literally depicted as a floating vessel, is the Constitution itself. Secondly, by drawing the legislative branch of the government as crewmen on board the ship, the anonymous cartoonist interpreted the Constitution as a floating foundation upon which the structure of American government rested. Thus, the Constitution is interpreted in this instance as a base of

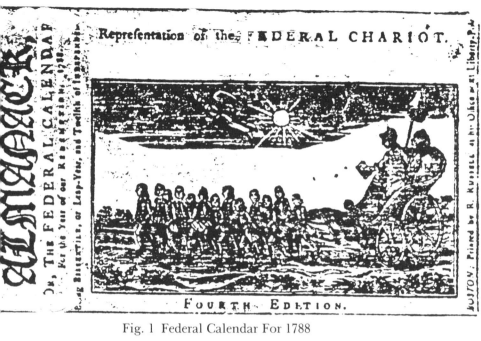

Fig. 1 Federal Calendar For 1788

Fig. 2 The Providential Detection

Fig. 3   Congress Embark'd on board the Ship Constitution of America bound
to Conogocheque by way of Philadelphia

government that must not be allowed to fall into dangerous straits.

A final cartoon from the early period of the Republic further emphasizes the Constitution as a vital, central component of the Federal government. "Church and State," drawn by B. Picart and published in 1816, dealt with the founding of the American Bible Society in 1816[8] (see figure 4). The cartoon depicts a horse-drawn church from which a cannon is being fired in an attempt to halt a U.S. mail coach on its journey. In the background is a Greek temple, with pillars labelled Paine, Franklin, Jefferson, Washington, and Lafayette. Upon the temple steps are engraved the phrases "Declaration of Independence" and "All Men Are Born Equal." The temple dome is labelled "Constitution." Columbia stands atop the dome, grasping a pole topped by a cap, the symbol of the French Revolution.[9] By depicting the Constitution as the dome of the temple of government, B. Picard interpreted the document both as the capstone of the Federal government by which the virtue of liberty is upheld, and as a document held up by the strength of the inheritance from the late-18th century political leaders.

Overall, it may be seen that the political cartoons of the early Republic symbolically venerate the Constitution. Several artists depicted the document as a harbinger of peace, prosperity and justice. Others interpreted it as an object of inheritance symbolizing Greek democratic principles. The Constitution was also regarded as a source of strength, either a ship of state that would carry the government, or the capstone of American principles of government. It is important to note that even in this early period of American history, the various symbols used to depict the Constitution glorify and upgrade its image to the extent of divorcing perception of the Constitution from the reality of what it is—a document outlining the principles of American government. As such, it is obvious that the myth of the Constitution began to evolve from the period immediately following its ratification.

In the era of Jacksonian Democracy, the myth of the Constitution received a new interpretation by political cartoonists. Most cartoons published in this period held a strong anti-Jacksonian orientation. Recurrent among these was the theme that the U.S. Constitution was being attacked and desecrated by the principles of Jacksonian Democracy. Several cartoons clearly reflect this theme. A well-known political cartoon of this period was published in 1832, entitled "King Andrew The First." Andrew Jackson is depicted as a king seated upon his throne, with a sceptor in his right hand and a scroll labelled "Veto" in his left hand. Jackson's left foot rests upon a torn paper labelled "Internal Improvements, U.S. Bank." His right foot rests on a torn piece of paper labelled "Constitution of U.S. of America."[10]

Several cartoons drawn by the well-known antebellum political

Fig. 4 Church and State

cartoonist David Claypoole Johnston (1799-1865) include iconographical interpretations of the Constitution. One of Johnston's most famous cartoons includes a symbolization of the Constitution in terms of desecration. "The Great Loco Foco Juggernaut, A New Console—A—Tory Sub-Treasury Rag Monster," is a mock 12½ currency bill in which Johnston satirizes the Jacksonian Democratic radicals known as Loco Focos (see figure 5). In the right-hand box of the bill, Jackson, dressed as an old maid under the title "Liberty," is standing on documents labelled "Vote of Congress," "People's Rights," and "Common Sense." In his left hand he holds a scroll inscribed, "veto," while his right hand holds a very ragged and torn flag, labelled "Constitution."[11]

Johnston's *Scraps (No. 6), For The Year 1935* included a cartoon condemning anti-Catholic fanaticism, entitled "The Triumph of Fanaticism." In the foreground of the cartoon Miss Liberty lies unconscious next to a stone altar. Scattered beside her are torn pieces of scroll, labelled "Constitution of U.S." In the background, a mob of people are setting fire to several buildings.[12]

Among cartoons that emphasized a non-Jacksonian Democratic theme, only one example was found that dealt with the use of the Constitution as an icon. Like the anti-Jacksonian cartoons, "Whig Candidates For The Presidency. Or Trying On The Whig," published in 1837, symbolizes the Constitution as being maligned. The cartoon satirizes three candidates for the Whig Presidential nomination—John Tyler (seated on the left), Nicholas Biddle (seated in the middle), and Henry Clay (seated on the right). Biddle wears a sign around his neck labelled "Hartford Convention," and is seated upon a chest labelled "Monetary Chest." In his right hand he holds a scroll labelled "U. States Bank Rechartered." Biddle's right foot is stepping upon a rolled-up scroll labelled "Constitution." The caption of the cartoon is a poem that Biddle recites:

> Uneasy is the head that wears a crown,
> But a wig is a different thing,
> It's the very first step to a National Bank
> And the next step is to be King.—
> So here's the Hurra! for the NO PARTY,—
> For the TEA PARTY, or what not,
> Nicholas Biddle shall pay the Fiddle,—
> Who pays the Piper I care not.—
> Of honest men in these panic times,
> I confess there's somewhat of a dearth,
> But Nicholas Biddle, is as rich as the devil,
> And MONEY'S the test of worth.—
> So here's Hurra! for the NO PARTY,
> For the tea party or what not,
> Nicholas Biddle shall pay the Fiddle
> Who PAYS the Piper, I care not.—

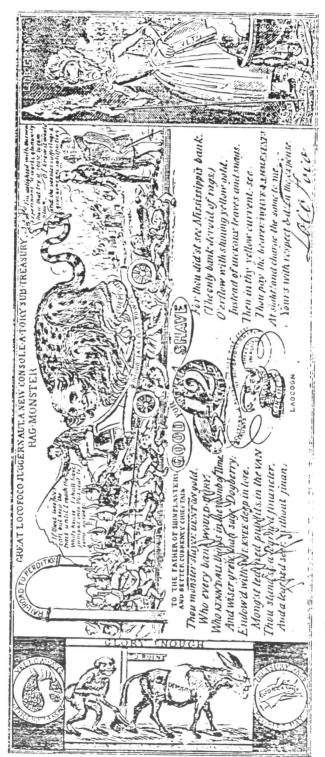

Fig. 5.   Great Loco Foco Juggernaut, A New Consol-a-tory Sub-Treasury Rag Monster:
A Cartoon Bank Note

"You won it, wore it, kept it, gave it me;
Then plain and right, must my possession be;
Which I with more than with a common pain
'Gainst all the world will rightfully maintain."

Fig. 6 Untitled

And all the People shouted,
From Nahant to Cape Cod,
Of a truth our noble Daniel,
Is a down-east god!!

As Biddle recites his poem, a figure of the devil places a wig, symbolic of the nomination, upon his head.[13]

An initial examination of the political cartoons described above may lead to the interpretation of the Jacksonian era as a period characterized by a lack of respect and veneration for the Constitution. Indeed, political cartoons of the period consistently depicted the Constitution as being torn to shreds or stamped upon—a far cry from the early Republic representation of the Constitution in "The Providential Detection," in which the cartoonist portrayed the document as being saved from harm before the protagonist Jefferson was able to inflict any damage upon it. Yet such symbolizations must be regarded as a continuance of the myth of the Constitution from the early Republic years. In each cartoon, the cartoonist attacked the opposition to his own political principles. By declaring the opposition as desecrators of the Constitution, the cartoonist argued that the political opponent's principles and actions were not only unfavorable but represented an attack upon the most venerated principles of American democracy, as embodied in the Constitution. In this manner, Jacksonian era political cartoonists interpreted the Constitution as a document of importance that must not be harmed.

Several political cartoons of the Jacksonian era represented a continuance of particular iconographical interpretations of the Constitution that were evident in the early Republic. Several cartoons symbolized the Constitution as a ship of state. A typical example is "The in Glorious Nineteen!—Or scenes at Annapolis," published in 1836. In this cartoon the devil perches atop a tree labelled "Hickory," Jackson's well-known nickname. Several men are clinging to the tree, while others have fallen off into a mud puddle. The trousers of the fallen men are labelled "Veto!" In the background, a ship labelled "Constitution" steams toward the shore. Three men witnessing the entire scene comment in the caption:

First Man: "Hurra! for the Constitution!"
Second Man: "Jack, they've put new timbers into 'Old Ironsides' and she FLOATS as well as ever!"
Third Man: "Yes, and they did it according to LAW too!!"[14]

As seen above, the iconographical depictions of the Constitution drawn during the era of Jacksonian Democracy represented both a transformation of the myth of the Constitution and a continuance of interpretations of the myth from the period of the early Republic. As will next be seen, the myth of the Constitution was defined in greater depth and complexity in the third distinct period of Constitutional iconography, that of the early 1860s.

The main theme of the majority of Civil War era political cartoons quite naturally centered around the issue of secession. Within these cartoons, the myth of the Constitution was greatly expanded. With the advent of the Civil War, the Constitution became the focus of patriotic symbolism, serving as a document around which the Union could rally. As a consequence, the meaning of the Constitution became ever more distorted, as political cartoonists literally placed the document upon a pedestal and mythicized the Constitution as a sacred and omnipotent document.

In several political cartoons of the day, the Constitution was venerated as a sacred inheritance from the Founding Fathers. "Columbia Awake At Last" depicts Columbia holding a slightly torn copy of the Constitution in her left hand, while choking a Southern man with her right hand. The man's trouser legs are labelled "Secession" and "Treason." As he is being choked, he drops two knives, a gun, a miniature Fort Sumter, and the torn corner of the Constitution. In the background of the scene hovers the wavering spirit of a Founding Father, visible from the waist up, wearing a powdered wig and colonial attire.[15] Interestingly, this is the first cartoon found in this study since "The Providential Detection" in which the desecrator of the Constitution is being punished for attacking the document.

"Political 'Blondins' Crossing Salt River," printed by Currier and Ives in 1860, explicitly emphasizes the sacredness of the Constitution. The scene is over the Salt River, with the right bank of the river labelled "North," and the left bank "South." Several leading political figures of the day are having difficulty crossing the river from the northern to the southern bank. Abraham Lincoln and Horace Greeley fall off a board balanced upon "Abolition Rock." Stephen O. Douglas falls off a rope labelled "non intervention" into Salt River. Joseph Lane teeters on a very frayed rope labelled "slavery extension." Behind these gentlemen looms a massive stone bridge spanning the banks of the river, labelled "Constitutional Bridge." John Breckinridge and Edward Everett stand on the bridge, holding hands. The caption of the cartoon reads as follows:

Breckenridge: "It's no use, Gentlemen, you'll all go overboard, because you were not satisfied to stand upon this bridge but must needs try some other way to get across...."
Everett: "Built by Washington, Jefferson, and the Patriots of 76 this bridge is the only structure that connects these two shores in an indissoluble bond of union, and woe be to the man who attempts to undermine it ...."[16]

By the cartoonist's choice of Everett's words, the image of the Constitution was mythologized far more than in any other cartoon previously examined. In his effort to emphasize its sacredness, the cartoonist distorted the myth of the document, portraying it as an inheritance from the Patriots of 1776, rather than the constitutional convention delegates of 1787.

The myth of the Constitution as a sacred symbol from the past is a common development of the evolution of tradition within societies. According to Edward Shils, one fundamental ground for tradition is awe before the sacred in the past. Authority possesses the quality of sacredness and is exercised by elders through whom "the past" is transmitted and by whom attachments to the past are fostered. There is an authority inhering in symbols which derive their weight and force through their connection with persons formerly existant, who once filled certain roles or were members of the collectivity at an earlier stage.[17] Shils' assumptions are evident in the two cartoons described above. In both, the quality of sacredness within the Constitution is upheld by symbolically correlating the document with elders through whom "the past" is transmitted.

The authority of the Constitution was emphasized in many Civil War era cartoons by symbolizing the document as a bound volume. Rather than realistically depicting it as a scroll or piece of paper, several political cartoonists expanded the myth as a respository of authority, in the form of a rule book or book of law. In "Mistress Columbia, Who Has Been Taking A Nap, Suddenly Wakes Up and Calls Her Noisy Scholars to Order," Columbia is depicted as a stern teacher seated at her desk. Atop the desk is a large, bound volume inscribed "Constitution." Students are scampering back to Northern and Southern seats from a line painted down the middle of the classroom, labelled "Mason-Dixon line."[18] In this cartoon, the Constitution is interpreted as the teacher's supreme law or word.

An untitled political cartoon published in *Vanity Fair* also included an icon of the Constitution as a bound volume (see figure 6). The scene depicts a seated Union officer with his right hand resting on the American eagle, and his left hand holding forth a scroll enscribed "To the People of U.S." Facing him is a standing Union officer with sword drawn and arms outstretched. The caption is a poem, recited by the standing officer:

> "You won it, wore it, kept it, gave it to me;
> Then Plain and Right, Must My Possession Be;
> Which I With More Than With A Common Pain
> 'Gainst All The World Will Rightfully Maintain."

In the background are three bound volumes, one untitled, and two labelled "Constitution."[19]

Many Civil War era political cartoons that dealt with the secession

issue included iconographical symbols that appeared in both the early
Republic period and the Jacksonian era. Again, the Constitution was
mythologized as a temple or base of strength. In "Sambo Agonistes," a
slave is portrayed as attempting to push apart two pillars of the temple of
the Constitution, labelled "Constitution 1787-1860" (see figure 7). The
caption reads, "Day Don't Budge."[20] By symbolizing the Constitution as
two immovable pillars, the cartoonist reaffirmed the myth.

An untitled cartoon that appeared in *Vanity Fair* symbolized the
Constitution as a temple of shelter (see figure 8). The cartoon depicts
Lincoln and Columbia tending a garden of Civil War figures. The caption
reads:

Old Abe: "Ain't there a nice crop? There's the hardy Bunker Hill flower, the
Seventh Regiment Pink, the Fireboy Tulip—That tricolored flower grows near
Independence Hall—that Western Blossoms and Prairie Flowers will soon begin to
shoot."
Columbia: (Pointing to small gallows): "What charming plant is this?
Old Abe: "That is rare in this country—it will bloom shortly and bear the
Jeffersonia Davisiana."

Behind Lincoln and Columbia stands a small garden shelter, erected
in the form of a temple, and inscribed "Constitution."[21]

An effective allegorical political cartoon interpreted the Constitution
as a rock of stability and strength, upon which the Union rested. The
anonymous cartoonist pictured "Justice on the rock of the Constitution
waving an American flag toward a happier scene, where the sun of
Universal Freedom is brightly shining." Behind her are hideous scenes of
disorder and national disaster. In contrast with the dark picture on which
Justice has turned her back is the bright vista of the future, "the Union as it
will be."[22] Rich with iconographical symbolism, this cartoon interpreted
the Constitution as a rock of strength around which the populace of the
North could rally.

The interpretation of the Constitution as a heritage derived from
Greek democratic principles was greatly distorted by Civil War era
cartoonists. In "A Record of the Day," the scene depicted is inside the
temple of the gods on Mount Olympus, within which the gods are
physically fighting among themselves. Sitting on a throne raised above the
gods is Zeus, who attempts to restore order by holding a paper inscribed
"Constitution of the U.S." in his right hand over the quarreling gods.[23]
While the earlier period cartoons included icons alluding to the
Contitution's Greek democratic heritage, "A Record of the Day" greatly
distorted this aspect of the myth. The Constitution is depicted as handed to
America by the gods themselves—an emphasis that serves to reinforce the
aura of sacredness surrounding the myth.

No analysis of political cartoons dealing with secession would be

Fig. 7 Sambo Agonistes

OLD ABE.—Aint there a nice crop? there's the hardy Bunker Hill flower, the Seventh Regiment Pink, the Fireboy Tulip—That tricolored flower grows near Independence Hall—the Western Blossoms and Prairie Flowers will soon begin to shoot.

COLUMBIA.—What charming plant is this?

OLD ABE.—That is rare in this country—it will bloom shortly and bear the Jeffersonia Davisiana.

Fig. 8 Untitled

complete without an examination of cartoons depicting the Southern viewpoint of the issue. During the Civil War, two periodicals were published in Richmond, Virginia, that became the main Southern sources of graphic illustrations. *Southern Punch*, published from August 15, 1863 to July 9, 1864, was a weekly magazine that emulated the well-known British Punch. *The Southern Illustrated News*, published from 1862 to 1864, was a carbon copy format of the New York-based *Harper's Weekly*.[24]

In all issues of both periodicals, only one cartoon dealt with the Constitution. "Schoolmaster Lincoln and His Boys," published in *The Southern Illustrated News*, satirizes the military performance of the Union armies in the early phases of the war. Lincoln is depicted as a stern schoolmaster, seated at his desk. His right hand holds a ruler labelled "Constitution." Facing Lincoln are four small boys covered with bandages and leaning on canes, symbolizing Union Generals McClellan, Pope, Banks, and Burnside. The caption reads:

Lincoln: "Waal, boys, what's the matter with ye; you hain't been hurt, hev yer?"
McClellan: "Them fellers that runs away has been beatin' us."
Lincoln: "What fellers?"
McClellan: "Bob Lee and Jeb Stuart and them"
Lincoln: "I sent you out to fetch them same fellers back, so's I could wallop 'em."
McClellan: "Yes, but Bob Lee took and bunged me in the eye."
Pope: "And Stunwall Jackson he kicked me in the rear until he broke my arm."
Banks: "Yes, and that same feller gouged me and run me until I run my leg off and hev to wear a wooden one."
Burnside: "All of 'em, Bob Lee, Stunwall and Stuart, jumped on me at Fredericksburg and give me fits; that's the reason my jaw is tied up, to keep my teeth from chatterin' for I've had a fit of the ager since."
Lincoln: "You are a worthless set, all of you. You hain't no spunk. I'm agoin' to spank every one of yer. Come up here."[25]

While the anonymous cartoonist ridiculed the North in this cartoon and depicted the Constitution as an instrument of punishment being misused by Lincoln, the myth of the Constitution as an acknowledged source of strength is evident. The Constitution is not depicted as a piece of paper that can be stamped upon or torn up, but as a source of strength (handruler as instrument of punishment), albeit a misused one.

Two cartoons that center upon Lincoln writing the Emancipation Proclamation include interpretations of the Constitution similar to those found in cartoons dealing with the secession issue. In "Abraham Lincoln Writing the Emancipation Proclamation, 1863," by David Gilmour ⊤lythe, the scene centers upon Lincoln seated in a chair, the Bible and the Constitution on his lap, writing the proclamation that he would issue publicly on New Year's Day, 1863. Surrounding him are piles of documents, petitions, maps, and books that he has set aside in his search for

Fig. 9 Abraham Lincoln Writing The Emancipation Proclamation, 1863

inspiration. From the bookcase hangs a map of Europe and a sword, while a map of the rebel states lies on the floor in front of him. Lincoln's own words appear inscribed across the bookcase cornice: "Without slavery the war would not exist, and without slavery it would not continue."[26]

The key to interpreting this cartoon is seeing that Lincoln has laid aside all sources of inspiritation for the Emancipation Proclamation save the Bible and the Constitution. In justifying the legitimacy of the Proclamation, the cartoonist interpreted it as being based upon the two most sacred literary works cherished by American society.

A political cartoon embodying the Southern reaction to the Emancipation Proclamation includes a similar symbolization of the Constitution. "The Emancipation Proclamation, 1864," drawn by Adolbert J. Volck deals with Lincoln writing the Proclamation. In contrast to Blythe's depiction, Lincoln's inspiration is maliciously demonic. Lincoln is seated at a table that has legs carved as cloven hooves. A carved object on the desk depicts a small demon holding a cup. Furniture carvings throughout the room symbolize demonic animals. As Lincoln writes, his left foot rests upon a bound volume entitled "Constitution."[27] Although this cartoon emphasizes a negative view of the Proclamation, the Constitution is portrayed in a somewhat positive manner. While Lincoln is literally stepping on the Constitution by writing the Emancipation Proclamation, the Constitution is depicted as a bound volume of law that supposedly should be revered and respected by the President.

Concerning post-Civil War intepretations of the myth of the Constitution, an entire separate study would be required for an adequate analysis, yet it may be seen that the accelerating rate of postbellum industrialization and urbanization left its mark upon the myth of the Constitution. A brief glimps of this interpretation can be viewed in Erasmus Field's painting entitled "Historical Monument of the American Republic" (see figure 10). Field's symbolic painting of an entirely urbanized America depicts several towers, of which the central and tallest commemorates Lincoln and the Constitution.[28] Thus, the Constitution as a symbolic myth continued to play a central role in iconographical interpretations of American nation-building.

In conclusion, it may be seen that iconographical interpretations of the Constitution in political cartoons reveal an intensification of the myth of the Constitution in the 19th century. During the early Republic, the Constitution was venerated as a symbol of progress and peace, was considered as an inheritance from Greek democracy, and was symbolized as the foundation or capstone of government. Sanctification of the Constitution intensified during the Jacksonian era, as tampering with or

Fig. 10 Museum of Fine Arts, Springfield, Massachusetts,
The Morgan Wesson Memorial Collection

non-adherence to the principles came to be expressly symbolized in negative terms. Early Republic aspects of the myth recurred in the age of Jackson, most notably the belief that the Constitution was a vital vehicle (ship of state) serving as a foundation of government.

Finally, in the Civil War era the sanctity myth of the Constitution developed to the point where the Constitution was interpreted as a sacred and omnipotent document or a supreme volume of law or rules. By the early 1860s, the myth of the Constitution was greatly distorted from its original cast, because of the need for a symbol around which the Northern populace could rally in a time of war, and because of the passage of three generations from the ratification itself. The effects of this distortion are apparent to the point where the document was depicted as a sacred product of the gods of Greek mythology, rather than a practical, present-day application of Greek democratic principles.

The phenomenon of both change in the myth of the Constitution between periods and a reaffirmation of particular aspects of the myth (i.e., Constitution as ship of state, inheritance from Greek democratic heritage) supports the assumption that the myth of the Constitution must be defined in terms of both continuity and change. As Shils writes, "new" traditions emerge as modifications of already existing ones. The degree of novelty can vary considerably, yet the fact remains that completely disjunctive novelty in the sphere of belief is out of the question. Creative innovations in tradition-making consist of an assimilation of inherited aspects of the tradition with new interpretations of the tradition. Adaptations are thus made without a sense that anything essential has been renounced.[29] As such, the myth of the Constitution embodied both past ideals and present aspirations, as 19th century political cartoonists adapted it to the national needs and issues of the day.

Notes

[1]Edward Shils, "Tradition," Comparative Studies in Society and History (April 1971), p. 139.

[2]Shils, p. 140.

[3]*Columbia Magazine* (Spring 1788), p. 1.

[4]Shils, p. 140.

[5]Michael Kammen, *A Season of Youth—The American Revolution and the Historical Imagination* (New York: Knopf, 1978), Chapter 3—"Revolutionary Iconography in National Tradition."

[6]William Murrell, *A History of American Graphic Humor (1747-1865)—Volume I* (New York: Whitney Museum of American Art, 1933), pp. 35-36.

[7]Murrell, p. 53.

[8]Murrell, p. 69.

[9]Murrell, p. 70.

[10]American Antiquarian Society Political Cartoon Collection, American Antiquarian Society, Worcester, Mass.

[11]Ibid.

[12]D.C. Johnston, *Scraps (No. 6), For the Year 1835* (Boston, 1835).

[13]American Antiquarian Society Political Cartoon Collection.

[14]Ibid.

[15]*Harper's Weekly*, June 8, 1861.

[16]American Antiquarian Society Political Cartoon Collection.

[17]Shils, "Tradition," p. 138.

[18]*Harper's Weekly*, Jan. 7, 1860.

[19]*Vanity Fair*, Nov. 16, 1861.

[20]*Vanity Fair*, March 3, 1860.

[21]*Vanity Fair*, May 4, 1861.

[22]Arthur Maurice and Frederic Cooper, *The History of the Nineteenth Century In Caricature* (New York: Dodd, Mead, 1904), p. 172.

[23]*Harper's Weekly*, Dec. 15, 1860.

[24]Murrell, p. 199.

[25]*The Southern Illustrated News*, Jan. 31, 1863.

[26]Dorothy Miller, *The Life and Work of David G. Blythe* (Pittsburgh: Univ. of Pittsburgh, 1950), p. 90.

[27]Murrell, p. 92.

[28]Bernard Bailyn, et al, eds. *The Great Republic: A History of the American People* (Volume II) (Lexington, Mass.: Heath, 1977), insert.

[29]Shils, "Tradition," pp. 144-155.

Architecture and the Constitution: Self and System

Dennis Alan Mann

Introduction
WHILE THOSE WHO HAVE STUDIED THE CONSTITUTION of the United States have written about both its strict and loose construction, a less than exhaustive reading provides very few direct references to buildings. The Constitution, itself, is a contract or a major bargaining document between a government and its sponsors. Therefore it is written to be as general as possible without being completely ambiguous. And when it does specifically mention buildings it is quite clear as to the type of building to which it refers. For instance, in Article I, Section 8 the Constitution gives Congress the power to "establish *post-offices* and *post-roads.*" In the same article Congress (meaning the Federal Government) was given authority over all places purchased from the states "... for the erection of *Forts, Magazines, Arsenals, dock-yards, and other needful buildings;...*" There are a few other direct references. In the Amendments to the Constitution Article III prohibits soldiers from being quartered in any *house* without the consent of the owner (except in time of war and to be prescribed by law). Article IV protects the rights of people to be secure in their *houses* (from illegal search and seizure), Article V prohibits any citizen from being deprived of *property* for public use without just compensation, and Articles V and XIV prevent a citizen from losing his life, liberty or *property* without due process of law. The Constitution also gives Congress the power to promote the progress of the

110

"useful *arts*" by securing to the authors their exclusive rights to their work for a limited period of time.

Yet in spite of these few direct references to buildings the Federal government has had an enormous influence on the built form in this country. This influence has been felt in both the area of Federal regulations and in programs supported by Federal dollars. Besides many projects built with a large percentage of Federal funds, like roads and highways, bridges, airports, public educational facilities, public housing and government buildings, the Federal government through some form of tax program contributes to the construction of nearly every building in this country. Revenue sharing programs with States, cities and counties provide federal dollars to augment local dollars. A complex tax code, both personal and corporate, allows investment credit on income tax. It encourages residential construction by allowing home purchasers to deduct the interest on their mortgages, provides a 25% tax credit on the renovation and restoration of property in historic districts and encourages rehabilitation in areas of the city which might otherwise deteriorate. Urban renewal programs, which since the 1950s have been a major factor in the rebuilding of the central core of nearly every American city, have largely been the result of Federal programs. In addition, zoning or the specified regulation of land use, first codified in the United States in the 1920s and upheld by the Supreme Court from arguments that it infringed on the free use of private property has had a direct impact on the shape and form of our physical environment. Most of these programs have fallen under the general rubric of promoting the general welfare.

But these facts should be rather evident to the informed student of government and current events. Although the programs mentioned are directly or indirectly responsible for many of the buildings constructed today, they do not lie at the foundation of what can be interpreted as one of the fundamental characteristics of the Constitution. This characteristic can be best summarized in the word "freedom." Surrounding the idea of freedom are the rights and responsibilities of the individual as they might infringe on the liberty of others. The framers of the Constitution wrote a thin line between individual freedom and the general welfare, between what is best for the individual and what is best for the community— between self and system.

A much broader interpretation of the Constitution in light of the demands of a democratic and pluralistic society would examine through architectural form the delicate balance that exists between the individual, the community and the idea of freedom. If the Constitution is used as a basis for establishing an attitude toward architecture, then it follows that both an anarchy of form and a conformity to community standards will continually vie for authority in an atmosphere of freedom. Learn to study buildings as representations of many values.

We The People ____

The idea of individual freedom and the promotion of common concerns is embedded in both the Preamble and the Bill of Rights. It was at the insistence of the writers of the Constitution to form a more perfect union, to establish justice, to insure domestic tranquility, to provide for the common defense, to promote the general welfare and to secure the blessings of liberty. Yet this set of goals did not resolve the debate between Alexander Hamilton who wished to concentrate power in a strong federal government and Thomas Jefferson who preferred to diffuse power throughout a wide democratic base. Should our system of government establish the boundaries within which the individual might find a place or should the United States be an egalitarian society whereby the government is created solely to protect the freedom and rights of the individual?

Architecture, like the Constitution, is capable of many readings and many interpretations. Popular architecture is even more ephemeral. It changes as rapidly as popular values emerge, flower and then disappear. This essay will explore, through a deliberate and careful examination of visual images and text, popular architecture as a reading of the relationships between the self and the system that can be interpreted within the Constitution. The success of the War for Independence was a force that would always make Americans suspicious of too much government.

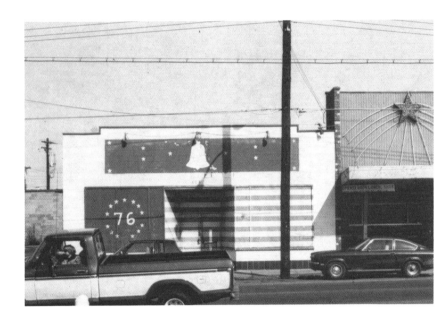

"...Preserve, Protect and Defend the Constitution of the United States."

When the President echoes these words during his oath of office he becomes the first among equals. His pledge to defend the Constitution reflects his belief in the values that it embodies. These unique values are in part symbolized by the American flag. Displaying the flag is a sign of the patriotic ideals incorporated into the Constitution. The monument to the American servicemen who died while capturing Iwo Jimo from the Japanese during World War II uses the raising of the flag as the theme for the sculptural composition..In another example the criticism and debate surrounding the design of the Vietnam Veterans Memorial in Washington, D.C. was not resolved until it was agreed that an American flag be flown as part of the monument. Government buildings prominently display the flag as an integral element in identifying its public use.

Yet the most explicit display of patriotism and love of country occurred in 1976 during this country's Bicentennial Celebration. The flag was not only flown more often and in more places but it often *became* the architecture itself. Popular architecture never hedges its bets. It is direct and to the point. Building facades became flags as the stars and stripes were freely interpreted. American patriotic values, expressed in the red, white and blue, symbolized a reinvestment in the American ideal.

"...Nor Be Deprived Of Life, Liberty or Property"

Owning property means the right to do with that property as the individual owner sees fit as long as it does not infringe on the rights of the community. The alternative is monotony. Self or system?

"... The Right of the People to Keep and Bear Arms"

Historically, Americans have defended their right to keep arms. This basic right, established during a time when the gun was necessary for the overthrow of the tyranny of England, became a fundamental requirement in a rough and threatening environment. Today the National Rifle Association is among the more powerful and influential lobbying groups in Washington. Opposed to gun control laws the NRA has been able to raise millions in support of Article II of the Bill of Rights.

While individuals are encouraged to purchase and maintain weapons for sport, as a hobby, or for self-protection, the United States government has been enjoined with the responsibility of providing for the common defense. The Constitution has given Congress a wide berth of power in Article I, Section 8 to raise armies and navies, to declare war and to erect military installations. And if the "self" is embodied in the free spirit of the popular architecture of Caristo's Gun Shop in Albuquerque, then the "system" can be characterized by the orderliness and regimentation of the architecture of the Air Force Academy in Colorado Springs.

" ... No Law Respecting the Establishment of Religion"

The Constitution guarantees an America of many religions—or, if you so choose, no religion. This free exercise of religious choice has resulted in an architecture which fills not only the byways but also the airways. Sunday morning features tele-evangelist Robert Schuller preaching from his magnificently inspired crystal cathedral designed by the award-winning patriarch of present-day American architecture, Philip Johnson. And while Schuller delivers the glad tidings on national television, gospel music flows out through the doorways of storefront churches all across America. Religious architecture has maintained an independent spirit characterized by the relative independence of each congregation. Where the larger system of ecclesiastical authority is exercised, like in the Roman Catholic or the Episcopal Church, religious buildings conform to a more recognizable typology. But the true spirit of the statement "... free exercise thereof" (religion—Amendments, Article I) is best exemplified by the individual and idiosyncratic interpretations found in popular religious architecture. Just as each religion finds its own way of celebrating its beliefs, it creates its own architecture as a stage for those celebrations.

"All Persons Born or Naturalized in the United States and Subject to the Jurisdiction Thereof, are Citizens of the United States..."

The richness and variety of popular American architecture stems, in part, from the wide variety of ethnic origins of the people who migrated to this country. The buildings that they constructed not only display regional variations but also reflect their unique interpretation of the American dream. That America has not become a melting pot is evident by the strong sense of pride in the ethnic traditions that set people apart from one another. People continue to cherish their roots and maintain connections to the institutions that support their common heritage. Part Old World, part ingenuity, part utility and part symbol of success, the architectural interpretations of these roots in popular American building types suggest connections to both the past and the future. While stylistic motifs from each culture maintain a connection to the past, the realities of a modern high-tech consumer society require a view into the future. Buildings unique to this modern American life style like service stations, detached single-family houses, drive-in restaurants and tourist attractions exhibit characteristics of both ethnic associations as well as present day functions.

The buildings that result from these double forces often display a split personality. While ethnic origins might suggest a culturally specific architecture, the urge to express the individual idiosyncracies that originate in merging a building's function with modern technology

require unique adaptations. And if a pledge of allegiance means a commitment to a new way of life it does not necessarily demand that the old ways be forgotten. Rather, it might mean a creative intepretation of two distinctly different and sometimes contradictory systems.

While immigration from Europe has slowed to a trickle, immigration from Spanish speaking countries and from Asia has increased. Little Havana in Miami and Little Saigon in Los Angeles have taken up where the Chinatowns and Little Warsaws have left off. New sources of immigrants continue to enrich our culture and our architecture. New interpretations of built form abound with the energy that is always present as new Americans reach for the American dream of success and security.

"...Or Abridging The Freedom of Speech"

Written or spoken language is the most common form of communication. Language in this form is encoded, transferred between parties and then decoded. Normally, written or spoken language is relatively explicit. Architecture as well as art is not the same as language although its surfaces are often used to write upon. Architecture is much more abstract than language. Architecture, unlike language, has no semantic component. Therefore it communicates nothing. But architecture can be interpreted. These interpretations, though, always tell more about the interpreter than the building that is being interpreted. For instance, would you say that the buildings at the top of the page represent a vision of the freedom of speech implied by individual expression? Or do the buildings at the bottom of the page portray the individuality that one sacrifices when he joins the corporate world—a world that insists on a carefully controlled party line? Could it be said that freedom *to* speak through individual expression exists in popular architecture but is stifled in the architecture of the establishment?

It could also be argued that architecture is far more ethereal. As Emerson wrote of art, architecture speaks to the imagination.

Conclusions

Attributing the diversity of American architecture solely to a broad interpretation of the language of the Constitution would be unreasonable. Yet it is not outside of reason to suggest that American architecture, especially popular architecture, is as much the result of the independent spirit, the imagination and ingenuity, and the unbounded energy of her people as it is the result of the freedoms that the Constitution makes possible. Fundamental to the formation of the Constitution was a basic apprehension of control by a powerful central government. Consequent of this fear and mistrust was the creation of the three branches of government: the legislative, the executive and the judicial. A system of checks and balances written into the Constitution guaranteed that no one branch could usurp power from the other branches. Yet this organization of government does not assure that an equitable balance will always exist between an individual and the community. While the sense of the independent spirit is alive in America the pressures to conform from large scale organizations is a constant threat. Conversely while large scale organizations work to establish democratic and egalitarian policies, individuals constantly vie for the power of authority within those organizations; self and system always parrying to maintain a delicate balance.

In *Megatrends*, one of the more popular best sellers of the past few years, author John Naisbitt forecasts ten new directions which he argues are transforming the America of the past, a centralized, industrialized and economically self-contained society, into an America of the future where a credo of self-reliance and local initiative would exist. He considers this new credo to be de-centralist in nature with a clear shift of responsibility from Washington back to the grass roots level. This concept of the self-acting, well-informed citizen is implicit in the egalitarian principles articulated by the court's interpretations of the Constitution's intentions. And it is this attitude which fosters the interpretations found in popular architecture.

This might suggest that we learn to look more closely at buildings. There, we might recognize the creative and imaginative energy unleashed by the liberties that are characterized by the American spirit of freedom. We must learn to interpret buildings as objects which reflect the values of the people who made them. We should ask how such values can generate buildings which are unique to a way of life found nowhere else in the world. Finally, we might wonder at this way of life with all its faults and all its possibilities and ask whether such diversity could ever be possible without the wisdom and foresight of the builders of the American Constitution.

The Constitutionality of Cable Television

Linda K. Fuller

FIRST AMENDMENT RIGHTS and responsibilities regarding cable technology have been neither defined nor decided by Congress and the courts, despite a nearly four-decade continuing debate on the topic. Unless and until a national policy is determined, both the cable industry and the citizenry are losers.

Aspects of Cable Technology

Cable television, as distinguished from transmission by electromagnetic waves in the air that characterizes broadcasting, involves transmission by coaxial wire over a wide communications spectrum. Cable operations are made possible upon receipt of television broadcasting signals from stations or satellites, which are then amplified for retransmission by cable wire or microwave to paying subscribers.[1] The important implications for First Amendment considerations from this method of reception is erasure of broadcasting's "scarcity of spectrum" argument and cable's potential for interactivity.

What began around 1948 as a system to aid reception from poor conventional broadcast signals due to geographic location has traditionally been referred to as Community Antenna Television (CATV). Where broadcasting began as an outlet for advertisers, cable's inception is based on a service for improving reception. Once federal regulations toward its development were lifted in 1972, audiences and multiple systems operators burgeoned, further enhanced by the introduction of satellite communications in 1975. Expanding programming and the promise of diversified services brought a great deal of attention to the industry, but throughout these developments the Federal Communications Commisions (FCC) has remained, in the opinion of Professor Don LeDuc[2] a "reluctant regulator."

According to the National Cable Television Association (NCTA), more than 15,000 communities across the United States are served by 5,800 cable television systems, with subscribers representing nearly 40% of all American households. Over-the-air broadcasters own approximately one-third of those cable television systems, newspaper and magazine publishers financially control another quarter, and the rest are in the hands of multiple-system operators.

Since the notion of cable's retransmission was not even in existence when the Communications Act of 1934 was drafted, there has been a constantly recurring question as to whether or not the FCC should have jurisdiction for it. If the FCC does have jurisdiction for cable, should it be at the federal and/or the state or local level? Above all, what needs to be addressed is the role of cable vis-a-vis its operators and its audiences.

Several key court cases are relevant. As early as 1958 (*Frontier Broadcasting Co. vs. Collier, 24 FCC 251*) the FCC declined to intervene with this new technology, a decision based on the grounds that it lacked the power to do so. By the time of its Second Report and Order (2 FCC 2d 725, 1966), however, carriage and nonduplication rules were extended beyond microwave relays to the cable system, and the Commission asserted its jurisdiction over cable television for the first time. By declaring which major markets' distant signals could not be brought into the top 100 television markets, which service almost 90% of American television households, the FCC virtually froze cable expansion and sustained its jurisdictional decisions in *U.S. vs.Southwestern Cable Co.* (392 U.S. 157, 88 S. Ct. 1984, 20 L. Ed. 2d 1001, 1968). The next applicable federal case came the same year in *Fortnightly Corp. vs. United Artists TV, Inc.* (392 U.S. 390, 88 S. Ct. 1084, 20 L. Ed. 2d 1176, 1968), which said that cable systems did not "perform" according to copyright laws, a decision later reaffirmed in *TelePrompt Corp. vs. Columbia Broadcasting System, Inc.* (415 U.S. 394, 94 S. Ct. 1129, 39 L.Ed. 2d, 415, 1974); the FCC's power over cable was established.

Two significant litigations have been decided in favor of the cable interests: *Intermountain Broadcasting vs. Idaho Microwave* (196 F.Supp. 315, S.D. Ida., 1961), which declared that television stations have no authority restricting their signals after they transmit them, and *Cable Vision vs. KUTR* (211 F. Supp. 47, S.D. Ida., 1962), which found that broadcasters could protect their programming only if they could "demonstrate a protectable interest by virtue of copyright laws, or bring themselves within the contemplation of some other recognized exception to the policy promoting free access to all matters in the public domain.[3] Although the *Red Lion* case (Red Lion Broadcasting Co. vs. Federal Communications Commission, 395 U.S. 367, 89 S.Ed. 1794, 23 L.Ed. 2d 37, 1969)[4] confirmed protection of free speech for broadcasting in its declaration that "It is the right of the public to receive suitable access to social, political, esthetic, moral and other ideas and experiences which is critical here," that notice has never been legally applied to broadcasting.

From the start, the FCC's regulation of cablevision has mainly been concerned with these areas:

1. jurisdictional division of regulatory power between the Commission, on the one hand, and local authorities on the other;

2. regulation of cable importation of distant signals and imposition of

requirements for mandatory signal carriage;

3. regulations requiring cable systems to render so-called "non-duplication" programming protection to local television;

4. regulations imposing affirmative obligations on cablevision systems to initiate their own programming and to make available to the public so-called "access" channels on which anyone has the right to purchase time;

5. imposition of regulatory strictures upon cable systems similar to those placed upon radio stations, such as rules limiting concentration of ownership and control, equal employment reporting requirements and, for cable origination programming, political and fairness requirements and anti-obscenity provisions.[5]

Rivkin[6] contends that the FCC mainly wants to protect local broadcasters, and sees its views of regulatory programs as intuitive and evolutionary. Some of the standards that the FCC imposes include: frequency boundaries of cable channel, frequencies of the usual boundaries of cable channel, frequencies of the visual and aural carriers, visual signal levels, variations, on voltage, peak-to-peak, channel frequency responses, ratio of noise to interference, terminal isolation, and external radiation.

Ross[7] points out how the proposal to change cable television's status from franchised private communications carriers to "common carriers" involves both practical and theoretical problems. While spectrum space has been reserved for use by common carriers, cable operators have had to negotiate rates for their services on a diminished bargaining power basis. According to the FCC's bifurcated jurisdictional structure, there is a dual licensing system recognizing local authorities that issue franchises or licenses, subject to federal standards by means of certificates of compliance. In addition to carriage and non-duplication rules, the FCC imposes regulations on cablecasting similar to those of broadcasting, such as the Fairness Doctrine, presentation of lottery information, prohibitions on obscene and indecent matter, identified sponsors, open records, and affirmative action in employment.

With recent passage of H.R. 4103, the cable deregulation bill, through the House of Representatives Energy and Commerce Committee, cable has scored a smashing victory over the telephone companies.[8] Yet, by way of example of the industry's lack of unity, not all segments are pleased with the provisions of the bill, as witnessed by Century Communications's suit vs. NCTA complaining that it has acted in restraint of trade and violated members' First Amendment rights in striking a compromise deal with the League of Cities.

The economic success of a cable system is dependent upon three factors: 1) total population base, 2) housing density, 3) market saturation,

4) number of channels available and 5) quality of reception for over-the-air broadcast television signals.[9] The industry as a whole is doing very well, with the *Wall Street Journal* reporting its pre-tax profits growing 614% since 1975's $26.8 million to $200 million in 1979, and anticipation of revenues of $8 billion by 1990.

Cable operators, needless to say, have been guided by the profit motive. As it has been far more profitable to bring cable to urban apartment complexes than to remote rural areas, that has been the common move. And the extra services that cable might offer are at this point still out of reach of most subscribers—extras such as interactive and enhanced capacities for home security, fire alarms, teleshopping, banking, polling, play-per-view, meter reading, energy management and home information services such as teletext, videotex and access to data banks and computerized sources of information.[10] Yet many of these services are being routinely offered in urban cable franchises.

As cable is basically a local issue, it is therefore essentially a political phenomenon. Stemming from authorization by the Communications Act of 1934 for Congress to regulate interstate commerce, cable television draws its federal regulation, as does broadcasting, "in the public interest, convenience, and necessity." State approaches to cable are discrepant, ranging from imposing further restrictions than the FCC requires to moving from substantial deregulatory politics. Delaware, Massachusetts, Minnesota, New Jersey, New York, Connecticut, Nevada, Rhode Island, Vermont, Alaska and Hawaii have regulated cable television on a comprehensive basis through state agencies since 1974, with the final six states assigning responsibility to state utility commissions.[11] States then transit franchising authority to local governments through legislative grants, and receive financial support from established state fee assignments. They also usually allow local municipalities to decide their ownership issues in the franchising process, determine proper content standards, privacy legislation, pole attachment rules, access requirements, service extensions and intercommunications, fraudulent reception laws and even maintain ongoing assessments of their cable television operations.

In most instances, final decisions rest with the local issuing autorities for franchises—a situation some media followers cite as another example of the FCC protecting local broadcasters. Still states are increasingly getting involved in the many complex issues surrounding cable television. State laws can be classified into three categories: 1. pre-empt, where jurisdiction is under the Public Utility or Public Service Commission; 2) appellate statutes, where "local municipalities retain some control over franchising, but the state has the power to review local agreements and be the final arbiter of disputes"; and 3) advisory statutes, serving as "general guidelines" for local governments.[12]

Reviewing the regulatory history of cable television by the FCC as exemplary of agencies faced with a technological or economic threat to their client industries, Owen, Beebe and Manning state: "The principal question to ask about the FCC's behavior with respect to cable television is whether it is in any way justified by its own public interest considerations."[13] The authors indict the FCC with myopia regarding cable, saying "it has never seen cable as what it really is—a chance to expand viewer choice, a chance to increase freedom of expression, and a chance to reduce the intrusion of government into the marketplace of ideas."[14]

The advent of cable paralleled a time of disillusionment with traditional broadcasting, a general public distrust of media. Schwartz and Watkins[15], calling the development of cable a paradigm of man evolving under the influence of his existing environment, contend that, "As well as citizen groups, product-oriented industries such as the telephone utilities, television broadcasters, and manufacturers of electronic technology see the cable as an extension of themselves."

Seen from the wider view of affirmative rights and nondiscrimination, cable promises specialized programming for minority groups and specialized audiences. Mainly, it offers diversity—such as the weather channel, C-span, movie and entertainment channels, the sports channel, MTV (music television), children's programming, ESPN (the sports channel), the health channel, Cable News Network, etc. Emphasis certainly is on "narrowcasting" for those who are willing to pay for these programs. Owen[16] submits that cable television offers a strong argument on balancing speaker rights with listener rights based on freedom of speech principles.

In one of the rare publications to concern itself with the wider implications of the communications revolution, Pool's "Technologies of Freedom"[17] states how "Civil liberty functions today in a changing technological context," and that despite a 500-year struggle for freedom of speech rights that the new communications technologies have not yet won legal immunities. Seeing a trifurcated communications system—print, common carriage and broadcasting—all with different laws, Pool sees a pattern of "soft technological determinism." He argues that spectrum space on cable television is abundant, but squandered and misused, sadly lacking in much-needed policy decisions.

Above all, First Amendment notions dating from Holmes and Brandeis' "free trade of ideas" encourage a laissez-faire relationship between government and the media, and the epitome of that notion is to be found in the concept of access.

The Particular Case of Access

According to Benno Schmidt[18] President of Yale, "Proponents of access requirements argue that guaranteed entry into modern mass communications media will increase diversity of expression, and that access obligations accordingly should be viewed as consistent with, and even supportive of, the First Amendment.

Access to cable television can be public, educational, governmental and/or by leased channels. When the FCC promulgated rules to its 1972 *Cable Television Report and Order* mandating cable systems in the top 100 television market with more than 3,500 subscribers to originate its own programming, the phenomenon of access via cable television began. In an effort to promote localism through cable's abundance of channels, the Commission stipulated that these channels would be available to the citizenry on a first-come, first-served, nondiscriminatory basis. Although this decision was abrogated by the Supreme Court's decision in the *Midwest Video* case (440 U.S.689, S. Ct. 1935, 1979), which said that the FCC had no jurisdiction imposing origination requirements, and that access requirements were outside its regulatory authority, Yet many cable operators continued to honor franchise agreements that already contained the provision and many local negotiations today continue to include it.[19]

There are several reasons for the continuation of access to cable television. Pre-eminently there is the promise: the promise of decentralized media; the promise of grassroots video where people talk to people, neighbors learn about one another and their common concerns, minority groups speak out; and there is the promise of personal programming, immediate feedback, democratic dialogue. The promises are infinite and intriguing. Second, there is the fact that many community groups are learning to get organized and involved, learning to re-orient their attitudes toward television as an active medium for their interests and causes. Organizations such as the National Federation of Local Cable Programming (NFLCP) currently report more than 800 community programming efforts in the United States. And, finally, the cable industries themselves are by necessity supporting public access as attractive to "bid items" in their frantic franchising proposals for major urban markets.[20]

Local cable community programming via access, of course, is nowhere near as costly as commercial operations. What keeps the cost down is the equipment, such as the portapak videotape recorder, which can be purchased for about $1,500 or rented for $50-$100 per day. Studios can be makeshift or state-of-the-art, usually costing about $10,000 or more, depending on what facilities and extras are desired. And then videotape is most reasonable, at about $15/half-hour reel. Most access centers are volunteer-dependent, but many also include paid administrators, technicians and/or cable company personnel.

Organizationally, local cable programming fits into one of these management models: 1. institution-based, such as schools, libraries, or churches; 2. cable company managed local originations; 3. urban access management corporations, incorporated as nonprofit, tax-exempt entities separate from the cable company and the city, overseers of access administration and development; and 4. independent citizens' organizations, the traditional grassroots structure where the governing board is elected by its own members and operation is dependent upon the system's townspeople. Support can come from members' contributions, grants, service contracts, and/or the cable company—but is most of all highly dependent on community members' efforts.

The issue of whether cable companies should be required to supply free access channels is at the crux of the dispute. Barron[21] argues that the First Amendment actually compels government to act affirmatively to insure freedom of expression while requiring citizen access to media. While municipalities are requesting the channels during franchising processes, cable companies argue that they are "electronic publishers," and that their constitutional rights to free speech are being infringed by these demands. Opponents, meanwhile, claim that "since cable companies have virtual monopoly control over their markets, they should be required to give up some of their many channels for public use.[22] Asking "Whose First Amendment Is It, Anyway?" Les Brown[23] remarks: "Cable is uniquely equipped among all media, to advance the ideal of free speech and create an open marketplace of ideas. And yet it is doing its utmost to be spared having to provide outlets for free speech—and doing it shamelessly in the name of the First Amendment."

Implications

In keeping with the 1980's trend toward deregulation, Stevens[24] finds the FCC "giving up most of its pretense about setting standards for cable or even off-the-air broadcasters." Similarly, the courts have tended to see constitutional distinctions between cable television and print media,[25] but have not made any uniform policy decisions regarding free speech protections. Commenting on the fact that the courts have apparently justified their contradictory decisions "on the ground that different media present different First Amendment considerations," Zuckman and Gaynes[26] state that the courts "do not often explain in any rigorous analytical detail how the differences in media result in constitutional distinctions; and it is even rarer for a court to test the breadth of scope of its holding against the constitutional justification for differences in regulation." Yet, Friendly[27] reminds us that "the genius of the First Amendment is that it prescribes what the government is restrained from doing."

Cable is but one of many newly emerging communications technologies[28] that need regulatory decisions. While it is unique in its multiplicity of channel offerings, cable television symbolizes the need for both public and private rethinking and advocacy toward a uniform legal approach to print and electronic media.

Freedom of speech as addressed by the framers of the Constitution was indivisible then and remains as such; application of the First Amendment to cable television and the other new communicatins technologies must remain a constitutional right. The time has come for a national policy dealing with the constitutionality of cable technology.

Notes

[1]Douglas H. Ginsburg, *Regulation of Broadcasting: Law and Policy Toward Radio, TV, and Cable Communications* (St. Paul, MN.: West Publishing Co., 1979), p. 335.

[2]Don R. LeDuc, *Cable Television and the FCC: A Crisis in Media Control* (Philadelphia: Temple Univ. Press, 1973).

[3]Morton I. Hamburg, *All About Cable: Legal and Business Aspects of Cable and Pay Television* (New York: Law Journal Seminars-Press, Inc., 1979), pp. 12-3.

[4]Fred W. Friendly, *The Good Guys, the Bad Guys, and the First Amendment: Free Speech vs. Fairness in Broadcasting* (New York: Vintage Books, 1975).

[5]Harvey L. Zuckman and Martin J. Gaynes, *Mass Communications Law in a Nutshell* (St. Paul, MN.: West Publishing Co., 1977), pp. 391-2.

[6]Steven R. Rivkin, *Cable Television: A Guide to Federal Regulations* (Santa Monica, CA.: Sage Publications, Inc., 1974).

[7]Leonard Ross, *Economic and Legal Foundations of Cable Television* (Beverly Hills, CA.: Sage Publications, Inc., 1974).

[8]Alan Pearce, "Cable Wins, But Lacks a Full House," *Computerworld On Communications*, Vol. 18, No. 31A (August 1, 1984), p. 13.

[9]Charles Tate, ed., *Cable Television in the Cities: Community Control, Public Access and Minority Ownership* (Washington: The Urban Institute,1971), p. 24.

[10]Nancy Jesuale and Ralph Lee Smith, CTIC Cablebooks, Vol. 1: *The Community Medium* (Arlington, VA.: The Cable Television Information Center, 1982), pp.24-33.

[11]Nancy Jesuale, Richard M. Neustadt and Nicholas P. Miller, CTIC Cablebooks, Vol. 2: *A Guide for Local Policy* (Arlington, VA.: The Cable Television Information Center, 1982), p. 12.

[13]Bruce M. Owen, Jack H. Beebe and Willard G. Manning, Jr. *Television Economics* (Lexington, Mass.: Heath, 1974), p. 143.

[14]*Ibid.*, p. 146.

[15]Barry Schwartz and Jay-Garfield Watkins, "The Anatomy of Cable Television," in Barry N. Schwartz, ed., *Human Connection and the New Media* (Englewood Cliffs, N.J.: Prentice-Hall, 1973), p. 80.

[16]Bruce M. Owen, *Economics and Freedom of Expression: Media Structure and the First Amendment* (Cambridge, Mass.: Ballinger, 1975), pp. 24-6.

[17]Ithiel deSola Pool, *Technologies of Freedom* (Cambridge, Mass.: Belknap Press, Harvard Univ., 1983), p. 1.

[18]Benno C. Schmidt, Jr. *Freedom of the Press vs. Public Access* (New York: Praeger, 1976), p. 29.

[19]Linda K. Fuller, "Public Address Cable Television: A Case Study on Source, Content, Audience, Producers and Rules-Theoretical Perspective," Unpublished doctoral dissertation, Univ. of Mass., 1984, pp. 1-2.

[20]Linda K. Fuller, "Television Of the People, By the People, For the People: Public Access." Paper presented to the International Television Studies Conference, London, England (July, 1984), p. 2.

[21]Jerome A. Barron, *Freedom of the Press for Whom? The Right of Access to Mass Media* (Bloomington: Indiana Univ. Press, 1973).

[22]Bill Kirtz, "First Amendment battle brewing over local control of cable tv," *Christian Science Monitor* (Nov. 10, 1983), p. 7.

[23]Les Brown, "Whose First Amendment Is It, Anyway?" *Channels of Communications* (Sept.-Oct. 1982), p. 25.

[24]John D. Stevens, *Shaping the First Amendment: The Development of Free Expression* (Beverly Hills, CA.: Sage, 1982), p.146.

[25]Michael D. Wirth, Thomas F. Baldwin and Jayne Zenaty, "Consumer Demand for Sex-Oriented Pay Cable Programming and the Application of Obscenity Laws." Paper presented at International Communications Association's Annual Conference, San Francisco, Cal. (May 1984), p. 2.

[26]Zuckman and Gaynes, p. 295.

[27]Friendly, pp. 235-6.

[28]David M. Rice, Michael Botein, and Edward B. Samuels, *Development and Regulation of New Communications Technologies: Cable TV, Subscription TV, Multipoint Distribution Service, and Direct Broadcast Satellites* (New York: Communications Media Center, New York Law School, 1980)

The Fairness Doctrine:
An Update

Richard J. Knecht

BROADCASTING IN THE UNITED STATES in the past fifty years has been to a great degree a critical as well as central element of society, shaping values and opinions to an extent unrivaled by all other other forms of media.[1] The structure, success and regulation of this industry did not just happen. Broadcasting has evolved to become the product of particular American values and needs, as well as a unique democratic method of applying values to implement needs.[2] Perhaps this continuing process is best illustrated in the evolution of the Fairness Doctrine in broadcasting and its application to the fundamental guarantee of freedom of speech under the First Amendment of the Constitution.

From its inception the Communication Act of 1934 has as its basic function the establishment of a national policy regulating telecommunications in the United States and the administrative machinery to execute its policy. The 1934 Act, which serves as the legislative yardstick that measures the scope of broadcast regulation makes two assumptions: 1) that the radio spectrum is in the public domain and 2) that the natural demand for radio spectrum space exceeds the available supply. Based upon this dual hypothesis the FCC over the past fifty years has theoretically attempted to treat those parties concerned, citizens and broadcasters alike, as equitably as possible. Implicit in the fostering of free enterprise and in the regulation of broadcasting is the notion that fairness plays a central role in the fiduciary responsibility of licensees—their role as holders of broadcast channels in trust for the general public,[3] is the foundation upon which the American system of broadcasting operates today. Simply stated the theory which underlies fairness is that in a scarce medium like broadcasting some affirmative government intervention is needed to insure that the public hears diverse ideas and viewpoints.[4]

In order to accomplish its own mandate the FCC in 1949 issued a report on editorializing by licensees, known as the Fairness Doctrine. The so-called historical FCC decision encouraged licensees to introduce controversial issues by means of an editorial—provided that they gave others access to their broadcast facilties to express opposing points of view.[5] This was not an entirely new position, but more of an affirmation of

132

two assumptions upon which broadcast regulation is built in this country. In effect the Commission was saying that it is a kind of unfairness for a licensee to program nothing but bland entertainment; avoiding all serious or provocative programming would deprive the public of an important First Amendment right that it had come to expect from broadcasting.[6] However, critics of the FCC's stand felt that the requirements levied by the Fairness Doctrine was a view markedly different from the traditional laissez-faire concept which had prevailed up to then. As a consequence it would be only a matter of time before the Fairness Doctrine would be challenged on constitutional grounds.[7]

Perhaps in hoping to avoid a confrontation, and in order to clarify and codify its position on the doctrine, the FCC in 1964 released its Fairness Primer. This guideline was to be used by those who may have questioned past FCC decisions as well as shedding light on other stations' practices and policies, showing where complaints may or may not meet Fairness Doctrine requirements.[8] However, still waiting, was a major legal test of the constitutionality of the Fairness Doctrine.

In November 1964 the Reverend Billy James Hargis in a program aired over WGCB and licensed to the Lion Red Broadcasting Company accused author Fred J. Cook, who had written a book, *Goldwater Extremist to The Right*, of an attempt to smear Barry Goldwater. Mr. Cook demanded an opportunity to respond to the charges of Reverend Hargis. The management of the station refused to allow Mr. Cook the use of its facilities claiming that the First Amendment guaranteed the station an absolute right to determine the content of its broadcast.[9] Eventually the Supreme Court upheld the decision of the FCC and in June of 1969 granted Mr. Cook the opportunity to reply to the charges leveled at him by Rev. Hargis five years earlier. The Court said:

Because of the scarcity of radio frequencies, the Government is permitted to put restraints on licensees in favor of others whose views should be expressed on this unique medium. But the people as a whole retain their interest in free speech by radio and their collective right to have the medium function consistently with the ends and purposes of the First Amendment. It is the right of the viewers and listeners, not the right of the broadcasters, which is paramount.[10]

With its historic decision the Supreme Court gave the Fairness Doctrine legal endorsement and presumably settled the controversy surrounding the question of its constitutionality. Since the time of the Red Lion decision legal appeals have not been concerned with the doctrine itself but its applicability in given cases.[11] However, the 1969 decision has done little to lessen the argument during the past fifteen years as to whether to retain or repeal the doctrine. Periodically during this time the FCC under its own initiative, in 1971, examined the doctrine and then again in 1976 at the request of citizen groups reaffirmed its position by supporting the licensees' responsibility to uphold the spirit of fairness in broadcast programming.[12]

Since that time, eight years ago, when they last issued a Notice of Inquiry on the subject, both the posture and the makeup of the FCC has changed dramatically. Within the past four years the current chairman of the commission, Mark Fowler, has asked that the Fairness Doctrine be eliminated altogether. On more than one occasion he said that broadcasters should be as free from regulations as the print industry that they share the press table with and compete with for advertising revenue. Mr. Fowler identifies his ambitious plan as "the print model," and has been quoted as willing to do everything that is consistent with legislation on the books to accomplish deregulation.[13]

The present chairman in an address before the North Carolina Broadcasters Association in the Fall of 1982 was quick to point out that in order to accomplish his goals a certain blueprint would have to be followed. His plan calls for a new statute passed by Congress so that a future commission would not turn back the regulatory clock to what had preceded the current administration's posture of less regulation, resulting in a freer competitive market.[14] The chairman's argument as well as that of others including Jeff Baumann (the National Association of Broadcasters senior vice president and general counsel),[15] is that the Fairness Doctrine was introduced and enforced at a time when a real scarcity of broadcast channels existed. However, they believe that recent developments in the tele-communications industry have invalidated this philosophy. According to the authorities in the industry, a plethora of electronic outlets now exists—namely as low-powered television stations and cable outlets which service most urban areas. The argument would follow that since technology can provide the community with real diversity allowing the competing viewpoints to be explored it is no longer necessary to saddle the industry with restrictions that do not apply in a competitive marketplace.

On the other hand, fairness doctrine proponents believe that expanding technology alone may be insufficient to address the concerns of those anxious to safeguard not only the ability of disempowered minorities to express their views but also access by the public at large to a multiplicity of opinions. Advocates of the doctrine would argue that the sheer number of electronic communications outlets cannot guarantee robust debate if no signals pulsate to a different drum.[16] It would seem that the proponents' worst fear would be that the conglomerates who already dominate the mass media would make it impossible for the individual expressing an unpopular viewpoint to be heard. The logic of their argument would lead one to conclude that by removing fairness obligations altogether, the public for whom the doctrine was intended would go uninformed.

It seems impossible to believe that both proponents and critics alike of the Fairness Doctrine applauded a five to four decision that was handed down by the Supreme Court in a case involving the Pacifica Foundation during the summer of 1984. Yet, closer scrutiny of the decision may cause proponents some real concern and leave critics of fairness less than enthusiastic about what might appear to be a technicality that the court believed should be examined.

Pacifica long heralded as championing the guarantee of the First Amendment so far as it pertains to broadcasting, challenged a federal law which prohibited public radio and television stations that receive federal funds from editorializing. The law, Section 399 of the Public Broadcasting Act of 1967, was enacted as the direct result of some members of Congress who feared that the financial assistance that was to be given under the act would be used by the government to transform public broadcasting stations into propaganda machines for the administration in office.[17] The significance of successfully challenging the law lies in the fact that for the first time the bench overturned a restriction imposed upon broadcast content on First Amendment grounds.[18]

Justice William Brennan, Jr., writing for the majority said:

Because Section 399 appears to restrict precisely that form of speech which the Framers of the Bill of Rights were most anxious to protect—speech that is "indispensible to the discovery and spread of political truth"—we must be especially careful in weighing the interests that are asserted in support of this restriction and in assessing the precision with which the ban is drafted.[19]

The glimmer of eliminating fairness altogether for critics of the doctrine seems to lie in a footnote of the recent Pacifica decision. The footnote says:

The prevailing rationale for broadcast regulation based on spectrum scarcity has come under increasing criticism in recent years. Critics, including the incumbent Chairman of the FCC, charge that with the advent of cable and satellite television technology, communities now have access to such a wide variety of stations that the scarcity doctrine is obsolete. See, e.g., Fowler & Brenner, A Marketplace Approach to Broadcast Regulation, 60 Tex. L. Rev. 207, 221-226 (1982). We are not prepared, however, to reconsider our long-standing approach without some signal from Congress or the FCC that technological developments have advanced so far that some revision of the system of broadcast regulation may be required.[20]

Citing Mark Fowler's position for eliminating fairness seems to add credibility to the argument of how advanced technology has demostrated that the demand for spectrum usage has been lessened or in some cases completely eliminated. While the court seems to be proposing a reexamination of telecommunications law in this country, it is quick to point out in another footnote that it must be demonstrated in some future landmark case that the decision made in Red Lion impeded rather than contributed to the guarantee of the First Amendment. The second footnote reads in part like this:

> As we recognized in Red Lion, however, were it to be shown by the commission that the fairness doctrine has the effect of reducing rather than enhancing speech, we would then be forced to reconsider the constitutional basis of our decision in that case.[21]

It would seem to suggest that in interpreting the two footnotes in regard to the constitutionality of Red Lion, the landmark fairness case will remain on firm legal footing until a time when it has been successfully challenged. To predict with certainty the future of the doctrine is sheer folly. Although the FCC has promised to survey the entire topic of fairness sometime after the 1984 election, the agency under the chairmanship of Mark Fowler, like the rest of the nation, must be vigilant to insure that in its haste for deregulation it does not produce a system in which the strength of one's vote is proportional to the size of his bank account.[22] After all, in settling the dispute over the constitutionality of the Fairness Doctrine the Supreme Court concluded that it was the purpose of the First Amendment to preserve an uninhibited marketplace of ideas in which truth will ultimately prevail.[23] The means of disseminating "truth" to the people through the years has changed with technology but "the people" as a whole retain their interest in free speech via telecommunications and their collective right to have the medium function consistently with the ends and purposes of the First Amendment just as they did over two hundred years ago.

Notes

[1] Erwin G. Krasnow and Lawrence D. Longley, *The Politics of Broadcast Regulation* (New York: St. Martin's Press, 1978), p. 1.

[2] Frank J. Kahn, *Documents of American Broadcasting* (New York: Appleton-Century-Crofts, 1973), p. 1.

[3] Sydney W. Head and Christopher H. Sterling, *Broadcasting in America* (Boston: Houghton Mifflin, 1982), p. 475.

[4] Krasnow and Longley, p. 49.

[5] Head and Sterling, p. 475.

[6] *Ibid.*, p. 475.

[7] Irving R. Kaufman, "Reassessing the Fairness Doctrine," *The New York Times Magazine* (June 19, 1983), p. 18.

[8] John R. Bittner, *Broadcast Law and Regulation* (Englewood Cliffs: Prentice-Hall, 1982), p. 149.

[9] Kaufman, p. 18.

[10] Byron White, (395 U.S. 367, 1969) cited in Bittner, *Broadcast Law and Regulation*, p. 167.

[11] Head and Sterling, p. 478.

[12] Bittner, p. 157.

[13] Broadcasting, Oct. 25, 1982, p. 24.

[14] *Ibid.*, p. 24.

[15] *Ibid.*, July 9, 1984, p. 27.

[16] Kaufman, p. 18.

[17]*Broadcasting*, July 9, 1984, p. 33.
[18]*Ibid.*, p. 33.
[19]William J. Brennan, Jr., cited in the United States Law Week (Washington: Bureau of National Affairs, 1984), p. 5013.
[20]*Ibid.*, p. 5011.
[21]*Ibid.*, p. 2012.
[22]*Kaufman, p. 19.*
[23]White (395 U.S. 367, 1969) cited in Bittner, *Broadcast Law and Regulation*, p. 167.

Sex, Pornography and the Constitution

William E. Brigman

PORNOGRAPHY PRESENTS A GREAT PARADOX of American culture. On the one hand, Americans buy and read as much or more sexually oriented material than any other society: two magazines which focus on sexual topics are among the dozen best selling magazines in the country and pornography is a multimillion dollar business. On the other hand, pornography and obscenity[1] are the subject of a long and vociferous national debate. Conservatives demand an end to pornography in order to maintain a decent society. They are joined in their demands by liberal feminists who view pornography as both a symbol and a cause of female subjugation and violence against women. Arrayed against them are liberals who insist that freedom of communication is essential in a free society and that no communication can be outlawed without inflicting a very great amount of actual harm.

The Origins of American Sexual Attitudes

How is it possible to account for the paradoxical American attitudes toward sexuality and pornography? Although the answer is fairly simple, it has two elements, one which is nearly universal and a second which is more culturally specific. First, the concept of sexuality which serves as the basis of public morality in most societies is inconsistent with the nature of sexuality itself. As Kingsley Davis has cogently demonstrated[2] the goals of sexual behavior in human beings is not inherently social. However, mankind has felt the need to relate sexuality to socially desirable ends, particularly to the bearing and raising of children, and has therefore attempted to restrict the morally legitimate expression of sexuality to the institution of marriage.

The general society goal of submerging "animal" sexual instincts into stable "human" institutions for child rearing and societal stability is reinforced in the American mind by Judeo-Christian concepts of sexuality which are highly negative. The eminent historian of sex, Vern Bullough, describes Christianity as a "sex negative" religion.[3] Christians inherited Greek dualistic thought which divided the world into two opposing forces, the spiritual and the material, or the soul and the body. The purpose of life was to achieve salvation, to escape the domination of the flesh. Sexual activity was evil because it represented the victory of the worldly over the spiritual.

This Greek asceticism was adopted by the early Christians not only because it was part of the culture in which they developed, but also in part because they believed that the end of the world and the resurrection was imminent. Because of this they eschewed the wordly concerns of the flesh and focused on spiritual matters. It is probably in this context that St. Paul offered his oft repeated advice in I Corinthians that "it is good for a man not to touch a woman. Nevertheless, to avoid fornication, let every man have his own wife, and let every woman have her own husband."

While St. Paul demonstrated a pronounced anti-sexual bias, it was the church fathers of the next three centuries who decided that physical pleasure of any type was inconsistent with spiritual progress. One scholar has concluded that "[t]he dominant attitude of the Catholic Church throughout the Middle Ages and Renaissance was that sexual love itself was an evil and did not cease to be so if its object were one's husband or wife."[4] For example, in the fourth century Athanasius argued that the primary message of Christ was the need for virginity and shortly thereafter Jovinan was excommunicated for stating that the married state was not inferior to virginity. In the following century Tertullian and Ambrose took the position that it was better that the human race cease to exist than to be propagated through sinful sexual intercourse.

Although St. Augustine was unwilling to go quite that far, he too was upset by the necessity of bestial desires and actions to propagate the race. Though coitus must be regarded as good since it came from God, and although marriage transformed the sex act from lust to a necessary duty thereby expiating the sinfulness, every specific act of intercourse was evil. The desire to produce children was holy and good but the passion which accompanies physical sex was sinful.

With such a philosophy, the Church condemned any sexual act which was not for the purposes of procreation and developed an obsessional horror that sex would be used for other purposes. The philosophy is expressed in a series of "Penitential Manuals" which praised celibacy and set forth lists of sexual regulations for the faithful: coitus could be performed only in the male superior position; it was improper on Sunday, Wednesdays and Fridays, for forty days before Easter and for forty days preceding Christmas; no parishioner could attend communion unless he had abstained for three days; sex on all religious rite days, including the wedding day, was strictly prohibited. Also emblematic of the medieval attitude was a special night shirt called the "chemise cagoule" which bore the church seal of approval—it had a strategically placed hole which permitted the husband to impregnate the wife without having to endure unnecessary contact with her.[5]

The essence of the attitude of the Church toward sexual intercourse is epitomized by a statement from a penitent manual of 1584 which states that

the husband, who transported by immoderate love, has intercourse with his wife so *ardently* in order to satisfy his passion,that even had she not been his wife he would wished to have commerce with her, is committing a sin.[6]

The rise of Protestantism caused a slight change in the religious attitude toward sexuality. Martin Luther rejected the medieval assumption that virginity was preferable to marriage as a state of grace and Calvin had a much greater appreciation of the positive role of sex in marriage. However, even he considered it inexcusable for a wife to touch that part of her husband's body "from the sight and touch of which all chaste women naturally recoil."[7]

While it appears that the Puritans were not nearly as prudish as subsequent generations have assumed and that they saw sexual activity in a positive light,[8] there was no massive breakthrough in the attitudes of Western civilization in its attitude toward sex for another two centuries. The first major religious group to look upon sexual activity as positive rather than evil appears to have been the Anglican bishops of England who reached the conclusion in 1930. However, it was not until the Second Vatican Council that the Catholic Church publicly and with qualifications acknowledged that

the acts by which the spouses intimately and *chastely* unite with each other are decent and worthy, and *exercised in their truly human way*, signify and foster a mutual giving by which with joyful and grateful spirit they reciprocally enrich each other.[9] (italics added)

The Vatican statement is only one of the developments of the last three decades which indicate a move from a negative to a positive assessment of sexuality. The new positive appreciation of sexuality is based in part on a perception that the viewing of the Bible through the eyes of Greek dualism has undermined the Hebraic understanding of the unity of body and spirit.

The Modern Argument over Obscenity and Pornography

Contemporary battles over pornography and obscenity are fought within the confines of a religious and philosophical framework which assumes a competing dualism of physical body and transcendental soul. Contemporary conservatives use arguments against pornography which parallel those the Church fathers used against sexual activity. The standard conservative argument is that obscenity degrades humanity by presenting individuals as mere objects of impersonal desire thereby reducing humans to a mere animal level. Conservatives argue that since obscenity is primarily calculated to arouse depersonalized desire and to separate sex from those social and moral elements which distinguish humans from inferior animals, censorship of obscenity is necessary to preserve the unique qualities of humanity.

While there are some "sexual radicals" who directly challenge the argument that human sexual activity is significantly different from that of other animals, the influence of the group has not been very great. Instead, the major opponents of sexual censorship have based their arguments on the contention that democracy requires a free exchange of idea, even about sex, and therefore any form of censorship carries a very heavy presumption against it. From a liberal perspective, a democracy cannot exist unless *all ideas* are given free rein. Therefore, pornography and obscenity must be allowed to exist unless it can be shown that they are completely without ideational content.

The most telling argument against censorship is the history of censorship itself. Virtually without exception, censors have enthroned one set of values at the expense of all others. In 387 B.C., Plato suggested that Homer's *Odyssey* be censored; in 1244, the *Talmud*, a book central to Jewish thought, was burnt on charges of blasphemy and immorality; four centuries later Martin Luther's translation of the Bible was destroyed by the Catholic Church.

In the modern world, the list includes the works of Dante, Michelangelo, Galileo, Shakespeare, Milton, Locke, Swift, Voltaire, and Jefferson. More recently the list includes Anatole France, George Bernhard Shaw, Mark Twain, Oscar Wilde, Sir Arthur Conan Doyle, Havelock Ellis, Jack London, James Joyce, Sinclair Lewis, William Faulkner, Walt Disney, John Steinbeck, Erskine Caldwell and Ernest Hemingway.

Censorship has not been restricted to books. The rock musical "Hair" was denied use of a public auditorium in 1975 on the grounds that it was obscene. (The Supreme Court disagreed.) The movie "Carnal Knowledge" was ruled obscene by the Georgia Supreme Court but once again the United States Supreme Court overturned the decision. A recently enacted Indianapolis law (which was declared unconstitutional by the supreme court) would prohibit motion pictures such as "Dressed to Kill," "Ten," "Body Heat," "Swept Away" and "Last Tango in Paris."

Not only have censors outlawed books which subsequent generations have judged to be outstanding, but, more important, they have attempted to prevent ideas from being advocated. In this connection it should be noted that some of the most censored material in America has been birth control information.

The traditional battle between conservatives and liberals has been altered in the last decade by the intervention of feminists, mostly liberal, who attack pornography as either implicit or explicit violence against women. Whereas traditional conservatives argue that pornography degrades humanity by reducing humans to the level of animals, the feminists contend that pornography is directly aimed at the subjugation of women. The entry of feminists into the battle has affected the balance of political and social forces. Perhaps even more important, feminists have challenged the legal framework within which decisions have been made in the past. In order to understand the importance of this development it is first necessary to sketch the development of the law of obscenity.

The Development of the Law of Obscenity

The development of the law of obscenity demonstrates its close relationship with both religion and politics. In the first recorded obscenity case in English law in 1663, Sir Charles Sidley was fined and jailed for appearing naked on a balcony, cursing the government and throwing bottles of urine on an applauding crowd below. Since the punishment was primarily for an action it is not obscenity as we use the term. In the second English case, *Queen v. Read* (1708), the court ruled that "writing an obscene book," as that entitled "The Fifteen Plagues of a Maidenhead" is not indictable, but "punishable only in the spiritual court." Obscenity was a spiritual, not a legal, offense. The religious theme arose again in the English case of *Rex V. Curl* (1727) involving a book entitled *Venus in the Cloister,* or the *Nun in Her Smock*. Since the book had a very strong anti-religious theme, it may have been punished as blasphemy instead of obscenity. In any case, it was not a clear case of an obscenity prosecution.

The American experience is similar. The only censorship case in colonial America involving erotica was the prosecution of one Marmaduke Johnson for having an unlicensed work in his printshop. Although he was fined five pounds, it is unclear whether it was for possessing the unlicensed material or a judgment on the material itself. In 1711, in what appears to have been an attempt to limit blasphemy and sacrilege, Massachusetts passed an act to punish anyone convicted of blaspheming religion by "composing, writing, printing or publishing of any filthy, obscene, or profane song, pamphlet, libel or mock sermon, in imitation or in mimicking of preaching, or any other part of divine worship." However, there appear to have been no prosecutions under the statute.

These facts led Theodore Schroeder, writing in 1911, to state:

The analysis of all the cases of obscenity that were reported in England before the American Revolution, as well as those authorities that came into existence immediately after, are conclusive upon the point, that mere "obscenity," as such was not a common law crime before the Revolution, and, therefore, never became part of the common law crime in America.[11]

In fact, early American practice was not hostile to obscenity and profanity. As historian Clifford Shipton has observed, the standards were quite relaxed: "babes, ladies, and even the most saintly of the clergy, in jest and in ordinary conversation, used language which today would startle an aviation mechanic.'"[12] As other scholars have pointed out, it is ironic that the post office which was to become a major censor in the 20th century, was founded by Benjamin Franklin, the author of the colorful *Speech of Polly Baker* and a much published and very explicit letter of advice to a young man on the glories of older women.

The first real obscenity case in America was *Commonwealth v. Sharpless* in 1815. Six years later the first true obscenity law was passed in Connecticut.[13] The same year also saw the first major obscenity case in Massachusetts. (The case involved the novel *Fanny Hill*.) It was another twenty-one years before the first federal legislation, a customs statute, was enacted and it was not until after the Civil War when Anthony Comstock created the Committee for the Suppression of Vice that there were any significant federal prosecutions.

Although several state courts had assumed the constitutionality of obscenity legislation, the United States Supreme Court did not rule on the issue until 1956.[14] By that time, two major constitutional developments had occurred which made the treatment of obscenity in the United States different from the way it was in England or had been in the earlier period in America. First, American law was based on separation of church and state and could not treat obscenity as a religious crime as English law had done. Second, starting in 1925 the United States Supreme Court began to apply the protection of the Bill of Rights to the states. This meant that the regulation of pornography and obscenity in the United States had to take place within the framework of the First Amendment.

Based on these concepts the Supreme Court in 1956 struck down a Michigan statute which made it a crime to publish "materials tending to incite minors to violent or depraved or immoral acts, manifestly tending to the corruption of the morals of youth...."[15] It was improper, stated Justice Frankfurter, to "reduce the adult population of Michigan to reading only what is fit for children." The decision effectively limited future obscenity litigation to questions of the impact of materials on adults.

In the 1957 term the Court finally reached the core constitutional issues regarding obscenity. In *Roth v. United States*[16] Justice Brennan took the position that "the dispositive question is whether obscenity is an utterance within the area of protected speech and press." He contended that the historical evidence was to the contrary and then went on to explain why obscenity was not protected by the First Amendment:

All ideas having even the slightest redeeming social importance—unorthodox ideas, controversial ideas, even ideas hateful to the prevailing climate of opinion— have the full protection of the guaranties .... But implicit in the history of the First Amendment is the rejection of obscenity as utterly without redeeming social importance. ...We hold that obscenity is not within the area of constitutionally protected speech and press.

By narrowly focusing on whether obscenity was "speech," Justice Brennan abandoned the earlier concept that obscenity should be defined in terms of its tendency to "deprave and corrupt." Since the old standard had used children as its benchmark, the new formula seemed to be more protective of freedom of speech than the older rule. After all, its purpose was to protect works having even the slightest redeeming social importance. However, in practice the definition assumed that obscenity was harmful and removed the necessity of censors having to show any harmful effect. The issue was whether the material created a "prurient interest," i.e., created sexual itching, desire or longing, and, if so, whether it had redeeming social qualities.

As numerous commentators have demonstrated, Brennan's logic limits the First Amendment to intentions and practices of 1790—a position which is contrary to virtually every other holding on the Supreme Court on the First Amendment since 1925. Many laws existing in 1790 could not survive constitutional challenge in 1957 or today. For example, would Justice Brennan uphold blasphemy statutes? The Alien and Sedition Acts? the Massachusetts law which provided for state collection of taxes to be disbursed to churches? Surely not.

The *Roth* decision was widely interpreted as judicial support for further obscenity prosecutions. However, the Court soon made it clear that it was going to define obscenity fairly narrowly. In *Kingsley Pictures v. Regents*[17] the Court unanimously overturned a New York decision denying a license to the movie version of *Lady Chatterley's Lover* on the grounds that the movie encouraged immorality. Advocacy of "improper" sexual ethics could not be the basis for an obscenity prosecution.

The next major step in narrowing the concept of obscenity was taken in *Manual Enterprises v. Day* when the Court declared that material had to be "patently offensive" before it could be considered obscene. Otherwise, according to Justice Harlan, many acknowledged masterpieces of literature might be censored since they might create a "prurient interest." Such a concept was probably inherent in *Roth* but this case made it explicit.

In 1964 a badly divided Court reversed the conviction of an Ohio theater manager for exhibiting the French film *The Lovers*.[18] Justice Brennan clarified his and the Court's view of what constituted the obscene:

...material dealing with sex in a manner ... that has literary or scientific or artistic value or any other form of social importance, may not be branded as obscenity and denied the constitutional protection. Nor may the constitutional status of the material be made to turn on a "weighting" of its social importance against the prurient appeal, for a work cannot be proscribed unless it is "utterly" without social importance.

The same day the Court, without opinion, reversed the conviction of several publishers.

On March 1, 1965 the Supreme Court unanimously struck down the practices of Maryland's film censorship board. A film censorship system must place the burden of instituting judicial action on the censor, not the exhibitor, and there must be prompt determination of the film's obscenity. The trend toward leniency culminated in *Memoirs v. Massachusetts* in 1966.[19] In finding that John Cleland's *Memoirs of a Woman of Pleasure*, popularly known as *Fanny Hill*, was not obscene, Justice Brennan restated the law of obscenity as it had developed since *Roth*. In order for an item to be obscene it was necessary to establish three elements: "(a) the dominant theme of the material taken as a whole appeals to a prurient interest in sex; (b) the material is patently offensive because it affronts contemporary community standards [of the nation as a whole] relating to the description or representation of sexual matters; and (c) the material is utterly without redeeming social value."

Two other cases[20] were decided the same day and one of them established a new principle regarding obscenity. In upholding the conviction of Ralph Ginzburg for sending his magazine *Eros* through the mails, the Court ruled that the manner of sale and publication of an item could be used to establish its obscene character. Although the magazine itself was not obscene the method in which it had been promoted could be used to outlaw it. The court also upheld the conviction of Edward Mishkin for publishing "sadistic and masochistic" materials contrary to New York law.

Throughout this period there was massive disagreement within the Court. From 1957 to 1967, the Supreme Court handed down 13 major obscenity decisions. Those 13 cases had 55 different opinions. The issue was so divisive that in 1967 the Supreme Court announced it was in a morass, and stopped issuing opinions in obscenity cases. For the next five years, with a few significant exceptions, the Court reversed obscenity convictions without written opinions (there were 31 such cases) because the divergent views of the Justices did not allow them to state reasons for their actions.

There were two issues on which the Court was able to reach a consensus. In *Ginsburg v. New York* (1968)[21] the Court by 6-3 upheld age restrictions on non-obscene materials. The following year in *Stanley v. Georgia*[22] it ruled that a person could not be denied the right to read even obscene material in the privacy of his home.

After the appointment of new conservative Justices, the Court in June 1973 reentered the fray with five opinions which dramatically changed the scope of obscenity law. The two key cases are *Miller v. California* and *Paris Adult Theatre I v. Slaton*.[23] The new majority, through Chief Justice Burger, argued that the government has a legitimate interest not only in protecting the community but also in protecting individuals from their own weaknesses and desires. In his view, the state may act "to protect the weak, the uninformed, the unsuspecting, and the gullible" from the exercise of their own volition. Ignoring the majority Report of the Presidential Commission on Obscenity and the bulk of sociological and psychological research, he cited the *minority* report of the Commission to argue that legislatures could base public policy on the judgment that the commercial exhibition of obscene materials might have "a tendency to injure the community as a whole, to endanger the public safety, or to jeopardize ... the States' right ... to maintain a decent society."

While the Court declined to define what it meant by obscenity and left the actual definition up to the states it offered a few examples of what a state could outlaw: "patently offensive presentations or descriptions of ultimate sexual acts, normal or perverted, actual or simulated" or "patently offensive representations or descriptions of masturbation, excretory function, and lewd exhibition of the genitals."

One of the most fascinating aspects of *Miller* was the dissent by Justice Brennan who had been the primary architect of earlier obscenity cases. He argued that all the past attempts had failed to develop a standard for obscenity which was not excessively vague and suggested that the new standards would also fail. He expressed his distaste at having to decide "whether a description of human genitals is sufficiently 'lewd' to deprive it of constitutional protection" and he also asked why the First Amendment should be limited to protect only *serious* literary or political value.

The new decision drastically altered the old definition of obscenity and made it much easier to get a conviction. First, it concluded that material was obscene if it lacked serious value. This is dramatically different from the old test which had protected material unless it was utterly without value: the new test allowed the offensiveness of the material to be weighted against its social value. In 1957 the Court had taken the position that obscene material could be censored because it was *utterly* worthless but in 1973 it argued that material charged as obscene was unprotected even if *not utterly* worthless. Second, while the earlier opinions had seemed to suggest that the nation was the appropriate community whose values were to determine what was offensive, the Court now determined that the proper "community" for that purpose was the local community.

Although the Supreme Court thought that its new definition would remove the ambiguities in the law of obscenity, it was proved wrong almost immediately when Georgia tried to outlaw the movie *Carnal Knowledge*.[24] It was necessary for the Court to step in and reaffirm its position that only hardcore pornography as suggested by the examples above could be outlawed.

Ironically, although the new guidelines made it much easier to get a conviction there appears to have been a drop in obscenity prosecutions since 1973. This decline probably reflects the development of a more liberal attitude toward sexual expression.

The Feminist Attack on Pornography

At approximately the same time that a conservative Supreme Court was rewriting the rules to make it much easier to prosecute obscenity, liberal feminists were opening a new front in the war on pornography. The first major battle in the new offensive took place in 1976 when a Los Angeles group called Women Against Violence Against Women (WAVAW) successfully forced the removal of a billboard advertising a new record by the Rolling Stones which depicted a woman in chains with bruises on her body. Two years later a national conference called by Women Against Violence in Pornography and Media (WAVPM) to examine "Feminist Perspectives on Pornography" attracted 5,000 women. By 1979 the movement had moved to the East Coast where a group called Women Against Pornography conducted tours of the Times Square area in New York City.

The original feminist attacks against pornography were founded on a widespread belief that there was a direct casual relationship between pornography and violence against women. As Robin Morgan phrased it, "pornography is the theory, violence is the practice." However, the more basic objection to pornography was the belief that it was pathognomonic of a broader society which objectified and disvalued women. Hence it was soon argued that pornography did not have to be overtly violent in order to constitute violence against females. Susan Griffin, for example, wrote:

For whether or not pornography causes sadistic acts to be performed against women, above all *pornography is in itself a sadistic act* (italics in original). Let us remember again that the central experience of sadsomasochism is humiliation. This degradation is the essential experiences of pornography. It can be argued that for a woman to be disrobed in public at all, given the values of this culture, is a degradation.[25]

For the new opponents of pornography, there is a conflict between the First Amendment which guarantees freedom of speech and the Fourteenth Amendment which guarantees equal protection of the law. The First Amendment protects all speech which is not lewd, obscene, profane, libelous, insulting or fighting words or child pornography. Moreover, the courts have consistently ruled that "speech may not be punished merely because it offends."[26]

Such a position is directly opposed to the feminist argument that any display of the female body, whether in advertisements for jeans or in hardcore pornography is degrading and must be outlawed if women are to attain their rightful place in society. The development of sexual equality in the society requires the abolition of all presentations of females in stereotypic or unflattering ways and if the First Amendment stands in the way it must be evaded. Radical feminist Andrea Dworkin represents the disdain which many feminists feel toward a First Amendment which protect works they find objectionable: "I find the civil liberties stance to be bourgeois hypocrisy a lot of the time. We're talking about the oppression of a class of people."[27]

True to her beliefs, Dworkin helped design a new legal approach which treats pornography as a form of sex discrimination against women. She and Catherine MacKinnon, a law professor at the University of Minnesota, persuaded the Minneapolis City Council in December, 1973 to define pornography as sex discrimination. Using a Fourteenth Amendment equal protection approach, pornography was to be treated as a violation of women's civil rights. The ordinance was heavily based on the feminist argument that exposure to pornography in contemporary society was both unavoidable and psychologically harmful to women. The Council accepted Dworkin's argument that "my rights as a citizen are violated because of those magazines that show me as an abject degraded person. They in fact subordinate me when I am in the supermarket. They change my civil status and make it different from yours because you're a man and I'm a woman."[28] Using this logic, the law allowed individual females to bring a civil suit for an injunction and damages against "a particular person, place, distributor, exhibitor." Since the damages would have been primarily psychological, and standards for establishing damage so unclear, the law would have been a major threat to any business displaying any item that any individual found offensive. However, the Minneapolis ordinance was vetoed by the mayor as a violation of freedom of speech.

Almost immediately Professor MacKinnon was invited to Indianapolis to assist in the development of a virtually identical ordinance which became law in May, 1984. In the adoption and subsequent amendment process the Indianapolis law was slightly altered from its original Minneapolis form but the basic underlying assumptions remained.

If viewed as obscenity laws, both the Indianapolis and Minneapolis ordinances are clearly unconstitutional. The major flaw in the legislative schema is an attempt to restrict non-obscene materials which presently have constitutional protection. While the amended law presently in force does not define "sexually explicit" (which itself is contrary to the requirements of *Miller v. California*), the original law defined the term to include "uncovered exhibition of the genitals, pubic region, buttocks or anus of any person." Such material obviously is not the "hardcore pornography" which the Supreme Court has stated is the only type which can be proscribed.

The law is also deficient in other ways. It does not refer to a "community standard" test and does not require that the material be "patently offensive" in order to be outlawed. The closest that the law comes to the constitutionally required balancing of "literary, artistic, political or scientific value" against the offensiveness of the material is an exemption for publicly funded libraries. In addition, the law restricts the private possession of pornographic materials despite the fact that the Supreme Court has ruled that a person may have even obscene material in the privacy of the home.

The law also creates a tort action which allows a legal claim against anyone in the chain of publication and distribution when a person is attacked by someone acting under the influence of materials they have viewed or read. Leaving aside the staggering difficulty of proving causation, the provision is directly contrary to a large number of precedents which hold that a producer of communicative materials cannot be held responsible for the action of third parties. To hold otherwise would have the unconstitutional effect of reducing what normal adults could view to that which would not adversely motivate the most impressionistic and/or morally bent person in the society.

Since the law cannot stand constitutional scrutiny as an obscenity statute, the question then becomes whether it is possible to use a civil rights law as a way to circumvent the limitations of obscenity law. The task, as the Indianapolis law illustrates, is extremely difficult. A valid civil rights law must establish that pornography differentially harms women or leads to violence against women. However, unless feminist assumptions and rhetoric are accepted without question, it is difficult to defend such a position. The argument that pornography leads to violence against women is flawed two ways. First, the feminists have misused the research on the relationship between film violence and violence against women. As Professor Edward Donnerstein, who was widely quoted by supporters of the antipornography law in the hearings in both Minneapolis and Indianapolis, has stated, the research has been misconstrued. "If you take the violent content out of pornographic films and leave only the explicit sex, there is no effect. It is violence, whether connected with sex or not, that results in desensitizing to violence."[29]

Second, contrary to feminist statements, there is little actual violence against women in mass audience pornography. Instead, the pornographic movie is a celebration of physical sexuality. As Cynthia Toolin has noted:

in all cases of [pornography], women and men are shown as weak; neither is in control. Passion is in control; genitals are in control. Women are controlled by their own desires, their insatiable passion, and/or the uncontrollable passions of men. Men are controlled by the desires and passions of women, and by their own insatiable desires and uncontrollable passions.[30]

The pornographic genre is about individuals overcome with lust—as a result there is almost no resistance to sexual overtures and little violence.

The feminist argument, which is adopted in the preamble to the Indianapolis law, is that pornography *uniquely* objectifies women and as such "differently harms women." If, as Toolin has shown, it is not just women but "people who are objectified in pornography" the argument fails. The Indianapolis law itself is logically inconsistent on this point. Although pornography is defined as written and pictorial works where women are "presented as sexual objects who enjoy pain or humiliation" or "as sexual objects for domination, conquest, violation, exploitation, possession or use, or through postures of servility or submission or display," *the word "women" is specifically said to apply to "men, children and transsexuals."*[31]

It is difficult to see how even a Supreme Court which shares traditional conservative values regarding obscenity, as the present one does, can uphold a law of this type. If the pornography-violence nexus cannot be established, and at this point it is highly doubtful that a case can be made, the feminist argument is reduced to an argument that pornography defames women. However, with one exception which seems to have been overturned *sub silento*, the courts have ruled that mere offensiveness is not adequate to permit censorship. If Nazis cannot be prohibited from marching and displaying materials offensive to Jews who have been in concentration camps, it is difficult to see how the Constitution could prohibit the display of materials some females find offensive.

Conclusion

Politics and pornography make strange bedfellows. It is doubly ironic tht traditional conservatives and liberal feminists have joined together to attack pornography. The most obvious irony is that on most policy issues feminists and conservatives are adamantly opposed. Even on the pornography issue feminists deny mutual interest with conservatives. Catherine MacKinnon, for example, has been quoted as saying that "right-wing men have too much staked on their dominance" to be allies in the anti-porn crusade.[32] However, despite denials from both sides, their objectives are the same.

The second, and less obvious, irony is that the intellectual leaders of the feminist movement have explicitly rejected the mind-body dualism which is at the root of conservative thought. Susan Griffin, whose book *Pornography and Silence* is the intellectual foundation for the feminist attack on pornography, argues that the dualism of body and soul result in a pornographic mind "in which we all participate." She argues that Christianity and pornography are merely obverse sides of the same coin.

Christianity incorrectly focuses on the spiritual to the detriment of the physical and pornography focuses on the physical to the detriment of the spiritual. "The metaphysics of Christianity and the metaphysics of pornography are the same ..." and "all the old shapes of religious asceticism are echoed in obscenity. And every attitude, every shade of pornographic feelings has its origin in the church."[33]

(While it may appear to be unfair to characterize the entire feminist movement on the basis of a radical writer, in this case it is not inappropriate because the concept of "objectification" of the female body is the central element in the thought of virtually all feminists, especially in regard to pornography.)

Thus the argument comes full circle. In the beginning of the Christian era sexual activity was a (perhaps necessary) evil because it reduced man to an animal level. Subsequently, obscenity was considered objectionable because it reminded man of his animal nature. In rebellion against this asceticism pornographers deliberately portrayed man as an animal overcome by lust. Feminists came along and rejected the mind-body dualism because it inevitably led to objectification which in turn led to the treatment of females as something less than total human beings. The result is that conservatives and liberal feminists end up advocating the same thing: censorship of images that both find objectionable but for totally opposed reasons.

Regardless of the outcome of the present controversy, the legal and constitutional battles over pornography will continue. The reason is simple: ours is both a pluralistic and a litigious society. Individuals and groups with one view of mankind and sexuality will continue to attempt to impose their views of proper sexual ethics on others using the legal process and those with differing views will respond in the same arenas—the legislatures and the courts.

Notes

[1]The terms "pornography" and "obscenity" almost defy definition. "Pornography" is derived from two Greek words meaning "writing of or about prostitutes" and is usually used to mean written or graphic descriptions of sexual organs or activity. Some writers, including Justices of the Supreme Court, try to distinguish between "softcore" and "hardcore" pornography but without much success. From a legal perspective, pornography, at least the softcore kind, cannot be outlawed.

The term "obscenity" is harder to trace and define. Etymologically, the term appears to be a derivation of a Latin concept meaning "offstage" and has been interpreted to mean things best left out of sight. Legally, the term is a verbal nightmare. As the discussion below indicates, the Supreme Court has tried since 1957 to define the term. From 1957 to 1973 the Court sought an intrinsic meaning for the word. However, in 1973 the Court moved to an extrinsic definition: items having sexually explicit, or excretory, content whose social or other value is outweighed by its offensiveness to contemporary local community standards. The result of this approach is that an item may be obscene in one locality and not in another which means that the obscenity is not in the item but in the location of the item!

[2]Kingsley Davis, "Prostitution," in Robert Merton and Robert Nisbet, eds, *Contemporary Social Problems* (New York: Harcourt, Brace & World, 1961), pp. 262-88. Ned Polsky, "On the Sociology of Pornography," in his *Hustlers, Beats, and Others* (Garden City, N.Y.: Doubleday, 1969), applies Davis' argument regarding prostitution to pornography on the grounds that they are functional alternatives.

[3]Vern L. Bullough, *Sexual Variance in Society and History* (Chicago: Univ. of Chicago Press, 1976) is the source of much of the material in this section. Chapter 8 of the book is entitled "Early Christianity: A Sex-Negative Religion."

[4]Leland Ryken, "Were the Puritans Right About Sex?" *Christianity Today*, April 7, 1978, p. 14 [830].

[5]Franklin S. Klaf and Bernhardt J. Hurwood, *A Psychiatrist Looks at Erotica* (New York: Ace, 1964), p. 50.

[6]J. Benedicti, *Somnes des Peches*, 1584, quoted by J.-L. Flandrin, "Contraception, Marriage and Sexual Relations in the Christian West," in R. Forster and O. Ranum (eds.) *Biology of Man in History* (Baltimore, 1975), p. 35.

[7]Quoted in Richard F. Hettlinger, "Sex, Religion and Censorship," in Harry M. Clor (ed.), *Censorship and Freedom of Expression* (Chicago: Rand, McNally, 1971), p. 76.

[8]There is at least one recorded instance in which a New England wife complained to her pastor and congregation her spouse was not performing his sexual duties with the result that the husband was excommunicated by the church! See Ryken, *op. cit.*

[9]Quoted in Hettlinger, *op. cit.*, p. 77.

[10]*Rex v. Sidley*, Mich. 15 car. II. B.R. (1663). The early cases are reproduced in Edward DeGrazia, *Censorship Landmarks* (New York: Bowker, 1969).

[11]Theodore A. Schroder, "Obscene Literature and Constitutional Law: A Forensic Defense of Freedom of the Press (New York: Privately Printed, 1911), p. 39.

[12]Clifford K. Shipton, *Isaiah Thomas: Printer, Patriot, and Philanthropist* (Rochester, N.Y., 1948), p.22.

[13]The 1978 New Jersey statute cited by Justice Brennan in *Roth v. United States* was directed at all shows for profit and was not a true obscenity law.

[14]The court had agreed to hear a case nine years earlier but because Justice Frankfurter was a friend of the author of the challenged book and did not participate in the case, the Court was evenly divided and could not decide the case.

[15]*Butler v. Michigan*, 352 U.S. 380 (1956).

[16]*Roth v. United States*, 354 U.S. 476 (1957).

[17]*Kingsley Pictures Corporation v. Regents*, 360 U.S. 684 (1959).

[18]*Jacobellis v. Ohio* (378 U.S. 184 (1964). Justices Black and Douglas argued that there was no power to censor movies; Justices Brennan and Goldberg restate the national community standard position; Justice Stewart argued that censorship must be limited to "hardcore pornography" which he could not define but knew when he saw it; Chief Justice Warren and Justice Clark wanted to use local rather than national standards. Justice Harlan dissented on the grounds that reasonable state limitations were permissible.

[19]*Memoirs vs. Massachusetts*, 383 U.S. 413 (1966).

[20]*Ginsburg v. United States*, 383 U.S. 463 (1966); *Mishkin v. New York*, 383 U.S. 502 (1966).

[21]*Ginsberg v. New York*, 390 U.S. 629 (1968).

[22]*Stanley v. Georgia*, 405 U.S. 645 (1969).

[23]*Miller v. California*, 4113 U.S. 15 (1973); *Paris Adult Theatre I v. Slaton*, 413 U.S. 49 (1973).

[24]*Jenkins v. Georgia*, 418 U.S. 153 (1974).

[25]Susan Griffin, *Pornography and Silence* (New York: Harper & Row, 1981), p.111.

[26]*Collins v. Smith*, 447 F. Supp. 676 at 697 (1978) summarizing United States Supreme Court decisions in the area.

[27]Quoted in Jean B. Elshtain, "The New Porn Wars," *The New Republic*, June 25, 1984, p. 16.

[28]*Ibid.*

[29]Quoted in *New York Times*, July 3, 1984.

[30]Cynthia Toolin, "Attitudes About Pornography: What Have the Feminists Missed?"

Journal of Popular Culture, 17, 2 (Fall, 1983), p. 173.

[31] Indianapolis Ordinance 35, 1984, Sec. 16-3 (q). For an extended discussion of the Indianapolis law, see William E. Brigman, "Pornography as Group Libel: The Indianapolis Sex Discrimination Law," *Indiana Law Review*, Vol. 18 No. 2, (1985), p. 479-505.

[32] *The New Republic*, June 25, 1984, p. 17.

[33] Susan Griffin, *Pornography and Silence* (New York: Harper & Row, 1981), p. 12.

The Bird, the Bible and the Constitution: Trinitarian America

Marshall W. Fishwick

America is truly the last bulwark of Christian civilization.

Billy Graham

AMERICAN RELIGION SOARS with the eagle. How high is that? That our rhetoric has been high-minded, no one can doubt. We did indeed want to build "a city on a hill," to make New England, a New Haven, complete with a New Canaan. Inevitably pietism became intermingled with pride and (once the colonies became a Republic) nationalism. The resulting civil religion has served the nation, and numerous God Pumpers, well. But what has it done to Christianity?

The term "civil religion" is Jean Jacques Rousseau's, appearing in *The Social Contract* (book 4, chapter 8). The state, he claimed as early as 1762, had no right to endorse any dogmas except the existence of God, the reward of virtue and punishment of vice, and the exclusion of religious intolerance. This has long been the tacit policy of many Western nations— including the United States. There are four references to God in the Declaration of Independence.[1] "We are one nation, under God." Every President from Washington to Reagan has paid homage to a kind of deity much more related to law and order than to love and salvation. But this God is intensely interested and involved in history—especially ours. And thereby hangs the tale. The tale—the term "saga" might be more appropriate—inspires preachers and politicians generation after generation. Its many parts (including symbols, rituals and fables) add up collectively to a religion—there seems no other word for it—while not antithetical to and sharing much in common with Christianity, is neither sectarian nor in any specific sense Christian. At a time when the society was overwhelmingly Christian, it seems unlikely that this lack of Christian reference was meant to spare the feelings of the tiny non-Christian minority. The civil religion expressed what those who set the precedents felt was appropriate. It reflected their private as well as public views. Nor was the civil religion simply "religion" in general. While generality was seen as a virtue, the civil religion was specific enough when it came to America. Because of this specificity, civil religion was saved from empty platitudes and served as a genuine vehicle of national religions' self-understanding.

The vehicle had to be built from the ground up. Being a new nation with old memories, we had no indigenous body of traditional imagery to draw from—and certainly didn't want what we had left behind in Europe. American Indians had been cast aside as barbaric and inappropriate for symbolic use until they finally surfaced on one-cent pieces toward the end of the nineteenth century (after they were no longer a serious threat to anyone). The nation's oldest traditions ran back only to the seventeenth century. Neither the Pilgrims, huddled on their New England rocks as self-conscious Protestants, nor the Virginia Cavaliers, dreaming of plantations on their more hospitable land, thought of themselves as a "race" or a "nation." From the first our condensed and diffused symbols have been in conflict. Liberty and pluralism have on repeated occasions, run head-on against the implications of the flag which, despite its arbitrary and changing design, has often functioned as a tribal totem. Why its popularity skyrocketed in the mid-1980s is a question later historians will have to answer.

But the settlers did have the Bible, which supplied the Exodus theme. George Washington made a splendid Moses, freeing us from bondage. The Liberty Tree provided a graphic symbolic center. Our *Pater Patriae*, Washington, was virtually apotheosized in Parson Weem's best-selling *Life of Washington* (1800), and the basic elements of what is now called "Civil Religion" were in place.[2]

When he came over a generation later, the astute French visitor, Alexis de Tocqueville, quickly spotted the phenomenon. Preachers were skillfully mixing Puritanism, patriotism and prosperity into a powerful brew:

It is difficult to know from their sermons whether the principle object of religion is to procure eternal felicity in the other world or prosperity in this.[3]

Writers of what came to be known as "the American Renaissance," Emerson, Thoreau, Hawthorne, Melville, added new elements (especially Transcendentalism). But it was the great crisis of Civil War with casualties far exceeding those undergone by Americans in any war before or since, that transformed civil religion. Now the theme of death and rebirth entered the formula, symbolized in the life and death of Abraham Lincoln. Nowhere is it stated more vividly than in the Gettysburg Address, part of the Lincolnian "New Testament" among the civil scriptures. Robert Lowell has pointed out the insistent use of birth images in the speech explicitly devoted to "these honored dead": "brought forth," "conceived," "created," "a new birth of freedom." He adds: "The Gettysburg address is a symbolic and sacramental act. Its verbal quality is resonance combined with a logical, matter of fact, prosaic brevity .... In his words, Lincoln symbolically died, just as the Union soldiers really died—and as he himself was soon really to die."[4] Much was made over Lincoln's recurring dreams, and the legend arose that he had received warnings of his impending death. An aura developed around Lincoln which elevated him to the status of a demi-god; a divine agent or perhaps a theios aner (divine man). The ready identification with the Christian mythos of one sacrificially slain made this apotheosis easier. On the one hand, Lincoln was the American Christ; on the other, he was our indigenous King Arthur—absent but not destroyed. We also got a new Judas: John Wilkes Booth. Civil religion was a double winner.[5]

With the Christian archetype in the background, Lincoln, our martyred president, was linked to the war dead, who "gave the last full measure of devotion." The theme of sacrifice was indelibly written into the civil religion. Memorial Day integrated local communities into the national cult, just as the less overtly religious Fourth of July had done years before.[6]

The primary vehicle for perpetuating these things was the public school system and schoolbooks. These books, of which the graded Readers of William Holms McGuffey were the most successful, self-consciously set about not only to produce universal literacy but also to provide the new generation of readers with a set of values and orientation that would equip them to deal with the experience of growing up American.[7]

The basic attitudes indicated were evangelical and ethnocentric. McGuffey's works were rather mild in this regard. While on the one hand they strongly emphasized such Protestant attitudes as the "work ethic," temperance and a belief in special providences, they refrained from the excesses of racism and nationalism that were characteristic of many other works of this genre. The collective purpose was to provide young people not simply with functional skills but with an entire world picture—a cosmos—that was religious in essence and Protestant in emphasis.

Popular songs help too. "America" was written by a Baptist minister, Samuel Francis Smith, in 1832. Julia Ward Howe's "Battle Hymn of the Republic" was full of strong Old Testament imagery. The less militant "America the Beautiful" was written by an English professor at Wellesley—a Congregationalist well immersed in the civil religion and love of the land.[8] They are all popular—almost sacred—today.

We cannot write about God Pumpers and the contemporary religious scene unless we acknowledge its presence and force still cloaked in Biblical archetypes: Exodus, Promised Land, Chosen People, Born Again, Covenant, Sacrifice, Rebirth. Working with this framework America has produced its own sacred heroes, places and events; its own special solemn symbols and rituals. Sometimes we have used civil religion to do things which make Christians shudder. Lincoln called us the "almost chosen

people." But most Americans—including theologians and preachers—
have blessed the secular and sacred as an organic unit.

That civil religion can be misused is obvious. Look how the
"American Israel" theme was avoided to justify the shameful treatment of
American Indians and immigrants; how the American Legion ideology
has branded numerous non-conformists or liberals "Reds" or
"Communists." The way the John Birch Society interprets patriotism
must make early American patriots turn over in their graves.[9]

Many critics of religion, the "American Way," or of American
Shintoism, are really talking about the civil religion. They find much to
criticize; yet civil religion, at its best, points to transcendent religious
reality as seen in or revealed through the experience of the American
people. Like all religions, it has suffered various deformations and
demonic distortions. At its best, it has neither been so general that it has
lacked incisive relevance nor so particular as to place American society
above universal human values. The leaders of the church may not have
represented a higher truth or vision than those (like Lincoln, Roosevelt
and Kennedy) who used the language of civil religion.

Unremitting pressure from civil religion, for example, helped find a
partial solution of our greatest domestic problem, the treatment of black
Americans. It remains to be seen how relevant it can become for our role in
the world at large, and whether we can effectively stand for "the
revolutionary beliefs for which our forebears fought," in John F.
Kennedy's words.

Civil religion has reached its third "Time of Trial." The first, in the
eighteenth century, wrestled with the question of independence, whether
we should or could run our own affairs in our own way. The second time
was over the issue of slavery, which in turn was only one aspect of the more
general problem of the full institutionalization of democracy. This we are
still far from solving though we have some notable successes. But we have
been overtaken by a third which has led to a crisis, in the midst of which we
stand: the problem of responsible action in a revolutionary world, seeking
to attain many of the things, material and spiritual, that we have already
attained.

Only since World War II have we had the power and wealth which
made the crisis inevitable.

So it is on the last forty years—post World War II—that we will
concentrate. Our massive power has had enormous effect around the globe.
In those years our Fourth Great Revival began.

After V-J day, *Time* heralded "The Great American Century." The
world was our oyster: American troops were coming home, but Americans
were going everywhere, to share the blessings of the "American Way of
Life."

The former British colonies had suddenly become Prime Minister of the world.

Sole possessor of the atomic bomb, with a giant Navy that roamed the world unchallenged, we created a new crusade: religion. European visitors, like Barbara Ward, were amazed. In her "Report to Europe on America" (1964) she wrote: "We don't need polls or statistics to confirm what we can so easily see—the walls of new churches rising in town and countryside wherever we went."[10] Tenors brayed and evangelists prayed; from sea to shining sea, the day of the Lord was at hand.

The spectacular growth of religion was good news: the nature and meaning of the growth was debatable. In 1955 Will Herberg noted that Americans think, feel and act in terms quite obviously secularist at the very time that they exhibit every sign of a widespread religious revival. Religiousness and secularism, he thought, derived from the same sources. The religious situation can be understood only when held up against the inner development of American society. What sort of religion did we produce in the Age of Eisenhower? A religion to end all religion? Or a religion that was no religion?[11]

Before attempting to answer we should recall the cliche which hung over the decade like smog over Los Angeles: "The American Way of Life." Because we *live* it, we seldom examine (let alone define) it. Yet it is always with us, expressing a special kind of idealism, evoking a warm, friendly feeling, affirming our basic values: success, self-improvement, education, "making it." Scholars can point to symbols, saints and *sancta*; ordinary people absorb it from newspapers, magazines, radio, television, item by item, one day at a time. "The American Way of Life" is the phrase by which we define ourselves and establish our unity.

What Americans believe in when they are religious is religion itself. Religion means *believing* and *doing*. This faith in faith—religion that makes religion its own object—is central to "The American Way." Whether you're Protestant, Catholic or Jew isn't important—so long as you *believe* . . . and follow "The Way."

A corollary is that every God-fearing, decent and virtuous nation is religious; that religion is the true basis of national existence and therefore the one sure resource for the solution of all national problems. On the level of personal life, the American faith in religion implies not only that every right-minded citizen is religious, but also that religion (or faith) is the best device for getting what one wants in life. "Jesus," the Rev. Irving E. Howard assured us, "recommended faith as a technique for getting results . . . . Jesus recommended faith as a way to heal the body and to remove any of the practical problems that loom up as mountains in a man's path.[12]

Not all the pop preachers of the 50s envisioned "Pie in the Sky." Instead, the fastest-rising star in the evangelical heaven, Billy Graham, took on the role of America's Joshua—warning that the prestige of his nation would go down and that the good name and cause of God would too. In the Old Testament, Joshua forced his people to rid themselves of sin. Seeing this, God approved and once more intervened on their behalf. Billy Graham seemed to be working the same formula.

God had given America victory over the British, the French, the Mexicans and Germans twice in one century. But in Korea, things began to look bad. Something had gone wrong. Sin must be moving in the camp, subversion in the land. Sometimes regarding sin and subversion as the same phenomenon, Billy Graham sought to persuade every American to confess his sins. America's prestige was at stake; so was God's. Subversion of America was a sin against God, and sometimes Billy committed the converse fallacy of thinking of sin (as defined by his evangelical faith) as subversion. But he caught the mood of the times, and played a key role in the civil religion.[13]

Not all Americans found this common religion equally useful. Among these were the immigrant-ethnic background churches. Groups that have an explicit theological concern, "orthodox," "neo-orthodox" or "liberal"; in varying degrees, found their theologies at odds with the implied "theology" of the American Way of Life. Finally, there were the ill-defined, though by all accounts numerous and influential, "religions of the disinherited," the many "holiness," pentecostal and millenarian sects of the socially and culturally submerged segments of society. Their "peculiar" religion was frequently still too vital and all-absorbing to be easily subordinated to some "common faith." But they did not affect majority opinion.

How can our culture become more religious yet more secular at the same time? Many observed it, but no one fully explained it.

The paradox is there, and it would be wrong to try to get rid of it by suppressing one or the other side of the apparent contradiction. We can't brush aside evidence of religious revival by writing off the new religiousness as little more than shallow emotionalism, "escapism" or pretense. The people who join churches, take part in "crusades," send their children to church schools, and identify themselves in religious terms are not fools or hypocrites. They are usually honest, intelligent people who take their religion seriously.

The widespread secularism of American religion, to which religion is made to provide the sanctification and dynamic for goals and values otherwise established, is difficult for Europeans to understand. In Europe the confrontation between secularism and religion tends to be much more explicit and well defined. In the United States explicit secularism— hostility or demonstrative indifference to religion—is a minor and manageable force. The secularism that permeates the American consciousness is found within the churches themselves.

This may have bothered some theologians, but not their President. To Ike both World War II and his presidential campaign were "crusades." He was called upon to fight against corruption at home, and "godless Communism" abroad. Knowing this, Americans could chant: "I like Ike." "The things that make us proud to be Americans," he said, "are of the soul and of the spirit."[14]

So the dream of the New Israel and the Promised Land continued; we still sought the new order (*novus ordo seculorum*), the divinely sanctioned new beginning that has been made, a new order of things established, different from and superior to the decadent institutions of the Old World. This conviction, emerging out of the earliest American history, was nourished through many decades into the present century by hopes and expectations of immigrants, for whom the New World had to be new if it was to be anything at all. This conviction still remains in American life, hardly shaken by the new shape of the world and the challenge of such "new orders" of the twentieth century as Fascism and Communism. They automatically become the "bad guys" against whom preachers and politicians rail. Certain key words take on cultic power: "democracy" in politics, "free enterprise" in economics, "equal opportunity" in the job market. How simple—and how satisfying. After the bumps and grinds of the 60s and 70s, we needed Ike again. Then he appeared: Ronald Reagan.

Just what does all this mean in the area of religion? Will Herberg notes contradictions and paradoxes: people flocking to church, yet forgetting about Christ when it comes to naming the most significant events in history; men and women valuing the Bible as revelation, purchasing and distributing it by the millions, yet apparently seldom reading it themselves. Every aspect of contemporary religious life reflects this paradox—pervasive secularism amid mounting religiosity, the strengthening of the religious structure in spite of increasing secularization.[15]

Paradox or contradiction? How can we have "total expression," Michael Novak asks, at the same time we court "universal harmony?" On the one hand, spontaneity—on the other, conformity and agreement. The real clue may be neither of these, but utilitarianism. "Do anything you want—just as long as it doesn't harm others." From this perspective, liberalism, conservatism and radicalism all become one homogenized national theme—just as Protestant/Catholic/Jew become one homogenized national religion.[16]

Presiding over this paradox, and central to it, was Dwight D. Eisenhower, who combined the genuine grandeur of success in battle with the familiar friendliness of the man next door. When things went wrong, he smiled; his good intentions were so obvious as to be axiomatic. They could be taken for granted, sufficient for all things; by it, men and politics could be measured and defended. Eisenhower himself seemed to be a believer in this part, as in other aspects, of his own myth: when challenged, criticized or disagreed with, he would cite the goodness of his own intentions. Thirty years later the same tactics worked for another smiling Republican President. Eisenhower also was a repository of the bi-partisan or suprapartisan national piety that surrounds the Presidential office and was particularly strong in the 1950s—the soft nationalism that knows there is a domain of the common and good and American that is more important than all the "things that divide us."

John Gunther, a pop writer who understood the Pop President, wrote a popular book on *Eisenhower: the Man and Symbol*, in which he described Ike's main characteristic as "drive . . . . Theory irritates him, and he believes in first things first." In *Eisenhower: Soldier of Democracy*, Kenneth Davis suggested that for Ike, ideas were valid "only in-so-far as they were scenes for immediate practical action."[17] Yet he was always friendly, team-minded, moralizing and reform-seeking: the archetypal American for the American century.

Who were Ike's counterparts in the pulpit? Almost everyone in the 50s put Norman Vincent Peale at the top of the list—a New York Methodist preacher specializing in "positive thinking," and writing best-selling euphoric self-help books; then Bishop Fulton J. Sheen, a highly literate Roman Catholic priest, and "Angel of the Airways"; and Billy Graham, a dynamic Presbyterian revivalist with lots of charisma. Religion spilled over into Hollywood. Bible "spectacles" with Hedy Lamarr as Delilah and Rita Hayworth as Salome filled movie houses across the land. Cecil B. DeMille parted the Red Sea and explored Moses' love life in even bigger spectacles. As for books, one out of every ten bought in America was religious. There was a rash of pop tunes, all "plugging" some spiritual truism or celebrating faith. Juke boxes, radio and television sets spewed forth religious ditties with references to God, telling everyone that everything would be all right.

In 1900 only 36% of the total American population was churched. That number reached 49% in 1940, and passed 60% in 1955. Thus, while it took four decades to increase the population from one-third to one-half, only fifteen years were required to go from one half to three-fifths of a rapidly expanding population. Other statistics are equally imposing. Contributions of 49 Protestant churches in 1955 totaled $1,687,921,729. The estimated value of new construction in religious buildings ran to $736 million.[18]

Religion in this manner tends to be compressed into arranged stereotypes and formulas of the mass media. It is "salable" religion, clearly and candidly cut to fit the requirements of ratings, box offices and newsstand sales. A large part of it is under commercial rather than churchly auspices. As salable religion it is "helpful"; does not challenge, offend or disturb. It is "useful" in fulfilling already established secular purposes.

The central theme of the popular revival is self-help. The American emphasis upon the technical is here applied to the problems of spirit and soul. The religious writers, as they constantly explain, teach the "formulas," the "methods," the "secrets" by which the self may attain its desires. They do not suggest that religion might challenge the goals given the self. Religion is a source of techniques by which these goals might be more effectively realized. The correlation between spiritually induced power and worldly success is complete. By practicing the right spiritual techniques, one achieves greater income, fame and position—in a word, success.

To William Lee Miller, the same ethos was operating in different parts of the culture:

> The illusion of American omnipotence, that America can do whatever she wants to, is part of the same ethos which a conversionist and revivalist heritage helped to produce. In short, the American religious tradition is geared to arouse enthusiasm and passion, not to produce wisdom and patience; it is more at home with single, simple, moral choices, than with complex, continuing political problems.[17]

The resulting popular potpourri brought together things as different, yet as inter-related, as Ike's prayer breakfasts, Billy Graham's "engineering of mass consent," Norman Vincent Peale's "Let the churches stand up for capitalism," Msgr. Fulton J. Sheen's equation of Christianity with Americanism, Rabbi Liebman's *Peace of Mind*, and various anti-communist crusades feeding upon McCarthyism, Korea and Cold War.

Critics found American religion to be less theological and liturgical, more chauvinistic and materialistic. Paul Tillich, a leading Protestant theologian, thought the revival was accompanied by loss in the dimension of depth. Perhaps the "Return to Religion" was nothing but a desperate and futile attempt to regain what has been lost. Our growth was horizontal, not vertical. The power of depth is most present in those who are aware of the loss—and are striving to regain it.

There was diminishing power of depth even in death—as Jessica Mitford's *The American Way of Death* showed. Following Evelyn Waugh's *The Loved Ones* and followed shortly by Ralph Hancock's *The Forest Lawn Story*, Mitford showed that deep human mourning was giving way to funeral directing. Avoidance and evasion took over, along with sympathy cards: bland, sentimental, shallow. One word seldom if ever used was *death*—let alone corpse, grave, worms or decay. The sting had been removed.

It is one thing to read about the "American way of death," and another to live through it, as I did when my parents died. Numb with grief, one must walk through the neon-lit supermarket for caskets, starting with a bronze model reminiscent of the Pharaohs, with a salesman mumbling, "For those who *really* care ..." looking down to the dimmer end, where the "cheap" gray caskets await—presumably for those who don't care. No need to go through the excruciating details. All told, we have commercialized grief and invented what Mark Twain called "a mean little ten-cent heaven about the size of Rhode Island."

Ho ho ho—what about Christmas, and other "religious" holidays? New secular-religious holidays emerge, and old ones change to fill symbolic vacuums in contemporary life. Peter Williams cites the perennially popular movie *White Christmas*, released in 1954 and seen by millions on television every Christmas since, featuring the Irish Catholic Bing Crosby and the Jewish Danny Kaye (born David Daniel Kaminsky). The sentimental plot involves two ex-GIs (Crosby and Kaye) who rally their old unit to the support of the post-war enterprise (a ski lodge) of their old commander. Their effort, after many complications, is successful. The film ends with a rendition of the title song. (Crosby's version remains to this day the best-selling recording by a solo vocalist.)

Despite the word "Christmas" in the title, this movie is hardly religious at all—like the gadget-laden candle-lit holiday. The *real* holidays, for many Americans, have become July 4, Memorial Day, Labor Day, the birthdays of Washington, Lincoln and (now unofficially) Martin Luther King—plus the November 22 recollection of John F. Kennedy's assassination. All these commemorate events of national tender significance. Sydney Ahlstrom thinks that the rescheduling of many of these occasions to convenient Mondays is an indication of their secularization into "long or lost weekends."[15]

There are still days which directly link our early history with today's sagging table—like Thanksgiving. In a country in which dieting has become both a passion and a mania, who needs all that food? And how best to forget one's gluttony and relax? Watch a televised football game, of course.

Then there is Easter—the new hats, rabbits and egg-rollings, even on the lawn of the White House. Little or no reference is made to resurrected Jesus.

The remaining icons and im•ges, in these holidays, are more American than Christian. We have a Santa who stops to enjoy Coca Cola, Frosty the Snow Man and Rudolph the Red-Nosed Reindeer—folklore has given way to fakelore. The movie *White Christmas*, Peter Williams writes, sums it up, ending with young girls dressed in fairy-princess costumes performing a ballet. They are surrounded by a large surrogate family (the reassembled World War II regiment) and dance in front of a large Christmas tree. The divine child motif is evoked, without any explicit religious reference. The group is drawn from all faiths (Kaye and Crosby being examples); even Jews can participate in this celebration, since it has little to do with Christian doctrine or practice. It is a nostalgic representation of Americans assembled into a voluntaristic rather than a biological family, bound together by war. They are now united in a common festival, drawn from a wide variety of sources, the meaning of which is purely human.[16]

Not only holidays, but the Power that provides them, has taken on a distinctly American flavor. God Himself became, in some quarters, "The Man Upstairs," a "Friendly Neighbor."

But the zenith of the "chumminess cult" was reached when God became, in Jane Russell's inimitable phrase, a "livin' doll." What relation has this kind of god to the biblical God who confronts sinful man as an enemy before He comes out to meet repentant man as a Savior? Is this He of Whom we are told, "It is a fearful thing to fall into the hands of the living God? (Hebrews 10:31).

One has only to read the bumper stickers on an interstate to see church and state blend in America: SMILE, GOD LOVES YOU. I FOUND THE ANSWER! I'M PROUD TO BE AN AMERICAN. LOVE IT OR LEAVE IT. WAVE OLD GLORY! HONK IF YOU LOVE JESUS! Yet one can find elsewhere universal themes too—a wide variety of strains and variants which make up any world religion that comprehends a wide and diverse population. At one level, theologians reflect and agonize about the compatibility of Civil Religion with Christianity, Judaism or humanistic ethics. Politicians, clergy, teachers and other public functionaries conduct the rites. The laity—the American public—participate and engage with varying degrees of self-consciousness in potentially devotional acts such as senior-class trips to Washington. Folk cults of American leaders spontaneously emerge from time to time, and range in their manifestations from supernaturalistic legends to commercialized souvenirs, verse and bric-a-brac.

Only slowly is the United States readjusting to a revised Christian Americanism. According to the older version, on the international scene America was almost omnipotent, omniscient and omnipresent. But brute empirical facts have cracked this structure. The Korean and Vietnam wars, and the Iranian hostage crisis, have dented the dogma of America's omnipotence.

Yet bounce back we did, under the warm and winning smile of ex-Hollywood actor, Ronald Reagan. He seemed, if possible, even more platitudinous than Eisenhower; but his 1984 presidential victory, in which he carried the largest number of electoral votes in America's history, showed that he must be doing something right. Certainly Reagan made an ideal father figure for civil religion—and what some call the new electronic Great Awakening. Putting aside the tourist souvenirs, bumper stickers and serious setbacks to *macho* America, one could see clearly that this latest revival will be associated with the rise of existential philosophy, neo-orthodox theology, the election of the first Roman Catholic President, the aggiornamento of Vatican II, the peace movement and the civil rights movement, the revival of pacifism, the war on poverty, the anti-nuclear movement, feminism and the quest for a new politics. In 1950, few could have foreseen this. Martin Luther King, Jr., was still in seminary; Adlai Stevenson and the Kennedy family were just entering national politics; Reinhold Niebuhr's books were just becoming influential. The new generation of hard-headed, realistic reformers in theology and politics was known only among the avant-garde intellectuals of the yet unborn "New Frontier." This Fourth Great Awakening is by no means over yet. Great Awakenings usually take a generation to mature. Ours is an intellectual revolution in search of consensus, the product of an Awakening still at high tide. No one can say how high the tide might rise, or what it will wash away. The one thing we can say about the future is that anything we say now may be wrong.

Notes

[1] William G. McLoughlin and Robert N. Bellah, eds., *Religion in America*, p. 8.

[2] Catherine L. Albanese, *Sons of the Fathers: The Civil Religion of the American Revolution* (Philadelphia; Temple Univ. Press, 1976). See also Marcus Cunliffe, *George Washington: Man and Monument* (New York: Anchor, 1977).

[3] Alexis de Tocqueville, *Travels in America*, I, p. 135. My own analysis of the period appears in *Gentlemen of Virginia* (New York: Dutton, 1960).

[4] Allan Nevins, ed., *Lincoln and the Gettysburg Address*, p. 88.

[5] Lloyd Lewis, *Myths After Lincoln*, part 2, "The American Judas."

[6] For a fuller treatment see W. Lloyd Warner, *American Life* (Chicago: Univ. of Chicago Press, 1962).

[7] See Richard D. Mosier, *Making the American Mind: Social and Moral Ideas in the McGuffey Readers* (New York: King's Crown Press, 1947). The Readers, reissued in the 1960s and 70s, enjoyed wide popularity.

[8] See Henry Wilder Foote, *Three Centuries of American Hymnody* (Cambridge: Harvard Univ. Press, 1949) and Albert Edward Bailey, *The Gospel in Hymns: Backgrounds and Interpretations* (New York: Scribners, 1950).

[9] For more on this, and problems presented by pluralism, see William G. McLoughlin and Robert N. Bellah, editors, *op. cit.*

[10] Barbara Ward, "Report to Europe on America," *New York Times Magazine*, June 20, 1954, p. 13. For a broader look at the long-range picture, see Oscar Handlin, *The Uprooted: The Epic Story of the Great Migrations that Made the American People*, p. 3.

[11] Here my chief source and interpretation is Will Herberg, *Protestant-Catholic-Jew: An Essay in American Religious Sociology*, See also A. Roy Eckhardt, "The New Look in American Piety," *The Christian Century*, November 17, 1954 and Alexander Miller, *The Renewal of Man*. Chapters 2 and 3 provide the titles from which two terms are taken: "A Religion to End All Religion" and "The Religion That is No Religion." The strongest warning in these years came from Reinhold Niebuhr, especially his article on "The Perils of Complacency in Our Nation," *Christianity and Crisis*, February 8, 1954.

[12] Irving Howard, "Random Reflections," *Christian Economics*, March 8, 1955. p. 12.

[13] The Joshua parallel is made by Joe E. Barnett, *The Billy Graham Story*, chapter 5.

[14] Paul Hutchinson, "The President's Religious Faith," *The Christian Century*, March 2, 1954.

[15] Will Herberg, *op. cit.*, p. 14.

[16]Michael Novak, *All the Catholic People*, p. 13.

[17]Both authors are quoted by William Lee Miller, *Piety Along the Potomac, Notes on Politics and Morals in the Fifties*, p. 15.

[18]These figures are quoted in Ronald E. Osborn, *The Spirit of American Christianity*, pp. 212-213. Christianity, he notes, had moved from a self-conscious minority to a prevailing cult.

[19]William Lee Miller, *op. cit.*, p. 131.

Cults, Crusaders and the Constitution

David G. Bromley

VIRTUALLY ALL SIGNIFICANT FORMS of human behavior are socially regulated in some fashion. However, few types of behavior are either totally prescribed or proscribed. Absolute normative regulations are by their very nature, therefore, both rare and dramatic. Historically there has been a great deal more study of absolute proscriptions, or taboos, than of absolute prescriptions, probably because taboos are surrounded by rituals, ceremonies and sanctions that are of particular interest to social scientists. The study of taboos comes out of anthropological research on small relatively static, homogeneous tribal societies. Primitive societies which were structurally undifferentiated, experienced little change, and were culturally homogeneous offered fruitful opportunities to study taboos, for such norms were prominent features of the cultural landscape.

In modern societies like the United States the study of taboos in the traditional sense is more problematic since there is more rapid change, greater cultural heterogeneity and greater institutional differentiation—all of which mitigates against the sense of absolute, consensual, permanent normative proscription conveyed by the concept of taboo. Historically, of course, taboos often have been connected in some fashion with religion because its transcendent symbolism supplies the requisite legitimation and sanctioning capacity for absolute proscription. However, in modern societies the religious institution is but one in a differentiated complex of institutions and therefore is no longer the symbolic hub of the social order. If there is any single institution which is the primary locus of symbolic and structural integration, it is the state. Indeed, it has been eloquently argued that rituals and ceremonies surrounding the political institution constitute a "civil religion" (Bellah and Hammond, 1980). Hence, when seeking expressions of fundamental values, principles, prescriptions and proscriptions, one of the major repositories is the founding political documents, the Bill of Rights and the Constitution.

Taboos represent behaviors against which there is enormous collective resistance. However, the social and cultural diversity of American society means that interests of various groupings do not coincide and that there is no perfect consensus on any single set of values. Still, general declarations of values and principles, like those contained in the Constitution and Bill of Rights, are widely acknowledged and there is support across the social order for this "public morality." Since there is such absoluteness associated with taboos, it is intriguing how violations of taboos associated with this public morality might be successfully negotiated (that is, in such a fashion as not to immediately discredit the violator) and how the aversive aura surrounding taboos is sustained in the face of violations.

To be sure there are constantly *individual* violations of all normative regulations which escape detection or which are discovered and result in the imposition of sanctions. This paper is not concerned with such individual deviance but rather explores attempts to organize and maintain a pattern of *collective* activity which could be interpreted as a violation of a constitutional taboo in such a way that a stigmatizing definition and possible sanctions are avoided. The case involves the occurrence of a "social scare" which yielded an organized effort to exert various forms of social control over a number of new religious groups, popularly referred to as "cults." The simultaneous emergence of a number of new religious groups in the United States produced a clash of interests between these groups and an oppositional movement. The aggrieved coalition of parties that formed the opposition attempted to translate their private troubles into a public issue, the cult problem. The resulting "cult scare" created the impetus and conditions for efforts to mobilize sanctions against new religious groups despite constitutional prohibitions on governmental regulation of religious activity. The occurrence of this social scare provides the occasion for gaining an understanding of how violations of taboos can be orchestrated and the consequences of such collective evasions. Briefly, I shall argue that the "cult scare" created the conditions necessary to morally over-ride normally unassailable proscriptions. The case study presented here demonstrates one way in which taboos can be contravened and suggests that violations have mixed effects on the influence of taboos.

Taboos

In all societies there are some behaviors that are, at least in theory, universally forbidden. In its original anthropological usage the term taboo referred to a normative proscription which, if breached, would result in automatic punishment. The use of the concept now has broadened to refer simply to behaviors which are absolutely forbidden, and the basis for individual avoidance has shifted to shared cultural values and interests which identify their violation as evil, sick, morally reprehensible, or personally and socially irresponsible. Thus even lacking otherworldly, automatic sanctions, the negative, aversive symbolism associated with taboos creates the impression that no one would even contemplate violating them.

In reality, of course, tabooed behaviors are violated more often than their forbidden status would suggest. Arguably, a most important reason for the existence of taboos is that there is such a substantial "natural" motivation for engaging in the prohibited behaviors that only a very strong emotional repellent will balance the motivational calculus. Just a cursory comparison of the proscriptions contained in the widely shared values expressed in the biblical ten commandments with actual conduct patterns in American society, for example, reveals that even these universalistic norms are rather regularly violated. The edict, "Thou shalt not kill," and widespread affirmations of the sanctity of human life notwithstanding, there is substantial motivation for and large numbers of cases of the taking of life. Normative proscriptions, even absolute ones, do not deter behaviors for which there are strong motivational impulses.

Taboos, Religion and the Constitution

The First Amendment of the Constitution states a prohibition so broad as to constitute a taboo: "Congress shall make no law respecting an establishment of religion nor prohibiting the free exercise thereof." This proscription has resulted in what is popularly regarded as the "separation of church and state." As in the case of other absolute proscriptions, of course, the boundary between church and state has not been nearly as impermeable as the constitutional taboo would suggest. Churches have supported the state by displaying national symbols in churches, holding prayer services and private consultations for governmental leaders, supplying chaplains for the armed forces, in some cases advocating specific candidates for public office, and supporting specific governmental policies such as racial segregation or declarations of war, which at least on their face violate theologically based moral principles. The state, in turn, has regulated specific religious practices by prohibiting snake handling and use of drugs in religious ceremonies, outlawing the Mormon practice of polygamy, denying uninoculated school children admission to school, and restricting the right of Jehovah's Witnesses to refuse blood transfusions for their children in life-threatening situations.

Still, the exception proves the rule, and these illustrations of state regulation of churches only demonstrate that no freedom or restriction is complete. The state has regulated religious practice in certain cases, but the measures of the proscription against governmental intrusion into religious affairs are the public celebrations of church-state separation, appeals to the principle when violations are revealed, the elaborate rationales provided when actions which could be defined as intrusive are contemplated, the public indignation that attends perceived violations, and the limited number of examples of state regulation (where resistance was offered) that have been successful. If state regulation of churches is possible but extraordinarily difficult, the issue remains of what social conditions weaken the taboo and facilitate regulation. Social scares, of course, offer one such set of circumstances.

Social Scares

One of the persistent features of American social history has been the occurrence of periodic "scares." In some cases these have been relatively short-lived incidents of collective behavior in which large numbers of people suddenly became aware of an outbreak of "dangerous" incidents (Cantril, 1940; Johnson, 1945; Kerckhoff and Back, 1968; Medalia and Larsen, 1958) such as the famous "windshield pitting" epidemic and the invasion from Mars. Public anxiety typically mounts rapidly and then subsides just as rapidly. Other types of scares have recurred as part of long-term, organized countermovements (Davis, 1960; Goldstein, 1940; Murray, 1955; Meyers, 1943). Organized anti-Catholicism, which reached several acute crisis points, and the periodic "red scares" illustrate these more enduring episodes in American history.

Scares are fueled by subversion mythologies which serve to arouse public sentiment and to create a fear and foreboding of destruction by evil forces. In essence such mythologies provide a conspiracy theory which asserts 1) a specific danger and a group associated with it, 2) one or more conspirators who have planned and direct the plot, 3) a set of base impulses that motivate the conspiracy leaders, 4) a manipulative process through which the conspirators involve others in their conspiracy, 5) an imminent danger for the entire society, 6) a remedial agenda that must be followed if catastrophe is to be avoided. Three examples of scares involving criminals, drug users and Catholics illustrate the common elements among scare myths.

The archetype of criminal activity in the United States is organized crime, the symbol for which has become the mafia (Albini, 1981). According to this mythology there is a monolithic, unified, national criminal organization called the mafia which is organized into secret families headed by "godfathers" who ruthlessly pursue power and wealth. Some individuals are involved in this organization through their ethnic heritages; others are corrupted, bribed or coerced to do the bidding of mafia leaders. Organized crime poses a variety of threats to law abiding individuals and institutions: its vast illegal economy, which drains federal revenues and competes unfairly with legitimate businesses; its corruption and coercion of government officials, law enforcement officers and businessmen; its undermining of public morality and fomenting of drug use, gambling and prostitution. Mafia mythology has been the product of political and law enforcement interests which have sought extraordinary legal authority.

According to drug scare mythology (Lindesmith, 1940; Reasons, 1972), the dangerous group of individuals is addicts. Addicts are created by other persons, pushers, who have as their goal the conversion of nonusers for the purpose of financial profit. Innocents are involved in drug use by being "hooked" by addicts and their dependence is then exploited to convert others in an ever expanding network. The dangers posed by addicts stem from their degenerate character and from their impulse to corrupt nonusers. Since addicts do not respond to the normal range of positive and negative sanctions, additional legal powers are required which, if granted under normal circumstances, would endanger constitutionally protected civil rights. Governmental bureaucracies have been particularly central in the creation of the drug scare feeding at different times upon public fear over increasing recreational drug use, public fear of criminal victimization, and organized crime (Dickson, 1968; Duster, 1970).

The nineteenth century Catholic scare (which also involved Mormons and Freemasons) constitutes a close parallel to the contemporary cult scare. In that case, Catholic immigrants comprised the dangerous group (Davis, 1960; Billington, 1963). According to nativists, the Catholic conspiracy was masterminded by the Pope and a group of unscrupulous, deployable agents—Jesuit priests. While most Catholics were viewed as simply innocent dupes with misplaced loyalties, there was also manipulation involved as priests wielded enormous power over individual Catholics through knowledge gained in confessions and through threats of eternal damnation. More coercive imagery was employed to describe Catholic nuns, however, who were depicted as virtual slaves in convents where they were exploited for the pleasure of sexually frustrated priests (Bunkley, 1955; Ricci, 1934). The primary danger to American society came from the political clout Catholics could wield if, as expected, they voted as a bloc upon papal instruction, although there were also widespread rumors during the nineteenth century that Catholics were forming an army in the West to launch a violent revolution. It was on the basis of such fears that a number of bills were introduced in state legislatures to limit the political rights of Catholics (Kinzer, 1964). The anti-Catholic scare served the interests primarily of Protestant/nativist groups who viewed the immigration of large numbers of Catholic workers from southern and eastern Europe as a threat to the values upon which Colonial America was founded. The scare fed upon the public concern over the rapid social transformations and unrest that were so characteristic of late nineteenth and early twentieth century American cities. Davis (1960:208) summarized this myth particularly well:

Behind specious profession of . . . religious sentiment, nativists discerned a group of unscrupulous leaders plotting to subvert the American social order. Though rank-and-file members were not individually evil, they were blinded and corrupted by a pervasive ideology that justified treason and gross immorality in the interest of the subversive group. Trapped in the meshes of a machine-like organization, deluded by a false sense of loyalty and moral obligation, these dupes followed orders like professional soldiers and labored unknowingly to abolish free society, to enslave their fellow men, and to overthrow divine principles of law and justice. Should an occasional member free himself from bondage to superstition and fraudulent authority, he could still be disciplined by the threat of death or dreadful tortures. There were no limits to the ambitious designs of leaders equipped with such organizations. According to nativist prophets, they chose to subvert American society because control of America meant control of the world's destiny.

The common features of subversion mythology are attributable to the structural situations which spawn them. In each case there is a source of social tension which is externalized. For example, Americans purchase large quantities of illegal products and services (e.g., gambling, stolen goods, prostitution) and then attribute the existence of this illegal market to a conspiratorial criminal organization. In the case of the nineteenth century Catholic scare, Protestants encouraged large-scale immigration to supply the labor force for the emerging industrial economy and then attributed political tensions arising from growing numbers and concentrations of Catholic workers and voters to a papal conspiracy. By externalizing the threat, subversion myths camouflage the internal sources of the problem at hand and construct a group of conspiratorial "outsiders" against whom opposition can be rallied. Constructed in this fashion a problem is no longer seen as a private clash between specific interest groups but rather becomes a public problem in which the fundamental values and institutions of the social order are at risk. It is a relatively simple matter under these conditions for an emotional, rhetorical version of a subversion myth to take hold and inflame public passions. Once a social scare has begun and the threat to the social order is perceived to be imminent, the grounds for morally over-riding normal restraints are established.

The Cult Scare

In the decade between the early 1970s and the early 1980s a number of groups in the United States, popularly referred to as "cults," rapidly gained members and visibility. These new religious groups included well known groups (e.g., the Unification Church, Divine Light Mission, Children of God, Hare Krishna, Scientology, The Way International) as well as a host of lesser known groups. The primary clientele for most of these groups was young adults. Particularly among the communally organized groups, the ages of recruits tended to cluster between 18 and 25. During the mid to late 1970s these groups grew rapidly although most never had more than a few thousand members.

The public reaction to new religious movements, in the form of a network of organizations referred to as the Anti-Cult Movement (Shupe and Bromley, 1980), formed shortly after conversions by these groups began. From the outset anti-cult organizations (with names like Love Our Children, Citizens Freedom Foundation, American Family Foundation) were comprised primarily of family members of individuals who joined new religious groups although the movement also gained a few supporters among clergy, social scientists and clinicians. Not surprisingly, parents of members of new religious groups were alarmed when their sons and daughters distanced themselves from family and friends; laid aside educational, career and domestic plans; and adopted new lifestyles and commitments. Despite the fact that these changes took place during a period of life typified by idealism and rebellion, many families concluded that their offspring would never have made such choices of their own volition (Shupe and Bromley, 1979). Reasoning from effect to cause, parents quickly determined that something had been done to their children. From this point it was a relatively short step to the brainwashing thesis which has been the core assumption of anti-cult mythology (Bromley and Shupe, 1981). The components of the myth underlying the cult scare are remarkably similar to those surrounding contemporary drug addicts, nineteenth-century Catholics and the mafia.

The Anti-Cult Movement has contended that there exists a class of groups called "cults" which can be distinguished from all other types of groups (Appel, 1983; Rudin and Rudin, 1980). The distinguishing characteristics of "cults" includes authoritarian leadership, suppression of rational thought, deceptive recruitment techniques, coercive mind control, a totalistic group structure, isolation from conventional society and former relationships, and exploitation of group members by leaders. Malevolent gurus are thought to be the driving force behind these pseudo-religious groups which have been cynically created to take advantage of religious liberty guarantees as a means of maximizing these individuals' power and wealth. The membership of these groups is comprised of young adults from the middle class whose naivete and idealism are being systematically exploited by these gurus. According to anti-cultists, cultic groups employ a combination of deception and sophisticated, coercive mind control techniques to subvert individual autonomy and free will.

There are, of course, a number of variants of anti-cult ideology. The most extreme form of this ideology alleges that cult membership is the product of isolation, food and sleep deprivation, hypnosis and relentless indoctrination. Milder forms of the ideology highlight deception and manipulation of trust and youthful idealism. The danger from "cults" is perceived to be substantial and imminent. It is alleged that these groups are numerous and rapidly growing; hence they constitute a real threat to all families as well as unsuspecting youth. In addition, these groups are allegedly amassing enormous financial empires on the energies of their brainwashed members and their leaders have thinly disguised political designs. The primary, and most novel, control technique advocated by anti-cultists is a process referred to as "deprogramming." Although this process has now evolved into a number of different procedures, in its original form deprogramming involved abducting adherents of new religious groups, physically detaining them and challenging their religious beliefs until they agreed to repudiate membership in their respective groups.

The key element in the ACM ideology is brainwashing. Unless individuals lack autonomy and independence most of the other anti-cult allegations lose their force and certainly the calls for formal governmental intervention in the affairs of these groups or their members become groundless. As is the case for the central components of the myths previously outlined, there is a great deal of prima facie evidence that brainwashing/mind control allegations are more rhetorical than descriptive: 1) The experience of Korean War POW's upon which anti-cultists draw shows a remarkable lack of success in converting Americans despite having prisoners under total control for several years. Only 25 of the 3,500 Americans held prisoner refused repatriation (Scheflin and Opton, 1978:89). 2) Coercive mind control techniques should yield high rates of recruitment; however, all of the empirical evidence suggests that even among those groups proselytizing most aggressively the conversion rate is well under one percent. Further, these groups have all experienced declines in even their modest conversion rates in recent years as young adults have become more concerned about future careers and less prone to experiments with idealistic crusades (Barker, 1984; Rochford, 1985). 3) Coercive mind control techniques should yield low defection rates; however, the retention rate for these groups is as abysmal as the conversion rate, with the annual membership turnover rates of at least twenty percent. Further, the way in which disaffiliation occurs is not consistent with brainwashing. It is a gradual process that occurs only after soul searching and analytic reflection is precipitated by factors such as failure of the group to achieve its goal or inconsistencies between the rhetoric and behavior (Skonovd, 1983; Wright, 1983). 4) The types of techniques allegedly employed by cults should be effective on any individual; however, virtually all the converts to new religious groups are between the ages of 18 and 25. 5) All of these groups have experienced frequent internal membership conflict and schism, which is totally inconsistent with the slave-like image of members conveyed by the brainwashing thesis.

In essence the anti-cult mind control argument converted the problems of youthful idealism and rebelliousness, disenchantment with conventional institutions, and the discontinuities between childhood and adulthood in American society into subversion mythology. Internal sociocultural problems were transformed into an external conspiracy masterminded by unscrupulous gurus. The belief that anyone was vulnerable to these subversive forces and that already large numbers of innocent youth had been helplessly ensnared recast what otherwise would have been private family conflicts as a public problem. By the late 1970s cult mythology was widely accepted and the cults were perceived to be a significant social problem. The fear of cults thus generated became the fulcrum upon which the Anti-Cult Movement sought to leverage its efforts to morally over-ride constraints on state intervention into religious practice.

The Interaction of Scare and Taboo

As the Anti-Cult Movement began its campaign against cults, it naturally sought access to state controlled legal sanctions. The anti-cultists quickly discovered that it was ineffectual for individual families, which lacked substantial resources or sanctioning power, to become involved in conflicts with a variety of groups over a number of different issues. It was much more desirable to define all the groups as essentially alike and to file complaints with public officials who would then coordinate sanctions against them. There were two major thrusts to these efforts to mobilize state power, and both involved circumventing the taboo on state intervention rather than denying its legitimacy. The anti-cultists sought to change the legal status of new religious groups, on the one hand, and to change the legal status of their members, on the other hand. Through either strategy the customary civil liberties protection simply would not apply.

Altering Group Status

The Anti-Cult Movement attacked the legal standing of new religious groups on three different fronts. The simplest and most direct tactic was to try to establish a difference between "cults" (i.e., pseudo-religious groups) and genuine religions. For example, a bill was introduced into the New York State Assembly as an amendment to the state's penal law entitled "Promoting a Pseudo-Religious Cult." The proposed amendment read as follows (Shupe and Bromley, 1980:185):

A person is guilty of promoting a pseudo-religious cult when he knowingly organizes or maintains an organization into which other persons are induced to join or participate in through the use of mind control methods, hypnosis, brainwashing techniques or other systematic forms of indoctrination and in which the members are participants of such organization engage in soliciting funds primarily for the benefit of such organization or its leaders and are not permitted to travel or communicate with anyone outside such organization unless another member or participant of such organization is present.

This tactic failed rather quickly because of its obvious contravention of the establishment clause of the First Amendment.

A second route was to impede public fundraising by new religious groups. As is common in fledgling social movements which lack any obvious skills or valuable commodities to generate financial resources, several new religious movements (most notably the Hare Krishna, the Unification Church, and the Children of God) solicited donations in such public settings as streetcorners and airports. Anti-cultists reasoned that if they cut off the economic lifeline of new religious groups that other activities, including proselytization, would also be suppressed. Once this tactic was discovered and publicized, literally hundreds of communities sought to restrict the ability of new religious groups to solicit in public by refusing to issue permits, elaborating the application process or placing cumbersome restrictions on the conduct of solicitation itself. This tactic was moderately successful for a short period of time as new religious groups found themselves continually confronted with new procedures, restrictions and delays. Local magistrates were supportive of such local ordinances, but as soon as new religious groups took cases to the appellate court level and raised First Amendment issues, restrictive ordinances were struck down. As one federal court judge put it in his decision (Shupe and Bromley, 1980:182):

It is well established law that distribution of literature and solicitation of funds to support a religious organization are well within the protection of the First Amendment.

Finally, attempts were made to get at "cults" through laws governing charitable organizations. Although charities are not as closely regulated as profit-making organizations, there are more controls over them than over religious organizations. Further, if new religions could be placed in this more comprehensive category, additional controls over this whole category could be introduced as a less obvious means of controlling the new religions. The Minnesota legislature did amend its laws on charitable solicitation (Shupe and Bromley, 1980:185), but the legislature's desire to avoid injuring "legitimate" charities prevented the enactment of regulations restrictive enough to impede fundraising by new religious groups.

Altering Individual Status
The most sophisticated and pervasive attempt to combat new religious groups through the use of law involved changing the status of individual members rather than the status of the groups themselves. If members of new religions had been brainwashed as anti-cultists alleged, it could be argued that they had not actually made autonomous, voluntary conversion decisions. As a result, anti-cultists contended, members of new religions should be removed from these groups and offered the opportunity to make an informed, independent choice. The implication was, of course, that no one would freely choose to return. The most articulate legal argument supporting the anti-cult position was that deception and mind control reduced or eliminated the individual's capacity for informed consent in the affiliation process. As Delgabo (1983:223) put it:

The process by which an individual becomes a member of certain cults appears arranged in such a way that knowledge and capacity, the classic ingredients of an informed consent, are maintained in an inverse relationship: when capacity is high, the recruit's knowledge of the cult and its practice is low; when knowledge is high, capacity is reduced.

Rather than seeking to create an entirely new law, anti-cultists sought to extend an already established legal concept. Virtually every state had enacted temporary guardianship and/or conservatorship legislation. These laws were designed for elderly individuals who were incapable of managing their own personal affairs. While specific provisions varied from state to state, in general such statutes permitted granting legal custody and power of attorney over mentally incapacitated family members for a limited period of time, ranging from a few weeks to a few months. Anti-cultists simply sought to extend the coverage of such conservatorship legislation to include adult individuals who had become mentally incapacitated through affiliation with "cults."

The amendments anti-cultists proposed typically identified characteristics of groups which anti-cultists deemed cults, processes associated with manipulative mind control, and symptoms of individuals subjected to thought control processes. Revisions and extensions of conservatorship legislation were introduced in a number of states. The bill which became the model for conservatorship legislation was originally introduced in New York and was passed by both houses of the legislature in that state in two successive years but was vetoed on both occasions by the governor.

The New York legislation (New York, 1981:3-4) provided for appointing a temporary guardian upon a showing that a person had "undergone a sudden and dramatic personality change." The characteristics which were specified as indicators of such change mirrored anti-cult mind control mythology. These included: 1) abrupt, dramatic personality change, 2) lack of "appropriate" emotional responses, 3) regression to child-like behavior, 4) physical changes (e.g., wooden, mask-like expression, dilated pupils, cessation of perspiration), 5) reduction of decisional capacity, 6) psychopathological changes (delusional thinking, hallucinations, obsessional ruminations).

No state actually passed such legislation, although bills modeled after the New York legislation were introduced and debated in a number of states. In a number of cases family members did go to court and successfully gain legal custody of their sons and daughters under the generic provisions of conservatorship bills. By identifying sympathetic magistrates in advance, parents were able to gain custody of their offspring for long enough to convince them to disavow their group membership. Gradually, however, appellate judges began issuing rulings against conservatorships for this purpose. The First Amendment taboo ultimately was always the key factor in overturning conservatorship legislation and rejecting individual requests for issuance. As the *New York University Law Review* (Note, 1978:1272) pointed out:

The extreme powers of temporary conservators ... not only interfere with but negate the members' free exercize rights .... (There is) a total and direct denial of the members' ability to practice their religion and a serious threat to the freedom of their co-religionists.

As the author (Note, 1978:1279), the government could only intervene if there was a compelling state interest, but

...the sect members do not engage in conduct that injures or threatens harm to the legitimate interests of others. The absence of any such injury distinguishes this case from virtually every decision in which the courts have found a compelling governmental interest sufficient to outweigh a religious claim. The state's interest in preventing self-endangerment should not, in and of itself, justify the granting of conservatorship.

So although parents continued to gain occasional conservatorships from local magistrates, constitutional proscriptions precluded this tactic as a general solution which would have allowed the anti-cultists to handle conversions on a case by case basis under the protection of the law.

Neither of these strategies succeeded, then, in creating legal change. However, the fact that crudely framed bills were proposed and seriously debated in a number of state legislatures and came very close to becoming law in New York indicates the degree of panic over cults. The anti-cultists were perceptive in attempting to circumvent rather than alter civil liberties protections. By arguing that religious liberties were not at issue because the groups and individual choices involved were not religious, anti-cultists nearly built enough support for their initiatives.

Relatively few of the opponents of these legislative initiatives defended the new religious groups themselves. Rather, opposition came from a variety of groups which were concerned about their own interests being undermined by such legislation: churches and minority group leaders who sensed dangerous precedents being set, civil libertarians who recognized that such measures could make defense of any fringe religious groups more difficult, charitable organizations which were not anxious to see governmental regulation expanded, and mental health professionals and jurists who recognized the administrative quagmire which would eventuate from enactment. However, even though the pressures to morally over-ride legislative barriers failed, non-legislative tactics were dramatically more successful.

Non—Legislative Tactics

In the face of a sympathetic hearing but a lack of tangible results from state legislators, anti-cultists developed two other strategies which depended upon private initiative: deprogramming and civil suits. Although both involved support from courts and law enforcement agencies, neither required formal revisions of the law. Both strategies also relied heavily on the cult scare for their success.

The more recent of these two developments has been the filing of civil suits against various new religious groups on charges such as infliction of emotional distress, false imprisonment and physical or mental abuse, fraud and clergy malpractice. While the specific charges were framed in terms of the legal grounds stipulated in state statutes, the testimony offered in support of the charges reflected cult subversion mythology as most plaintiffs alleged in one fashion or another that they had been the victims of mind control practices. Civil suits offered an intriguing alternative to criminal prosecution under existing law or new legislation for four reasons. First, civil suits are brought at the discretion of the party alleging injury and do not require unanimous jury verdicts; thus action was possible without state initiative and legal victories could be achieved on the basis of less compelling evidence. Second, by operating under existing statutory provisions, anti-cultists were not faced with the prospect of having to build sufficient political strength in each state to revise conservatorship or other laws. Third, judges and jurors did not have to agree to support action against all "cults" in all situations. Rather, the plaintiff simply had to convince the court of injury in one specific case. Finally, there could be substantial monetary awards which would not only damage the "cult" but would also create in the process financial resources that could be used to support other initiatives against these groups. In at least one case an attorney actively recruited disgruntled former cultists as clients for civil actions with the goal of using monetary awards to underwrite future suits.

Recent trends suggest that there is considerable potential in bringing civil suits although virtually all cases have been appealed or remain unsettled. In 1985 the largest civil award against a new religious group, nearly $35,000,000, was granted in a suit brought by a disaffected member (Julie Christopherson) against the Church of Scientology. In 1980 a former member of the Children of God, Una McManus, won a settlement of $1,500,000. The extent to which moral outrage is reflected in these settlements in this and other cases is reflected in the presiding judge's remarks. Judge William Gillie stated (McManus, 1981:xi-xii):

Frankly, young lady, I've been appalled by this case. I've heard few stories in this courtroom to equal it. It's shocking that religion can become so twisted that even the lives of little children are endangered. How could religious teachings become so perverted that immorality is considered a sacred duty? Obviously, money can't recompense you for the physical and emotional damages done .... This court awards Una McManus one million dollars in compensatory damages and one-half million dollars in punitive damages ... for alienation of her husband's affection and for misrepresentation of their ideals.

In a suit brought against Hare Krishna by a former member, Robin George, for false imprisonment, intentional infliction of emotional distress and other charges, an award of $23,500,000 was made in a highly emotional trial. It seemed clear in that case that all "cults" were on trial. The prosecuting attorney commented after the decision (Carlson, 1983):

The decision sends a message to all cults in this country .... It's the first case of its kind in the country, and it's very important to the children of America. If there are other people who have suffered this kind of abuse at the hands of people who manipulate the minds of minors or other citizens, lawyers will know that the courts will redress this kind of action.

In these and other cases, the merit of the specific legal charges aside, the testimony almost always centered on mind control practices of the group being sued, and sometimes other groups as well. This type of testimony appeared to substantially influence the juries, was vehemently objected to by defense attorneys and served as one major basis for legal appeals. What is most important is that this testimony almost inevitably involved the kind of delving into religious belief and practices that the First Amendment was intended to exclude. Any specific, legally grounded charges typically were obscured amid allegations and counter-allegations over the much more elusive and emotionally charged issue of brainwashing. The mind control allegations which became the primary trial agenda, formally or informally, created the conditions necessary to over-ride normal limitations on investigation of religious group observances. The defense attorney in the George case observed as much when he labeled the settlement "a runaway verdict" and contended that (Carlson, 1983):

The jury was obviously influenced by all the improper testimony that Judge (James A.) Jackson allowed. I think all religions should worry a little bit about this decision.

In any event, whatever the final disposition of these cases, there were major consequences for new religious groups. Allegations and trial testimony were widely reported and served to further reinforce the already pervasive cult scare.

As noted earlier, deprogramming has involved the abduction and physical restraint of individuals affiliated with religious groups which their families regard as "cults." This self-help tactic developed in the mid-1970s and spread rapidly during the next several years until civil suits and criminal prosecutions substantially raised the legal risks. A network of deprogrammers gradually developed who could be contacted and hired through the anti-cult movement. Again, this tactic was attractive because the initiative could be taken by the aggrieved party and family conflicts could be resolved without the necessity for direct intervention by law enforcement or judicial officers. The best available data on deprogramming for three religious groups which were the major targets of deprogrammers indicates that at least 400-500 members of the Unification Church, 100 members of the Hare Krishna and 150 members of The Way International have been abducted and deprogrammed over the last decade. Thus it would appear likely that at least 1,000 individuals were forcibly deprogrammed during this period from all new religious groups. This tactic was successful in a relatively high proportion of cases and thus made counteraction by the target groups difficult. Once the successfully deprogrammed individuals renounced membership, they naturally refused legal action and the group was without legal recourse. In virtually every case deprogrammers relied on convincing the deprogrammees that they had been brainwashed (rather than converted) and that the beliefs of the groups they had joined were false (Patrick, 1976). Thus, by its very nature deprogramming involved a direct attack on religious belief and affiliation, and the scale on which it was practiced was possible only because of the widespread acceptance of the cult subversion myth.

Despite the fact that deprogrammings were carried out through an informal network, deprogrammers did gain protection from the courts and police agencies. Deprogrammers could not abduct cultists in public settings without some incidents coming to the attention of the police or being sued in cases where deprogrammings were unsuccessful. In many cases, when police did encounter such incidents they sided with the deprogrammers and against the individual being abducted. The most famous of the deprogrammers boasted of his escapades. He recounted numerous incidents in which abducted individuals managed to attract police attention only to be rebuffed in their requests for assistance. For example (Patrick, 1976:119-120) reported the following encounter with a local police chief:

"What the hell is going on here?" he demanded.
"I'll be happy to explain," I said. I had with me copies of the *New York Times* account of my acquittal in the Dan Voll case a few weeks before in New York. That case had made national news, and the chief had heard about it. He'd also heard about the Sinunu case in Seattle.
"So you're the guy," he said.
"I'm the guy," I smiled.
"All right, fill me in on the particulars."
I did. When I was through, he was very sympathetic. "Yeah," he said, . . . "these damned cults. I've been reading about them. Kids getting all screwed up. But damn it, Patrick—why did you have to pick this little town to stop for gas? We ain't equipped to handle stuff like this."

The Federal Bureau of Investigation also rebuffed requests for assistance when individuals were abducted, even when this involved transportation across state lines. The agency chose to view the conflicts as a family matter. The sympathies of the Bureau were evident in an article prepared by two special agents (Luckstad and Martell, 1982:21):

A more realistic law would aim at and criminalize the less controversial areas of cult behavior—misrepresentation in recruitment and in proselytizing activities, preventing a member from contacting individuals outside the organization, or preventing members from leaving the cult . . . . The coercive acts of some cults in recruitment and proselytizing activities should not go unchallenged. Nor should some cults be allowed to hide behind the first amendment, while at the same time denying constitutional rights to some of their followers.

What civil suits and deprogramming shared, then, were that each relied on individual rather than state initiative, that state support was in some fashion integral to the strategy, and that state support was elicited by creating sufficient moral indignation as to over-ride normal First Amendment restraints. The moral indignation, in turn, clearly was attributable to the cult subversion mythology.

Conclusions

Taboos which enunciate absolute proscriptions of specific social behaviors continue to play an important role in regulating human behavior even in modern societies like the United States. Although there is much less social and cultural homogeneity in modern societies, taboos do demarcate the boundaries of public morality. These boundaries are defended both because interests coalesce around the norms (and the opportunities and restrictions they create) and because values which form the basis of collective identity make individuals and groups loathe to violate these dramatic proscriptions. There is then great collective resistance to violation of taboos; they come to constitute "social scarecrows" which warn off intruders from this forbidden social landscape. This resistance has naturally and gradually developed through American history as various groups have strengthened, shaped and adjusted this generic taboo to the times and their own interests.

Taboos do not, however, exist in a vacuum. Like all features of the social order, they are subject to challenge and change. In this paper I have considered one type of challenge to normative boundary maintaining devices such as taboos, the social scare. Scares are a significant social force for through subversion mythologies they capture and focus malaise in such a way as to produce great impetus for action. When scare meets taboo, an intriguing situation is created which is perhaps best captured by the popular imagery of the irresistible force meeting the immovable object. The case study presented here of the interaction between the cult scare and the First Amendment taboo on state intervention in religious observance is revealing on several counts. First, the resilience of taboos was again demonstrated. There was great pressure for legislative change generated by the cult scare. Yet despite this heavy pressure, virtually all of these initiatives were rebuffed. The true basis of strength of such taboos also is revealed to be coincidence of interests. Even though publicly proclaimed values exert influence in their own right, in the long run their persistence is due to a coalition of common interests. Had a variety of interest groups not viewed themselves as at risk, restrictive legislation almost certainly would have been enacted.

Second, the anti-cult campaign demonstrated that there are effective means for escaping any normative prescriptions or proscriptions. The informal strategies anti-cultists developed to resolve the cult problem as they defined it were in fact rather successful. In the face of state inaction the anti-cultists developed a sufficient degree of public outrage over "cults" to over-ride the constitutional protections that theoretically shield such minority groups. In essence the anti-cultists created a public drama much like those Americans are accustomed to viewing in the media. In many of the westerns, detective stories, soap operas and similar genre which pervade television and cinema the plot develops around a succession of outrageous, callous acts by the villains. By the time the heroic figure arrives on the scene to avert catastrophe the audience is well prepared for the total disregard for due process and even basic humanity which is to follow. So it is in this case. The specter of innocent youth being swept into virtual slavery to maniacal gurus laid the groundwork for inflated monetary awards from indignant juries and indifference to forcible deprogrammings by the public and law enforcement agencies. Creating and then exploiting moral outrage is a time honored strategy, and this case indicates that such inflamed passions can, at least temporarily, overcome even apparently well-entrenched values and traditions.

Finally, this case suggests that taboos can in certain respects be strengthened by their violation. The anti-cultists constantly reaffirmed their commitment to religious liberty and made every effort to circumvent rather than challenge the First Amendment taboo. They consistently argued that religion was not involved in the dispute and hence constitutional safeguards did not apply. From one perspective, of course, the recurrence of such sequences could yield simple hypocrisy, with all parties offering ritualistic affirmation of the very values they were undermining in practice. From another perspective, however, violators can have the effect of strengthening the very norms they defy. Not only do violators call up sanctions for their offenses but also they typically seek to reaffirm their own commitment to the values they have contravened in order to minimize the sanctions and ostracism they might face. It is in this fashion that taboos are honored in the breech.

References

Albini, Joseph
    1981   "Reactions to the Questioning of the Mafia Myth," Pp. 125-134 in Israel Barak-Glantz and C. Ronald Huff (eds.) *The Mad, the Bad and the Different.* Lexington, MA: Lexington Books.

Appel, Willa
    1981   *Cults In America: Programmed for Paradise.* New York: Holt, Rinehart & Winston.

Barker, Eileen
    1984   *The Making of a Moonie: Brainwashing or Choice?* Oxford, UK: Basil Blackwell

Bellah, *Robert and Phillip Hammond*
    1980   *Varieties of Civil Religion.* San Francisco: Harper & Row.

Billington, Ray
    1963   *The Protestant Crusade, 1800-1860: A Study of the Origins of American Nativism.* Gloucester, MA: Peter Smith.

Bromley, David G. and Anson Shupe
    1981   *Strange Gods: The Great American Cult Scare.* Boston: Beacon Press.

Cantril, Hadley.
    1940   *The Invasion from Mars.* Princeton: Princeton Univ. Press.

Carlson, Timothy
    1983   "Landmark Case Awards Cult Victim $32.5 Million: Jury Says Krishnas Brainwashed Teen." *Los Angeles Herald Examiner*, 18 June.

Davis, David Brion
    1960   "Some Themes of Counter-Subversion: An Analysis of Anti-Masonic, Anti-Catholic, and Anti-Mormon Literature." *The Mississippi Valley Historical Review* 47:205-224.

Delgado, Richard
    1983   "Limits to Proselytizing." Pp. 215-233 in David G. Bromley and James T. Richardson (eds.) *The Brainwashing/Deprogramming Controversy.* Lewiston, NY: Edwin Mellen Press.

Dickson, Donald
    1968   "Bureaucracy and Morality: An Organizational Perspective on a Moral Crusade." *Social Problems* 16: 143-156.

Duster, Troy
    1970   *The Legislation of Morality.* New York: Free Press.

Goldstein, Robert
    1978   *Political Repression in Modern America.* Cambridge, MA and New York: Schenkman Publishing and Two Continents Publishing.

Johnson, Donald
    1945   "The Phantom Anesthetist of Mattoon: A Field Study of

Mass Hysteria." *Journal of Abnormal and Social Psychology* 40:175-186.
Kerckhoff, Alan and Kurt Back
   1968   *The June Bug: A Study of Hysterical Contagion.* New York:
Appleton-Century-Crofts.
Kinzer, Donald
   1964   *An Episode in Anti-Catholicism: The American Protective
Association.* Seattle: Univ. of Washington Press.
Lindesmith, Alfred R.
   1940   "Dopefiend   Mythology."   *Journal   of   Criminal   Law,
Criminology and Police Science* 31:199-208.
Lucksted, Orlin and D.F. Martell
   1982   "Cults: A   Conflict   Between   Religious   Liberty   and
Involuntary Servitude?" *FBI Law Enfocement Bulletin* (June).
McManus, Una and John Cooper
   1980   *Not for a Million Dollars.* Nashville, TN: Impact Books.
Medalia, Nahum and Otto Larsen
   1958   "Diffusion and Belief in a Collective Delusion: The Seattle
Windshield Pitting Epidemic," *American Sociological Review* 23:180-186.
Murray, Robert
   1955   *Red Scare: A Study in National Hysteria, 1919-1920.* New
York: McGraw-Hill.
Myers, Gustavus
   1943   *History of Bigotry in the United States.* New York: Random
House.
New York
   1981   "Proposed Act to Amend the Mental Hygiene Law, in
Relation to the Appointment of Temporary Guardians." New York State
Assembly, Albany, New York (April 10).
Note
   1978   "Conservatorships and Religious Cults: Divining a Theory
of Free Exercise." *New York University Law Review* 53:1247-1289.
Patrick, Ted
   1976   *Let Our Children Go!* New York: Ballantine Books.
Reasons, Charles E.
   1972   "Dope, Fiends and Myths." Paper presented to the annual
meeting of the American Sociological Society, New Orleans.
Rochford, Burke
   1985   "New Religions, Mental Health and Social Control." Paper
presented at the annual meeting of the British Sociological Association
Study Group on Religion. Durham, UK.
Rudin, A. James and Marcia Rudin
   1980   *Prison or Paradise? The New Religious Cults.* Philadelpha:
Fortress Press.
Scheflin, Alan and Edward Opton

1978   *The Mind Manipulators.* New York: Paddington.

Shupe, Anson and David G. Bromley

1980   *The New Vigilantes: Deprogrammers, Anti-Cultists and the New Religions.* Beverly Hills, CA: Sage Publications.

1979   "The Moonies and the Anti-Cultists: Movement and Countermovement in Conflict." *Sociological Analysis* 40:325-336.

Skonovd, Norman

1983   "Leaving the Cultic Milieu." Pp. 91-105 in David G. Bromley and James T. Richardson (eds.), *The Brainwashing/Deprogramming Controversy.* Lewiston, NY: Edwin Mellen Press.

Wright, Stuart

1983   "Defection from New Religious Movements: A Test of Some Theoretical Propositions." Pp. 106-121 in David G. Bromley and James T. Richardson (eds.) *The Brainwashing/Deprogramming Controversy.* Lewiston, NY: Edwin Mellen Press.

Age Group Music:
Democracy, Rock & Roll
and the Constitution

Jack Santino

1986 sees the inauguration of the Rock & Roll Hall of Fame in New York. The first ten inductees are the founding fathers of this genre of music: Elvis Presley, Chuck Berry, Buddy Holly, The Everly Brothers, Fats Domino, Little Richard, Sam Cooke, Ray Charles, James Brown and Jerry Lee Lewis. Of the performers listed here, six are black, all were from modest if not poor beginnings and several have had problems with drugs, alcohol or the law. All are major American artists who have contributed significantly to the cultural life of this country. After thirty years, rock & roll music is being recognized as a vitally creative art form, and its early progenitors, many of whom were vilified at the time of their first successes, are today being enshrined in those cultural temples we call museums.

In 1985 the world witnessed another event that demonstrated the magnitude that rock music has achieved, the Live-Aid concert, held to raise money for the millions starving in Ethiopia. Generated through the efforts of rock musician Bob Geldoff, of the Irish band the Boomtown Rats, Live-Aid was a tremendous success both logistically and critically. As an international media event, the concerts (held in Philadelphia and London, as well as in other cities throughout the world) relied extensively on sophisticated satellite, cable and video technologies. As a humanitarian event, it helped to clean up the image of rock music in the 1980s, an era of androgynous stars, explicit lyrics and outrageous performances by heavy metal and hard-core punk bands. Bob Geldoff has since been nominated for the Nobel Peace Prize. Ironically, during the same period of time as the efforts to organize the Live-Aid concert, and the charitable Band-Aid and U.S.A. for Africa recordings that preceded it ("Do They Know It's Christmas," "We Are the world"), pressure was mounting in Washington to bring legislation to the floor of the House of Representatives that would establish a system for rating the lyrics of rock albums in terms of sexually explicit, violent or drug and alcohol related lyrics. This effort has been led by a group of women who call themselves the Washington Wives Group, because each of them is married to a United States Congressman. These women head up an organiztion entitled the Parents Music Resource Center

(PMRC). So while rock music was enjoying its finest moment as a concerned, humanitarian industry, it was once again under attack, accused by some segments of society of being a socially disruptive, negative influence that, if it must be tolerated, should at least be done so under the close and watchful eyes of the United States Congress.

In this article we will first address rock as a democratic art form and look at the ways in which it embodies the society of its birth. We will then examine the negative and the positive reactions to it, both of which have been and continue to be extreme. Concomitant with the music's continued success and popularity is the fact of the ongoing attacks upon the music as an art form. We will try to delineate some of the paradoxes inherent in the music that might give rise to the controversial, divisive emotions it generates, and finally we will examine some of the recent episodes concerning freedom of speech and the constitutionality of many of the attacks on rock & roll over the decades, especially with regard to attempts to establish a congressionally sponsored system of regulation over the lyrical content of rock music.

If popular music, or the popular arts, are the democratic arts that they have been called, then rock & roll is among the most democratic of them all.[1] It is a music which is a result of the intermingling of Afro-American and Anglo-American sources, of the Blues and Country-Western music. Both of these were in turn derived from the traditional musics of Africa and Northern Europe, especially Great Britain. A kind of folk music itself, rock & roll developed out of a variety of folk sources during the middle years of the twentieth century. In different areas in the United States, similar syntheses occurred, but each had its own unique regional characteristics, its own particular flavor that reflected the history of its place. Memphis became the home of an exciting countrified, uptempo version of the twelve-bar blues which became known as rockabilly. In Chicago, Chuck Berry (born in St. Louis) worked with the electrified blues musicians who recorded for Chess Records, added in some country guitar licks and novelty songs, and created some of the earliest, most fully realized, and most influential rock & roll songs ever recorded. In the urban centers of the North and Northeast, young Black singing groups, influenced by popular recording groups such as the Ink Spots, and Jubilee style gospel music, sang acapella four- and five-part harmonies on street corners, using the human voice to do what the instruments they could not afford to buy would otherwise do in the recording studio.[2] As Charlie Gillet has pointed out, throughout the United States at about the same time similar styles of music were being born, and they were all eventually to be known as rock & roll.[3] If ever a music is to be considered a truly American art form, it is rock & roll.

Likewise, examples and illustrations of many of our most cherished beliefs about America are all exemplified in rock—beliefs that anyone, no matter how poor or humble one's beginnings, can succeed; beliefs that hard work and talent will lead, almost inevitably, to this success; beliefs that America is a classless society, that our greatest resources are our people, and that the greatest of these are those "sprung from the earth," so to speak.[4] We look at our rock pantheon and see Elvis Presley, a man who was born in a two-room shack (as it is inevitably described) in Tupelo, Mississippi, who went on to become a King. We see poor boys from Lubbock, Texas (Buddy Holly), Ferriday, Louisiana (Jerry Lee Lewis) and Brownie, Kentucky (The Everly Brothers). We see a blind man from Albany, Georgia (Ray Charles), a gospel singer from Chicago (Sam Cooke) and one from Georgia (James Brown). None of these men was born wealthy, most were born into poverty. All have known great wealth in their lifetimes. So there we have rock & roll: sprung from the earth, grown from our folk roots of country, gospel and the blues. Sung enthusiastically, joyously by a generation of youthful performers (in a country that worships youth). It was uninhibited, it was spontaneous, it was emotional, it was irresistible. It was sexual. And, from the beginning, it was persecuted.

Rock & roll took America and the world by storm, and by surprise. As Peter Guralnick succinctly states, "The world was not prepared for Elvis Presley."[5] There was an enormous resistance to this apparently new thing on the face of the earth (and on everyone's radios). Rock & roll was condemned from the pulpit, ridiculed in newspapers, banned on radio stations and crusaded against in cities across America. At first, its opponents saw it as a fad that would quickly disappear. This, of course, was not to be. Thirty years have gone by, and this same music—the early rock & roll—is being heralded as a great national treasure by those who grew up with it. The new music stuck, perhaps because it was drawn so deeply and so unselfconsciously from its many folk roots; because it was so relevant to post-World War II American, baby-boom teenagers, who had money to spend on products that set them apart from adults; and because of developing technologies in the media (rock & roll could not have become the national popular music of its day without the previous development of top-forty radio).[6] The music itself, a synthesis of Black and white musical and cultural styles (including hair styles, clothing and perceptions as to what was appropriate public behavior) evolved mostly in Southern cities such as Memphis and New Orleans at the same time that E.D. Nixon and Martin Luther King Jr. were beginning to lead boycotts and freedom marches in protest against segregation. Moreover, the early "package tours" in which several rock & roll acts would perform together on the same bill brought out integrated audiences. Buddy Holly and Sam Cooke and their respective bands travelled together on the same bus, against the wishes of some and to the surprise of many, and according to all accounts, got along famously. Rock & roll did not happen in a social vacuum.

The music, of course, not only survived but thrived. Exported to other countries, it became the inspiration for the Beatles in Liverpool, who in turn sparked a wave of musical creativity, first in England, then, starting in 1964, in America. Today, the music continues to grow, change and develop. What were once new styles of music, created from dynamic processes of borrowing and syncretism became in turn the raw materials for new generation of young musicians. Called either rock & roll or simply rock (there are arguments as to how these terms should be used and which styles of music they should be used in reference to; some want to limit the use of the term rock & roll to the various styles of music that became popular in the 1950s, as described above, and contemporary styles obviously derived from them such as the music of, for instance, John Fogarty of Credence Clearwater Revival; I prefer to use the terms more or less interchangeably, while recognizing the potential taxonomical problems involved) this music, in all its many contemporary permutations is arguably the most popular music in the world and is one of the most profitable industries in the United States. All the while, its most refreshing and revitalizing artists continue to arise, as it were, from small towns (Hibbing, Minnesota, e.g., Bruce Springsteen from Asbury Park, New Jersey) while ethnic minorities including Blacks and Hispanics rely upon their own cultural heritages and those available to them throughout the great American popular culture to create musical syntheses that are consistent with tradition, and at the same time, new (Prince, e.g., or East Los Angeles' *Los Lobos*, or the dynamic blend of folk poetry and funk called Rap music). American rock & roll, now reflecting international influences (such as the Talking Heads' adaption of Nigerian JuJu music into their stylistic repertoire), and new technologies such as the synthesizer, continues to be fresh, vital and original. Perhaps it is not surprising, then, that rock music continues to be vilified.

The paradox of rock & roll, then, can be stated as follows: it is a quintessentially American art form, which embodies many of our most cherished cultural myths, but it has been seen as ignorant, threatening, evil and, for these reasons, unAmerican. Actually rock & roll is a music of many paradoxes. Some of them might be outlined as follows: Although it is a multimillion dollar industry, its fans, its consumers, demand an honesty in it, a sense of true, personal expression from its artists, even though it is mediated through a labyrinth of records, radio, video and tape. In short its fans want to hear in it the voice of individuals like those described above: naturals, unaffected and untainted by commercialism, even though the rock music industry is an intrinsically commercial enterprise.[7]

Thus, although rock has always been associated with youthful rebellion and social criticism as part of this rebellion (implicitly in the 50s, explicitly in the 60s), rock is a major economic force within the capitalistic system it often decries. The paradoxes continue: rock came from the working class, the rural and urban poor, but it became the music of white middle-class youth; it is a "grass roots" music that is nationally and even internationally popular; although it is nationally and internationally popular, it is greeted with suspicion and denunciation by many segments of our society. It is demonstrably American in its origins, it greatest practitioners, from Chuck Berry to Bruce Springsteen, have in their songs addressed familiar American themes, and as a field of endeavor it represents the American democratic ethos, that bundle of beliefs, symbols, wishes and fantasies we call the American dream. Biographies of rock stars read like the tales of the rough-hewn frontier heroes of the 19th century, wherein young men, poor but pure, naive but honest, youthful but wise beyond their years, armed only with talent, ambition and good intentions, rise above their station to become leaders and heroes, or today, idols, stars and celebrities.[8] Generally speaking, the actors in these cultural dramas have been males, and by far the most successful of these have been white males. In fact, it was not until the rise of Madonna as a "superstar" (as they are known in today's parlance, rock stars being equated with superheroes, and superstardom with a kind of charismatic divinity, as in *Jesus Christ, Superstar*) that young females have had a rock star of their own sex as a fantasy model, a rock star they could dress like, that they could pretend to be, rather than someone they had to dream of marrying, like Elvis, or Paul McCartney, or Michael Jackson. Madonna has been called "that quaintest of things, a sex symbol," because of her provocative stage show and the lyrics of her most popular songs (e.g., "Like a Virgin" and "Material Girl").[9] Once again, vast success and mass popularity are mixed inextricably with controversy and condemnation of a sexuality that is central to rock music.

Before attempting to unravel this tangled skein further, I would like to examine three episodes in the ongoing negotiation of the proper place of rock music (and rock musicians) in American society. Hopefully, these will serve as jumping off points that will allow us to delineate more precisely the terms of this negotiation, and what values and assumptions underlie them. First, I will describe an episode that occurred in a 1972 film which documents a tour of Evis Presley. Then, we will discuss the famous incident of the invitation which was extended and later rescinded to the Beach Boys, to perform at the National Mall in Washington, D.C. for the 4th of July. Finally, we will discuss the success of Bruce Springsteen in the 1980s, and the varying ways he and his work have been interpreted.

In the movie *Elvis on Tour* there is a scene in which Elvis is being awarded the keys to the city of Roanoke, Virginia. The mayor, an elderly looking man, is rattling off what appears to be a prepared spiel for the television cameras, as Elvis, bedecked in a sequined jump suit, fiddles with the paper-mache guitar he has been given as a gift. "I broke the strings," Elvis says, "I broke *all* the strings!" The mayor prattles on. "Are you gonna play 'I Ain't Nothin' But a Hound Dog' tonight? That was my favorite," asks the mayor, in an unconvincing effort at spontaneous camaraderie (correct lyric: "*You* ain't nothin' but a hound dog"). Elvis, called back to the moment, slips easily into what has become for him a trademark routine of polite, public deference for his elders. "Ah, yes sir, ah, we'll be doing that one," he says, obviously bored to tears by the thought of singing this song one more time. When his version of "Hound Dog" was released in 1956, Elvis was the most exciting and controversial performer in America, but on this day he impatiently stands, undergoing an empty little ceremony, receiving an honor bestowed upon him by a man who probably knows no other song Elvis ever did, who probably ignored and perhaps despised the record at the time of its popularity, and, more than likely, has no real appreciation of the worth of Elvis' originality and contributions to American culture. Elvis fidgets. His eyes dart around the room, searchingly, a bit helplessly. The two men talk past each other. Mayor: "The girls down at the office made this guitar for you." Something connects. For the first time Elvis perks up. He directs his attention to the mayor: "I played here several times. Yes sir, I was in Roanoke when I first started out." Mayor: "Now these little names on it are from your fans . . . ." The mayor seems not to hear Elvis. He seems not to be *listening* to Elvis. Has he ever listened? He comes to honor Elvis, not to pay attention to him, not to take him seriously. "Now if there's anything I can do for you . . . ." "Thank you very much . . . ." "Thank you, thank you . . . ."

In 1956, Elvis was seen as the great beast slouching toward Bethlehem by men such as this, the embodiment of the growing evil that threatened to corrupt the morals, and the youth of white America. Before his national breakthrough, Elvis and his band (Bill Black and Scotty Moore) played throughout the South. Although many feel that this period was Elvis' peak in terms of creativity, the mayor of Roanoke had not, of course, noticed. The Elvis he was giving the key to the city to was not, as far as he was concerned, the Elvis who, in an earlier era, along with Little Richard, Jerry Lee Lewis and so many others, was the demonic embodiment of chaos. Even relatively tame performers, such as New Orleans' Fats Domino, were viewed as part of this great and growing cancer called rock & roll, largely because their skin was black or their music was derived from African as well as Anglo sources. While rock is an arena in which America's democratic and political myths are worked out and lived through, rock is also rebel music, outlaw music that by its very existence challenges and calls into question those myths and the government that espouses them. Add to this the fact that rock is in large part developed out of blues, gospel and other Afro-American musics, coupled with the everpresent, undeniable racial prejudice long entrenched in our society, and the perceived threat of rock's rebelliousness becomes confused with the color black as the traditional color of evil and the devil and of Afro-Americans as well.

Rock & roll contains many of America's contradictions. Elvis Presley, of course, not only conforms to the rags-to-riches pattern articulated in the popular novels of Horatio Alger; he improves upon it. Not only riches but royalty—a kind of folk royalty, to be sure, but royalty nevertheless—could be had in this land where everyone is born free of class restrictions and has an equal chance, this great experiment in democracy called the United States of America. There is an obvious contradiction in the idea that royalty attained is a proof of democracy, but there are many such contradictions in the life and career of Elvis Presley. He was a good boy and a bad boy, a poor boy who became king, a rebel who loved his parents, a man who loved sacred music and sang dirty blues, a sex symbol who was shy, a white man who sang Black music, a symbol of the vibrancy of youth who grew inexorably old. Somewhere between the poles of these contradictions lies his appeal. When he died in 1977, it was of drug abuse. If the world had not been ready for him in the beginning of his career, it was completely shocked by his death. The national outpouring of grief was comparable to that of the death of John F. Kennedy. President Jimmy Carter issued a statement in which he said that Elvis embodied the best of America: its youth, etc. and that, with the death of Elvis Presley America lost a part of itself. Not only is this the same Elvis Presley who was banned by church groups, teachers' groups and parents' groups, and whose performances were secretly filmed by the police in order to bring him up on charges of obscenity; this is the same *government* that secretly taped the telephone conversations of John Lennon in the 1970s, and which today threatens to initiate a rock ratings system that many people see as a kind of incipient censorship.

These are the ambivalences and ironies being dramatized in the spectacle of Elvis Presley being given the keys to a city where, a decade and a half earlier, he brought something new, different, something important, and was at best ignored and at worst reviled. What he brought was not Black music, exactly, but a white music with the spirit and feel of Black music (precisely the qualities his first producer, Sam Phillips, had been looking for);[10] music with the attitude of Black music, a freer, less constrained, more open, more honest, more downright *physical* music.

The ambivalence toward rock as a mass cultural phenomenon which is thought (sometimes correctly, sometimes not) to endorse values and lifestyles that are antithetical to American middle-class society has more recently been dramatized in the incident involving the invitation extended to the Beach Boys to perform on the National Mall in Washington, D.C. on the 4th of July, 1982. Rescinded by Secretary of State James Watt as inappropriate, the invitation was hastily re-endorsed by the former Governor of the Beach Boys' home state, President Ronald Reagan. Although Watt had said that rock music attracted a "bad element," the

First Lady, Mrs. Reagan, later announced that she was a fan of the group. Clearly the spectacle was a political one: a first term president who could not afford to alienate the millions of fans who buy or have bought Beach Boys records and who are of voting age.

On a deeper level, however, we begin to approach the Constitutional questions having to do with freedom of speech. The Beach Boys performed that year, and on subsequent years, and drew record audiences for outdoor performances on the Mall, crowds that numbered in the several hundreds of thousands. Still, Beach Boys fans, and rock fans generally, despite their large numbers, remain a minority in this country. It is because of this fact—that rock is accepted, often passionately, by millions of Americans but is of no interest or even denounced by many millions more—that Robert Cristgau has termed it "semi-popular" music.[11] The issues then become: do millions of Americans have a right to celebrate with a style of music, and to celebrate musical groups, who are felt by those who represent the majority to espouse values which are counterproductive, perhaps even treasonous, to the commonweal as they understand it? Do such groups have a right to perform on the National Mall on the 4th of July, or does this validate those negative values? The issue is complicated by the fact that most of those who favor rock & roll, who see it as *their* music are young. Parental guidance of youth is said to be the issue, not freedom of speech. Nevertheless, rock fans may be overwhelmingly young, but they are not necessarily overwhelmingly minors. The irony is that the Beach Boys are a particularly tame band, whose songs and lyrics generally celebrate America, through the image of California, as a land of youth, surf, beach parties, and in the words of one of their hits, "Fun, Fun, Fun."

Again we find the paradox: the Beach Boys are an American phenomenon and are typically American in theme (the west as golden land of unlimited good and opportunity, the accent on youth, and so forth). Moreover their musical style is typically American in that it derives in equal measure from Black and white sources (Black group harmony singing, also known as doo-wop; Chuck Berry; and the Four Lads, among others). With these resources as a base, group leader Brian Wilson worked out a creative synthesis that came out sounding new and different. The music of the Beach Boys became representative of a new genre within rock & roll music, known as surf music, or the California sound. Nevertheless, for all their creativity, and whatever their particular genius, the Beach Boys were pronounced guilty by association. They were a part of the entity known as rock music. Rock is bad, therefore the Beach Boys are bad.

Did the Beach Boys audience perceive the band the way James Watt did? Because they have become so much a part of American culture, the Beach Boys were seen as an appropriate choice for the 4th of July. But because they were asked to perform on a day that is in its way nationally sacred, and to perform among the statues and symbols of that sacred nation (between the Lincoln Memorial and the Washington Monument on an east-west axis, between the White House and the Jefferson Memorial on a north-south axis, and in sight of all four), rock music was seen as an inappropriate genre of entertainment for the occasion. Nevertheless, someone in the government must have thought the Beach Boys were entirely appropriate for the occasion of the annual celebration of the birth of the United States; presumably these people saw the Beach Boys as a harmless slice of American culture—America's band, as they are sometimes called.

The final incident that embodies the cultural schizophrenia we have toward rock & roll music and the attitudes and qualities contained in various aspects of it, concerns Bruce Springsteen and his work. During the 1984 Presidential election campaign, one of the more amusing incidents occurred when Ronald Reagan, campaigning in New Jersey, quoted New Jersey native Bruce Springsteen in a speech, as if to imply an identification with the rock superstar. Springsteen later wondered aloud which album it was that the President had been listening to. Surely not *Nebraska*, he said, alluding to an album he wrote and recorded that features a bleak and desolate view of an America hit hard by unemployment. Springsteen had recorded *Nebraska* prior to his next album, *Born in the U.S.A.*, which was a major success and has been greeted as an indication of the return to patriotic values among contemporary youth, even though a single listening reveals a continuing questioning of the American capitalistic value system that places money before honor, and profit before pride. The album is about the U.S.A. to be sure, and features a picture of the artist standing in front of the American flag on the jacket cover. There *is* a kind of pride expressed within its tracks, a pride born of trying, of remaining optimistic in the face of grinding poverty and a non-caring government. But the kind of blind patriotism that translates into follow-the-leader, -surely-he-knows-what's-best-for-us-all is simply not there.

During the widely acclaimed tour of 1985 Bruce Springsteen was not allowed to perform in Foxboro Stadium in suburban Boston. A year earlier, Michael Jackson was also prohibited, on the grounds that rock shows attract bad crowds into an otherwise peaceful community. Banned in Boston is still a truism. However, the weekly football crowds that attend the regularly scheduled New England Patriots games at the facility are known to be extremely rowdy and disruptive to the surrounding community, and yet the stadium was *built* for them. Why is it rock that is the *bete noire*? Rock videos are condemned for being sexually explicit, and sexist, at the same time. But so are the television series *Dallas* and *Dynasty* (among several others) as well as many advertisements to at least the same degree. Why is rock the regular target for groups who want it off the airwaves, who want to control it? The question returns us to the issue of a rating system for rock music.

The Washington Wives Group, and their organization, the Parents' Music Resource Center (PMRC) has proposed a ratings system that, they say, will not censor lyrical content but rather indicate to parents the nature of the material in the album or tape. Granted that there is such a thing as pornography, and that children should not be exposed to it, this ratings proposal is still very disturbing for several reasons. Some of these have to do with the ever troubling definition of pornography. Prince uses sexually explicit material, but many critics find his work emotionally and artistically honest, if at times unsettling. Who decides? Other artists who would not be affected by a ratings system because of the lack in the work of material that the PMRC would find objectionable may in fact be producing music that is coy and cynical. Questions of relative artistic merit are invariably thorny and ultimately arbitrary. Therein lies one of the problems. All of the proposed ratings systems (and they always include plans for eventually rating rock videos and rock concerts as well) are based on a singular, particular set of aesthetic judgments based on one certain set of moral and religious beliefs. Can these be legislated into law?

Beyond aesthetic questions of artistic merit, and the unresolved questions of the nature and extent of the effects of the mass media upon members of its audience, are questions which are raised by the actions of politicians' spouses lobbying in behalf of a certain kind of legislation, legislation which contains within it a great many ideological and moralistic value judgments. As wives of congressional leaders, these women have an access to power that exceeds the right we all have to speak out. This legislation has received the attention of the Congress of the United States of America—hearings have been held—because of the relationships of its proponents to the lawmakers. This would seem to be a conflict of interest.

Moreover, at the time the hearings were held—during the summer of 1985—the recording industry had been sponsoring legislation of its own in hopes of creating new copyright and royalty rulings for protection against unauthorized tapings of their products. In an age of videocassette recorders and home recorders of all kinds this has become a problem for the recording industry. The hearings on the ratings systems, with the strong implicit message that the industry should begin to police itself, amounted to a kind of blackmail; "perhaps we will be more kindly disposed to your royalty problem if you clean up your act." To maintain that these actions are not censorious is to overlook the repercussions of such sabre rattling. Material thought to be offensive to one particular group—the PMRC and the Washington wives—will tend to be recorded and released. It is perhaps a final irony that many of the politicians involved, when dealing with other social issues, generally maintain that they are against government interference, that they want "big government" off our backs and out of our lives. For that reason, for instance, they oppose gun control.

No, it is rock & roll music that continues to outrage and be the target of outrage. Again we must ask why. One reason is because rock & roll as we understand it, referring to the music that became nationally popular in the mid 1950s has always been used by adolescents as a badge of separateness from their parents. It has always been a sign of age-identity, of identity with one's peers and a way of measuring the distance between oneself and one's parents. Parents prove their "age," which really means their social and cultural distance from their children, their lack of understanding, by not knowing who's in and who's not, by being offended and repulsed by what they hear and see, by not getting the joke. Parents are *not hip*, they simply *don't get it*. The kids do, most of the time, but find themselves in a position in which they have to defend singers, groups, songs and styles they themselves might not like. Rock is theirs, it belongs to them the way some musics belong to certain ethnic groups or regional areas. Rock belongs to an age group. To attack it is to attack all of it, and all of its youthful audience.

More serious, however, is the possibility that the ongoing, continual outcry against rock & roll has to do with the nature of the music itself. The rhythms of rock are Black. The music is, as we have seen, in large part Afro-American in origin (there are many who would say that it is overwhelmingly, if not *entirely* Afro-American in origin.)[12] Certainly it derives its rhythms from Black dance music. Over the years, it has been the "beat" of rock that has been centered on as the most insidious aspect of the music, the beat that would allegedly hypnotize and brainwash its listeners. Because of the Afro-American styles to which rock owes so much, the music and its white performers were greeted with racist reactions. From the beginning, rock was referred to as "Nigger music," as "jungle music," and has been persecuted by a number of racist groups. Rock today continues to be based on Black music, music which is sensual, physical, involving. These qualities are deeply cultural, and are threatening to the more reserved Northern European sense of what is proper, which underlies our public behavior. It is beyond the scope of this article to investigate this point in depth, but it should be recognized that the conflict does not begin and end with Elvis Presley being shown only from the waist up on television, or of Michael Jackson being banned from Foxboro Stadium, or of a group of lawmakers' wives attempting to impose their sense of order on a society that is changing in ways they cannot control. Rather these are episodes in an ongoing American drama. This drama concerns black people and white people in our society, and it concerns the interchange of cultural styles and aesthetics (rock music reflects this dynamic, or rather, rock *is* this dynamic, or a sample of it). The conflict reflects very different and centuries-old traditions, and it has to do with the freedom under the Constitution of all peoples to be free to practice their unique cultural inheritances without being forced to assimilate or compromise their integrity, artistic or otherwise.

Notes

¹Ray B. Browne, "Popular Culture: Notes Toward a Definition," in Christopher D. Geist and Jack Nachbar, eds., *The Popular Culture Reader*, 3rd edition (Bowling Green, Oh.: Popular Press, 1983), p. 16.

²Jack Santino, "The Spirit of American Music: 'Nobody Ever Told Me It Was the Blues," *Journal of American Culture*, V: 4, 1982.

³Charlie Gillet, *The Sound of the City* (New York: Pantheon, 1970, 1983), p. 23.

⁴See for example, "Popular Myths" in *The Popular Culture Reader* (Bowling Green, Oh.: Popular Press, 1984), pp. 37-96; and Greil Marcus, "Elvis Presley," in Greil Marcus, *Mystery Train* (New York: Dutton, 1976).

⁵Peter Guralnik, "Elvis Presley," in Jim Miller, ed., *The Rolling Stone Illustrated History of Rock and Roll* (New York: Random House/Rolling Stone Books, 1976), p. 19.

⁶Philip K. Eberly, *Music in the Air* (New York: Hastings House, 1982. I am grateful to Samuel Brylawski, Division of Recorded Sound, The Library of Congress, for this reference and for the suggestion.

⁷Simon Frith, *Sound Effects* (New York: Pantheon, 1981), esp. pp. 39-41.

⁸Richard M. Dorson, *America in Legend* (New York: Pantheon, 1982.)

⁹Ken Tucker, *The Philadelphia Inquirer*, May 30, 1985, p. E1.

¹⁰The story of Sam Phillips and the young Elvis Presley has been told so often that it is by now common knowledge. Phillips repeated to me in 1983 in a personal interview how he was looking for a white man who sang with the feeling and intensity that was found in Black music at the time.

¹¹Robert Cristgau, *Cristgau's Record Guide* (New Haven and New York: Ticknor and Fields, 1981), pp. 5-6.

¹²Nick Tosches, *Unsung Heroes of Rock and Roll* (New York: Scribner's 1984).

Nineteen Eighty-Four and the Constitution

W. Russel Gray

Since World War II no political book ... fiction or nonfiction ... has passed more thoroughly into the English language and the popular consciousness

TIME HAS CONFIRMED Lawrence Malkin's 1970 appraisal of George Orwell's masterpiece.[1] A rarity among novels, *1984* is distinguished as a literary work yet immensely popular. How popular? Thirty-five years after initial publication tens of millions are estimated to have read it in sixty-two languages.[2] More than 150,000 hardcover and ten million paperbacks are in print, and paperback sales entering calendar 1984 averaged 62,000 monthly at the sixty-sixth printing.

Manifestations of *1984*'s impact have been curious, even ominous. Yale's freshman yearbook for the class of '84 contained 302 pictures of Orwell, substituted by a "Big Brother" editor for students who failed to submit a photo. *The Big Brother Book of Lists* (December 1983) cited: eleven CIA-supported governments that fell, three ways to remove Castro (supposedly suggested to JFK by Ian Fleming), the ten most frequently censored books in American high schools, and J. Edgar Hoover's eight ways to identify a car driven by a communist. Also on sale at holiday time, the Big Brother Calendar for 1984 noted 250 dates its devisers considered anniversaries of government intrusion into the lives of individuals.[3]

The key word in Mr. Malkin's tribute—*political*—suggests why Orwell's 1949 novel is popular, influential and feared. As we entered 1984 an article in a political journal stated that Orwell's gloomy vision had come to pass in the United States. The "omnipotent Big Brother" was none other than Ronald Reagan, and we would not have to look far for counterparts of "Newspeak," the "Thought Police," and the "Ministry of Truth." The journal that published the article is the weekly *New Times* of the Soviet Union, where, ironically, the authorities never have allowed publication of *1984* and routinely confiscate copies brought in by travelers from the West.[4] Of course any Russian acknowledgment of validity in 1984 seems a favorable development after the reception *Pravda* gave it in 1950:

It is clear that Orwell's filthy book is in the spirit of such a vital organ of

American propaganda as the *Reader's Digest* which published this work, and *Life* which presented it with many illustrations.

Thus, gruesome prognostications, which are being made in our times by a whole army of venal writers on the orders and instigations of Wall Street, are real attacks against the people of the world . . . .

But the people are not frightened by such fears of the instigators of a new war. The people's conscience is clearer today than ever before. The foul maneuvers of mankind's enemies become more clearly understandable every day to millions of common people.[5]

It is not difficult to infer why the USSR suppresses *1984* even today. No totalitarian regime can acknowledge the rights and freedoms satirically defended by Orwell—many of which are in America's Constitution. Orwell's account of life in a modern state without such a covenant makes *1984* particularly germane.

Seeking a literary parallel to *1984*, Lawrence Malkin made a more than fortuitous connection with the eighteenth century when he suggested that we look "beyond the nineteenth century English novel with its romantic conception of man as problem solver and into the eighteenth century, where life is larger than man and the world is a wicked place."[6] Though not primarily a literary document, the Constitution, drafted in 1787, ratified in 1789, and modified by twenty-six amendments (1791-1971), reflects America's awareness of eighteenth century social and political injustice and, as well, our nineteenth and twentieth century efforts to solve problems democratically. Like the Constitution, *1984* addresses the suppression of basic freedoms (religion, speech, assembly, right to petition, press), unfair search, denial of due legal process, cruel and unusual punishment, self-incrimination, slavery and oligarchy.

*   *   *

Congress shall make no law respecting an establishment of religion, or prohibiting the free exercise thereof; or abridging the freedom of speech, or of the press; or of the right of the people peaceably to assemble, and to petition the government for a redress of grievances.

Because Orwell's Oceania has no congress, constitution, or First Amendment protection, readers of *1984* can scarcely imagine the "comrades" under Big Brother practicing religion or free speech, or daring to petition or assemble without authorization; the term *free press* would be an oxymoron.

The *proles* (eighty-five percent of Oceania) accept Party announcements of industrial productivity in the face of shortages and overseas victories over powers that the day before were allies. The proles seem content with Victory beer, utensil sales, pornography, pop songs, lotteries, martial parades, and public execution spectacles. No one stirs up this large bloc of citizens at election time, for there are no elections. Potentially dangerous Outer Party members do not indulge in or agitate for basic freedoms. Such activities do not violate specific laws, of which there are none, but would be reported to the Thought Police, who can make comrades disappear into "unpersons." Children spy for Big Brother and inform on parents. Adult Party agents may be anywhere; a kindly appearing old "shopkeeper" entraps and betrays Winston and Julia. Two-way telescreens monitor home life. This electronic spy detects not only facial expressions and conversations, but heartbeat changes as well. Too late Winston and Julia discover that the Party can even stake out a clandestine love-nest with camera and microphone. And who will start a conspiracy or organize an unauthorized meeting when Two-Minute Hate Periods reinforce state loyalty at one's place of employment, censors open mail, and closed circuit TV surveils even lavatories?

Our basic freedoms have not fared well in Oceania. Religion is non-existent. St. Martin-in-the-Fields has become a military museum and poet/editor Appleforth becomes an unperson for rhyming "rod" with "god." There is no freedom of speech even in one's sleep; telescreens always must be on. Unauthorized assembly or even a meeting of lovers in a public place is difficult to manage; telescreens are all around the pediment where Winston and Julia meet at Victory Square. And, considering the Party's entrapment of Winston by leaking him a copy of a subversive book, any petitions in Oceania likely will be Party fabrications to snare thought criminals.

War-time BBC writer Orwell knew what happens to freedom of the press during emergencies. Thus we have a startling demonstration of how a party in power can manipulate print and electronic media. Posters of Big Brother (with his apparently moving eyes) seem ubiquitous. Winston's office "speakwrite" facilitates his alterations of history for Minitrue, the state produces and distributes pornography, machines write novels, editors steadily shrink the Newspeak dictionary, ever-turned on telescreens emit not only state propaganda but possibly post-hypnotic suggestions to sleepers, and movie newsreels feature atrocities to which even Winston seems inured early on in the novel.

Media information and entertainment content in *1984* underscores the affinity between totalitarian governments and narrow, utilitarian programming. About battles (of war or production) only good news is announced. When and if it suits the state, "traitors" and "enemies" are stridently denounced (no equal-time provision), and phony production bulletins offset the perception of shortages, shoddiness, and errors in state planning. Entertainment includes martial tunes, machine-written novels and pop songs, pornography, compulsory TV calisthenics (Outer Party), and, presumably, coverage of prisoner parades, Hate Week festivities, and public hangings.

Unreasonable search of one's person reaches fantastic limits in a society where telescreens can observe, listen, and even detect heartbeat irregularities during news bulletins or speeches by Big Brother. Besides lack of Fourth Amendment protection there is no Fourteenth Amendment due legal process. Children can easily incriminate parents or strangers for real or imagined reasons and become heroes in the bargain; after an arrest there is no *Habeas Corpus* protection (Article I: Section 9). Orwell suggests the farcical aspect of Winston and Julia's arrest by means of an accumulation of auditory and visual grotesqueries: a crash of breaking picture glass, trampling boots below, a rolling clang, a ladder crashing through the window frame, a stampede of boots, the smashing of the glass paperweight on the hearth, and Julia's being doubled up like a pocket ruler and hoisted and carried off like a sack.

Winston's physical and psychological torture at the Ministry of Love is cruel and unusual enough to make Americans appreciate the Eighth Amendment. Beaten, insulted, kept in a constantly lighted and windowless room, menaced by ravenous rats about to feed on his face, and electroshocked by grand inquisitor O'Brien, he breaks. More than once he would have welcomed the brutalizing public hanging dispensed to some and attended by Party members and their children.

The Party obviates the possibility of martyrdom by driving its accused to self-incrimination. Winston, Julia, Tom Parsons, Ampleforth and the trio of Jones, Aaronson and Rutherford have no Fifth Amendment shield, nor does a charge of treason require two witnesses to the same overt act (Article III: Section 3). Of course even the U.S. Constitution waives the witness requirement if there is a confession in open court. Every accused confesses in *1984*, but the "court" is hardly "open."

*   *   *

Orwellian events in America in the past two decades have posed remarkable threats to Constitutional freedoms. First there is eavesdropping. An electronics company marketed a closed circuit telescanner that enables a supervisor to look in on branch offices or time coffee breaks. Also, a federal judge fined an auto dealer for bugging his showroom to eavesdrop on customers; the defense attorney claimed it was a common regional practice. Soon we were into behavioral modification. A chemical company marketed the ultimate deodorizer. It anesthetizes nose nerve endings, making it impossible to smell bad odors while leaving intact nerve endings that sense "good" smells. Why clean up foul odors from a factory when we can readjust the noses of workers and neighbors? Another measure seemed to cause a sharp decline in shoplifting losses. Subliminal commands not to steal were transmitted along with a department store's background music.

Popular support of the First Amendment's free press provision may be a thing of the past. A *Time* cover story quoted the National Opinion Research Center's finding that from 1976 to late 1983 the percentage having "a great deal of confidence in the press" slipped from 29 to 17.7 per cent. More evidence of mistrust surfaced when the Reagan administration invaded Grenada and excluded reporters from the action. After sounding the alarm on NBC's *Nightly News,* John Chancellor was probably astounded when letters and phone calls supported the press restrictions 5 to 1. *Time*'s 225 letters on the matter ran almost 8 to 1 against the press.[7]

There were other examples of the administration's growing interest in secrecy. Federal employees are now randomly subjected to lie detector tests, apparently to discourage press leaks by keeping workers with access to classified information on edge.[8] Also, the administration has placed time limits on the Freedom of Information Act, and required of 113,000 officials lifetime vows that they will clear anything that they ever write that touches on "sensitive" material or intelligence activities of any kind.[9] This restriction includes books, articles, letters to the editor, and even fiction.

One's faith in due process and protection from self-incrimination must be further shaken by disclosures that the CIA operated entrapment/blackmail apartments in Greenwich Village and San Francisco, using prostitutes, see-through mirrors, cameras, microphones disguised as electrical outlets and tape recorders. Add to that a state's successful effort to use a toll-free hotline on which citizens could anonymously accuse relatives, neighbors and others of welfare cheating.

Advocates of cruel and unusual punishment are alive and well in the republic. David Goodman observes:

> In the U.S. a well-known Texas politician recently recommended public hangings as a deterrent to crime after the Gary Gilmore incident. More generally, the increasing acquiescence of the American public toward violence in the movies and TV bears a close resemblance to the mood of savagery that marks the people of Oceania. The vicarious pleasure taken in violence is one of the strongest parallels between modern society and the world of *1984.*[10]

The Philadelphia *Inquirer* ushered in 1984 with a January 1 article that for some readers laid too heavy a stress on the advantages of castrating rapists. There are more mundane but disturbing examples. In one of our public schools, a sixth grader was called a "nonperson," confined to a topless and bottomless appliance carton for ninety minutes and jeered at. The offense? Talking to a girl in class. School officials called the treatment "reality therapy," and a spokesperson referred to the penalty box as a "social adjustment center." In a sectarian school, a summer Bible teacher gave children a twelve-volt shock by pressing a button to an electric stool—to aid them in "hearing the word." Few parents objected. One said she was not worried because her eight-year-old was learning about God.

*   *   *

FREEDOM IS SLAVERY goes one of the Party's slogans in *1984*. Indeed, freedom from the existence of specific protective laws turns out to be the worst form of slavery. The only crime is thoughtcrime, but the Party can stretch it to cover almost any violation. One stays within his decreed station—prole, Outer or Inner Party; nonproles wear overalls of a prescribed color. Party members must love Big Brother exclusively: to marry they must convince a committee that they are not in love but wish only to make babies for Big Brother.

One reason for *1984*'s extraordinary hold on the popular mind may be its affinity to a popular American protest novel that prepared the way for enactment of our Thirteenth (Anti-Slavery) Amendment—*Uncle Tom's Cabin*. Herb Greer remarks cogent parallels. Both novels aroused public feelings about their focal issues (the totalitarianism of slavery, and the slavery of totalitarianism). Both authors contributed words of political abuse still current (Uncle Tom, Simon Legree; Big Brother, Doublethink). Both books had similar literary flaws (excessive melodrama, sentimentality), and both authors expressed hatred of "principled human cruelty"; and for both writers the political effect of the latter concern proved far more significant than their novels' aesthetic faults.[11] In fact, just before starting *1984* Orwell himself practiced "doublethink" in a favorable reference to Mrs. Stowe's novel. In an essay entitled "Good Bad Books" he developed the point that "art is not the same thing as cerebration":

> Perhaps the supreme example of the 'good bad' book is *Uncle Tom's Cabin*. It is an unintentionally ludicrous book, full of preposterous melodramatic incidents; it is also deeply moving and essentially true; it is hard to say which quality outweighs the other. But *Uncle Tom's Cabin*, after all, is trying to be serious and to deal with the real world.[12]

The heart of Constitutional protection against oligarchy is the separation of powers in Articles I-III. While power to declare war is vested in congress, the President is commander-in-chief; he has treaty-making powers but subject to the advice and consent of the Senate, with two thirds concurrence. Judicial power is reserved to the courts.

Big Brother's Oceania (and, presumably, East Asia and Eurasia) have no legislative and judicial checks and balances. Government is by *oligarchical collectivism*: unchecked power is exercised by the Inner Party (approximately two percent of the population), whose figurehead is Big Brother. Matters of production, distribution, education, law enforcement and even warfare are managed by the Party. If it so wills, yesterday's ally is today's historical enemy. In one of *1984*'s farcical scenes a Hate rally orator silently reads a message during his speech and redirects his animus to East Asia, an ally at the start of the speech—without breaking syntax or inflection.

For Americans two end-runs around Congress' war-making powers in the 1960s and early seventies had distinctly Orwellian overtones. These were the Gulf of Tonkin affair and the secret bombing of Cambodia.

Reporter Joseph Goulden probably thought 1984 came two decades early when he was unraveling the government's untold side of alleged attacks on U.S. destroyers in August 1964. He later surmised that government selectivity in releasing details influenced *Time, Life* and later *Newsweek* to report in a flurry of flag-waving more appropriate to Big Brother's Ministries of Peace and Truth than to ostensibly free news organs.[13] Lest we forget, in this overheated patriotic climate a sympathetic congress in effect delegated to the President its war-making prerogative by enacting a broadly worded resolution that Mr. Johnson had been carrying for months, waiting to fill in geographic particulars when an occasion arose.

Philadelphia *Inquirer* reporter Goulden was taken aback at the Senate's Tonkin Gulf hearings in 1968. Under close questioning by Senators Fulbright, Morse and McCarthy, Secretary of Defense MacNamara appeared to contradict some of his 1964 testimony on the Tonkin affair. In the story he sent to Philadelphia, Goulden highlighted this dramatic turn of events. However, after his Philadelphia editors finished revising the story, Goulden had a lesson in the mutability of past and present. The lead of the published story flatly contradicted what Goulden had heard and reported the previous day: "The United States did not provoke the 1964 Gulf of Tonkin incident, previously secret naval communications indicated Saturday."[14]

Goulden left the *Inquirer* to become a free-lance writer and sought out crewmen and others involved in the Tonkin incidents. His detailed findings cast considerable doubt on the administration's 1964 and 1968 claims that our destroyers had been attacked without provocation.[15]

Many Orwellian developments surfaced during Goulden's research. A mysteriously sanitized transcript of the 1964 hearings, released two years later by the Pentagon and State Department, carried no mention of connections Senator Morse had noted between South Vietnamese naval raids and concurrent U.S. patrol activity just before our destroyers allegedly were fired upon. Also, the Fulbright Committee had to prepare for its hearings in 1967 and 1968 without a crucial cable in which the skipper of the destroyer *Maddox* had expressed doubt that the second "provocation" (4 August 1964) involved hostile North Vietnamese actions. And, by February of 1969, when the Committee was questioning Secretary MacNamara, it never knew of Sonarman Patrick Park. During the alleged attack of 4 August Park wisely balked at a direct order to fire at a "big target" in the Tonkin overcast. That target, which the *Maddox* had been about to blow out of the water, was not an attacking North Vietnamese torpedo boat, but the *Maddox's* companion patrol ship, the *Turner Joy*! Strangely, Sonarman Park's name was missing from the "complete list" of destroyer crewmen the Pentagon gave Goulden as late as July 1968. To the Pentagon, Park had become an "unperson." Also, when Goulden finally got to read the biographical sketch of *Maddox* skipper Herrick in the Internal Regulations Division of the Navy Office of Information, there was no mention of the second attack, of 4 August, the questionable one that government hearing witnesses claimed took place. Finally, a commander who had read cable traffic about the August 4 incident leaked helpful leads to Fulbright. After confessing his action to his superior, he was subsequently subjected to a psychiatric examination. He passed, but was given another. The second examination board also found him fit for duty.[16]

Implausible as they seem, these events occurred. One lesson is that even a solid constitution can be circumvented when a government exploits classic behavioral principles to influence thought. One such principle, the willingness of many to accept a polarization of reasonable differences into good-guy/bad-guy conflicts, was used in two ways. First there was card-stacking, as when the Senate, news media, and later the Fulbright Committee got only one side of the Tonkin Gulf story. The other way was by the ancient ploy of name-calling. The Navy applied it rather subtly by subjecting an officer who helped Fulbright to two psychiatric examinations. In more explicit shoot-from-the-hip fashion President Johnson characterized Senate adversaries of his hawkish policy as "Nervous Nellies," a disrespectful epithet earlier applied to Coolidge's Secretary of State in response to his (Kellogg) pact to outlaw war.[17]

As all opinion molders know, the tendency to conform, imitate and follow the crowd when in doubt makes citizens vulnerable to the bandwagon effect. Thus, despite intriguing questions raised about the possibly provocative nature of our activities in Tonkin Gulf before the alleged attacks, the Senate followed the lead of the popular press and voted 88-2 for the Tonkin Resolution, which gave the President what amounted to war-making powers. In a carefully cultivated climate of uncertainty, few senators risked seeming to be unpatriotic.

The principle of association worked well enough through the use of "virtue" words or glittering generalities. Fed only a smattering of the Tonkin action reports, and none that reflected on-the-scene doubts about the second attack, the media were primed to laud the pilots of our retaliatory air strike on North Vietnam as "the nation's newest battle veterans," "heroes of the Tonkin Gulf," and "Policemen of the Pacific."[18]

Thus by the end of the sixties readers of *1984* were in for a shock of recognition when Goulden's disclosures appeared in his book *Truth Is the First Casualty: The Gulf of Tonkin Affair—Illusion and Reality.* There were more to come during the "secret" bombing of Cambodia, as when an

Air Force officer berated the media in Doublespeak for using the term "bombing" instead of "air support."

Orwell indeed had shown how a strong-willed government propagandizes with the same methods. Examples of card-stacking and name-calling abound in *1984*. From youth citizens learn only the state's side of debatable matters and are conditioned to accept it. They lack objective knowledge of history, know only the negatives of capitalism, and get only good news about military and productive matters. Old news items are altered when embarrassing, and a depleted language prevents thought about alternatives to *Ingsoc*. Finally, Outer Party members are kept ignorant of the positive, fulfilling aspects of sex. Name-calling, another dirty trick, frustrates reasoned inquiry. Troublemakers—those who show inclinations to deviate—are labelled "unpersons" and forgotten. Those who think for themselves are "thoughtcriminals." Eurasia, when the Party pleases, is "the enemy." The sexually unregulated proles are "animals." The ritual epithet for Goldstein is "Swine." "Capitalist" is always a nasty word.

Also masterly is the Big Brother government's use of organized meetings and special membership groups to instill and reinforce the bandwagon effect. Control is so complete during the Two-Minutes Hate and the Hate Week festivities that citizen behavior seems competitively imitative. Also, belonging to the Spies, Junior Anti-Sex League, Outer, or Inner Party makes individuals feel part of an approved group while the state reinforces its desirable attitudes to the point of uniformity even in attire within groups. Indeed, bandwagon is so prevalent and favorably regarded that one time Julia averts suspicion of sex-crime by taking more than the usual number of hikes and being seen rolling bandages or packing munitions a few evenings at the Community Center.

Also prominent in *1984*, especially in Party nomenclature and rhetoric, are glittering generalities. In odd antitheses the official slogans contain the virtue-associated abstractions *Peace, Freedom* and *Strength*. Ministries have similarly ironic names (*Peace, Love, Plenty, Truth*). Misleadingly innocent titles are "Comrade" and "Big Brother." The ubiquitous brandname which guarantees generically inferior consumer good is *Victory*.

*   *   *

To regard *1984* as essentially a work of predictions is to overlook a more important function. Orwell's novel was not meant to be a self-fulfilling prophecy, but the opposite. By extrapolating his fears into both a literary and popular success he created an instant myth—a construct that has made us increasingly aware of the anti-Constitutional implications of otherwise random-seeming events and trends. *Nineteen Eighty-four* provided a frame of reference to put Tonkin, Cambodia and other "managed" events into critical perspective, perhaps enabling us to respond in a more timely manner to other intimations from our press—as during the Pentagon Papers and Watergate affairs of the early seventies. If he had addressed himself to the Constitution explicitly, Orwell might have approved of its proven adaptability to reform, amendment, addition—by a rational, people-based process not at all at odds with the Fabian goal of gradual social and political amelioration rather than the "quick" solutions of revolution or statism.

First though he might have had us squirm a bit. The glittering generalities in the Preamble (Justice, Welfare, Liberty) certainly do not jibe with the compromise at the Great Convention which provided that in enumerating state populations to determine degree of representation, southern states could add to their total number of white persons three fifths of the non-voting Negro slaves within their borders. At that point in time the prematurely idealistic "All men are created equal" of the 1776 Declaration was temporarily inoperative.

Then, as now, the crucial question is not to what extent are we in *1984* but to what extent is *1984* in us?

Notes

Some of the *1984* material in this article originally appeared in the author's April 1983 *English Journal* article "Slouching Toward Relevance, or What To Do with *1984* until 1984" (National Council of Teachers of English).

[1]"Halfway to 1984," *Horizon*, XII (Spring 1970), 33.

[2]Paul Gray, Anne Hopkins, and John Saar, "That Year Is Almost Here," *Time*, Nov. 28, 1983, p. 46.

[3]Ron Givens, "Cramming for 1984," *Newsweek* (On-Campus edition), Oct. 1983, Book Section.

[4]"Let it be duly noted," (editorial), Philadelphia *Inquirer*, Jan. 14, 1984, p. 8-A.

[5]I. Anisimov, *Pravda* article of May 12, 1950, reprinted in *George Orwell: The Critical Heritage*, ed. Jeffrey Meyers (London: Routledge, 1975), pp. 282-3.

[6]"Halfway to 1984," 34.

[7]William A. Henry III, "Journalism Under Fire," *Time*, Dec. 12, 1983, p. 76.

[8]Jane Edenbaum, "Where Have You Gone, George Orwell? *1984*'s already Here!" *Swarthmorean* (weekly newspaper, Swarthmore, Pa.) Jan. 6, 1989, pp. 1,5.

[9]Edwin Guthman, "Grenada News Blackout Set a Dangerous Precedent," Philadelphia *Inquirer*, Dec. 4, 1983, p. 7-D.

[10]"Countdown to 1984: Big Brother May Be Right on Schedule," *Futurist*, XII (Dec. 1978), 352.

[11]"Orwell in Perspective," *Commentary*, 75 (March 1983), 52.

[12]*Tribune*, Nov. 2, 1945, reprinted in *Collected Essays, Journalism and Letters of George Orwell*, Vol. Iv, eds. Sonia Orwell and Ian Angus (Middlesex: Penguin, 1980), 39, 40

[13]Don Stillman, "Tonkin: What Should Have Been Asked," *The Age of Communication*, William D. Lutz, ed., (Pacific Palisades: Goodyear, 1974), pp. 296-7.

[14]Stillman, p. 299.

[15]Mr. Goulden's book, *Truth Is the First Casualty: The Gulf of Tonkin Affair—Illusion and Reality* (Chicago: Adler/Rand McNally,1969), is not to be confused with Phillip

Knightley's similarly entitled study of manipulated war coverage from the Crimea to Vietnam, *The First Casualty* (New York: Harcourt Brace Jovanovich, 1975).

[16]Goulden, pp. 202-219.

[17]Goulden, p. 178.

[18]Stillman, p. 297.

Matrix for Development:
The Fiction of Louis L'Amour and the U.S. Constitution

Michael T. Marsden

"Those who went West were unknowing carriers and transmitters of the Spirit which took on the mantle of the spirit of Americans. Fundamentally for Hegel, Spirit is Freedom, and the Western movement was just one more instance in world history which exemplified that Spirit in a concrete manner."[1]

No American storyteller has more widely proclaimed the American spirit than Louis L'Amour through his bestselling Western fiction. The recipient of both a Special Gold Medal given by the United States Congress in 1983 and of the Medal of Freedom given by President Ronald Reagan in 1984 in recognition of his life's work, Louis L'Amour has been able to count Presidents Eisenhower, Johnson, Carter and Reagan among his devoted readers.

In the midst of this master storyteller's considerable body of fiction exist his tales in which he explicitly talks about the viability of the United States Constitution, a topic on which he is quite clear concerning the nature of his feelings:

"... I have a very strong feeling for the country .... And I have a very strong feeling for the Constitution. And I don't want anybody to bother it, actually, because I don't believe they're ever going to improve on it."[2]

Louis L'Amour's future writing schedule includes a novel about the American Revolution in which he will discuss how the framers of the Constitution created harmony of thought through the utilization of democratic communication systems.[3]

Through L'Amour's considerable body of frontier novels are woven fictionalizations of the First Amendment (freedom of religion, speech and the press), the Second Amendment (the right to keep and bear arms), the Fourth Amendment (the right of the people to be secure in their property) and especially the Tenth Amendment (the essential power of the people). In fact, his fiction will no doubt survive the test of time alongside the Constitution, commenting on its tenets and dramatizing its actors, famous and common.

In a recent essay, Tom Sullivan notes that "a L'Amour hero often not only must fight and kill to defend a community, but also remain to live in the community.''[4] He further adds that many of L'Amour's readers "wanted to receive this reassuring message of a L'Amour Western, that not only was such violence necessary, but that one simply had to learn to live with one's national pistol under one's national pillow in order to maintain the good life.''[5]

The genius of L'Amour's three family history of the American frontier experience is that it allows not only the trailblazing and the pioneering, but the settling and the civilizing to be worked out in his fiction. Through his fiction the United States Constitution is acted out; his fiction applies the tenets of the Constitution to the specific realities of frontier America. Reminiscent of Jefferson's famous saying that the price of freedom is eternal vigilance, his fiction demonstrates that the Constitution truly is a remarkable document which, like the American spirit, has survived a long time and still captures our imaginations, and in so doing allows the growth and development of such masterful creators of popular culture as L'Amour.

Notes

[1]Gerald F. Kreyche, "The Relevance of Philosophy to the American West," *DePaul University Magazine*, Fall 1984, p. 32.
[2]Interview with Louis L'Amour by Michael Marsden and Kristine Fredriksson on March 17, 1985 in Los Angeles, California.
[3]Ibid.
[4]Tom Sullivan, "Westward to Statis with Louis L'Amour," *Southwest Review*, Winter 1984, p. 78.
[5]Sullivan, p. 86.

Futuristic Comic Books and Contemporary Society

Phillip R. Seitz

FANTASY ALLOWS US to express feelings that have been set aside during the process of intellectual development but have not been removed from our minds altogether. Within the safely defined context of imaginary speculation we can re-create and enjoy some of the immediate urges we normally keep in check—dreams of glory, beautiful playmates and unlimited power. Futuristic settings in comic books likewise free their creators from the conventions required by the "present day," allowing artists and writers to let their imaginations more fully shape their work.[1] As a result, futuristic stories offer a revealing glimpse into the comic-book subconscious. Fantasy stories and images reveal the attitudes and fears which often shape our behavior.

The United States Constitution, however, is based on a carefully reasoned set of abstract values and morals which by its very nature seeks to transcend the impulse for action in selfish interest. Abstract moral systems are essential for the creation of modern governmental and legal systems, and it this moral foundation that most Americans adhere to by the time they have developed into mature adults. Thus when we express faith in our commonly held ideals we proclaim our belief in such things as equality, the virtues of a fair hearing in case of conflict, and the value of property. These beliefs are codified in the provisions of the Constitution so that every individual will have a voice in government, a plurality of views will contribute to the strength of government, and due process of law will be made the essential foundation of a just society. Comic books strip away this veil of maturity and show us the elemental forces we have stored away. They ponder the shapes society might take if we follow those instincts which are kept under wraps in a democratic society, and help us recognize some of the forces inside us that are in antipathy to the principles we usually espouse and support.

The imagined worlds of outer space are not governed by the tenets of the Constitution, nor is constitutional government an important feature in stories set on Earth. In fact, futuristic comic books assume the failure of collective government and glorify a set of undeniably appealing ideals that are totally incompatible with our present form of government. We enjoy reading this kind of material despite its inherent conflict with our principles. By understanding the appeal of these comic-book societies we learn about the forces in all of us which must be mastered if 'our constitutional government is to survive and thrive.

While it is necessary to understand the materials themselves, there is also the question of the role the medium plays in the broader context of American culture. In some cases futuristic comic stories include material that is directly related to constitutional issues, but a broader reading is useful when the goal is to understand the forces in our society. The comic format is inherently unsuited to anything but bold strokes and large themes. With limited space and a format that is primarily pictorial it is difficult to treat complex issues. The functions of bureaucracy, for instance, make for unappealing copy despite their importance in developing and enforcing the mandate of the Constitution. The accepted style of comic-book storytelling is also a limiting factor; the social and technological character of each imagined world serves largely as a context for heroic activity. Comic-book plots and characterization are usually based on authoritarian relationships where power, weakness and competition shape all aspects of the social order. This hardly changes from issue to issue of the same magazine, and hardly more so from one title to another. The study of a wide variety of titles is therefore most useful when assessing the role of comic books in contemporary culture.[2]

The superhero's role in society does vary depending on the time setting. In comics of the present, the superhero is a glorified vigilante who functions outside of, but in conjunction with, the authority of society. Batman, Superman and Spiderman pursue criminals beyond society's limits, but they invariably surrender their quarry to the authorities. The police may need assistance from time to time, but it is they who are in charge. Thus the heroes' activity can be seen as an endorsement of society's values and fundamental stability; without Batman there might be more crime in Gotham City, but society would not collapse. This situation is further demonstrated by the example of those present-day heroes who are part of society's elite. Speaking of millionaires Bruce Wayne and Tony Stark (Batman and Iron Man, respectively), Bernt Kling found that their high social standing, when combined with their alter-ego relationships as superheroes, suggested a social condition "tantamount to pretending that an elite of the society sacrifices itself for everyone in its secret super-heroism."[3] The Avengers, with their own mansion and butler, also fall into this category. Noblesse Oblige dictates that those beyond the mainstream of common society are bound by honor to serve it; it implies a subjugation of self for the greater good. Like his heroic counterpart, the Earth-bound villain is also someone who doesn't fit into society. Batman's arch enemy, the Joker, is a typically anarchistic criminal who acts unpredictably and whose goal is to bring the world around him down in chaos. The troublesome Mr. Mxyzptlk, Superman's bane, is similar. The criminal is an outcast who rejects society's rules by virtue of his criminal activity.

But the futuristic bad guys play a role different from those on present-day Earth. In the future it is the bad guys (usually aliens) who run the show (and therefore define the structure of society), and the forces of chaos that have triumphed. This is the case in half of the comics set in the future, with *Buck Rogers* numbered among them.[4] The futuristic bad guy is much like his present-day counterpart, who is both egotistical and power hungry. He is motivated only by a thirst for power, and is less interested in acquiring resources or manipulating politics than in subjugating the universe and bending it to his will. This threat is especially serious because the aliens are more advanced technologically. Jules Feiffer comments:

One of the self-denigrating laws of science fiction is that every other planet is better than ours. Other plants may have funny looking people but they think better, know more languages (including English), and are much further along in the business of rocketry and destruction.[5]

The alien's visual appearance is also threatening; most comics feature aliens who are both morally and visually repulsive. Reptilian features are common, as are fangs, scales and other grotesque features. Commenting on this point, Arthur Berger observes that, "on the visual level alone the grotesque is significant. Its ugliness is an affront to society and suggests that something is wrong with the social order."[6]

Bad guys, of course, have always appreciated the virtues of despotic government, but the investiture of authority in the hero requires a pretext. This is provided by the failure of collective society to repel the forces of evil, namely, the aliens. While intra-planetary government is relatively stable, relations between the planets can be intensely hostile and alien attacks often come as a complete surprise. Society has lulled itself into a sense of false security and relaxed its defenses. At best this shows that society has become weak and ill prepared, but at worst it suggests that feudal or totalitarian rule provides the only defense against chaos. It has failed to hold off threats which may result in its total destruction; technology has failed to equalize differences between individuals and races; armies prove useless in the face of alien attack. The futuristic superhero therefore becomes the savior of the people, living proof that humanity is incapable of governing or protecting itself without the aid of a self-appointed, militaristic super-leader. He stands as the last line of defense against chaos, and those without extraordinary powers will only be spectators at the battle which decides their future.

Obviously one of the standard attributes of the hero is the possession of super-normal power, but there are numerous visual and thematic clues which reinforce the image of the mythical hero/protector. Given the emphasis on fighting and combat in adventure comics it's hardly surprising that the future means new weaponry; here the destruction of entire planets is commonly made possible at the touch of a button. Even so, new technology generally enters warfare on the personal level, with laser pistols, ion blasters and plasma weapons appearing frequently. Since personal combat is a staple of all comic action, futuristic products of technology increase the stature and destructive power invested in the hero. Oddly enough these weapons are rarely found in the hands of the people, indicating that the right to bear arms, as well as the "well regulated Militia ... necessary to the security of a free state," have fallen by the wayside.

A curious variation on the weapons theme is the endowment of obvious anachronisms with futuristic capabilities. Comics contain plasma crossbows, high-tech swords, or other weapons which are clearly past/future hybrids. These old elements add to the mythic quality of the plot. Speaking of Flash Gordon, one scholar comments:

Especially striking is the contrast between the feudal society and advanced technology: the fighting uses both swords and atomic cannons; the hero and his opponent are like mythological figures who decide the fate of a people by technological means, while the people only celebrates (sic) the victorious hero or kneels before the evil antagonist.[7]

It is interesting that the effects of these weapons are not significantly different from those of old-fashioned firearms. In visual terms, enemies are always blasted rather than burned or disintegrated. Push-button warfare is too impersonal to be a satisfying exercise of power, and therefore comic book editors stick to more accepted means of destruction.

As with other visually-oriented media the settings in comic books are defined by details of appearance. Of the features which commonly identify the future, the "technological look" is the most important, and most future interiors are packed to the ceilings with piles of computer-like equipment. A typical scene in the *Avengers*'s mansion, for instance, shows Jarvis the butler seated in the "communications center," surrounded by control panels and television screens. Conversely, many present-day objects are simply souped-up for modern living, resulting in floating armchairs and holographic billboards. This device has been used in comics for years, and a good example is the "Space Cabbie" story republished in Michael Uslan's *Mysteries In Space: The Best of DC Science Fiction Comics*. Here the old element is

the tough, street-wise New York-type cabbie, long a 20th century legend. Loath to give him up, DC called him Space Cabby, moved him beyond Earth's atmosphere, and gave him crowded space lanes, jammed space intersections, meteor swarms, asteroid billboards and cosmic cops to worry about.[8]

Flying furniture, cosmic cabfares and other peripheral futurisms are valuable because they bridge the gap betweeen present and future, and, furthermore, demonstrate that the attitudes of the present are being projected into the future.

It should be noted that technology, not science, is made heroic in the future. This reveals the anti-intellectual strain long prominent in American society. Berger noted this trend in our earliest futuristic comic, *Buck Rogers*, and his point can be justly applied to recent ones as well:

> It is technology that is romanticized in *Buck Rogers*, not science per se .... In this respect, *Buck Rogers* is a rather faithful mirror of basic American values (for we have developed a remarkable technology and seem more interested in practical applications of the laws of science than basic research) ...[9]

Intelligence and intellectualism are regarded with suspicion, especially when they don't bear fruit in technological achievement. Bernt Kling comments on Superman in *Science Fiction Studies:*

> ... yet another quality can be found in his super enemies which is missing in Superman: they are intelligent. The Superman writer Jerry Seigel said, 'We do not emphasize the intellectual side of Superman. People do not dream of becoming super-intelligent.' Only his enemies have intelligence, and are often Mad Scientists who because of their intelligence do not fit into the desired simple order of a Superman America.[10]

Most often science serves as the enabling factor that provides vague justifications for super powers. Peter Parker, for instance, was a normal high-school student until he visited a local science fair and was bitten by a radioactive spider; he acquired many of the insect's powers and went on to become the wall-crawling Spiderman. The same applies to villains. Salvatore Mondello, in "Spiderman: Superhero in the Liberal Tradition," notes that "many of the supervillains degenerate into knaves as a result of scientific accidents."[11]

The popular *Micronauts* offers the best example of the degenerate scientist. Degrayde, chief scientist for Baron Karza, knows that the Baron himself once occupied this science position, but sees that the Baron now draws power from mysticism and the unknown. "I despise mysticism," he muses, "only science can subjugate the universe!"[12] Degrayde scoffs at things he can't understand and sees science as the tool by which to achieve his own selfish goals. In stark contrast to this sorry figure stands Reed Richards of the Fantastic Four, himself the most widely respected scientist in comics. He lives in the Baxter Building amidst the most dazzling array of gadgetry imaginable. He uses his knowledge to build machines, not to do research, and is a champion of the pragmatic. He has wisely avoided the boring details of research that ruined the minds of so many others.

These portrayals of the intellectual are also in marked contrast to those held by the men who framed our government. Numbering among the so-called founding fathers were some of the finest minds our nation has produced, and their writings reveal a steadfast concern for principle tempered by the needs of everyday reality. But pragmatism is all in the comic-book world; the carefully reasoned structures of science and government are dismissed as eggheaded, and the motives of those who live by principle are misconstrued. The behavior of the comic-book hero varies widely from the performance of our real-life American heroes. George Washington refused a third term as president; Thomas Jefferson, though himself elected to the presidency, was a champion of the common man. These were men who would not allow fear of instability to compromise their democratic principles. They had the opportunity to become the new aristocracy but defined it in deference to constitutional government.

While the details of structured social relations and especially of government are almost never directly addressed by futuristic comics, those few glimpses that are offered show autocracy and aristocracy as having replaced democracy (or, for that matter, every other form of collective government).[13] The traditional social contract has collapsed and the possibilities of cooperative action are simply ignored. The comic world rejects all semblance of constitutional order, whether in structure or principle, and celebrates the power and authority of the hero. This authority is justified by the constantly impending threat of alien reprisal; if the aliens do not already reign in tyranny, they are undoubtedly contemplating attack. The result is society without proportionate representation, with no legal system to speak of, and with few guaranteed rights. The assumption of equality is abandoned, the principle that "No Title of Nobility shall be granted" cast aside. Admiration for the powerful has lead to an abdication of popular responsibility.

The xenophobia described here has its parallels in real life. Michael Uslin points this out in his work on the comics of the early 1960s:

We were involved in a cold war with Russia, were hunting down Communists among our neighbors, and lots of us were protesting the Supreme Court's efforts to make racial integration the law of the land. In short, we ran the gamut from suspicious to destructive when it came to anything strange—'alien.'[14]

The alien vs. society relationship, like the real world conflict between democracy and communism, is an outgrowth of the individualism, fear and conservatism that is based on deeply felt insecurities. The realization of these insecurities lies in the assumption of individual authority, often on the pretext of defending traditional values, that can be found in almost every aspect of the comic-book future. This suggests that the readers of futuristic comic books are the bearers of unfulfilled longings which are satisfied by the vicarious experience of power and glory.

Sword and sorcery comics also serve this purpose. The reader uses the comic tale as a vehicle for realizing fantasies that would be considered egotistical, if not outright antisocial, in the context of the real world. Since the reader sympathizes with or identifies with the heroic characters, the implication is that the reader uses the individualistic heroic experience to win the power and praise due to the aristocrat. This experience differs somewhat, but not widely, from the identification with a present-day character such as Batman; in the future the self-sacrificing imposition of secrecy has been stripped away to allow for a full-scale recognition of the heroic individual's moral and physical superiority. Present-day themes merely receive a bolder treatment when set in the future.

Comics appeal to feelings that nearly everyone experiences during his growth and development. This is especially so during those years when aggression is admired as a vehicle for self definition. That there are also many adults who enjoy the same material suggests that the desires and motives of adolescence are overcome but not eliminated by the arrival of adulthood. Comics allow us to retreat into a fantasy world of idealized scenarios where authority is universally admired, right and wrong easily distinguishable, and sexual success, albeit of an immature variety, is easily achieved. The passing of adolescent years does not necessarily entail the eradication of its emotional forces.

Does this mean that comic fans are neo-fascists? Many adults subscribe to the same cold-war mentality that flourishes in the comic-book future, and sometimes take these ideas to extremes that go far beyond those depicted in comics. We can identify and denounce anti-social extremists who would alter the freedoms and representative character of our society. This does not, however, release us from individual responsibility to examine our own actions and their implications for a society based on the principles defined in the Constitution. It was the support of "ordinary" people that gave authority to leaders like Tom Watson, Father Coughlin, or Sen. Joseph McCarthy. These and others became most dangerous when their advocacy of disenfranchisement, racism and selective persecution gained support beyond fringe groups by touching the dormant spirit of fear and intolerant individualism that can be found in most people. The greatest danger to our society arises when normally reasonable people allow their sense of social responsibility to be sacrificed to the powers of fear and self-interest. When this happens it is easy to suggest that unconstitutional actions and ideals be pursued in the effort to stave off imagined threats. Set in comic-book terms, the immediate and personal fear of aliens (or chaos) is used to justify the disassembly of a government based on principle and the adoption of one based on strength alone.

Our enjoyment of comics shows that there is a side to most of us which is prepared to abandon the difficulties of collective government for the simplicity of protection. Yet we live in a constitutional society in which everyone is expected to uphold the principle of plurality, where a certain level of equality is essential for the system to work. To assume that democratic structures are sufficiently strong to resist the forces of chaos is imperative. A personal commitment to honor the individuality of others, and to maintain the collective structures that provide us with governmental necessities is fundamental to the Constitutional system. Our enjoyment of comics does not indicate our willingness to abandon democracy, but it should alert us to forces within ourselves which must be recognized and controlled if our current forms of representational government are to continue.

Notes

[1] For the purposes of this study those comics that feature action set in the future or in outer space will be considered futuristic, as well as those set on present-day Earth that include futuristic concepts (such as the viability of inter-stellar travel) and technology.

[2] Thirty-six comics were used in this study, consisting of 35 separate titles purchased in November of 1983. The list of titles includes some of the best-known, longest running, and most popular comics: *The Micronauts, Camelot 3000, Rom, Firestorm* and *The Legion of Super-Heroes* are listed in Richard Overstreet's *Comic Book Price Guide: 1983-1984* (New York: Harmony Books, 1983, pp. A-25, A-33) as "hot titles." Old copies of *Avengers, X-Men,* and *Justice League of America* are rapidly appreciating in value. Other heroes, like Superman, have enjoyed immense popularity for decades.

[3] Bernt Kling, "On SF Comics: Some Notes For a Future Encyclopedia," *Science Fiction Studies,* 4, No. 3 (Nov. 1977), p. 281.

[4] This is demonstrated in titles such as *Powerlords, They Were Chosen To Be The Survivors, Atari Force, Rom, Camelot 3000, Bold Adventure, Dreadstar, Starslayer, Vanguard Illustrated, Alien Worlds, Micronauts* and *The Omega Men.*

[5] Jules Feiffer, *The Great Comic Book Heroes* (New York: Dial Press, 1965), p. 27.

[6] Arthur Berger, *The Comic-Stripped American* (Baltimore: Penguin, 1973), p. 200. For some really ugly aliens, see *Powerlords.*

[7] Kling, p. 277.

[8] Michael Uslan, *Mysteries In Space: The Best of DC Science Fiction Comics* (New York: Simon and Schuster, 1980), p. 14.

[9] Berger, p. 94.

[10] Kling, p. 280.

[11] Salvatore Mondello, "Spiderman, Superhero in the Liberal Tradition," *Journal of Popular Culture,* 10, No. 1 (Summer 1976), p. 233.

[12] *The Micronauts,* 1, No. 56 (Jan. 1984), p. 16.

[13] For example, aristocratic government is the norm in *The Micronauts, Omega Men* and *Powerlords.* This type of government is frequently used in shorter pieces as well. The same is true for the government of Asgard, home town of the popular thunder god Thor.

[14] Uslan, p. 11.

Before the F.B.I.: Hoover's First Cases

Richard G. Powers

The United States had been at war for four months when the twenty-two-year-old J. Edgar Hoover joined the Justice Department on July 26, 1917. Those had been months of war hysteria, and the Justice Department was at the center of the hysteria. Starting as a file clerk, Hoover was soon promoted, but though he quickly was given a degree of responsibility unusual for someone of his age, his work during the war did not involve him in policy-shaping or decision-making. Hoover's wartime experience was significant, however, because it put him near the center of the government's effort to eliminate dissent against the war. Hoover was not directly involved in this, since his job had him helping administer the Department's program to supervise German aliens during the war. After Armistice on November 11, 1918, the Department's attention shifted to another group of aliens, this time immigrant radicals. Hoover was ready with the reputation and credentials of being an alien expert, and so it was his wartime experience that put him in line for promotion to his first position of real authority.

While Hoover was dealing with the affairs of German aliens, the Justice Department was responsible for some of the most egregious violations of civil liberties and political rights in American history. The Department broke the back of the country's most militant radical organization, the International Workers of the World, at a show trial in Chicago. It tried and convicted the perennial Socialist candidate for President, Eugene Debs, for opposing the draft, which was also the Department's grounds for sending Emma Goldman and Alexander Berkman to jail.

During the war the Justice Department organized a civilian army of 260,000 amateur detectives, the American Protective League, supplying them with credentials and badges identifying them as Justice Department Auxiliaries, and turned them loose to hunt for spies and disloyal neighbors. The Justice Department used the A.P.L. to enforce the draft by rounding up huge numbers of draft-age men on suspicion of being "slackers."

Ironically, the Justice Department's repressive policies during the war were directed by two men with authentic credentials as civil libertarians, Attorney General Thomas Gregory and Special Assistant to the Attorney

General for War Work, the eminent attorney John Lord O'Brian. As patriotic Americans, Gregory and O'Brian were as susceptible to tribal emotions as any of their fellow citizens, but they fought vigorously to preserve constitutional processes and to make it clear that restrictions of individual rights during the war were emergency measures that should endure only for the duration of hostilities. Without Gregory and O'Brian, things could have been much worse.

If Gregory's first war-legislation advisor, Assistant Attorney General Charles Warren, had had his way things might have been much worse. The country at large was not prepared for the war, but men like Warren definitely were fully ready. They saw the war as a heaven-sent opportunity to settle old scores against their enemies. For Warren, the immigrants had always been a threat to American society, while other superpatriots eyed the chance to use the rough rules of wartime against domestic "reds," anyone who was dissatisfied with the established order. The Justice Department was far from merely being the nation's law office during these years; it was the militant headquarters of an effort to create and maintain national conformity, and Hoover was a witness to a debate between constitutionalists and those bent on fostering tribal unity by stigmatizing or exiling anyone who spoke out against the status quo, between those who wanted the law to protect individuals against the government, and those for whom it was a tool to protect the government against dangerous citizens.

There were three battles raging in the Justice Department when Hoover joined in the summer of 1917. The most public was the Department's war against German spies, in reality more of a publicity campaign to persuade the public the government was dealing competently with a largely illusory spy threat. The second was a bureaucratic battle between Gregory's Justice Department and its rivals within the government (primarily the Treasury Department's Secret Service and the War Department's Military Intelligence Division) for jurisdiction over disloyalty and espionage cases. The last, and most important in terms of influence on Hoover's development, was the battle between those, like Gregory and John Lord O'Brian, who wanted to preserve due process and the principle that criminal guilt was always personal, and others who were willing (or eager) to use the emergency to justify proscribing whole groups of citizens and aliens because of their disloyal associations. The chief spokesman for this repressive point of view in the Justice Department was Assistant Attorney General Charles Warren. Held in check by Gregory and O'Brian, Warren's point of view was shared by many subordinate members of the Department, and it became Justice Department policy when O'Brien and Gregory left in 1919 and A. Mitchell Palmer became Attorney General.

Thomas W. Gregory, the first of the nineteen Attorneys General under whom Hoover would serve, was a Mississippi-born Texan, an early supporter of Wilson who was credited with persuading the indispensable Colonel House to support Wilson for the Presidency. Gregory entered the cabinet in 1914, succeeding the politically inept James C. McReynolds after McReynolds' elevation to the Supreme Court. He definitively ended the Department's traditional alliance with industry in its clashes with unions and redirected the Justice Department's energies toward enforcement of the antitrust laws. A progressive-era liberal reformer, he also encouraged the chief of his Bureau of Investigation, A. Bruce Bielaski, to enforce the federal white slave law (the "Mann Act"), in those days regarded as a progressive reform.[1]

Like many of Wilson's early supporters, Gregory had an instinctive sympathy for reformers. He urged Wilson to appoint Louis Brandeis to the Supreme Court, saying that "one radical in nine is not such a bad thing on the Supreme Bench."[2] Wilson had such respect for Gregory's intellect and character that he wanted to appoint him to the Supreme Court when Charles Evan Hughes resigned to seek the Presidency in 1916, but Gregory, who was almost deaf, refused because of his handicap. And so Wilson's administration, which was soon to preside over atrocious assaults on civil liberties, entered the war with at least two civil libertarians in the cabinet, Gregory and Secretary of Labor Wilson, to help stem the legal collapse.

When Wilson signed the declaration of war against imperial Germany on April 6, 1917, the country had been subjected to almost three years of war news and war propaganda, almost all of it calculated to enflame the country against Germany. The nature of the sea war—British control of the ocean's surface countered by German submarines—had made it inevitable that when Americans got hurt, it would be the Germans who hurt them. Even though the British, with their paper blockade of Europe, had also violated American neutrality rights, their offenses had been outweighed, even eclipsed, by American loss of life in the sinking of the *Lusitania* in May 1915 and the French passenger ship *Sussex* in 1916.

During the three years of neutrality, German and British agents in America both ignored American sovereignty, but the acts of German agents were what alarmed the public. British agents attempted to stir up Czechs, Yugoslavs and Poles to support American entry into the war, while the Germans conspired with Irish- and Indian-Americans to keep America out and to block munitions shipments to England.

Because of Secretary of the Treasury William McAdoo's pro-English bias, Secret Service agents investigated "German intrigues" and produced spectacular disclosures about the German underground. In August 1915 a Secret Service agent managed to steal documents from a German commercial attache that proposed a propaganda campaign in America. McAdoo got Wilson's approval to leak the plans as proof of a German plot.[3] In September 1915 Treasury agents revealed a plan by the Austro-Hungarian embassy to persuade their nationals in America not to work in war materials plants. A few months later Wilson, in an attempt to stampede Congress into passing his military preparedness program, leaked papers linking German agents to plots with Mexican revolutionaries against American interests in that country.

The public's fear of German plotters swelled to a panic in July 1916 when a munitions depot exploded on Black Tom Island in New York harbor. While the cause of the explosion was not legally established until decades later, Americans assumed that only German agents could have been responsible.[4] On March 1, 1917, Wilson released the famous Zimmerman telegram, supposedly a proposal from the German Foreign Secretary to the German Ambassador in Washington for an alliance between Germany, Japan and Mexico if America should enter the war, the plan calling for the dismemberment of the Western United States after the war.[5] That same month Secret Service Agents, aided by British intelligence and the New York police, rounded up aliens from East India thought to be working with German agents to stir up a rebellion against British colonial rule in India.[6]

The accumulated effect of three years of stories about "German intrigues" was to convince much of the public that enemy agents had organized vast numbers of aliens, particularly Germans and Austro-Hungarians, into a secret army poised to sabotage the nation's preparations for war. At the time of Wilson's war message, according to one observer, "many Americans believed that a declaration of war would transform the United States into a battlefield, with every one of the million resident German aliens an agent for the Kaiser. Mexicans in league with Germany would march north, retake Arizona and New Mexico, and cut off California from the rest of the country. Japanese would then land on the Pacific Coast and invade California. In the East, German submarines would shell New York City. Sabotage would be particularly widespread in the heavily industrialized Northeast. Spies, of course, were believed to be everywhere.[7]

Even in advance of the declaration of war there was hysteria over the "enemy alien" threat. In March 1917 the War Department began ostentatiously guarding public utilities and railroad bridges, and distributed weapons to factory owners.[8] On the West Coast, especially, public opinion was out of control. Power plant owners surrounded their facilities with barbed wire and electric fences,[9] gun clubs mobilized to protect their neighborhoods, and citizens were warned to arm themselves. On March 25 the War Department imposed a blackout on all news of military movements, and in the absence of hard news about military preparations rumors about the danger of enemy agents ran wild.[10]

Under those circumstances government officials who refused to give in to the hysteria were accused of "lack of concern" and of failing to do their duty. Within Wilson's cabinet there were only a few who stood their ground against the hysteria. Secretary of State Robert Lansing and Secretary of the Treasury McAdoo were in favor of a sweeping round-up of aliens, while Secretary of War Baker and Attorney General Thomas Gregory were skeptical that any critical threat existed, and advised proceeding against individual aliens only when incriminating evidence of disloyal activities developed.[11]

Attorney General Thomas Gregory's principled opposition to calls for sweeping abrogations of civil liberties, whether for aliens or citizens, later stood in sharp contrast to the conduct of his successor, A. Mitchell Palmer. Gregory called attention to the dangers wartime security measures posed to civil liberties, and he denounced the abuse of these measures to stifle legitimate political or industrial (union) activity. Gregory's Justice Department portrayed its security measures as necessary evils, while Palmer's Department used the same laws as happy opportunities to stifle dissent. What for Gregory was an unfortunate effect of the security laws, repression of political dissent, was reinterpreted by his successor as having been the real intent of Congress all along.

Despite the repugnance Gregory felt for wholesale abridgments of political rights, three factors compelled him to swim with the current. First was his loyalty to the administration in which he was a leading figure, and to a President he admired greatly. With the country and the press screaming for government action against the alien threat, it was clear that inactivity would be political suicide. Gregory deeply distrusted Secretary of the Treasury McAdoo and his Secret Service, and the penalty for Justice Department inactivity against aliens would be to concede the internal security field to the Treasury, which he felt would eventually discredit the government.

Secondly, Gregory's chief legal advisor was Assistant Attorney General Charles Warren, who was in favor of the most sweeping measures against disloyal aliens and citizens. Moreover, Warren was not adverse to making alliances with Gregory's rivals in the cabinet to promote his policies. Eventually Warren would even propose using military law and courts martial against disloyal aliens, and he offered these proposals to the Congress and the press without Gregory's approval. Gregory had too much strength of character (and was too highly respected within the administration and Congress) to live in terror of disloyal subordinates engaged in the common ploy of building congressional alliances against their superiors, but he was too politically astute to recklessly antagonize the powerful political forces who were Warren's allies.

Lastly, the emotional fear of the alien threat had affected even Gregory, particularly at the beginning of the war. While Gregory publicly scoffed at the more outlandish accounts of the danger the country faced from the German alien population, he had his private worries. On April 20, 1917, shortly after the declaration of war, Gregory wrote the Chief of his

Bureau of Investigation:

My butler is an unusually reliable man, although a negro; he told me last night that Mrs. J.L. Besson, 1329 14th St., and her daughter, were very much excited for fear they might be prosecuted for concealing information they had in regard to German spies. My butler thinks the Bessons are French, though he is not sure about this, and thinks possibly they may be German. I wish you would send someone around to interview these people and run this thing down.[12]

During the neutrality period and until the fall of 1917 Gregory relied on Assistant Attorney General Charles Warren for advice on the Justice Department's response to the German threat, to the public's cries for action, and to the competition of the Treasury Department. Warren was one of Hoover's first Justice Department superiors, and during Hoover's first months in the Department Warren's star was ascendant. In view of Hoover's war work as attorney to the Alien Enemies Bureau, and his postwar efforts to deport alien radicals, it is relevant that Charles Warren was one of the five founders of the small but influential Immigration Restriction League, which was organized at a meeting in Warren's home in 1894. This organization's purpose was to lobby for literacy tests and for other ways of stemming the tide of immigrants whose impact on America was so detested by blue-bloods like Warren.[13]

Charles Warren drafted the Espionage Bill that Gregory sent to Congress in June 1916. The bill died in 1916, and again in March 1917, but it was passed in June 1916. The bill died in 1916, and again in March 1917, but it was passed in June 15, 1917, during the special session of Congress.[14] Warren was also responsible for shaping government policy dealing with German merchant ships that had berthed in American ports to avoid the blockade.

Warren's prestige was its highest in April 1917 when he discovered a way of making use of the old 1798 Alien Act as the basis for Woodrow Wilson's April 6 proclamation placing the disposition of German "alien enemies" at the pleasure of the President and delegating their treatment to the Attorney General.[15] John Lord O'Brian, who later fought Warren over civil liberties and was instrumental in forcing his resignation from the department, also admired Warren's service in the early days of the war. O'Brian wrote:

We seemingly had no laws adequate to deal with the insidious methods of internal hostile activities. There were laws under which forgery of passports could be punished and there was the old Logan Act, which made it a crime to set on foot military expeditions against friendly countries. The only statute of any real use was one enacted in 1798 as part of the so-called Alien and Sedition Laws. This statute conferred on the President the power in time of national emergency to seize and intern without trial alien enemies who, in his opinion, were dangerous.

Under this statute and a presidential proclamation framed by Assistant Attorney General Charles Warren, many of the active German and Austrian master secret agents were, on the night war was declared, seized and imprisoned for the duration of the war. The importance of this action and the boldness and resourcefulness of Mr. Warren in executing it may have never been adequately emphasized. For the time being it paralyzed the operations of the German espionage system in this country. Subsequently this power of internment was used to such an extent that at the end of the war more than 2,500 dangerous alien enemies had been seized and interned—most of them agents or helpers in the German espionage system.[16]

Warren helped convince Gregory to bow to the public's demands for action against German aliens at the outset of the war. He wrote Gregory shortly before the declaration of war to urge that aliens be arrested even before the declaration, "I am confident," he wrote, "from my consideration of the reports of the special agents, that Germans and German sympathizers in the United States intend to commit widespread crimes of violence at the very outbreak of war. No time will be lost by them, and in my opinion, no time must be lost by us to guard against their actions."[17] Warren drafted the Department's regulations on zones from which enemy aliens were to be prohibited, and, according to an official history of the Justice Department, "the policing of the system became one of the heaviest tasks of the Department of Justice throughout the war."[18] It was, specifically, the task that kept Hoover busy for the duration.

Warren was also instrumental in prosecuting the I.W.W. leaders in Chicago, and was responsible for drafting and guiding through Congress the Trading with the Enemy Act that became law on October 6, 1917.[19] This law established the office of the Alien Property Custodian which was filled by future Attorney General A. Mitchell Palmer. Palmer's chief investigator was Francis P. Garvan, who had been chief of the Homicide, Insurance and Banking Division of the New York City District Attorney.[20] Garvan succeeded Palmer as Alien Property Custodian when the latter became Attorney General, and then joined Palmer and Hoover in June 1919 as Hoover's immediate superior during the Red Scare Raids of 1919 and 1920. Thus while Hoover cannot be said with any certainty to have had direct relationships with such officials as Palmer and Garvan during the war, nevertheless he was traveling in circles that would be highly important to him a few months in the future.

Once O'Brian entered the Justice Department, most of Warren's responsibilities, except "Trading with the Enemy and a few odds and ends," as O'Brian put it,[21] were transferred to O'Brian's War Emergency Division. Warren, who eventually became a Pulitzer Prize winning historian, utilized his remaining time in the department to write an article for the *Yale Law Review*, "What is Giving Aid and Comfort to the Enemy?" He argued there that aliens, like citizens, were punishable under the treason statute and thus were liable to the death sentence.[22]

Gregory eventually lost confidence in Warren when he began to lobby in Congress for extra-legal measures against subversion and espionage. "For a man working within the civil branch of the government," according to one critic, "Warren had an amazing disdain for the judicial process when it came to disloyalty."[23] During World War II he argued that German war criminals should be punished without trials because of their "barbarous crimes against civilization."

Warren alienated Gregory by insisting that the military should be in charge of trials for spying or disloyalty. Knowing that the President and the Attorney General were opposed to his position, he nevertheless went to the Senate with a bill that would have turned espionage investigations and trials over to the army. "One man shot, after court martial, is worth a hundred arrests by this Department," was his statement to Gregory.[24] When Gregory showed some signs of weakening under the furious public and congressional pressure to approve of Warren's proposal to revise the Articles of War to permit military trials of spies, O'Brian wrote Gregory "I have already expressed my opinion to you that such legislation is not only unconstitutional but embodies the worst possible policy."[25]

Gregory wrote the Senate that Warren had prepared his bill without Gregory's knowledge or approval, and that Warren's recommendations were "exactly contrary to those approved by the assistant to the Attorney General in charge of the problems involved [O'Brian] and the Attorney General himself. I entirely disapprove of the action taken by Mr. Warren, and it would not have been permitted if I had known it was contemplated."[26] As a consequence Warren resigned on April 19, 1918.

Beginning with the German submarine note of January 31, 1917, Attorney General Gregory's Justice Department took steps to stay abreast of official and public alarm over the enemy alien threat, and to stay ahead of its rivals in the Treasury Department. Gregory's highest priority during the war was prohibiting any other agencies, military or civilian, to alter the traditional arrangement that gave the Justice Department the federal government's primary and general law enforcement responsibilities, while restricting other government investigative agencies to enforcement of specifically delegated regulations. Specifically, Gregory was concerned about Secretary of the Treasury McAdoo's efforts to make the Secret Service the government's principal counterespionage agency, or, failing that, to set up a new umbrella agency under his control in which the Secret Service and the Bureau of Investigation would alike play subordinate parts.

Starting in February 1917, immediately after the German submarine note, Gregory, with Warren's aid, began maneuvering the Justice Department into a leadership role in dealing with the German "threat." Nearly every one of Gregory's wartime initiatives either involved a great deal of paperwork or promised to involve the department in a flood of paperwork once hostilities were declared. This created an opportunity for someone with the talent, even genius, for bureaucratic organization that

Hoover would soon show that he possessed, along with his incredible ability to impose a brutal order on the flood of paper that poured into the department in those pre-computer days.

On April 6, immediately after signing the declaration of war, Wilson issued a proclamation invoking the 1798 Alien Acts. Specifically, the principal statute (Section 4067 of the Revised Statues) stated:

Whenever there is declared war between the United States and any foreign nation or government ... and the President makes public proclamation of the event, all natives, citizens, denizens or subjects of the hostile nation or government, being males of the age of fourteen years and upwards, who shall be within the United States, and not actually naturalized, shall be liable to be apprehended, restrained, secured, and removed, as alien enemies. The President is authorized, in any such event, by his proclamation, thereof, or other public act, to direct the conduct to be observed, on the part of the United States, toward the aliens who become so liable; the manner and degree of the restraint to which they shall be subject, and in what cases, and upon what security their residence shall be permitted, and to provide for the removal of those who, not being permitted to reside within the United States, refuse or neglect to depart therefore; and to establish any other regulations which are found necessary in the premises and for the public safety.[27]

Wilson then listed twelve regulations that prohibited "alien enemies" from possessing guns or explosives, radio transmitters, documents "printed in cipher or in which there may be invisible writing." They were banned from within one-half mile of military installations or munitions plants. They were banned from zones to be designated later by the President (chiefly the Capital and the Port of New York) and were prohibited from entering or leaving the United States. The regulations raised the possibility of the registration of all alien enemies at a later date and threatened prison for any about whom "there may be reasonable cause to believe may be aiding or about to aid the enemy." The regulations also sought to silence enemy propaganda, about which there was almost superstitious dread: "An alien enemy shall not write, print, or publish any attack or threats against the Government or Congress of the United States, or either branch thereof, or against the measures or policy of the United States, or against the person or property of any person in the military, naval, or civil service of the United States, or of the States or Territories, or of the District of Columbia or of the municipal governments therein.[28]

The President on April 6 also charged the Attorney General with the responsibility of enforcing this proclamation by arresting aliens and drawing up procedures for their registration.

On April 16 Gregory set a deadline of June 1st for alien enemies to remove themselves from prohibited zones. He ordered the marshals to issue permits for aliens to continue to work or reside in the prohibited zones if their presence posed no danger to the country. He also ordered the Attorneys to wire the Attorney General with the names of such alien enemies as they felt ought to be summarily arrested under the terms of the proclamation, but not to arrest anyone until securing approval from Washington, unless there was an extraordinary degree of danger in allowing the alien to remain free.

Gregory pointed out that the "plan" of the department was to "take up the case of each individual alien enemy arrested separately and decide ... what disposition the interests of the country and of justice required."[29] His instructions to officers issuing permits mentions that they should transmit information to the "Permit Officer, Department of Justice, Washington, D.C." Even at this early date Gregory realized that he was facing a formidable job in dealing with the paperwork generated by the department's authority over alien enemies.[30] Before O'Brian recruited Hoover for his own operation, Hoover, along with many other clerks, was presumably filling the role of "Permit Officer."

Hoover's first four months in the Justice Department are undocumented. His name first surfaces in a letter from John Lord O'Brian submitted to Attorney General Gregory on December 14 describing the organization of O'Brian's War Emergency Division. The contents of this paper had been informally approved by Gregory on December 4, so it may be assumed that O'Brian had decided to have Hoover work in his Division's Alien Enemy Bureau some time before that. It is also probable that Hoover had been working in that area for several months before O'Brian formalized his assignment.

It may seem strange that so much of the Department's attention was being directed to alien affairs, but the reason was largely forced on Gregory by the nature of the work. He was able to delegate or control the tempo of almost all of the other war-related work, but there was no way for the Washington office to avoid handling the administration of the Alien Enemies regulations. Under the Draft Law of May 18, 1917, the Justice Department had the responsibility of prosecuting persons failing to register on June 5 or attempting to persuade others not to register. Under Attorney General Gregory, in some cases his hand forced by eager U.S. Attorneys, the department had prosecuted and obtained the convictions of several prominent enemies of the draft, most notably Emma Goldman and Alexander Berkman. Gregory's general policy, however, was to proceed slowly relying on the threat of prosecution to "get the eligibles into the Army [rather] than to confine them in jail."[31] Gregory and his Chief of the Bureau of Investigation, A. Bruce Bielaski, had delegated the work of locating and arresting draft violators to the volunteer operatives of the American Protective League. He was also relying on the A.P.L. to supervise the vice- and liquor-free areas around military installations.

Gregory had also prepared legislation for Congress to give the government the power to proceed against opponents of the war, and this legislation, drafted by Assistant Attorney General Charles Warren, was enacted as the Espionage Act of June 15, 1917. Gregory praised the law as finally giving the government the "power to deal with disturbing malcontents." This law would add to the burdens of the Department's attorneys and special agents, but once again the bulk of the work could be done by the A.P.L., and the work load could be made still more manageable by the usual prosecutorial discretion in choosing how many and which cases to prosecute.

Where the Department was faced with an uncontrollable volume of work was in its third area of responsibility, control of enemy aliens. President Wilson's proclamation on April 6, 1917 regulating the activities of German males fourteen years of age and older charged the Attorney General with the "duty of execution" of the regulations.[32] Gregory had already prepared a list of particularly dangerous enemy aliens and immediately arrested 63 Germans. After June 1 he also had to administer the thousands of appeals from German aliens who wanted to be exempted from the prohibited zone regulations so that they could keep their jobs and homes.

The paperwork mounted fast. According to Red Cross regulations all interned enemies had to be registered. Forms had to be prepared to allow them to apply for parole. Aliens who resided or worked in the forbidden areas, which included many large concentrations of the foreign-born, had to register with the Department to apply for permission to remain where they were. A complete registration of all German male aliens, and later, registration of alien females (there were, in all, 480,000 German alien enemies in the country, as well as nearly 4 million Austro-Hungarians), was deferred at the outset because of the need for extensive preparations, but on November 16, 1917, Wilson ordered the registration of all German males,[33] and on April 19, 1918, the regulations governing registration and permits were extended to German women.[34]

Hoover's first assignments in the Justice Department seem to have been processing the paperwork resulting from the internment of German aliens, particularly seamen. A severe labor shortage was already developing, so employers were desperate to have their interned alien workers released to fill out their work forces and so the Department had to begin processing parole applications almost as soon as the internments began. This work too seems to have been given to Hoover.

John Lord O'Brian, who was to be Hoover's superior for the duration of the war, did not arrive at the Justice Department until October 1. O'Brian's first task was to organize the war work of the department. He submitted a plan to Gregory around the end of November, and Gregory approved it in principle on December 5.[35] O'Brian formally submitted the structure of what he proposed calling the "Emergency War Division" or "Temporary War Division or ... some other similar title" to Gregory on December 14. The work of what was finally called the "War Emergency

Division" would consist of:

"1. Supervision of litigations, special arguments in aid of the United States Attorneys, supervision of liquor and vice zones and miscellaneous business chiefly relating to litigation, Mr. Bettman, special assistant to Attorney General, aided by Mr. Mothershead, attorney.

"2. Registration of Aliens. Mr. Sprague, special attorney, assisted by Mr. Blanchard, special agent; other subordinates to be named.

"3. Supervision of water-front protection in connection with the Army authorities to be assigned to Mr._____. (For the present in charge of Mr. Kenefick, attorney).

"4. All work relating to the internment and parole of enemy aliens and supervising issue of permits, etc., to them, to be handled by a subordinate 'Alien Enemy Bureau' in charge of Mr. Storey, as attorney.

"Within this Bureau, work to be sub-divided as follows:

"All subordinates reporting to Mr. Storey and Mr. Storey reporting directly to Mr. O'Brian, namely:

"(a) Questions affecting arrest and internment of alleged alien enemies Mr. Storey.

"(b) Questions relating to the parole of men in detention including the important work to be done in connection with the Department of Labor, relating to interned seamen, Mr. Saxon, assistant to Mr. Storey, aided by Mr. Hoover, special agent.

"(c) Questions effecting permits for aliens, barred zones, supervision of United States Marshals, etc., including miscellaneous correspondences, Mr. McGuire assistant to Mr. Storey."[36]

By December Hoover was a part of the Alien Enemy Bureau routine. His job was to review cases, summarize them, and then submit them to O'Brian with a recommendation for action. Most cases were very clear-cut. For example, an eighteen year-old German named Ernest Loehndorff was arrested in El Paso trying to enter the country from Mexico. "Loehndorff stated that he reported to the German Consul in each city and offered his services on behalf of his country. He also refused to promise that he will not aid enemy and states that 'if there is anything any of the high officials tell me to do I shall try to do that thing even if it costs me my life'." Hoover concluded the summary, "The facts in this case lead me to recommend that Ernest Loehndorff be detained for the duration of the war."[37]

O'Brian's procedure in any case in which anyone, whether in Washington or the field, expressed any doubts about an alien, was to intern him for the war. This means that he nearly always overruled pleas for clemency, evidently feeling that it was his responsibility to intern any alien who appeared dangerous to any authority. Nevertheless, Hoover and Hoover's immediate superior, Special Assistant Attorney General Charles W. Storey, frequently recommended action less harsh than internment for the rest of the war. For the most part Hoover simply passed along the district attorney's recommendation to O'Brian without comment.

In certain cases, however, Hoover was overruled by his superiors; from these cases some insight into Hoover's early attitudes can be gained. On

December 28 Hoover wrote a memorandum to O'Brian on a German seaman who had been refused permission to work on shipboard or near the waterfront after hostilities began, but who nevertheless took a berth as a deckhand on a coastal vessel. Hoover noted that "the attitude of this alien enemy is stated to be sullen and uncommunicative. The Special Agent in charge recommends that Dieriches be interned for the duration of the war." All the same, Hoover recommended that "in view of the circumstances of the case a parole may be safely granted at the end of thirty days, provided the limits of such are restricted to a rural community." Charles Storey disagreed vigorously: "A willful violation of our most important regulation. I see nothing to do but recommend detention for the war. Resp. CES. P.S. This is in line with our regular policy in these cases." O'Brian concurred: "Intern for War."[38]

In another similar case a German was arrested for "selling liquor to soldiers in uniform and soliciting men for immoral women." Hoover's comment was that "this is a case in which parole may be safely granted, provided Schachman is able to secure a competent supervisor and furnish a bond of not less than a $1000." Storey concurred: "If the man were a spy he would hardly have acted the way he did in regard to petty larceny and women. I fancy he is harmless in this respect and am inclined to recommend we remove him from the Naval Base and parole him in some inland town on a bond as stiff as he can put up." Bettman disagreed, noting "I think he should be interned for duration [of the] war. Has violated laws passed to further war." O'Brian interned him for the duration.[39] In still another case Hoover recommended parole for a German train conductor who had said "It is a shame that the best blood of the United States should be sent to Europe to fight England's war."[40] Again he was overruled.

On the other hand, there were cases in which Hoover was more severe in his recommendation than his immediate superior, although in all these cases O'Brian's final action was, as usual, to intern the alien for the duration of the war. In one case an Otto Mueller called President Wilson "a cock-sucker and a thief," and later, when asked about how he liked America, answered "fuck this god damned country." Hoover characterized these as "various vulgar and obscene remarks about the President" and "the most pronounced Pro-German expressions." Therefore he seconded the recommendation of the United States Attorney who "recommends that Mueller be interned for the duration of the war, in which recommendation I concur." Charles Storey disagreed with Hoover, saying that "Mueller has unquestionably overstepped the rights of free speech but still his offense is no more than a failure to keep his mouth shut, and I feel that internment for the war for mere talk is rather severe. Three or four months in jail will be equally effective."[41]

Another instance in which Hoover recommended more severe treatment than his immediate superior involved a German who, according to Hoover, "engaged in a conversation with a negro in which he indulged in pro-German utterances and in derrogatory [sic] remarks regarding the United States Government. He also made disloyal statements to other parties." Hoover passed along without comment the Attorney's request for the permanent internment of the alien. Storey protested that the alien had been in the country for 30 years; although he agreed that the fact that he had been overheard speaking "in this manner to a negro lends color to the idea that he was trying to influence the latter against the United States," Storey recommended that he be given a month or two in prison followed by parole. "The additional facts that this man is a drunkard and abuses his wife cut two ways and I do not feel that they should be considered in this case." O'Brian interned him for the duration.[42]

There seems to be a pattern in the cases involving disagreement between Hoover and O'Brian. O'Brian seemed determined to base his decision about internment only on the specific actions of the accused, or on the fact that someone with first-hand experience of the alien thought him dangerous. Hoover seemed equally determined to probe the beliefs and attitudes of the aliens; he showed himself willing to excuse illegal actions by well-meaning aliens, but was harshly punitive toward aliens whose actions might be innocuous but whose opinions were repugnant or dangerous.

Apparently Hoover continued to summarize the case files of interned alien enemies until April 1918, dealing also with administrative problems arising from the November 16, 1917, registration of German males. On April 19, 1918, German females were required to register, and it appears that Hoover was heavily involved in this operation, perhaps even in charge. On July 3, 1918, he sent a memo to O'Brian enclosing an editorial from the New York *Sun* praising the "efficient work of the Department in the registration of alien females." It would not be unrealistic to assume that Hoover was calling attention to the success of his own work. Beginning in the summer of 1918 letters begin to appear with O'Brian's signature, but bearing Hoover's "JEH" initials, indicating that he was the attorney who had drafted the letter and to whom replies should be routed. Most of these deal with the registration of German alien females, and they show Hoover exercising increasing authority, a remarkable advance considering his age (23 in 1918).

Further evidence of the reputation Hoover was developing is the extent to which superiors began to give him tasks outside his formal responsibility. The Justice Department had reason to be anxious about the number of German aliens living on Staten Island, since it was close to the prohibited area of the Port of New York. Hoover collected data allowing him to estimate the number of Staten Island Germans, together with the names and addresses of the police officers supervising them.

By August 26 Hoover was no longer simply summarizing files and attaching a tentative recommendation. He was evaluating cases from a legal standpoint and was furnishing final decisions to his superiors for their signature. He was no longer simply reporting to Charles Storey, but was also working for Albert Bettman, who was in charge of war litigation for O'Brian. Since in December Hoover had had to report to one of Charles Storey's assistants, this would indicate that he had moved up at least one echelon in the Justice Department bureaucracy.

In 1918 Hoover finally received his promotion to the rank of attorney, when O'Brian also gave Hoover the assignment of "reviewing aliens who volunteered for military duty and wanted to become citizens."[43] Since this law went into effect on May 9, 1918, it was presumably this assignment that accounted for Hoover's promotion on June 8, 1918.[44] By the end of September Hoover was also furnishing O'Brian with decisions on complicated cases involving travel permits for German aliens; he was now handling difficult cases from all areas within the Alien Enemy Bureau, although Armistice Day (November 11) found Hoover still busily compiling registration statistics on alien enemies.

According to John Lord O'Brian, "at the end of the war, at the time of the Armistice, [Hoover] told me he would like to continue in the permanent side of the Department of Justice, and I took that up personally with the new Attorney General, A. Mitchell Palmer, who had him transferred to the Bureau of Investigation."[45]

Both Gregory and O'Brian had notified President Wilson that they wished to leave government service at the end of the war. However, since Gregory and Secretary of Labor Wilson had asked Congress for the power to deport dangerous interned aliens (Feb. 5, 1919), O'Brian decided to stay on the job to review the files of all interned aliens to make sure that none who were not a menace during peacetime would be jeopardized by still being imprisoned. O'Brian released all except German seamen who had refused repatriation during the war and 150 aliens who had been convicted of violations of the wartime laws. He also reviewed all convictions he had obtained under the Espionage Act, and had Wilson issue three pardons and 102 commutations.[46]

O'Brian stayed in the Justice Department until April 30. Since the decision to name Palmer was not made until February 26, 1919, and he assumed the duties of the office on the date of Gregory's resignation, March 3,[47] O'Brian must have spoken to Palmer during March or April, and so the recommendation would have been fresh on Palmer's mind when radical aliens blew up his house in June and he needed someone who knew about aliens to hunt them down.

But while World War I *had* taught Hoover all about the care and handling of enemy aliens, it had taught him nothing about constitutional methods. The essential logic of the Alien Enemy Bureau was the same as that of the Immigration Bureau: administrative procedures as a swift, easy and unappealable substitute for the time-consuming delays, uncertainties and case-by-case approach of the legal process.

Hoover had spent a heady year and a half as a novice lawyer with freedom or prison as his gift with a stroke of a pen, his whims kept in check only by the sober responsibility of conscientious superiors. The end of the war would remove those superiors from government and replace them with ambitious and unscrupulous politicians eager to use talents like Hoover's for their political profit. Under A. Mitchel Palmer, techniques developed for dealing with aliens would be proposed as a means of combatting citizens with unpopular views; the entire Justice Department would become an Alien Enemy Bureau.

Notes

[1] Jean M. Jensen, *The Price of Vigilance* (Chicago: Rand McNally, 1968), p. 15 (Hereafter referred to as Jensen).

[2] Jensen, p. 16.   [3] Jensen, pp. 13-14.   [4] Jensen, p. 15.   [5] Jensen, p. 21.   [6] Jensen, p. 21.   [7] Jensen, p. 27.   [8] Jensen, p. 27.   [9] Jensen, p. 26.   [10] Jensen, p. 27.   [11] Jensen, p. 29.

[12] Gregory to Bielaski, April 20, 1917, Archives RG 60, DJ File 190470. (All National Archives files are from Record Group 60, hereafter referred to as NARS.)

[13] John Higham, *Strangers in the Land: Patterns of American Nativism 1860-1925* (New York: Atheneum, 1973), p. 102.

[14] Homer S. Cummings and Carl McFarland, *Federal Justice: Chapters in the History of Justice in the Federal Executive* (New York: Da Capo, 1970; originally published in 1937), p. 414. (Hereafter referred to as Cummings.)

[15] Jensen, p. 107.

[16] John Lord O'Brian, "New Encroachments on Individual Freedom," 66 Harv. L. Rev. I (1952) in *John Lord O'Brian Commemorative Issue, Buffalo Law Review* (1974), p. 92.

[17] Cummings, p. 417.   [18] Cummings, p. 418.   [19] Cummings, p. 423.

[20] Stanley Coben, *A. Mitchell Palmer, Politician* (New York: Columbia, 1963), p. 130. (Hereafter referred to as Coben.)

[21] Memo from O'Brian to Attorney General, Oct. 7, 1918, DJ File 190470, Gregory Box 2735, NARS.

[22] Jensen, p. 107.   [23] Jensen, p. 107.   [24] Jensen, pp. 106-7.   [25] Jensen, p. 121.

[26] Jensen, p. 121; Cummings, 424; New York *Times*, April 23, 1918; DJ File 44-4-4, Sec. 1, Feb. 167, 1918, NARS.

[27] *Report of the Attorney General for the Year 1917*, p. 57 (hereafter referred to as *AG Report 1917*).

[28] *AG Report 1917*, p. 58.   [29] *AG Report 1917*, p. 67.   [30] *AG Report 1917*, pp. 70, 71.   [31] *AG Report 1917*, p. 74.   [32] *AG Report 1917*, pp. 57-8.   [33] *AG Report 1918*, p. 29.   [34] *AG Report 1918*, p. 28.

[35] Gregory to O'Brian, Dec. 5, 1917, DJ File 190470 Gregory Papers Box 2735, NARS.

[36] O'Brian to Gregory, Dec. 14, 1917, DJ File 190470 Gregory Papers Box 2735, NARS.

[37] Hoover to O'Brian, Dec. 17, 1917, DJ 9-16-12-1384, NARS.

[38] Hoover to O'Brian, Dec. 28, 1917, BuFile 9-16-9-414 NARS.

[39] Hoover to O'Brian, Dec. 28, 1917, DJ 9-16-9-4-4; Hoover to O'Brian, Dec. 28, 1917, DJ 9-16-9-4-1 NARS.

[40] Hoover to O'Brian, Dec. 28, 1917 DJ 9-16-1726 NARS.

[41] Hoover to O'Brian, Dec. 18, 1917, DJ 9-16-12-1400 NARS.

[42] Hoover to O'Brian, Dec. 29, 1917, DJ 9-16-12-1689 NARS.

[43] Ovid Demaris, *The Director: An Oral Biography of J. Edgar Hoover* (New York: Harper's Magazine Press, 1975), p. 53.

[44] *AG Report 1919*, p. 28.

[45] Demaris, p. 53.

[46] Jensen, p. 267.

[47] Coben, p. 154; Cummings, p. 427.

The Constitution and the "People":
A Modern Intellectual Looks at the Constitution

Robert W. Schneider

IN THE YEARS FOLLOWING WORLD WAR II probably no historian struck a more responsive chord in the minds of young American historians than Richard Hofstadter. Arthur Schlesinger, Jr., the spokesman for a wider segment of the intellectual community, was better known, but it was the work of Hofstadter which excited the graduate seminars of the land and brought a flood of graduate students to Columbia University.

A number of factors, both internal and external to the discipline, have been put forward to explain Hofstadter's rise to a place of prominence in the post-war academic community. It was a time when Americans were becoming convinced that the great battle between good and evil on the international scene was far from completed; the frightening forces of Germany and Japan had been defeated, but a new force of potentially greater danger to the American dream was emerging from the ranks of the victorious Allies themselves. Led by nervous politicians and repentant intellectuals who only a few years before had had their youthful spirits moved deeply by the promises and hopes of Marx, the American people were quick to respond to the new dangers posed by those who blamed all of America's problems upon the evil machinations of international Communism and the duplicity of its domestic sympathizers who had infiltrated the most sensitive areas of American life.[1] A generation of writers and intellectuals who had been nurtured during their youth in the prewar depression by the hopes of international cooperation against the forces of Fascism without and of rampant capitalism within, now turned their minds and their pens against the malignant forces of the new devil—the Soviet Union.

And the new depression which so many had feared would accompany the demobilization of American troops and industry did not come. Instead American capitalism regeared itself to the demands of a peacetime economy and produced goods that a newly prosperous consumer could buy in ever increasing amounts. The New Deal had indeed succeeded in spreading the unique American system of a middleway between laissez-faire and socialism into an economy that seemed to provide the necessities of life to a mass society.

The new analysts of the American past had grown up in the dark yet intellectually exciting days of the 1930s. The ideas of Marx and the new intellectual currents had stimulated them for a while, but the disenchantment did not survive the Nazi-Soviet Pact and the apparent dangers of the cold war which shaped up more and more to be an intellectual battle between outmoded and discredited ideologies and the actuality of a functioning, growing American "pluralism."[2]

For American historians of Hofstadter's generation the problems and the solutions seemed to hang in the air. They had been raised on the writings of the so-called Progressive historians led by Turner, Beard and Parrington. These pioneers had guided two generations of historians in the study of the influence of the frontier, of sections, and of economic forces in American history and letters. Reacting to the myriad problems that had faced American liberals between 1890 and 1917, they had stressed the conflicts that had characterized the American past—battles between the haves and the have-nots. As Turner had explained that the uniqueness of American history lies in the existence of the unbounded free land of the frontier, so Beard and Parrington had shown how the development of that history had been determined by the conflict between various entrenched economic interests and the democratic lower classes that had struggled to overcome their oppressors.

In other disciplines writers like Louis Hartz in political science, Daniel Bell and Seymour Lipset in sociology—among a host of others— were emerging to challenge these established interpretations of the American past and to explain the American present. They minimized the old conflicts of the Progressive generation of scholars and stressed the beliefs, interests and political-economic structures which the bulk of Americans had shared over the centuries and which separated them from their old world forebears. Sometimes by implication and sometimes by direct analysis, they indicated that agreement on broad and perhaps transcendent essentials had characterized not only the American past but the American present as well. The Progressive school came to be replaced by the "consensus" school which wrote not about a dichotomized society but a "pluralistic" one which the new disciples of American studies, led by Henry Nash Smith, wrote about in terms of "symbol" and "myth," terminology adopted from cultural anthropology.

As the prosperity of the 1950s and early 1960s continued, the American writer and scholar seemed to find a home in the halls of academe as acceptance replaced alienation. For a time it escaped their notice that women, Blacks, Indians and the dispossessed had disappeared from the history books, while the poor of their own day became invisible.

At first as a trickle and then in a mounting stream, this new scholarship came under attack from every angle—just at a time when the Black movement stirred the lethargic sentiments of middle class America and their alienated sons and daughters jarred the social fabric with a blistering attack on the whole establishment. From half-way around the world came the screams of napalmed Vietnamese children that echoed not only in the White House and the halls of Congress but in the classrooms of academe itself. Conflict and violence were real in the American present and historians insisted that they were real in the American past as well. Women, Blacks, radicals, ethnics and homosexuals began exciting quests for their own histories. Critics of America's role in Vietnam joined with Marxists and neo-Beardians to show that the history of the United States had been one long imperialistic quest for new markets which would support a doomed capitalistic system.

Consensus history was denounced as being homogenized; it ignored the real and meaningful conflicts which had characterized American political debates. Status interpretations of such movements as Populism and Progressivism were found misleading if not completely false, as historians rediscovered the real problems which American reformers had faced in their battles to save American society. Postwar historians were condemned as elitists; they had buried the life and death struggles which submerged elements of society had faced in their daily lives. American Studies scholars were guilty of most of the same sins. On the one hand, they had been parochial in trying to show that the United States was unique and, consequently, they were misguided in searching for some fictional construct which they labeled American Character. The whole culture concept which lies behind and gave theoretical support to studies in both history and American Studies was attacked. Both disciplines were guilty of studying the thoughts and actions of a highly articulate, educated elite and projecting their analyses upon the unlettered elements who were concerned about hard economic realities. Modern scholarship had buried the old class conflicts and anatagonisms and distorted the very nature of man himself. It is with the last of these charges that I want to deal most explicitly here.[3]

The acknowledged authority on American ideas about human nature is Merle Curti who has been a life-long student of this subject. The culmination of his work was *Human Nature in American Thought,* published in 1980. He does not deal with post-World War II historians in this otherwise inclusive book, but he did analyze their writings in an earlier book entitled *Human Nature in American Historical Thought.*[4] In the latter work he suggests that, although few historians have dealt with the subject directly, they have made certain assumptions about human nature that color and, perhaps, even direct their interpretations of the oftimes dusty records they diligently search out. He believed that these assumptions are colored by such factors as the period in which they live (the so-called climate of opinion), as well as by their position in life, their personal temperament, and by the observed behavior of their contemporaries. In Curti's view the modern scholar has been made more acutely aware, particularly by the revelations of modern psychology and the events of recent history, that men are closer to the old Puritan view of them than to the beliefs of Jeffersonian democracy or Transcendentalism. These convictions led him to believe that the old Progressive synthesis which he, along with Turner, Beard and Parrington had embraced was unrealistic; it was unable to explain the tragic movements of the twentieth century.

Hofstadter clearly shared the new generation's reservations about the analyses of the Progressive historians, but—at the same time—he traced his own intellectual heritage directly to Beard. Yet such scholars as Gene Wise have contended that there is a break like that of a paradigm change in scientific theory between the writings of the Progressive school and those of the consensus, pluralistic, myth and symbol, culture-oriented studies of the post-World War II period.[10] Wise, along with Curti, and many of the critics of the newer scholars, has suggested that this dichotomy is brought about—at least in part—by a change in the view of man himself.

Curti's sympathetic picture of Beard's ideas about human nature show that he, like the leaders of the New History, wanted to call upon science to provide a history which would clear away the myths and irrelevancies of the past to make room for a history which would proclaim man's capacity to solve his current problems and direct his future. According to their view of things, human nature—a combination of both rational and irrational elements—was sufficiently plastic to make new responses to a changing world despite the pull of institutions and traditions. Indeed, man was capable of changing his institutions and his environment to improve both human conditions and social behavior. Man's plasticity gave him the capacity to respond to the changes brought on by an industrial world and, guided by the new science, he could and would work for the public good. Even war itself was not a product of man's innate aggressiveness but of existing institutional forces.[6]

Curti suggests that Beard's view of man, which did not essentially change over his long career, was never systematically stated but could be reconstructed from the bulk of his writings. It was influenced by the classics and his early Quaker environment, as well as by such obvious sources as Madison, Darwin, Lester Ward and the contemporary social sciences. He expected less from man, both individually and collectively, than some of his contemporaries but he rejected that notion that "human behavior in time can be reduced to a mathematical formula or understood by an analogy with physics or biology." While allowing a wide latitude for human choice, he admitted that man's freedom was bounded by hereditary and environmental forces. With the functional psychologists, he held that heredity and environment are inseparable components of the human organism.

While believing that the intelligence and talents of human beings are widely varied, he "rejected the doctrine that human nature inevitably points to an elite, whether based on sex, class or race." Unlike his mentor, James Madison, Beard contended that classes are rooted in historical circumstances, not in human nature. Still, in a modern, technological society man needs help to overome mass indifference and to prevent the selfish side of his nature from taking over. That is the function of a democratic, positive government.[7]

Curti disagrees with the view set forth by Robert Skotheim in his *Intellectual Histories and Historians* about the function of ideas in relation to Beard's view of human nature. According to Skotheim, Beard tended to see conservative ideas of which he disapproved, as mere rationalizations of the status quo; progressive, reform ideas, on the other hand, were given autonomous origins. Curti contends that Beard never "assumed that ideas develop and are transmitted apart from human agents responding in one or another way to problems in their environment. He firmly believed, however, in the power of ideas, as well as ideals and intelligence, to guide man toward his goals."[8] It is this belief that the cold war scholars supposedly lost, and it is this loss that helped to turn them into conservative defenders of the status quo.

Unlike the Progressive historians, Hofstadter and his friends were products of the new eastern, urban culture, not that of the WASP midwest. His family left Cracow when his father, Emil, was a youth and came to the United States in steerage in 1899. Rebelling against the extreme orthodoxy of his Jewish parents, Emil ran away from home when he was sixteen. In Buffalo he learned the fur trade of his father, married a German Lutheran, and prospered in his business. Richard Irving Hofstadter was born on August 6, 1916, and christened in his mother's church. His mother's death brought an early end to his childhood and apparently also ended any interest he may have had in religion.[9]

As a youth, he found an intellectual home with the Swados family that brought about a return to his Jewish intellectual roots and the allegiance was a permanent one. Felice Swados, whom Hofstadter later married, was the child of the dominating educational leader in Buffalo; she was two years ahead of him in school, and the sister of the leftist novelist and organizer Harvey Swados.[10]

In high school, Hofstadter was an attractive and scholastically outstanding young man whom everyone liked. He was a cheerleader, played tennis and golf, and became a member of a fraternity that did not normally admit Jews. President of his senior class and valedictorian, he won a state scholarship to the University of Buffalo.[11]

The Student League for Industrial Democracy and the National Student League competed for the participation of the small percentage of the University of Buffalo students who were politically active in the early years of the Depression. Felice, a tall, powerful woman and an extravert who made an immediate impression on people, had become an important member in these groups before Hofstadter arrived on the scene. It was in the fall of 1934 that he became involved with Felice in left-wing politics. He became a member of the Young Communist League, read Marx and Lenin, and became active in the efforts for radical social change.[12]

It was while he was involved in such activities that Hofstadter first read Beard's *Rise of American Civilization*. His senior thesis, dated May 1936, was an attempt to document the Beards' interpretation of the Civil War. Part of his investigation supported the Beards' thesis and another did not, but Hofstadter's concentration was strictly on economic causation and his criticism of their interpretation (what there was of it) came from the left of the Progressive analysis.[13]

Hofstadter and Felice left Buffalo in the fall of 1946 and went to New York City where they were married and where, coerced by his family, he entered law school to take advantage of his uncle's standing in the legal profession.[14] Living in a two-room flat near the docks in Brooklyn Heights, they wrote plays and stories about the life of the proletariat. At the time, he was going to New York Law School at night and working as an errand-boy at a law firm during the day. From the beginning he found law school dull and his own work equally uninspired.[15]

When he decided to abandon the legal profession, he wrote his wife's family that if he did not become a journalist, he would become an historian.[16] As late as 1940 he described himself as a "suppressed literateur who couldn't make the grade just writing good prose and had to go into history."[17]

At that time he was very concerned about the splits in the Communist Party and already searching for some way to combine the discipline of party loyalty with a legitimate opposition.[18] As late as January of 1938 he wrote Harvey Swados that he would never join the Party, but by April he had changed his mind. He stated that his reason for joining was that "I don't like capitalism and want to get rid of it. I am tired of talking. I am ashamed of the hours I have spent jawing about the thing...."[19] By the fall of that same year, however, he informed Swados that, having joined the Party, he found himself disgusted with the conduct of the party leaders; in February of 1939, the following year, he said that he was fed up with a lot of things involved with the Party and had decided to quietly ease himself out of it.[20] He still had enough interest in Russia and the Communist Party to be extremely disillusioned by the Nazi-Soviet Pact. He told Swados after the Russian invasion of Poland that "There is nothing so crude as the Stalinist mentality."[21] But even as he was separating himself from the Party, he felt anguish over his separation from the working class. As he said, he and his friends had discovered that they were "petty bourgeois intellectuals and that there is a certain inherent alienness between us and the working class."[22]

It was through Felice—a talented writer in her own right—that Hofstadter became associated with some of the brightest and most promising young radical intellectuals on the New York literary scene. Perhaps most important among them was Alfred Kazin who became his close and lifelong friend.[23] The literary critic has written of the group's sense of themselves as a trouble-laden generation. They engaged in endless discussions about the state of the nation and of the world and debated the responsibilities of the writer in their disintegrating society. In this radical milieu Hofstadter developed his fascination with politics, his awareness of human frailty, and his disdain for ideological stances.[24]

By all accounts, Hofstadter was not the stuffy academic one might expect him to be; rather, he was an easy and accomplished story teller who frequently had his audiences rolling with laughter. Kazin has described the young law student as "a natural conservative in a radical period, with a melancholy knowledge of the shoals and traps of human nature...." "He was strikingly passive, he took things in, he thought them over and waited them out; he let other people take the initiative, but was always more penetrating."[25]

By the time of World War II, Hofstadter seemed to stand outside all ideologies. He said that he used to sneer when he heard Communism described as a substitute for religion, but did so no longer. "I hate capitalism and everything that goes with it. But I also hate the simpering dogmatic religious-minded Janizaries that make up the CP."[26] While he disavowed the Marxists, he still did not trust Roosevelt (whom he considered to be neither intelligent nor honest) and this added to his sense of isolation.[27]

It does not seem to have mattered greatly to Hofstadter's fundamental ideas whether he was a member of the Party or not—his basic views seem to have remained much the same. And even in his mature years he was closest to his friends from the thirties.[28]

Hofstadter's MA thesis—"The Southeastern Cotton Tenants under the AAA, 1933-35"—was a technical, statistical study done under the direction of Harry Carmen. His path beyond strict economic determinism and class conflict models probably resulted from his relationship with Merle Curti. In Curti, Hofstadter found what he felt was a kindred Marxist soul who was also a successful academic historian.[29] The young scholar felt that his paper for Curti on Jefferson's ideas about class relations was a breakthrough for him.[30] At that time he believed that history moved strictly through the clash of economic interest groups and that Jefferson's failure to make the class struggle part of his social theory resulted from the fact that the great democrat hoped that such struggles in the United States would vanish in the triumph of agrarian democracy.[31] In this, his most developed academic effort done from a strict Marxist perspective, Hofstadter believed that Jefferson's problem stemmed from the fact that he, himself, was not from the ranks of the small farmer class whose interests he defended. As he was later to argue, Jefferson was too much absorbed by the American middle-class liberal mind to provide an alternative course for the nation.

It was in another paper done for Curti—on Wendell Phillips—that Hofstadter became personally identified with his subject, a man whose formative influences clearly were not derived from his own economic background.[32] This piece seems to mark the beginning of his later position that Marxist categories did not fit events in the United States.

Still, Hofstadter did not break with his Marxist past in the way that became common for so many of his contemporaries. While teaching at Maryland in the immediately succeeding years he met frequently with his fellow historians Kenneth Stampp and Frank Freidel, and the sociologist C. Wright Mills. In their conversations they agree on their continuing dislike for American capitalism and its current leader, FDR.[33] Frank Freidel has suggested that Hofstadter was the least radical of the group, but he did become a fast friend of the more radical Mills, and it seems to have been through their discussions that Hofstadter developed some of the major sociological theories that were to influence his later work.[34]

According to Hofstadter himself, what attracted him to history was a sense of engagement with contemporary problems, and he retained that sense of engagement throughout his life.[35] Writing about the supposedly conservative historian and the more radical Mills, Richard Gilliam noted in later years, "It was not the sociologist but the historian who protested publicly and loudly when McCarthyism came home to roost at Columbia." During the same traumatic years when McCarthyism seemed to be invading the heart of American life, Hofstadter still refused to join the intellectual's citadel against Communism—the American Committee for Cultural Freedom.[36] Instead he became a founding member of the National Academy of Education.

This action was probably a result of his uneasiness about the future of the American university which he felt was coming under direct attack from two separate not altogether different forces—the hysterical anti-communism associated with McCarthy and from what he viewed as the "false piety for populistic democracy."[37] Throughout his life he continued to publish articles analyzing the political and social issues that faced the country. Too late to be any kind of leader in the anti-war movement, but before most of his peers adopted such a stance, he denounced America's most flagrant imperialist adventure in Vietnam, as a "hideous war."[38]

It is difficult to judge to what extent Hofstadter's mature work was influenced by the Marxism that was so important to him during the 1930s. In later years he contended that "my own assertion of consensus history in

1948 had its sources in the Marxism of the 1930s."[39] Yet the bulk of his writings would tend to modify this contention. Much more convincing is his statement that, "I took up American history under the inspiration that came from Charles and Mary Beard's *The Rise of American Civilizaton*,"[40] (*Prog. Hist.*, xiv)

Events of his own time, "and among these some of the most ominous and appalling," launched Hofstadter and his contemporary scholars upon a "restless search for new methods of understanding."[41] The work being done in other disciplines had made modern historians conscious of the complexity of human behavior in ways that were not available to Beard's generation. Depth psychology and the newer work of the social scientists and literary scholars made the modern historian more aware than they had ever been that politics was a field in which feelings and impulses that are only marginally related to so-called real issues are of crucial importance and gave the historian a greater feel for the non-rational side of politics.[42] Daniel Bell, who became a good friend of Hofstadter's at Columbia, contends that the neo-orthodoxy of Reinhold Niebuhr (whom Hofstadter first heard speak when he was an undergraduate) was probably a more important influence on the historian than almost any other.[23] Such a contention fits in with the emphasis that Hofstadter placed on the non-rational and selfish side of man that perhaps as much as anything else separates him and his generation from the Beardian Progressives.

Although he disclaimed any real interest in the theoretical side of history,[44] he was particularly interested in individual and social character types, "in social mythologies and styles of thought as they reveal and affect character, and in politics as a sphere of behavior into which personal and private motives are projected." He found Mannheim of use for his link between ideas and social situations, and cultural anthropology essential for the study of styles of life. So far as Freud was concerned, Hofstadter believed that, although historians may hate to admit it, "they do work with certain general psychological presuppositions."[45] His friend, Kazin, remarked on the thorough study which Hofstadter had made of Freud.[46]

To what extent (if at all) does Hofstadter's view of man allow room for the rational man of the Progressive historian who sought his own self interest through recurrent political battles? Essentially Hofstadter's writings embrace the interpretation of American political history that is closely associated with Louis Hartz's *The Liberal Tradition in America*. In this view the side of the left, the side which had supported popular causes, has been free of the need to combat feudal traditions, on the one hand, or proletarian and social democracy of the kind found in the other countries of the West, on the other. Even the American Revolution "was a legalistic and socially conservative affair ...." Because it was always possible to assume a considerable measure of both social equality and of subsistence, reform in America was directed not so much toward social democracy or social equality as toward greater opportunities.[47]

This does not mean that sharp conflicts have been absent from American politics. Such encounters have been "a recurrent fact of American political life, with a fairly severe crisis taking place about once in a generation."[48] American political thought has had a long tradition of economic materialism and consciousness of class that can be seen in the writings of such men as Harrington, Madison, Adams, Webster, Calhoun, Hildreth and Brownson.[49] And the anti-trust movement which has been so strong in American history "must be understood as the political judgment of a nation whose leaders had always shown a keen awareness of the economic foundations of politics."[50] (205)

One of the criticisms of Hofstadter's picture of American history has always been that he homogenized history by removing any and all important conflicts, especially in the political area. Here the significant element may be the kind of conflict which he sees operating in American history, a view which differed from both those of the Founding Fathers and those of the Progressives. In America, he suggests, ethnic animosities have been almost a substitute for the class struggle. He does not deny that material interests and questions of power are present in the American political drama but he maintains that politicians also have had to cope with mass emotions that they cannot really create or manipulate. At one point he stated, "I have no interest in denying the reality, or even the primacy, of the problems of money and power," but he suggested that his purpose was to draw attention to the human context in which they arise.[51] He was quite willing to admit that American political history had involved conflicts between such special interests as landed capital and financial capital, but he denied that "at least until recently" crucial struggles between "propertied and unpropertied classes" had been a crucial factor.[52]

From the beginning of his analysis of "the ideology" of the American political structure he was convinced of the need for an interpretation of her traditions which would emphasize a common climate of opinion. And while he contended that class has always been an unacceptable term in American political debate, he does state that it is "beyond dispute that the parties do have a different class basis" and that "Party allegiance was reflected in socioeconomic breakdowns."[53]

For those of us who came of intellectual age in the 1950s it seemed clear that Hofstadter was not part of the attempt by so many of his age to rescue the tradition of American liberal thought in any recognizable form. It seemed to us a delicious heresy for him to write as he did in *The American Political Tradition* that the American experience had been completely dominated by capitalism and that the heroes of that tradition were really not very different from those we had been taught to look upon as villains. Hofstadter seemed to be so different because he could not and did not identify himself with those we had come to believe were naive progressives.

In an article on "Parrington and the Jeffersonian Tradition" which had originally been written as a graduate paper for Curti, he planted the germ of his later, more developed, notion that the Progressives had gone astray by trying too hard to find a heritage for their own political ideas in the writings of the treasured liberals of the past. He did this by the quite simple method of showing that on many fundamental questions Jefferson was much closer to his arch-enemy Hamilton than he was to modern liberal ideas.[54]

Perhaps because he did not believe that the working historian should be a theorist, Hofstadter nowhere expressed a developed interpretation of human nature. He was concerned, however, with the views on that topic that were expressed by the subjects of his studies. He was particularly interested in the thoughts about man that were expressed by the Founding Fathers. The Constitution, as he viewed it, was founded more upon experience than upon abstract theory; nevertheless, its authors "had a vivid Calvinistic sense of human evil and damnation and believed with Hobbes that men are selfish and contentious." As men of affairs they had witnessed human nature on display in the daily activities of their fellow citizens and they recognized all its frailty. "To them a human being was but an atom of self-interest." Man was a creature of rapacious self-interest; yet the Founding Fathers wanted him to be free. "They accepted the mercantile image of the life as an eternal battleground, and assumed the Hobbesian war of each against all; they did not propose to put an end to this war, but merely to stabilize it and make it less murderous."[55]

In Hofstadter's analysis the main structural features of American society were implanted during the colonial period when political participation was based upon widespread property ownership and broad suffrage. In relative terms, literacy was widespread and the people were accustomed to participating in public affairs. Leadership and office holding were dominated by the patrician (not aristocratic) class, but between this group and the mass of voters there existed general confidence and respect. "Colonial history had its record of class resentments, class conflicts, and even rebellions, but it had left no legacy of class hatred nor any fixed patterns of class hostilities."[56]

Hofstadter actually rejected the worshipful view of the Founding Fathers as much as Beard had done and his picture of them reflects his view of human nature as combining both reason and self-interest. "They were impelled by class motives more than pietistic writers like to admit," he continued, but (as Beard himself recognized) they were also directed by a scrupulous regard for republican philosophy.[57] It was as clear to him as to his Progressive precedessors that the Founding Fathers did not trust the common man or democratic rule; the Constitution was designed to confine the popular spirit that had been abroad in the land since the days of the Revolution. Modern Americans, Hofstadter felt, tend to view democracy and liberty as two sides of the same coin, but the liberty that the Founding Fathers were most concerned to establish was linked to property—as an extension of human nature—not to democracy. Democratic ideas, in Hofstadter's opinion, appeal to discontented and oppressed classes, rising middle classes, or perhaps to some sections of a partially disinherited aristocracy; they do not appeal to an established class, such as the Founding Fathers, that is still enjoying its privileges.[58]

He hastened to point out, on the other hand, that the Fathers were direct heirs of seventeenth century English republicanism that rejected arbitrary rule and demanded a form of popular sovereignty. The masses were by nature turbulent and their actions demonstrated that they were a threat to the established property arrangements. Yet the new government must be approved by them and based on their suffrage.

How can a government be built upon these seemingly divergent principles? "One thing that the Fathers did not propose to do, because they thought it impossible, was to change the nature of man to conform with a more ideal system. They were inordinately confident that they knew what man always had been and what he always will be."[59] This does not mean that Hofstadter interpreted the Founding Fathers' views of man as one which pictured him as simply selfish and evil, or that the lower classes must be "kept in their place." It does indicate that from the beginning he was aware of the divergent interests in American politics, and it would seem that this question seemed more important for him as the years passed. Compare, for example, the stress he puts on the importance of the differences in the conflict between the Federalists and the Jeffersonians in the early *American Political Tradition* and the later *Idea of Political Parties.*

When the Constitution was written and put into operation, the leaders still had to deal with the Founders' view of human nature, now as it expressed itself in factions or parties. This they deplored, but they knew they had to work with it. Speaking of Washington's view on the spirit of party, he writes, "As he saw, this spirit is unfortunately a part of human nature. It therefore exists under all governments, somewhat stifled and controlled, but it is at its very worst in popular governments."[60]

Then, as later, the American political tradition, however it might have been at odds on specific issues, shared a set of beliefs that was associated with human nature. Political and intellectual leaders believed in the rights of property, the philosophy of economic individualism, and the value of competition. In short, they have accepted "the economic virtues of capitalistic culture as necessary qualities of man."[61]

When Hofstadter wrote about the views of human nature espoused by the Founding Fathers, it sounds as if he is giving them his stamp of approval. Yet this is not the case. He contends that:

no man who is as well abreast of modern science as the Fathers were of eighteenth-century science believes any longer in unchanging human nature. Modern humanistic thinkers who seek for a means by which society may transcend eternal conflict and rigid adherence to property rights as its integrating principles can expect no answer in the philosophy of balanced government as it was set down by the Constitution makers of 1787.[62]

Still, he admits that in the modern era, influenced by a decade of neo-orthodoxy and existential thought, "a thinker like [Jonathan] Edwards, with his keen sense of human limitation, is always likely to seem to some of us profounder and in many ways more rewarding than, say, such a genial and externalized mind as Benjamin Franklin's."[63]

His analysis of the role of class conflict in understanding the American political tradition continued throughout the course of American history. When the battle between factions of the old established aristocracy of the early republic passed from the scene, a new force arose from the more democratic elements that Hofstadter saw in the new party men like Martin Van Buren. These were men from the middle or lower middle class, often self-made men with no direct connections with the leading families in their area. They came from a social class that valued the marginal advantages and limited prominence of lesser offices as they made their way to the top. "What they had was, by and large, hard earned, and there was a distinct edge of class resentment in their attitude toward patrician politicians . . . ."[64] In *The Idea of A Party System* he seems to be celebrating the ability of the professional politicians, "the people," to meet the new conditions of their own day by making the needed innovations in the system that their patrician opponents could not understand. The dynamism of the age had clearly passed from the hands of the old patricians to a group that was more closely in tune with the needs of "the people."

During those same years a few American analysts were actually developing an interpretation of American society that had a class basis. He cites Calhoun as one of the few American politicians, along with such intellectuals as Richard Hildreth and Orestes Brownson, who had a real sense for both social structure and class forces. "Before Karl Marx published the *Communist Manifesto*, Calhoun laid down an analysis of American politics and the sectional struggle which foreshadowed some of the seminal ideas of Marx's system"[65] In Hofstadter's interpretation, however, both Calhoun and Marx "overestimated the revolutionary capacities of the working class." The northern working class rather easily adjusted to the profit system. What Calhoun failed to see was that, by providing broad opportunities for the lower and middle-classes, the emerging Northern capitalist system provided a safety valve for popular discontents.[66]

Wendell Phillips was another prominent American who, as he moved from a concentration on abolition to a concern for the interests of labor "began to interpret American history as a series of class struggles." Hofstadter presents Phillips' views with obvious approval, but he adds, "except for his reliance upon the working class and his general economic interpretation of politics there was little of the Marxist in the American labor reformer."[67]

Examples of self-interest pursued by rational man continue as Hofstadter moves through American history. Although he emphasized the role of the Agrarian Myth and status explanations in the rise of the Populist movement, he was also aware that, "As a businessman, the farmer was appropriately hardheaded; he tried to act upon a cold and realistic strategy of self-interest."[68] The same concerns caused him to question Frederick Jackson Turner's interpretation of the West itself. The sectional principle of organization that Turner advocated, Hofstadter felt, could cause the historian to ignore other important elements of causation. "It may cause him to play down class or group conflict within the sections. It may cause him to describe people too much in terms of *where* they were, geographically, not enough in terms of *what* they were, vocationally and socially."[69]

According to Hofstadter, some of the readers of his analysis of the reasons for American imperialism at the time of the Spanish-American War viewed it as an attempt to present a psychological alternative to the economic interpretations. "I consider it," he countered, "less psychological than institutional; less an alternative than a necessary supplement to any economic interpretation that is to avoid running around on certain stubborn facts." Further, he believed that he had common ground with Walter LeFeber's economic interpretation on the long preparation for the open outbreak of imperialism in the 90s. The jingoism, which was by no means new in the 1890s, was used, according to Hofstadter, by politicians who wanted to divert the public mind from the real internal discontents that stemmed from the depression of 1893.[70] Still, he contends that the expression of that discontent by the Populists was not an attempt to develop a fundamental critique of industrial capitalism; they were simply trying to make it work.[71]

Hofstadter's understanding of the importance of economic issues for "the People" is evident. In explaining why the Mugwump reformers of the post-Civil War era found such a small following, he argues that:

reformers who concentrated upon a Civil Service Act, the tariff, or exposing the peccadilloes of politicians did not excite mass enthusiasm. Single-minded concern for honesty in public service is a luxury of the middle and upper classes. The masses do not care deeply about the honesty of public servants unless it promises to lead to some human fruition, some measurable easing of the difficulties of life.[72]

In the writings of the Progressive generation, he finds both a lower class bias and a rejection of the view of man presented in economic interpretations and Marxist ideas. For example, he states that Lester Ward's views on the role of the new state were "prompted by a lower-class bias," and that his rejection of Sumner and Spencer was motivated, at least in part, "by his sense of their aristocratic preferences."[73] But when he discusses Progressives in general what he finds is that what appealed to them about the economic interpretation of history was that it provided a rationale for the doctrine of progress. He points out that Beard himself belonged "both morally and materially to the possessing classes ...." "His radicalism, insofar as we can think of him as a radical, was like that of many other writers of the Progressive era, in that it reflected the conscience of the well-to-do as well as the critical spirit of the emerging American intelligentsia." For the Progressives in general, when they thought of the Marxist conceptions at all, they considered them over-generalized. Unlike Marxism socialists, they had no sentimental or moral attachments to the proletariat. They believed that they were dealing with a system that could be changed and reformed under the existing economic order, and "they would have shrunk from the conclusion that the existing state should be destroyed and supplanted by a new one based on a single class. What they sought was an open and pluralistic theory that would have the feeling of Marxism for hard realities without its monolithic implications.[74]

For Hofstadter the years since World War II continued to see this combination of interest and status concerns. He admits that he had been strongly drawn to a study of ethnic animosities, "which in America have been at times a substitute for the class struggle, and in any case has always affected its character." Even the McCarthy phenomenon which so troubled him and stirred him to action could not be identified with a social or economic class, "although its power probably rests largely upon its appeal to the less-educated members of the middle class."[75]

All of this implies that there actually is a class structure in the United States, but even the race struggle he basically saw as only the most poignant of America's ethnic problems. Indeed, throughout his career Hofstadter demonstrated little understanding of American racism apart from the continuing ethnic struggles that so concerned him. For example, in discussing the three major areas of the American past where he felt consensus history really broke down, he picks out the genuinely revolutionary aspects of the Revolution, the Civil War, and, finally notes, "It disposes us to turn away from one of the most significant facets of American social life—the racial, ethnic, and religious conflict with which our history is saturated."[76] Early in his career he believed that race prejudice arose from the economic circumstances surrounding it but he moved quickly to a position that concentrated on the psychological side of the slavery argument.[77]

Hofstadter readily conceded that earlier scholars had been aware that non-economics played a role in political behavior, but he felt that they lacked adequate analytic tools to deal with them. Consequently, scholars have placed much emphasis upon the obvious differences they have seen in the role assigned to reason as an important component of human nature in the writings of the Progressive historians and in those of a later period. It is obvious that Hofstadter did not place the same emphasis on reason as a determining factor in mass political behavior that Beard attributed to it. Hofstadter argued that modern scholars have a need for such tools as status considerations in studying political behavior precisely because of the excessive emphasis on rationalism that had characterized the preceding two generations of scholars who thought of political man "basically as a rational being who reckons as well as he can what his economic interests are, forms pressure groups and parties to advance these ideas—and as a citizen casts his vote in order to see them realized." Depth psychology and public opinion polls have made historians aware that politics can be a field for feelings and impulses that may be only marginally related to real issues. Modern historians and political writers, while they do not discount reason, interests and values, believe that man also expresses himself in politics according to identities, fears, and aspirations.[78] This does not mean that the modern historian dismisses reason as an aspect of human nature. "History is neither philosophy nor science," Hofstadter contends, "but it is rational discourse that has to proceed in accordance with certain rules . . . ." And it is through a study of history that man is provided with "an enormous area of thought in which we define our values and realize some of the possibilities of our own minds."[79]

In America one of the most pervasive notions which limited the rational operation of politics, in Hofstadter's opinion, was the Agrarian Myth. As he noted, "Here was the irony from which the farmer suffered above all others; the United States was the only country in the world that began with perfection and aspired to progress." By myth he meant, not "an idea that is simply false, but rather one that so effectively embodies men's values that it profoundly influences their way of perceiving reality and hence their behavior. In this sense myths may have varying degrees of fiction or reality. The agrarian myth became increasingly fictional as time went on." Originally the myth was not a popular one, but a literary product of the upper classes; by the last half of the eighteenth century, however, it was clearly formulated and almost universally accepted by the English mainland colonies. Although it came from English classical writers as a cultural importation, it took on new dimensions in the new world setting.[78]

In the imagery of the agrarian myth "the earth was characteristically a mother, trade a harlot . . . ." If an individual or a society deserted the ancestral ways, it was an invitation to Providential punishment. Farmers were not part of the overall business enterprise, sharing in its risks and rewards, but innocents who were victimized by some distant conspiracy. The myth was powerful in the first half of the nineteenth century because the nation was predominantly composed of literate and enfranchised farmers. Paradoxically, the myth came to be more and more widely embraced as it ceased to become a picture of reality.[79] As a matter of fact, the myth of the yeoman farmer had never expressed the actual aspirations of that group. "The ideal of the simple yeoman living close to nature, applying himself with loving care to the soil, and supplying virtually all his modest needs with his own labor and that of his family was an ideal first of the educated elite who read pastoral poetry and later of agrarian ideologues and politicians who wanted to claim a moral superiority to the farmer."[80] In fact, the American west was an arena for the expansion of the operation and methods of an expanding middleclass. The pioneer went West, not to live as a simple yeoman farmer, but to recreate the American standard of life that already existed in the east; he went "not to forge a utopian egalitarian society but to reenact the social differences of the older world—with himself now closer to the top."[81]

As America matured this irrational side of the ideal increasingly came into conflict with reality. America was richly endowed with land and resources; according to the myth, the natural result should be prosperity for the industrious yeoman. If such was not the case, it had to be because of a conspiracy against "the people." This enabled the Populist leaders to put forward what Hofstadter regarded as a basically crude conspiracy theory that saw the government and the new forces of big business enslaving the people through their philosophy of laissez-faire. This image of the Populists as increasingly bound up by the irrational doctrines of the agrarian myth was by no means Hofstadter's total picture of the reform movements of the late nineteenth century, but it was enough to convince his critics that he had abandoned the rational man fighting real economic deprivations that had inspired earlier generations of historians.

In fact the analysts are correct when they contend that this emphasis on irrational beliefs that leads people to see their enemies as engaged in a vast conspiracy as an important part of Hofstadter's picture of the political behavior of Americans, both in the past and in his own day. At the grass roots of American politics he found a strong tendency to believe that there is an essentially simple conspiratorial force out to destroy them. He hastens to add that the majority of Americans do not normally embrace these beliefs, but all too often politicians and intellectual leaders accept the notions of conspiracy and "so we go off on periodical psychic sprees that purport to be moral crusadses ...."[82] In the post-World War II era this paranoid style was clearly manifested in the extreme right-wing "who believe that we have lived for a generation in the grip of a vast conspiracy," but in the earlier periods of American history it had manifested itself on the left in democratic movements from anti-Masonry to Populism.[83]

Connected with the force of the Agrarian Myth was the whole concept of status anxieties. Hofstadter stirred up many scholars when he introduced the concept of status into the study of American political behavior. In doing so he was seemingly denying that man was basically a rational creature who utilized his reason to pursue his real economic interests. He was instead portraying human nature as basically emotional and irrational.

In fact he suggested that American political behavior had always been an inextricable mix of interest and status politics. In hard times, and in times of national emergency, politics is largely a matter of interests; in good times "status considerations among the masses can become much more influential in our politics."[84] He went on to make the controversial assertion that status considerations come into play both when a group's status is going up and when it is going down. Among old family, white, Anglo-Saxon, Protestants status becomes predominant when it is declining; on the contrary, it becomes important to many immigrant groups—notably Catholics—when they are gaining in their standing. In either case, its manifestations are not, as many fear, fascist or totalitarian, but peculiarly American.[85]

It was his contention that status anxieties of the newly affluent and fundamentalist groups were emphasized by the several scholars who wrote for Daniel Bell's *The Radical Right* because the authors felt that this was a neglected and unexplained side of the movement. Again, he does not deny the force of real social and economic factors, but he contends that earlier scholars had not taken sufficient notice of the fact that people also have deep emotional commitments—in religion, culture, race relations, etc.—which they hope to see realized in political action.[86] For his own part, Hofstadter states, "Although I am concerned here to discuss some of the neglected social-psychological elements in pseudo-conservatism, I do not wish to appear to deny the presence of important economic and political causes." McCarthyism itself, he contends, had no economic program. Unlike Father Coughlin's movement of the 30s, it did not appeal to the economically deprived but won support from the middle and upper ranks of society.[87]

Although he probably first embraced the status concept as a tool for understanding the troubling political climate of his own day, Hofstadter found it useful in explaining the unusual situation of a reform movement aprising, not, as was the usual case, in a time of economic problems, but in the midst of the generally prosperous years between 1900 and 1920. "It is my thesis," he wrote, that the old middleclass, "who might be designated broadly as the Mugwump type, were Progressives not because of economic deprivations but primarily because they were victims of an upheaval in status...."[88]

Among the most conspicuous losers from the status revolution who were intimately involved in the Progressive movement were the clergy; the academics who joined them in their call for reform came to that position from the opposite direction:

> The challenge they made to the *status quo* ... especially in the social sciences, was a challenge offered by an advancing group, growing year by year in number, confidence, and professional standing. Modern students of social psychology have suggested that certain social-psychological tensions are heightened both in social groups that are rising in the social scale and in those that are falling; and this may explain why two groups with fortunes as varied as the professoriate and the clergy gave so much common and similar support to reform ideologies.[89]

It is interesting that in one of his last books, a study of the development of the concept of party government in the early United States, the politicians and other spokesmen are presented as well rounded men who made distinctions on differences in ideology and reason and there is no mention of status in the whole book.

To whatever extent Hofstadter may have been "beyond innocence" in his interpretation of human nature and the structure of the American political system, there is no question that the moral nature of man was of considerable concern to him. He points out that even Beard in his economic interpretation of the Constitution did not question the moral nature of the Founding Fathers.[90]

Moral considerations clearly rose above economic considerations in his analysis of the abolitionist movement. For the most part the abolitionists "had no material stake in the conservation or destruction of the slave system, which was in the most literal sense none of their business." Nor does he make any reference to status considerations in their activities.

Among this group, Hofstadter writes most favorably of Wendell Phillips whom he describes as "a man of conscience" who "had an unconquerable faith in moral progress." Even such a successful politician as Abraham Lincoln could be imbued with moral idealism. Writing of one of Lincoln's statements, Hofstadter contends, "There is self-portraiture in the remark: one sees the moral idealism of the man; it is here, unquestionably ...." Even the Robber Barons, for all their faults, were men of conscience who firmly believed in the American mythology of opportunity for the common man and that "what they were doing would work to a final good."[91]

Speaking of the American political system in general, he notes that "the most prominent and pervasive failing is a certain proneness to fits of moral crusading that would be fatal if they were not sooner or later tempered with a measure of apathy and of common sense."[92] Even his disparaging comments on the old agrarian and entrepreneurial dreams are not designed to destroy them as real ultimate values. His interpretations of them are designed to safeguard them against their political misuse and to salvage those parts of them that are still meaningful for the development of the just society. Indeed, Hofstadter found moral and metaphysical aspects of human nature in instances where some other historians saw only the more distasteful forms of self-interest. In writing about the Spanish-American War, he contends that "the most striking thing about the war was that it originated not in imperialistic ambition but in popular humanitarianism," and "even those who talked about material gains showed a conspicuous and symptomatic inability to distinguish between interests, rights and duties."[93]

It was in discussing the reform elements of the turn of the century that Hofstadter got most involved in analyzing the moral aspects of American politics. Success in the great corporate world seemed to have only tenuous relations to character building; when one examined the behavior of the new plutocracy, it appeared to be little related to civic responsibility. This did not mean that the reformers of the day looked toward the future with despair for they believed that the nation could be redeemed if the good citizens were made aware of their duties. Their efforts were directed toward the restoration of an economic individualism and political democracy which they believed had existed in an earlier age. These traditional values had been almost destroyed by the trusts and the corrupt political machine, but civic purity and political morality could be restored by the efforts of the people. Moral qualities were indestructible and when decent men were once again installed in office they would lead the country forward.[94]

In their efforts to correct the evils of existing society, the Progressives adopted a philosophy of pragmatic liberalism that seemed on the surface to destroy the old absolutes. Hofstadter agreed with the contemporary analyst J. Allen Smith and the later historian Eric Goldman that there were dangers in this approach, but his reservations about Progressives were just the reverse of theirs. "My criticism of the progressivism of that period," he stipulated, "is the opposite of Smith's—not that the Progressives most typically undermined or smashed standards, but that they set impossible standards, that they were victimized, in brief, by a form of moral absolutism."[95]

Elsewhere he softened his criticism of the role of morals in politics by presenting the Progressives as the pioneers of the welfare state. He says that,

they were determined to remedy the most pressing and dangerous social ills of industrial society, and in the attempt they quickly learned that they could not achieve their ends without using the power of the administrative state. Moreover, they asserted—and they were the first in our history to do so with real practical success—the idea that government cannot be viewed merely as a cold and negative policing agency, but that it has a wide and pervasive responsibility for the welfare of its citizens, and for the poor and powerless among them. For this, Progressivism must be understood as a major episode in the history of the American conscience.[96]

But the line between Progressivism and the New Deal was far from direct in Hofstadter's opinion. The pragmatic spirit of the Roosevelt years, with its emphasis upon results, was a real change from the Progressive view of society which linked economic life with character building. Indeed, he saw a reversal of the ideological roles of conservatives and reformers in the two periods. In all ideologies, he suggests, there is an appeal to both moral principles and to the practical necessity of making society work. Before the New Deal, however, the strength of the conservative side had been their appeal to the hard facts of institutional structure; it was the reformers who appealed to moral sentiments. This had definitely, in his view, been the case during the Progressive era. "During the New Deal, however, it was the reformers whose appeal to the urgent practical realities was most impressive .... It was the conservatives ... who represented the greater moral indignation ...."[97] He presented Thurman Arnold, the hard-headed realist who was willing to forfeit the morality and sentimentality of the past, as the spokesman for the New Deal. Yet he did not feel that Arnold answered, or even posed "the very real and important questions ... concerning the relations between morals and politics, or between reason and politics." In his analysis of the New Deal, Hofstadter says he was merely trying to be descriptive. There were important questions of political ethics with which he did not deal. He certainly did not intend to imply that the morals of the New Dealers were inferior to those of their critics.

My essential interest is in the fact that the emergency that gave rise to the New Deal also gave rise to a transvaluation of values and that the kind of moralism that I have identified with the dominant patterns of thought among the Progressives was inherited not so much by their successors among the New Dealers, who tended to repudiate them, as by the foes of the New Deal.[98]

Another aspect of Hofstadter's view of politics that does not fit in with the rational man pursuing his own self-interest as described by the Progressive historians—not even with his own status interpretation—is the paranoid style. Unlike the regular working politician, the paranoid is a militant leader who does not view social conflict as something to be mediated and compromised. The enemy is seen as an amoral, superhuman menace, not part of the stream of history but the product of someone's will, whose methods may be imitated in order to achieve the final victory. Throughout history, from Maria Monk to contemporary ex-Communists, renegades from the enemy cause are particularly valued by the paranoid leader.[99]

This element in American politics and thought tends to secularize the Manachean side of the Christian tradition. Social issues are reduced to a battle between Good and Evil. The evil may be Communism or an international bankers' syndicate, but the rhetoric manifests itself in the same crusading mentality which supposes that all the ills of society can be solved by some final victory over the real or imagined evil force. The feelings of persecution systemized in grandiose theories of conspiracy are directed not against the individual, as in clinical paranoia, but against the whole nation or culture.[100]

More general than the paranoid style in America has been a deep distrust of authority. Madisonian pluralism in politics, Hofstadter suggests, owes a great debt to the example of religious liberty and toleration that had developed in the eighteenth century colonies. The tradition of dissenting Protestantism foreshadowed the American political tradition. "That fear of arbitrary power which is so marked in American political expression had been shaped to a large degree by the experience men of dissenting sects had had with persecution."[101] Freedom of religion became an example for freedom in the other spheres of society, and the libertarian writers in England who had meant so much to the colonists came from the tradition of religious dissent. If error could be tolerated in the crucial sphere of religious faith, Americans could also learn to tolerate error—however much they might dislike the factional influence of parties—in the wider social and political arena. A fear of authority, the sense that they might be divested of control over their own affairs, became an established trait in the American national character. It could be turned against government, as it had been during the years leading up to the Revolution; it could be used to justify secession or postpone for decades the governmental responsibilities for the good of society that had been adopted far earlier in Western Europe. Even later it could be used to combat the innovations of the New Deal. On the other hand, it could be utilized against business as it was in the bank war and in the Progressive period when Americans developed a widespread suspicion that business was becoming a closed system.[102]

William A. Williams, one of Hofstadter's early critics, attacked *The Age of Reason* as a transformation of history into an ideology. Whether it was consciously done or not did not matter to Williams. "However reached," he contended, "the conclusion indicates that the predominant group of American intellectuals is so wholly immersed in contemporary American society that no member of it can deal with the past, present or future save in terms of the present."[103] Hofstadter, himself, despite his early attachment to a Marxian analysis, denied that ideology played a real part in American political thinking. Even Darwinism had a dual potential; it was capable of being used to support opposing ideologies. The ascendancy of the rugged individualist's interpretation of the new science was due to the fact that American society saw its own image in the tooth-and-claw version of Darwinism. When the American middle class shrank from this principle the flimsy logic of the social Darwinists was easily demolished.[104]

The two party system as it had existed in the United States, far from being the ideological battle that Beard and Parrington had portrayed, hinged upon the recognition that the other party constitutes a loyal opposition; each side accepted the good intentions of the other. Major parties had always been coalitions of diverse elements with a strong premium placed on practicality rather than ideology.[105] An essential feature of the American political parties has been "their lack of ideological orientation." Even third parties in American politics have functioned largely as pressure groups, "and in this respect they are a curious combination of European ideological or special-interest parties and American interest groups." Even in Jackson's day, when the idea of party government was really coming to be accepted, the newly formed Democratic party, "even though founded on a commitment to republican principles, became an anti-ideological force."[106]

His only real admission that ideology may have been involved in American history before the Post-World War II period came in connection with the Civil War. In that conflict, he conceded, "one may differ as to whether to call the impassioned arguments of the North and South 'ideological' differences—but if this was not an ideological conflict (and I think it was), we can only conclude that Americans do not *need* ideological conflict to shed blood on a large scale."[107]

He was deeply concerned that the Goldwater campaign of 1964 was changing this non-ideological character of American politics. He emphasized that in the past, the American political party had been a consensual arrangement, a non-ideological group run by experienced and practical men whose every intention was to draw together a coalition of interests that were broad enough to win the presidency and then to run the country effectively. But Goldwater changed all this by making an ideological faction dominant. "If he is successful, whether elected or not, in consolidating this party coup, he will have brought about a realignment of the parties that will put the democratic process in this country in jeopardy."[108]

When it came to ideas as opposed to ideology, the mature Hofstadter was less certain about cause and effect. Just as the Progressive generation of historians (and perhaps especially Beard) were ambiguous about what role ideas played in the makeup of human nature, Hofstadter had some difficulty in dealing with the same problem. The position he usually espoused emphasized the interconnection between social causes and ideas. "Ideas," he wrote in his only real study of intellectual history, "have effects as well as causes," but he made it clear that the abstract truth and logic of ideas are less important than their suitability to the intellectual currents and the social conditions of the age.[109]

This is not to say that ideas are of no importance in changing the belief systems of society. The vital contribution of the pragmatists, for example, was their belief in the effectiveness of ideas, a position that was essential to the reform efforts of the turn of the century. Whereas Spencer and the Social Darwinists had stood for determinism and the control of man by the existing environment, the pragmatists argued for man's freedom to think and act and in so doing to change the environment itself.[110] Rational men were agreed that intellectual power, the ability to think and act, is one of the fundamental aspects of human nature and an attribute of human dignity.[111] Mind and consciousness are "not merely passive or adaptive," they can change the environment and when they do "the conditions of biological evolution are not only superceded, they are in a sense reversed." "I agree that ideas do have effects in history," he wrote, and he hastened to add that these effects are not always for the good. "I insist that ideas, though they have consequences, must also be thought of as *being* consequences themselves."

Hofstadter makes it quiet clear, however, that ideas do have an inner dialectic of their own. In explaining the change from the conflict emphasis of Progressive historians to the consensus views of the later era, he denied that this was due solely to the changes in the political environment. Progressives had pushed polarized conflict as an historical explanation as far as it could go; younger historians had to follow the inner dialectic of ideas and look in another direction if any new insights into American history were to be found. In the process the old Progressive "antimony" between ideas and interests was dissolved and was replaced "by an ability to recapture the meaning of ideas in history by seeing how they function in their pragmatic institutional setting ...."[13]

But while Hofstadter believed that ideas constitute an important aspect of human nature, he made it very clear that such ideas do not operate in a vacuum. In the body of his book on social Darwinism in America he discussed the ideas of the various interpreters of the new biology much as though each was a logical interpretation of a formulative idea; in the conclusion, however, he made his position clear. Here he stated that the changing interpretations of the new scientific principles was "a clear example of the principle that changes in the structure of social ideas wait on general changes in economics and political life. In determining whether such ideas are accepted, truth and logic are less important criteria than suitability to the intellectual needs and preconceptions of social interests."[114]

While ideas are an important part of human dignity, new ideas have a difficult time being heard in a society that is such a flourishing success as the United States has tended to be. Practical politicians, except in revolutionary times, are circumscribed by a rather narrow range of ideas that fit in with the existing climate of opinion and sustain their culture. "They differ, sometimes bitterly, over current issues, but they also share a general framework of ideas . . . ."[115]

In light of the fact that they are supposed to be polar opposites, it is interesting to take a closer look at Hofstadter's own account of the way Beard himself dealt with ideas as an aspect of human nature. As Hofstadter looked at the Progressive historians's work he found a dynamic relationship between interests and ideas which Beard set down in re-evaluating his own most famous book in 1937. As he expressed it, "In political history, if not in all history, there are no ideas with which interests are not associated and there are no interests utterly devoid of ideas."[116] Hofstadter agreed with this but pointed out some dangers that are involved in the position. "The first is that ideas—or all those intangible, emotional, moral and intellectual forces that may roughly be combined under the rubric of ideas—will somehow be dissolved and that we will be left only with interests on our hands." There is the further danger that the historian may think he is more capable than he is of ascertaining where interests begin and ideas leave off. Hofstadter sees Beard as picturing men as simply perceiving their interests out of thin air and then drifting into an acceptance of those ideas that would further those interests. He suggests instead that interests are, in large part, a reflection of inherited ideas and experiences. Ideas, in other words, "themselves constitute interests, in that they are repositories of past interests and that they present us with claims of their own that have to be satisfied.'" He contends that Beard was inept throughout his career in dealing with the ideas-interests formula and that he was far "less interesting as a historian of ideas, of moral impulses, of literature and culture, than when he wrote about the sweep of economic forces."[117]

Mind and its operation on the ideas that were part of human nature were an integral part of Hofstadter's view of the American past and present. In those long discussions with Kazin and their friends in the dark days of the 30s the role of the intellectual occupied a central place. For Hofstadter, it is through the intellectual that the life of the mind naturally expresses itself. "For the life of thought, even though it may be regarded as the highest form of human activity, is also a medium through which other values are refined, reasserted, and realized in the human community." The intellectual, consequently, believes that the world should be responsive to "his capacity for rationality, his passion for justice and order; out of this conviction arises much of his value to mankind and, equally, much of his abilty to do mischief." Historically, this quest has placed the intellectual on the left politically. This is not a peculiarity of the United States, but the American intellectual has usually been associated with causes and positions that are liberal, radical, utopian or anti-institutional. Hofstadter suggests that even the spokesmen for anti-intellectualism, "are almost always devoted to some ideas, and much as they may hate the regnant intellectuals among their living contemporaries, they may be devotees of some intellectuals long dead—Adam Smith perhaps, or Thomas Aquinas, or John Calvin or even Karl Marx."[118]

Respect for the intellectual and for the life of the mind has clearly varied during the course of American history. In the early days the Puritan clergy came as close to being an intellectual ruling class as anything America was to see, but even during the Revolution and the early years of the Republic the political leaders could be classed as intellectuals.[119] Hofstadter's main concern as he looked at his own society and at the history of America, however, was why this aspect of human nature had been consistently downgraded. What were the common strains that bound together the suspicion and resentment of the life of the mind and worked to minimize the influence of that life?

The first strain was the religious evangelicalism that began in the Great Awakening and gained strength in the decades after the Revolution. For the evangelical the source of knowledge was God or nature—the difference between the two was not always evident—which gave a clear preference for a wisdom of intuition which was thought to be natural or God-given, as opposed to the rationality of the Puritans which was artificial or cultivated. Anything that diminished the role of rationality and learning in religion often later diminished its role in secular culture. There was nothing distinctive about American religious anti-intellectualism, but in this country the balance between traditional established religion and revivalist or enthusiastic movements was shifted early and drastically to the latter.[120]

The second strain came along with the rise of popular democracy. In the American outlook the belief that the common man could, without much preparation, pursue the professions and run the government was fundamental. As popular democracy became strong and dominant,

it reenforced the widespread belief in the superiority of inborn, intuitive, folkish wisdom over the cultivated, oversophisticated, and self-interested knowledge of the literate, and the well-to-do. Just as the evangelicals repudiated a learned religion and a formally constituted clergy in favor of the wisdom of the heart and direct access to God, so did advocates of equalitarian politics propose to dispense with trained leadership in favor of the native practical sense of the ordinary man with its direct access to truth.[121]

In the absence of either a hereditary aristocracy or state patronage, art and learning in the United States were dependent upon commercial wealth and the personal views of the business class were always a matter of special importance to the intellectual life. In the stratified society of the eighteenth century when a significant part of the upper class which controlled business was fairly cosmopolitan, this fact was not particularly destructive to intellectual pursuits. But, as the nineteenth century progressed and businessmen withdrew from both culture and politics to devote all of their energies to the economic development of the nation, it became increasingly important. It was not that business was more anti-intellectual or more philistine than other major segments of society but simply that it was the "most powerful and pervasive interest in American life."[122]

Intellectuals may have lost their influence upon American society during the booming decades when the United States was building its industrial plant but they reasserted themselves in the generation that produced Beard and Parrington. As Hofstadter put it:

> Whenever an important change takes place in modern society, large sections of the intellectuals, the professional and opinion-making classes, see the drift of events and throw their weight on the side of what they feel is progress and reform. In few historical movements have these classes played a more striking role than in Progressivism.[123]

The coarse, materialistic society that had emerged during the latter decades of the nineteenth century had produced among the cultivated middle class a coterie of alienated intellectuals such as this country had not witnessed for a long time. These intellectuals could find no place for themselves in either the dog-eat-dog world of business or the shoulder-hitting world of boss-ridden politics. Even during the Progressive Era these sons and daughters of the Mugwumps had to reexamine their commitment to laissez-faire and their aristocratic notions and replace both with a new enthusiasm for popular government and a concern for the discontented.[124]

As the machinery of the society became more complex during the Progressive Era, however, the intellectual—especially in the form of the expert in various fields—rose to a new position of importance. These men did not hark back to the ineffectual civil service reforms of the late nineteenth century, but forward to the brains trust of the New Deal. As the Progressive movement emerged from the state level (most notably in Wisconsin), the university became the training ground for the new civil servants. The horizons for the intellectual broadened as he found himself in touch, not only with the higher reaches of political power but with the national mood as well. The long-standing estrangement between the life of the mind and the life of politics was temporarily overcome as scholars like Dewey, J. Allen Smith and Beard emerged with empirical, specialized skills fostered by the new university movement.[125]

This new unity between the intellectuals and the broader society was short-lived. The people soon turned on the intellectuals as prophets of war and of needless reform, while the intellectuals rejected their earlier supporters as boobs, Babbitts, and fanatics. The intellectuals, upon whose activities the political culture of the Progressive Era had depended, retreated from public careers toward the personal and private spheres.

During the 1920s, "even in those with a strong impulse toward dissent, bohemianism triumphed over radicalism."[126]

It took the trauma of the Great Depression and the advent of the New Deal to bring the popular cause in politics and the dominant mood of the intellectuals back into harmony. During the 1930s "the New Deal brought the force of mind into closer relation with power than it had been within the memory of any living man—closer than it had been since the days of the Founding Fathers."[127]

Paradoxically, in the years following World War II, while intellectuals resented the continuing strain of anti-intellectualism in society, they were troubled in a more profound way by their acceptance. During the upsurge of anti-intellectualism that was associated with McCarthyism, the intellectuals (especially of the middle and older generations) did not—as they had in the 20s—respond with a counterattack on the values of "the people." Hofstadter points to the famous *Partisan Review* interviews in 1952 as proof of the fact that the great bulk of intellectuals accepted American society and values. When such a pseudo-intellectual as Adlai Stevenson came on the national scene in 1952 he was embraced by intellectuals "with a readiness and a unanimity that seems without parallel in American history."[128]

Yet this was not a situation with which Hofstadter was completely comfortable. In an interview he said, "I think there is something valuable in the intellectual's alienation. David Riesman once said that he thought that American intellectuals did best for their country when they were most against it. And I think there is a lot to that."[129]

Earlier scholars, Hofstadter realized, had known that non-economic factors influenced political behavior, but they had few analytic tools to deal with them. Their rationalistic bias was broken down by his generation of scholars through the impact of political events, public opinion polls, and depth psychology. The wealth of the country and the absence of sharp class-consciousness had blunted direct economic conflict and made politics, at least in times of prosperity, an arena for the expression of emotions and prejudices; but, according to Hofstadter's view of human nature, "men often respond to frustration with acts of aggression and allay their anxieties by threatening acts against others."[130] If this is not a universal characteristic of human nature, it is at least characteristic of Western man and is by no means uniquely American. It has, however, been an important aspect of the history of the United States. The primary significance of the Spanish-American War, for example, was that it served "as an outlet for expressing aggressive impulses while presenting itself, quite truthfully, as an idealistic and humanitarian crusade."[131]

Domestically, Hofstadter contended, Americans have been able to convince themselves that they are peaceful and well-behaved in spite of the fact that their history is the story of violence, but he agreed with Beard that man has a proclivity for violence. Despite the extraordinary frequency and commonplaceness of violence throughout our history, such instances have been circumscribed and on a small scale and "the primary rationale for violence comes from the established order itself." "It has been unleashed against the abolitionists, Negroes, Orientals, and other ethnic or racial or ideological minorities, and has been used ostensibly to protect America, the Southern, the White Protestant, or simply the established middle-class way of life and morals." While almost commonplace in America, violence has lacked cohesion and an ideology. It has been "too various, diffuse, and spontaneous to be forged into a single, sustained, inveterate hatred shared by entire social classes." Intermittent group warfare, based on racial-ethnic antagonism has taken the place of class warfare.[132]

In spite of the violence that Hofstadter so clearly recognized, one of the major criticisms that has been leveled against Post-World War II historiography, especially as it carried over into the developing American Studies movement, was the notion that the United States was unique, that here man's interests and perhaps his nature were different from what they were in the rest of the world. Hofstadter stated baldly—with perhaps a hint of irony—"the United States was the only country in the world that began with perfection and aspired to progress."[133] The American attitude toward the past was an egalitarian protest against the institutions of the old world with its monarchies, its aristocrats and its exploitation of the people. It was a rationalistic reaction against superstition, a forward-looking and ambitious protest against the pessimism and the passivity of the old world.[134] In consequence, if not intent, this attitude has been anti-cultural, but what elements of truth did it contain for a scholar like Hofstadter?

Hofstadter seems to have agreed with Crevecour that the American was a new man. He says of Frederick Jackson Turner that he was the first American historian to see that if the peculiar nature of American history and the American character is to be understood it is necessary to analyze certain repetitive economic and sociological processes that have shaped men and institutions in the American environment.[135] The followers of Turner greatly over-estimated the force of the frontier; yet in the colonial period (when there was so much frontier and so little society) "the leverage of the frontier was at its greatest, and it cannot be minimized." Indeed, if one can get away from Turner's contention that the frontier was the source of democracy in the United States and look at the element of American uniqueness, there is a sound basis for rehabilitating (at least to some degree) the frontier thesis. Turner correctly saw the United States as an open society with a growth potential that was irresistible. His theory rested upon his conception of the intangible psychological and moral effects of the West; it oriented the American mind toward space and expansion and gave it a different cast from the European mind. It developed American confidence, optimism and adaptability.[136]

It was not only the boundless frontier that made America unique; its peculiarity was produced by the very nature of its formation. The English colonies on the mainland were the basis for the first post-feudal nation, the first to grow from its beginnings under the influence of Protestantism, nationalism and modern capitalism. Its inhabitants were gathered together by men with secular motives of profit and empire. Here, too, the English system of competitive pluralism in religion, as an attraction for immigrants, of earning profits from land and trade, was decisively superior to the French and Spanish church-state systems. That the fate of the inhabitants in this new society was varied, Hofstadter was quite willing to concede. He devoted considerable attention to the story of the large number of unfree servants and slaves who formed an important part of the early labor force. He noted that students of American mobility had destroyed the old myths about the possibilities for these groups; their chances to rise to positions of wealth and prominence were "statistically negligible." Yet free labor throughout the English mainland colonies was well paid from the beginning. What emerged was a labor force that was free, not only with the direct forms of need, but also free from a spirit of subservience. New Englanders in particular "had quite unwittingly devised an economy as close to egalitarianism as anything in the Western world."[137]

By the eighteenth century, America was a middle-class world—middle class in the sense that most of the people were neither conspicuously rich nor distressingly poor. It was a society where the poor man (if white) could edge himself into the middle class, and in which the upper classes who governed had to do so with an eye to conducting themselves in such a way that they did not alienate the numerous, aggressive, and largely enfranchised middle class. Eighteenth century America recognized classes in their own way, but what one saw among all these classes "was the disciplined ethic of work, the individual assertiveness, the progressive outlook, the preference for dissenting religions, and the calculating and materialistic way of life associated with the middle class." Even the mercantile upper crust in the cities and—given the entrepreneurial ways of most planters—in the South, was an open class with few other barriers to acceptance beyond wealth.

This middle class world was different from the post-industrial world in that it was a rural middle class society, peopled by farmers and small planters and by those who were in some way dependent on them. It was different in that those who started life below the middle class "not only shared its aspirations but had a significant chance to realize them within a lifetime. And in this America was supreme."[138]

The unique origins of the American colonies helped the United States to develop the first political party system. The United States was the pioneer nation in the development of broadly based social structures which mediated between the public and the parliamentary decision-making process in a regular manner. American priority is still more impressive if one takes into account mass participation in the political process. The unusual thing here was the development of a responsible and effective political opposition, "an immensely sophisticated notion," that was never followed by other nations. "The American system remains unique, distinguishable even from the British system to which it owes so much."[139] Because it had little to block it by way of aristocratic or labor-socialist theories, the idea of competition as an economic, political and moral force also developed stronger roots in the United States than elsewhere. Competition was a way of life, a creed, which was manifest in the irrational attack on the Second Bank of the United States and in the long history of the anti-trust movement.[140]

The anti-European thinking which had begun early in the United States and which continued to remain a strong component of its outlook throughout the nineteenth and twentieth centuries was given new impetus by World War II. "The collapse of Europe, the horrors of the war and death camps, brought about a revulsion from European society and politics, a disposition to look once again for the promise of the future on native grounds, a revival of the old feeling that the United States is better and different."[141]

This examination of Hofstadter's writings would seem to confirm many of the criticisms of his ideas and working hypotheses, and, in effect, the bulk of the work of the post-World War II establishment. It is clear that he, along with the scholars in the American Studies movement, was guilty of over-emphasizing what has been called "holism" or the organic view of American culture. He was aware, however, of the role of sub-cultures (which he preferred to analyze under the rubric of ethnic groups) and he wrote about them at length. In most of his writings he failed to deal adequately with Blacks (except as yet another ethnic group) but he handled their story at least as adequately as Turner and Beard did the problem of slavery. Critics have argued that he failed to take account of the very different concerns and attitudes of working class groups, but this is not really a valid charge. Through most of his works he did deal with this problem. In his last effort, perhaps responding to such criticism of his earlier works, he devoted a sizable part of the study to indentured servants and Blacks. But, while he stressed the importance of both groups in American colonial history, he still insisted upon the crucial role of a middle class value system which permeated that society. While he studied both the role of violence and the thrust of imperialism in American history, it is clear that he did not consider gender as an independent variable.

As many have pointed out, he probably did less basic work in research in primary materials than most major historians. Still, as Merle Curti once suggested, perhaps there is room in an age of increasing specialization for the interpretive generalist—especially one of such synthetic abilities as

Hofstadter.

In terms of the fundamental criticism that Hofstadter emphasized the irrational man in his studies of American political thought and behavior, some have suggested that perhaps status considerations are as rational in their own way as the more usual economic concerns that were stressed by the Progressives. I believe that both Hofstadter and most of his critics would have rejected this notion. Beard put forward a rational man who clearly understood the "hard" economic realities and acted rationally to improve his conditions. Hofstadter recognized "hard" economic realities, but he was particularly concerned with such additional considerations in political decision making as status—which to both him and his critics were emotional and essentially irrational factors.

This does not mean that the differences between Beard and Hofstadter constituted the kind of paradigmatic split that has sometimes been suggested. Neither believed that man was completely the rational man of classical economics; both believed that progress was possible. Hofstadter was simply much less certain that it would come about in the near future than Beard had been in the more confident era during which he wrote most of his seminal works.

Nor does it follow that Hofstadter's view of man and his interpretation of the American past were, as has so often been asserted, basically a complacent surrender to the general prosperity of the post-World War II period or a paranoid reaction to Communism. To fully analyze the explanations for the differences between the interpretations of Hofstadter and his contemporaries and those of the Progressive generation would require a book-length study. But it does seem clear that the differences were not as great as many have argued and that those which are most significant are the result of a different climate of opinion that had many manifestations—including great advances in the state of the social sciences during Hofstadter's lifetime and the inner dialectic of ideas which almost determined that he would have to reject some of the basic preconceptions of his admitted intellectual progenitors.

Notes

[1] See Les K. Adler and Thomas G. Patterson, "Red Fascism: The Merger of Nazi Germany and Soviet Russia in the American Images of Totalitarianism, 1930s-1950s," *American Historical Review*, LXXV (April, 1970), 1046-64.

[2] See Edward A. Purcell, Jr., *The Crisis of Democratic Theory: Scientific Naturalism and the Problem of Value.* Lexington: The Univeristy of Kentucky Press, 1973.

[3] Some of the more interesting criticism of the postwar scholarship are to be found in the following: John Higham, "The Cult of the 'American Consensus'; Homogenizing Our History," *Commentary*, XXVII (February, 1959), 93-100; and "Beyond Consensus: The Historian as a Moral Critic," *American Historical Review*, LXVII (April, 1962), 609-25; Barton Berstein, ed., *Towards a New Past: Dissenting Essays in American History*, New York:

Random House,1968; Jesse Lemisch, *On Active Service in War and Peace*, Toronto: New Hogtown Press, 1975; John P. Diggins, "Consciousness and Ideology in American History: The Burden of Daniel Boorstin," *American Historical Review*, LXXVI (February, 1971), 99-118; Robert Berkhofer, "Clio and the Culture Concept: Some Impressions of a Changing Relationship in American Historiography," *Social Science Quarterly*, LIII (September, 1972);. David Thelen, "Social Tensions and the Origin of Progressivism," *Journal of American History* LX (September, 1969), 323-41; Norman Pollack, "Hofstadter on Populism: A Critique of the *Age of Reform*," *Journal of Southern History*, XXVI (November, 1960), 478-500; Mariam J. Morton, *The Terrors of Illogical Politics: Liberal Historians in a Conservative Mood*, Cleveland: The Press of Case Western Reserve University, 1972; Cecil F. Tate, *The Search for a Method in American Studies*, Minneapolis: Univ. of Minnesota Press, 1973; and Gene Wise, *American Historical Explanations*, second edition, revised. Minneapolis: Univ. of Minnesota Press, 1980. Two other studies of post-World War II intellectuals need to be mentioned. Robert F. Fowler, *Believing Skeptics: American Political Intellectuals, 1945-1964*, Westport, Conn.: Greenwood Press, 1978; and Bernard Sternsher, *Consensus, Conflict and American Historians*, Bloomington: Indiana Univ. Press, 1975.

[4]Madison: Univ. of Wisconsin Press, 1980; and Columbia: Univ. of Missouri Press, 1968.

[5]*American Historical Explanations*.

[6]*Human Nature in American Historical Thought*, pp. 63-73.

[7]*Ibid.*, pp. 66-69.

[8]Skotheim, Princeton: Princeton Univ. Press, 1966, pp. 95-98, 100-03, 105-08; *Human Nature in Historical Thought*, pp. 70-71.

[9]Susan Stout Baker, "Out of Engagement, Richard Hofstadter: The Genesis of a Historian," Ph. D. Dissertation, Case Western Reserve, 1972, pp. 133, 136.

[10]*Ibid.*, pp. 148-9.

[11]*Ibid.*, pp. 150-1.

[12]*Ibid.*, pp. 165-73.

[13]*Ibid.*, pp. 203-14.

[14]*Ibid.*, pp. 227, 151.

[15]*Ibid.*, pp. 236-41.

[16]*Ibid.*, p. 245.

[17]Undated letter to Kazin, c. 1940. Cited in *Ibid.*, p. 394.

[18]RH to Harvey Swados, 11-7-37; cited in *Ibid.*, p. 241.

[19]RH to Swados, 4-30-38; cited in *Ibid.*, p. 267.

[20]RH to Swados, 2-16-39; cited in *Ibid.*, p. 331.

[21]RH to Swados, 10-20-39; cited in *Ibid.*, p. 341.

[22]RH to Swados, 12-16-40; cited in *Ibid.*, p. 357.

[23]See Lawrence A. Cremin, "Richard Hofstadter, 1916-70: A Biographical Memoir," Syracuse: National Academy of Education, 1972; and Alfred Kazin, *Starting Out in the Thirties*, New York: Vintage Books, 1980, p. 100; and Kazin, "Richard Hofstadter, 1916-70," *American Scholar*, XL (Summer, 1971), 39-40.

[24]Cremin, p. 3.

[25]Kazin, *Starting Out in the Thirties*, p. 100.

[26]RH to Swados, 9-20-39 and 10-20-39; cited Baker, pp. 343-4.

[27]See Baker, p. 339.

[28]*Ibid.*, p. 345.

[29]See *Ibid.*, p. 302.

[30]RH to Swados, 11—1—38; cited *Ibid.*, p. 302.

[31]See "Jefferson's Ideas on Class Relations," Manuscript in Richard Hofstadter Collection, Butler Library, Columbia University.

[32]See Baker, pp. 317-25.

[33]Baker interview with Stampp, April 2-3, 1981; cited *Ibid.*, p.382.

[34]See David W. Moore, "Liberalism and Liberal Education at Columbia University: The Columbia Careers of Jacques Barzun, Lionel Trilling, Richard Hofstadter, Daniel Bell and C. Wright Mills," Ph.D. Dissertation, Univ. of Maryland, 1978, p. 89 and 171.

[35]"Richard Hofstadter, C. Wright Mills, and the Critical Ideal," *American Scholar*, XLVIII (Winter, 1977-78), 79.

[36]*Ibid.*,

[37]See Moore, p. 119.

[38]Quoted in *Ibid.*, pp. 318-19. See also papers and letters in the Hofstadter Collection.

[39]*The Progressive Historians: Turner, Beard, Parrington.* New York: Knopf, 1968, footnote 9, p. 452.

[40]*Ibid.*, xiv.

[41]*The Paranoid Style in American Politics*, New York: Knopf, 1965, ix.

[42]*Ibid.*

[43]Cited in Moore, p. 211.

[44]See David Hawke, "Interviews: Richard Hofstadter," *History*, III (1960), p. 140.

[45]"History and the Social Sciences," in Fritz Stern, ed. *The Varieties of History*, Cleveland: Meridian Books, 1956, p. 362.

[46]Baker interview with Kazin, 11-18-80, cited Baker, p. 383.

[47]*The Age of Reform*, New York: Knopf, 1956, p. 10.

[48]"Political Parties," in C. Vann Woodward, ed., *The Comparative Approach to American History*, New York: Basic Books, 1968, p. 207.

[49]See "Beard and the Constitution: The History of An Idea," *American Quarterly*, VII (Fall, 1950), 196.

[50]*The Paranoid Style in American Politics and Other Essays*, New York: Knopf, 1965, p. 205.

[51]*Ibid.*, p. x.

[52]*The American Political Tradition and the Men Who Made It*, New York: Vintage Books, 1956, vii-viii. Originally published in 1948.

[53]Woodward, p. 216.

[54]See "Parrington and the Jeffersonian Tradition," *Journal of the History of Ideas*, II (October, 1941), 391-400.

[55]*American Political Tradition*, pp. 3, 16; see also *Ibid.*, p. 7.

[56]*The Idea of a Political Party: The Rise of Legitimate opposition in the United States, 1780-1840*, Berkeley: Univ. of California Press, 1969, pp. 74-75.

[57]*American Political Tradition*, p. 15.

[58]*Ibid.*, pp. 4-5.

[59]*Ibid.*, p. 7.

[60]*Idea of a Party System*, p. 98.

[61]*American Political Tradition*, viii.

[62]*Ibid.*, pp. 16-17.

[63]*America at 1750: A Social Portrait.* New York: Random House, 1973, p. 243.

[64]*Idea of a Party System*, p. 241.

[65]*American Political Tradition*, p. 69.

[66]*Ibid.*, p. 88.

[67]*Ibid.*, pp. 158, 161.

[68]*Age of Reform*, p. 46.

[69]*Progressive Historians*, p. 97.

[70]*Paranoid Style*, pp. 146, 148-52.

[71]*Ibid.*, 238-86.

[72]*American Political Tradition*, p. 177.

[73]*Social Darwinism in American Thought.* Philadelphia: Univ. of Pennsylvania Press, 1944, p. 82.

[74]*Progressive Historians*, pp. 200, 168, 186.

[75]*Paranoid Style*, pp. xii, 44.

[76]*Progressive Historians*, p. 459.

[77]Unpublished manuscript, Hofstadter Collection.

[78]*Paranoid Style*, pp. 90, ix, vii-ix.

[79]*Ten Issues in American Politics.* New York: Oxford, 1968, xii.

[78]*Age of Reform*, pp. 36, footnote p. 24, 25-26.

[79]*Ibid.*, pp. 33, 35, 29-30.

[80]1750, pp. 176-77.

[81]*Progressive Historians*, p. 160.

[82]*Age of Reform*, pp. 16-17.

[83]Paranoid Style, xi.

[84]*Ibid.*, p. 53.

[85]See *Ibid.*, pp. 54, 64-65.

[86]*Ibid.*, pp. 82-83, 86-87.

[87]*Ibid.*, p. 49.

[88]*Age of Reform*, p. 135.

[89]*Ibid.*, p. 153.

[90]*Progressive Historians* p. 207.

[91]*American Political Tradition*, pp. 144, 140, 102, 165.

[92]*Age of Reform*, p. 15.

[93]*Paranoid Style*, pp. 145, 179.

[94]See *Age of Reform*, pp. 5-11, 201, 221.

[95]*Ibid.*, 15-16.

[96]*The Progressive Movement*, p. 15.

[97]*Age of Reform*, p. 315.

[98]*Ibid.*, footnote, p. 322.

[99]*Paranoid Style*, pp. 31-32.

[100]*Ibid.*, xi-xii.

[101]*Idea of a Party System*, p. 55.

[102]See *Age of Reform*, pp. 227-32.

[103]"The Age of Re-forming History," *Nation* (June 30, 1956), 552.

[104]See *Social Darwinism*, pp. 201-2.

[105]*Paranoid Style*, pp. 100-07.

[106]Woodward, 210-11, and *Idea of a Party System*, p. 246.

[107]*Progressive Historians*, p. 461.

[108]"Goldwater and His Party," *Encounter*, xxiii (October, 1964, 3.

[109]*Social Darwinism*, pp. 203-4.

[110]*Ibid.*, p., 125.

[111]See *Anti-Intellectualism in American Life.* New York: Knopf, 1963, p. 46.

[112]"Darwinism and Western Thought," in H.L. Plaine, ed., *Darwin, Marx, and Wagner: A Symposium.* Columbus: Ohio State Univ. Press, 1962, pp. 59, 62-63.

[113]*Progressive Historians*, pp. 439, 443.

[114]*Social Darwinism*, pp. 203-4.

[115]*American Political Tradition*, viii-ix.

[116]Quoted from "Historiography and the Constitution," in Read, ed., *The Constitution Reconsidered*, cited in *Progressive Historians*, p. 243.

[117]*Progressive Historians*1, pp. 244-45.

[118]*Anti-Intellectualism*, pp. 28-29, 38-39, 22.

[119]See *Ibid.*, pp. 59, 145-52.

[120]See *Ibid.*, pp. 47-55.

[121]*Ibid.*, 154-55.

[122]*Ibid.*, 237.

[123]*Age of Reform*, p. 148.

[124]*American Political Tradition*, pp. 206, 143.

[125]*Anti-Intellectualism, pp.* 198-205; and "The Revolution in Higher Education," in Arthur Schlesinger, Jr., and Morton White, eds. *Paths of American Thought.* Boston: Houghton Mifflin, 1963, pp.287-88.

[126]See *Anti-Intellectualism*, p. 213; *Age of Reform*, p. 284.

[127]*Anti-Intellectualism*, p. 214.

[128]*Ibid.*, pp. 393-94, 220.

[129]"Conversation," in A. Alvarez, *Under Pressure: The Writer in Society*. Baltimore: Penguin, 1965, p. 112.

[130]*Paranoid Style*, pp. 90-92, 185.

[131]Stern, 62; *Paranoid Style*, p. 161.

[132]*American Violence: A Documentary History*, with Michael Wallace, eds., New York: Knopf, 1970, pp. 6, 30, 11, 3, 19-20.

[133]*Age of Reform*, p. 36.

[134]*Anti-Intellectualism*, p. 36.

[135]See Hofstadter and Seymour Martin Lipset, eds., *Turner and the Sociology of the Frontier*. New York: Basic Books, 1968, p. 5.

[136]1750, pp. 172-73; *Progressive Historians*, pp. 136, 152.

[137]1750, p. 143.

[138]*Ibid.*, pp. 134, 138-39, 134.

[139]Woodward, 206, 209.

[140]*Paranoid Style*, pp. 195-96.

[141]*Progressive Historians*, p. 438.

John Brown:
The Man, the Legend and the Alternative Constitution

W. Russel Gray

IF JOHN BROWN HAD BEEN HENNY YOUNGMAN, he might have encapsulated the Founding Fathers' attitude toward slavery in a one-liner such as : "They took a dim view of it; in fact, they didn't see it at all." Indeed to the chagrin of Brown and other abolitionists, the word "slave" appeared nowhere in the U.S. Constitution. Also, the curiously pre-Orwellian language of Article 1: Section 2 refers to slaves as "all other Persons," yet for purposes of representational apportionment and taxation of their owners the slaves were counted as three fifths human beings.

Of course small farmers and the nonpropertied elements were counted among the free whites of their time, but since their interests were virtually unrepresented at the 1787 convention, it was not difficult for the delegates to stunt the growth of majority voting power.[1] The apprehensions of many of the delegates about the potential political clout of the common man led to a variety of safeguards. Many of the delegates believed that democracy would mean popular tyranny. Thus came such "auxiliary precautions" as the separation of powers and the checks and balances system.[2] Other measures also thwarted the growth of majority rule. Until the seventeenth amendment, in 1913, the populace could not vote directly for senators, who were to be selected as state legislators decided; also, the method for amending the Constitution itself was not based on a simple majority vote.[3] And, despite the Constitution's silence on certain specific personal liberties, the Federalists had some success in propagating the belief that the Constitution reflected the popular will. By sponsoring some of those liberties in what became the Bill of Rights, the new government enhanced the Constitution's popularity.[4]

But the floodgates did not swing open to a wave of democracy. Rather, it was as if a lock slowly admitted a limited amount of water and raised only it to a higher level; Constitutional machinery kept much of the democratic surge in check. For example, in 1789 President Madison submitted several rights amendments that states had proposed. Of these, the popularly elected House passed seventeen. The Senate, not directly elected by the populace, approved twelve. Of these, ten survived the ratification-by-the-states process. Many personal liberties were yet to be guaranteed; not until

1865 did a provision abolish slavery.

Though he could not have had abolitionist John Brown in mind, Thomas Jefferson once said that every generation might need a new Constitution.[5] So far as the slave question was concerned, the raider of Harper's Ferry stood ready not only to liberate slaves through insurrection but, as well, to impose his own constitution upon the liberated areas. Like many nineteenth-century Americans, John Brown had become sold on the practical and symbolic necessity—the idea—of a constitution. But the one he had in mind, and hand, would have abolished not only slavery but perhaps the federal constitution. And, there being no West Virginia, the two-fold abolition strike occurred in what was part of Jefferson's own home state.

More than 125 years after the fateful strike, John Brown remains controversial. Historians, popularizers and ideologues have left contradictory images of the most violent of the premature emancipators. But all of them would agree that Brown's 1859 raid, trial and hanging raised sectional feelings to the boiling point and, in Frederick Douglass' words, turned a conflict of "words, votes and compromises" into civil strife "over the chasm of a broken Union."[6] And, despite unheroic quibbles and denials after his capture, Brown had hoped to foment slave rebellions, then impose a "Provisional Constitution" upon the liberated areas. This was heady stuff. Even that unequivocal opponent of slavery Horace Greeley thought Brown misguided.[7] Lincoln and Seward, both free-soil Republicans, condemned his methods.

But a legend was in the making. At the time of Brown's trial Henry Ward Beecher sermonized: "His Soul was noble; his work miserable. But a cord and a gibbet would redeem all that, and round Brown's failure with a heroic success."[8] Abolitionist tributes from Wendell Phillips and Ralph Waldo Emerson made execution seem martyrdom; Emerson predicted that Brown would make the gallows as glorious as the cross. Novelist Louisa May Alcott dubbed Brown "Saint John the Just"; Thoreau compared him to Jesus. Julia Ward Howe, whose husband was one of those who had supplied Brown with arms and money, wrote *The Battle Hymn of the Republic*, and Union troops marching to the melody of her stanza about Christ sang of "John Brown's body ... a mouldering in the grave."[9]

Jules Abels has recorded how Brown's "heroism" was bruited before as well as immediately after the hanging.[10] A week before the execution a twenty-five cent book, mainly an account of the trial, was on sale; a month after Brown's death came James Redpath's 400-page *The Public Life of Captain John Brown*, written in about a month. At a dollar a copy it sold well and, though in part fictionalized by the admiring author, would be the standard work for twenty-five years. Two weeks after Brown's death came a melodrama. During a successful (sixteen-week) New York run Mrs. J.C. Swayze's *Ossawattomie Brown* took factual license but managed to appeal to both pro and con views of Brown.

Not all northerners admired Brown. By 1869 even Emerson had lost enthusiasm. The Concord transcendentalist not only acknowledged the foolhardiness of the raid but removed from his earlier essay on courage references to Brown and his saintliness. But by then the "John Brown's Body" stanza had worked its magic on many others, even though the origin of that marching verse, like the legend of Brown itself, may not have been exactly what it seemed. A Massachusetts militiaman claimed to have been present when the song was born. According to George Kimball, in 1861 the men in his unit at Fort Warren (Boston harbor) sang to a popular Methodist hymn tune waggish lyrics about a Scotsman named John Brown (no relation) when he did not appear, or reported late for work details. There were joking references to Brown's being dead, his body mouldering. Soon applicability to the *other* John Brown spread the song to other units. The Twelfth Massachusetts sang it with popular effect in Boston and in New York while marching on Broadway on their way to the front.[11]

In pictures as well as words and music, the legend grew. An 1863 Currier and Ives lithograph depicted Brown meeting a slave mother holding a baby as he descended jail steps on his way to the gallows. In 1883 Thomas Hovenden's *The Last Moments of John Brown*, since reproduced in history texts, further enhanced the pathos of that scene on the jail steps: the white bearded Brown pauses to kiss a slave child. The incident was mythical, a product of the mind of an imaginative reporter.[12]

In this century regionalist painter John Steuart Curry transferred his interest in heroic posturing and theatrical figure arrangement from a canvas titled *John Brown* (1939) to a rotunda mural in the capitol at Topeka. In the Curry mural the artist's enjoyment in "the hyperbole of pictorial statement" is apparent in Brown's gigantic, bearded, Moses-like stature and "exaggerated gesture and contorted body animation."[13] Brown appears 'with wild expression, holding a Bible in one hand and a rifle in the other, towering over free-soil and proslavery forces in Bleeding Kansas.[14] In the background are a Kansas prairie fire and a tornado. Because of such artistic and governmental attention some Kansans no doubt regarded Brown as a popular hero despite his involvement in the grisly Potawatomie Creek murders of proslavers.

In 1942 black artist Horace Pippin painted a primitivist expression of social protest. *John Brown Going to His Hanging* has been called "stirring and macabre."[15] As huddled citizens watch the horse-drawn wagon carrying Brown (tied and sitting on his coffin), a black lady in the right foreground scowls at the viewer.

Other arts fostered the legend. By 1941, in American literature alone Brown had been the subject of at least 245 poems, 58 novels, 31 plays and 11 short stories.[16] The most distinguished of these, written in Paris by Stephen

Vincent Benet, won the 1929 Pulitzer Prize in poetry. *John Brown's Body* celebrated the spirit of Brown, and more broadly of America in a retelling of the Civil War that begins shortly before Harper's Ferry and ends after Lincoln's assassination. Though lacking the conventions of a central hero and a unifying metrical pattern, the poem was epic in scope if not in intention. The editor of a 1941 edition observed:

The epic ... is rich in action and suspense, with characters expressive of many moods and drawn from various sections and walks of life. The episodes are divided one from another by lyrics, and musical interludes planned to prepare the reader's mind for each new scene and contrasting character.[17]

The dramatic possibilities of Benet's long poem were further realized in 1953 and 1961 with stage and television adaptations. Soundtrack albums followed. In Charles Laughton's stage adaptions Tyrone Power and Judith Anderson were joined by Raymond Massey, who had been popularly identified with the Lincoln role. Significantly for the Brown legend, Mr. Massey was both John Brown and Abraham Lincoln in the modern dress dramatic reading. In 1955 a black-and-white Allied Artists film offered Mr. Massey again as Brown, whose image was not tarnished by, in the words of one reviewer, "Massey's steadying, low-keyed performance ... a script that sticks to simple narrative" ... (and) direction that "sidesteps psychology and dips into dramatic compromise near the end."[8]

Historical circumstance further glossed Brown's image. Harper's Ferry and its aftermath involved a stunning supporting cast. George Washington's body had been a-mouldering for sixty years, but for the "moral effect" that the Washington name might lend his cause, Brown had the first President's great-grandnephew seized with other local hostages.[19] And, taken from Colonel Lewis Washington's nearby farm and worn by Brown during the siege at the arsenal was a magnificent sword allegedly given George Washington by Frederick the Great.

There were other curious ironies. The officer in charge of the besieging federal troops was Brevet Colonel Robert E. Lee. Also present was another Virginian and West Pointer soon to be famous in Confederate gray. The attacking party that broke into the engine room to subdue Brown and his raiders and rescue their prisoners was aided by a daring truce flag maneuver by Lieutenant J.E.B. Stuart. Less than two months later at Brown's hanging one of the 1,500 cavalry and militia on hand to frustrate any rescue attempt and otherwise maintain order was a Richmond enlisted man, John Wilkes Booth. Ten days after the hanging Tennessean Andrew Johnson (to become President on Lincoln's death) reminded his Senate colleagues of Brown's unsavory role in the Pottawatomie murders of 1856.[20] Two days later a Senate subcommittee began investigating whether any "subversive" organizations had aided Brown; the chief inquisitor was Jefferson Davis of Mississippi.

Another factor that no doubt enhanced the Brown legend is the popularity of underdogs and comebacks in America. Before Harper's Ferry Brown was "a lifelong failure, a bankrupt, sometimes a thief, eccentric, fanatic, liar, and perhaps insane."[21] Certainly by 1852 his life had been darkened by family tragedies and business failures. He had lost his first wife and a total of nine children—two by his second wife. There had been some fifteen business failures in four states—as tanner, land speculator, woolgrower and merchant.[22] Harper's Ferry became an occasion for redemption—of his past and of the abolitionist conviction that all men are born free and equal.

Brown's image was further enobled by his composed, even chivalric behavior during and after the raid. Biographers, notably Stephen B. Oates, have preserved numerous examples.[23]

Twice while under siege Brown sent forth truce flags and a third time tried to negotiate by note. Colonel Washington later testified that although Brown condemned the shooting of his son Watson under a white flag, he made no threats to prisoners or besiegers. Even with a dead and a wounded son nearby, Brown impressed Washington as "the coolest and firmest man I ever saw." Upon capture Brown maintained poise even with a lynch mob calling for his head. His demeanor during three hours of questioning prompted Governor Wise to call him "the gamest man I ever saw."

And Brown's trial and hanging became a stage for martyrdom. Though the trial began less than a fortnight after his capture and took place in Virginia and not a federal court, Brown did not protest. Throughout the trial his injuries required him to lie on a cot. Early on though he rose to repudiate his counsel's efforts to lay groundwork for an insanity defense. After sentencing, he made a stirring address. Then, in the weeks before his execution, advised of a plan to rescue him, he rejected it. Permitted to write to his family and friends and answer mail from sympathizers, he composed replies so moving that the sheriff assigned to read them before posting cried. At his hanging, Brown's composure and resolution earned respect even from his accusers.

Such conduct did much to obscure or minimize some of Brown's less heroic aspects. Three years before Harper's Ferry he and a small band murdered and mutilated five proslavery sympathizers near Pottawatomie Creek, Kansas. Later, in an engagement against a numerically superior body of Missouri militia near Osawatomie, Kansas, Brown achieved a tainted victory. Dishonoring a truce flag, he put a gun to the chest of the Missouri captain to oblige the rest of his force to surrender.[24] Thus the poetic justice of J.E.B. Stuart's starting the final assault on the Harper's Ferry raiders by first approaching with a white flag, conferring, then signalling for the attack while in the truce area. Stuart had served in Kansas and knew of "Osawatomie" Brown.

Furthermore, for any who wanted to look closely, the planning and execution of the Harper's Ferry raid was not the work of a military genius. For one thing, pre-raid security left much to be desired. At least 80 people knew of Brown's plan, and one even mailed a warning to the Secretary of War, who failed to act on the tip.[25] Also, with the hindsight of history, armchair abolitionists might question Brown's selection of Harper's Ferry as a place to start a slave revolt. The arsenal indeed was well stocked and relatively undefended, but half of the 2,500 populace already were freed blacks and most of the whites were transplanted northerners.[26] Nor was ordnance Brown's forte. The 200 Maynard revolvers he obtained for his "Provisional Army" were useless; he had bought percussion caps rather than the tape primings they required.[27] Tactically Brown also seems to have been remiss. He split his 21-man party into three units, got cut off from his rear guard, allowed a train to continue on its way to where telegraph lines were open, and lingered the first morning to order breakfast for the prisoners. Finally, at the rented farm was an easily discovered slew of incriminating documents: maps, his "Provisional Constitution," his "Vindication of the Invasion" (sic), and a number of compromising letters from supporters.[28] Considering that the latter were in a carpetbag, Brown inadvertently may have given Southerners a special connotation to the name of that item.

Stephen B. Oates traced the history of that "Provisional Constitution" in his Brown biography *To Purge This Land With Blood*. At least one form of it existed twenty months before the raid. On Washington's birthday, 1858, Brown discussed the document with Franklin B. Sanborn and Edwin Morton in Massachusetts. That May, Brown held a secret constitutional convention—at Chatham, Canada. To 34 blacks and 12 whites he presented the 48-page document. It prompted much discussion and debate, but was unanimously approved and signed. In the ensuing election, perhaps not surprisingly, Brown was elected Army commander-in-chief by acclamation. The separate office of President remained unfilled when two nominees declined and Brown moved to postpone the election. Rather interestingly, the elected Secretary of State was an English-born published poet, Richard Realf.

Seventeen months later, on the Sunday morning before the night attack on Harper's Ferry, one of Brown's officers read the Provisional Constitution to the raiders, for Brown intended to use it as the basis for governing "liberated" areas.[29] In addition to providing for a separate Army commander-in-chief and President, Brown's constitution authorized a Vice President, a Supreme Court, and a one-house Congress—the latter to be a house of representatives of at least five but no more than ten elected members (three-year terms). Enactments of this body required approval of the President and the Commander-in-Chief. Officers were to be a Treasurer and Secretaries of State, War and Treasury.

One of Brown's 48 articles provided that the President and the Secretary of State set up a network of friends and facilities, especially in the northern states. Also, in free or slave states property of the "enemy" and those willfully holding slaves would be confiscated (Article 36). To reunite broken families, "intelligence" officers would be established (Article 42). Had Brown's revolt succeeded, his Provisional Constitution might have established a latter-day Puritan Commonwealth. An article dealing with "Irregularities" prohibited "profane swearing, filthy conversation, indecent behavior, or indecent exposure ... intoxication ... quarreling ... unlawful intercourse of the sexes." The first day of the week was to be reserved for "moral and religious instruction and improvement, relief of the suffering, instruction of the young and ignorant, and the encouragement of personal cleanliness." Except in urgent cases there was to be no manual labor on that day.

Though it seems almost an afterthought, there was a disclaimer. The forty-sixth of the 48 articles stated that the articles were not to be construed as encouraging the overthrow of any government—state or federal—and the flag would be that of the American Revolution.

The preamble to Brown's Constitution was a biting thirteen-line denunciation of slavery, perhaps composed with one eye on Article 1: Section 2 of the federal Constitution. It must have annoyed Brown mightily that, the Declaration of Independence notwithstanding, enslaved blacks had no rights and were reckoned as three fifths human beings in taxation and apportionment ratios. The latter provision eventually was changed by Section 2 of the Fourteenth Amendment, one of three Emancipation-related amendments passed from 1865-1870. With the Thirteenth and Fifteenth Amendments it achieved rights for Blacks that Brown no doubt would have rejoiced at: abolition of slavery, citizenship for former slaves, right to due process of law, and right to vote regardless of color.

It is of course impossible to gauge the degree to which John Brown— man and myth—influenced conditions that led to passage of these three amendments. But it is undeniable that before Harper's Ferry there had been no Constitutional Amendments since 1804; with the conclusion of the war his raid had helped to ignite, three slavery-related amendments passed in five years. It would be 43 more before any further Amendment would occur.

John Brown made the most of his moment in history. It could be said that he set the stage for the Civil War with his trial and, later, his words as he boarded the wagon that would bear him and his empty coffin to the scaffold:

I John Brown am now quite certain that the crimes of this guilty land: will never be purged away; but with Blood. I had as I now think: vainly flattered myself that without very much bloodshed; it might be done.[30]

The coffin would return with the dead John Brown, and soon there would be a marching verse about John Brown's body to rival "Dixie," which had been composed the year of Brown's death. But before slavery died, much blood would be shed. Congress, as always, could have changed the Constitution, but would not do so for a song.

Notes

[1]Harry J. Carman and Harold C. Syrett, *A History of the American People*, Vol. I (New York: Knopf, 1958), pp. 212-213.

[2]James MacGregor Burns, J.W. Peltason and Thomas E. Cronin, *Government by the People* (Englewood Cliffs: Prentice-Hall, 1984), p. 24.

[3]Carman, p. 213.

[4]*Ibid.*, p. 228.

[5]Burns, et al., p. 34.

[6]Frederick Douglass, "John Brown," in Louis Ruchames, ed. *John Brown: The Making of a Revolutionary* (New York: Grosset & Dunlap, 1969), p. 298.

[7]Irwin Unger, *These United States: The Question of Our Past*, Vol. I, (Boston: Little, Brown, 1982), 373.

[8]David Burner, Eugene Genovese, et al., *An American Portrait: A History of the United States* Vol. II (Jersey City: Revisionary Press, 1982), 295-96.

[9]*Ibid.*, 297.

[10]Jules Abels, *Man on Fire: John Brown and the Cause of Liberty* (New York: Macmillan, 1971), pp. 389-90.

[11]*Ibid.*, pp. 391-92.

[12]Ruchames, p. 268.

[13]George M. Cohen, *A History of American Art* (New York: Dell, 1971), p. 184.

[14]Abels, p. 113.

[15]Cohen, pp. 205-06.

[16]Abels, p. 394.

[17]Mabel A. Bessey, ed., *John Brown's Body* (New York: Farrar & Rinehart, 1941), pp. x-xi.

[18]Review of *Seven Angry Men* in *New York Times Guide to Movies on TV*, Howard Thompson, ed. (Chicago: Quadrangle Books, 1970), p. 174.

[19]Stephen B. Oates, *To Purge This Land With Blood* (New York: Harper & Row, 1970), pp. 291-92.

[20]Abels, p. 79.

[21]Burner, et al., 296.

[22]Oates, pp. 79, 209.

[23]Detailed accounts of the following incidents appear in Oates, pp. 293-352.

[24]*Ibid.*, pp. 153-54.

[25]Burner, et al., 295.

[26]Oates, p. 274.

[27]*Ibid.*, p. 276.

[28]*Ibid.*, p. 287.

[29]The text of this unusual document and the minutes of its adoption are in *Mass Violence in America/Invasion at Harper's Ferry*, Richard E. Rubenstein and Robert M. Fogelson, eds. (New York: Arno Press, 1969), pp. 45-59.

[30]Burner, et al., 296.

The Law and Human Cannonballs: Reflections on the First Amendment and the Popular Mass Media

Norman L. Rosenberg

... above all else, the First Amendment means that government has no power to restrict expression because of its message, its ideas, its subject matter or its content.
Police Dept. v. Moseley 408 U.S. 92, 95 (1972)

We learned more from a three-minute record, baby, than we ever learned in school.
Bruce Springsteen, "No Surrender," (1984)

IN AN AGE of carefully packaged pop cultural products, Hugo Zacchini, identified by the United States Supreme Court merely as an "entertainer," was a throwback to an era of individual artistry. Although for legal purposes, his "act" could be reduced to a scant fifteen seconds, the Great Zacchini took considerable pride in his ability to exit (with explosive assistance) a cannon, fly across some 200 feet of terra firma, and land in a well-used safety net. During the summer of 1972, visitors to the Geauga County Fair in Burton, Ohio, as part of the general admission price to the fair grounds, could marvel at the human cannonball's skill and daring. One admirer, a free-lance photographer, was impressed enough that he asked permission to record this rare pop art form for television. After Zacchini turned him down, the reporter returned the following night, at the request of Cleveland's WEWS-TV, and filmed a successful launch. WEWS-TV then covered Zacchini's activities as part of its regular evening newscast.

Even though the "happy talk" that accompanied footage of the flying Zacchini urged viewers to visit the fair and see a live performance for themselves, the human cannonball sued the television station. Although the various courts that considered Zacchini's case framed his cause of action in slightly different ways, the television station's defense remained straight-forward. Relying on a line of Supreme Court precedents, beginning with libel case of *New York Times v. Sullivan* (1964), the station insisted that the First Amendment immunized it from all common law tort actions such as those for defamation and invasion of privacy, brought by "public figures" like Zacchini.

The highest court in the Buckeye state agreed. The First Amendment, in the words of the Supreme Court of Ohio, gave the media "a privilege to report matters of legitimate public interest, even though such reports might intrude on matters otherwise private" or infringe upon individual property rights. Whatever Zacchini's own reasons for wishing to avoid the evening news, they must give way to the public's "right to be informed of matters of public interest and concern." In cases like this, the Ohio Court continued, the community's need for wide-ranging public discussion demanded that broadcasters be allowed a generous editorial and artistic license to determine what might be offered to their audiences. The Ohio Court dismissed Zacchini's lawsuit (433 U.S. 562, at 568 [1976]).

The United States Supreme Court in a 5-4 decision reversed the Ohio Supreme Court, ruling that the First Amendment mandated no such broad, constitutional protection, especially in a situation where WEWS-TV had "appropriated" Zacchini's act against his wishes. Justice Byron White, who had once entertained people by playing football for money, sympathized with Zacchini's desire to protect his unique talents from unpaid media exposure. Justice White argued that WEWS-TV had broadcast Zacchini's *entire* act, not simply a portion of it, and had aired footage that Zacchini had desired never be shot in the first place. Throughout his opinion, Justice White alluded to various kinds of property rights—such as copyright considerations and control over publicity—that the law guaranteed to Zacchini. Moreover, this case raised no issue of censorship since Zacchini was not attempting "to enjoin the broadcast of his performance; he simply wants to be paid for it." (433 U.S. at 578)

Viewed only as a legal precedent, *Zacchini v. Scripps-Howard Broadcasting Co.* will likely never be considered a "landmark" Supreme Court decision; even when collected in legal casebooks dealing only with mass media issues, *Zacchini* appears merely as a supporting act, not as one of the "leading" precedents.[1] Yet, if one looks beyond the rather routine way in which the Supreme Court's majority disposed of *Zacchini*, this case can actually help to highlight several fundamental questions about the ways in which legal institutions have come to view controversies involving the First Amendment and the media's coverage of popular culture.

I

Judicial opinions, including ones that originate in the hallowed chambers of the United States Supreme Court, are more than narrow legal documents; they are also political and cultural statements about issues— vital and not-so-vital—of the day. The extra-legal dimensions of judicial opinions loom especially large when judges talk about "THE FIRST AMENDMENT," a brief constitutional provision that carries, along with its black-letter legal meanings, deep historical and cultural connotations. As one historian of free speech argues, the First Amendment has "become a basic element of our national identity," an essential part of the popular conception of what a free, marketplace society is supposed to be all about. Thus anyone who rejects legal, political or cultural arguments based on "THE FIRST AMENDMENT" must proceed cautiously; no Justice of the United States Supreme Court ever wants to appear as an enemy of "free expression." Historians, for example, have generally dealt harshly with the authors of the Sedition Act of 1798 and with the "purity crusaders," such as Anthony Comstock, of the late nineteenth century.[2]

As a result of the powerful cultural symbolism connected with "THE FIRST AMENDMENT," the collected rhetoric of the Supreme Court is replete with glowing praise for the value and importance of "freedom of speech and of the press." Often forgotten, however, is that many (though certainly not all) of the Court's most effusive statements about First-Amendment freedoms—such as Justice Oliver Wendell Holmes, Jr.'s earliest "free-speech" statements—appeared in legal opinions that *rejected* the claims of defendants whose expression was about to be curtailed or punished. In addition, supposedly "black-letter" judicial statements, such as that in *Police Dep't v. Moseley* about the illegitimacy of First Amendment distinctions on the basis of content, can *really* turn out to mean something different in practice.

Justice White's *Zacchini* opinion followed this general pattern. Although he flatly rejected WEWS—TV's First-Amendment arguments, thus opening them to further litigation by Zacchini, White and the four justices who joined his majority opinion still genuflected toward the First Amendment. White even emphasized that the First Amendment protected entertaining expression, not simply political or informational works. "There is no doubt that entertainment, as well as news, enjoys First Amendment protection. It is also true that entertainment itself can be important news." (433 U.S. at 578)

Nonetheless, because of the competing legal considerations and the unique facts outlined earlier, Justice White ultimately held that "THE FIRST AMENDMENT" did not apply to WEWS-TV's footage of the human cannonball. Although White's opinion reinforced, and perhaps even extended, the central symbolism of "THE FIRST AMENDMENT," those who watched after the legal health of the media took no comfort from the *Zacchini* decision's rejection of the constitutional "newsworthy" privilege that had been extended by the Supreme Court of Ohio.

It would be easy, and even a little reassuring, to view holdings like *Zacchini* as belated victories for Richard Nixon and as tangible signs of the "Burger Court's Counter-Revolution," the "conservative" reaction of the 1970s to the "Warren Court Revolution" of the 1960s. Certainly, most mass media executives have insisted that the generally favorable First-Amendment decisions of happier days have been eroded by cases handed down by Chief Justice Warren Burger and his colleagues. Similarly, the dean of free-speech scholars, Thomas I. Emerson, has vigorously condemned the Burger Court for its failure "to take proper account of the dynamics of suppression" and to provide free expression with "the special protection to which it is theoretically entitled." Franklyn Haiman, another prominent First-Amendment scholar who shares Emerson's broad, libertarian perspective, lists *Zacchini* as only one of many Burger Court decisions that should be counted as defeats for defenders of freedom of expression.[3]

As with most "easy" interpretations of "the law," this view of *Zacchini* carries some force. Even the fact that Byron White, a nominee of the "liberal" John Kennedy, authored the decision can be explained away, once it is remembered that, on a whole range of legal issues, Justice White has been the most "Burgerish" member of the post-Warren Supreme Court.

Yet, the Warren-to-Burger, libertarian-to-conservative shift can also obscure as much as it clarifies First-Amendment decisions. In reality, Justice White's *Zacchini* opinion flew a considerably shorter distance than the human cannonball; against the friction of four dissenting votes, it barely made it out of the Supreme Court's Chambers. And it was an appointee of Richard Nixon himself, Justice Lewis Powell of Virginia, who challenged White's view of the free speech issues in *Zacchini*.

It should be emphasized, however, that Justice Powell's dissent offered no advanced, innovative response to White's majority opinion; rather, Powell's opinion remained rather firmly within fairly traditional bounds. Touching conventional First-Amendment themes, it relied upon a view of American culture based upon shopworn images of a "free marketplace of ideas" and familiar policy arguments such as the need to maximize the "free flow" of useful information. And consistent with Burger-Court decisions that brought the "speech rights" of business advertisers and large corporations within the confines of the First Amendment, Justice Powell's dissent implicitly embraced the superficially appealing but fundamentally deceptive idea of the "public's right to hear."[4]

Most important, Powell's dissent helped to underscore the inherent contradictions in the free-speech approaches urged by prominent First-Amendment scholars (especially "libertarian" ones) during the 1940s and 1950s and ultimately accepted by the Supreme Court in cases like *Times v. Sullivan* in the 1960s and 1970s. Seeking to avoid what they considered the dangers of a case-by-case approach in which courts balanced, on an ad hoc basis, conflicts between "the right of free speech" and competing legal "rights" such as protection of individual property interests or of public order, the "libertarians" of the cold-war era searched for a "general theory" (or theories) of the First Amendment. At the same time, they sought to bolster and fill out the general theory approach by devising various "categorical" legal formulae which attempted to define objectively the precise reach of the First Amendment's protection by "reliance on broad and abstract classifications of protected or unprotected speech."[5] While Justice White accentuated the property rights of the individual pop cultural "celebrity," Justice Powell drew upon the "general theory" and "categorical" approaches to First Amendment adjudication to emphasize the interests of the media and, by extension, its viewers. Thus, Powell's dissent, even more than the majority opinion of Justice White, is instructive for its conventionality rather than for any really new approach to the complex issues lurking within the *Zacchini* case.

Returning to a First Amendment theme that had played a prominent role in decisions of the Warren Court (especially in *Times v. Sullivan*), Justice Powell argued that White's ruling could cast a giant "chill" over the media's coverage of potentially "hot" news. In the future, Justice Powell feared, "whenever a television news editor is unsure whether certain film footage received from a camera crew might be held to portray an 'entire act,' he may decline coverage—even of clearly newsworthy events or confine the broadcast to watered-down verbal reporting, perhaps with an occasional still picture." (433 U.S. at 580-81). Film footage that even remotely threatened legal entanglements would likely never be shown. "The public is then the loser," concluded Justice Powell. "This is hardly the kind of news reportage that the First Amendment is meant to foster." (433 U.S. at 580-81)

White's opinion, Justice Powell also argued, gave too little weight to the trained, editorial judgment of media professionals and too much to the interests of those people who became the legitimate subjects for public discussion. The Great Zacchini, the dissent acidly noted, was not complaining about receiving free media exposure; he was only concerned that he himself be able to "retain control over means and manner" of the media's coverage. (433 U.S. at 582). If Justice White seemed solicitous of the property interests of Zacchini, Justice Powell (and Justices William J. Brennan and Thurgood Marshall, who joined his dissent) seemed equally as concerned about protecting the professional perquisites of the mass media's management. At least in theory, a holding in favor of Hugo Zacchini gave him—and presumably other "public figures" in similar situations—at least some leverage over how the mass media could portray them.[6]

As the differences between the justices suggested, the *Zacchini* case highlighted basic conflicts in recent free speech theory, ones inextricably linked to the broader issues of "general" theories, "categorical" approaches, and the application of the First Amendment to popular culture. One of the underlying problems, in fact, is quite familiar to students of the law of defamation. Reduced to its simplest terms, the question is this: should the legal protection afforded by "THE FIRST AMENDMENT" (and by state guarantees of free expression) extend equally to all expression in the "free marketplace of ideas" that proves "*of* interest" to the public; or, alternatively, should the fullest protection of the Constitution be reserved only for expression, such as "political speech," that courts determine is actually "*in* the public interest" to see, hear and read.[7]

This dilemma has arisen most often—and perhaps most clearly—in the area of defamation law. In fact, legal historians can hear echoes of earlier libel decisions in the opinions of both Justices Powell and White, with the former emphasizing the legal doctrines associated with a generous reading of *The New York Times v. Sullivan*, and the latter reflecting the general effort to limit the implications of this important defamation suit for those who featured "celebrities," such as Hugo Zacchini, in their pop cultural products.

The *Sullivan* case of 1964 brought much-publicized, and ultimately controversial, changes to the law of defamation. Growing out of the civil rights struggle in the Deep South and decided in the heyday of 1960s-style liberalism, *Times v. Sullivan* held, as a matter of constitutional law, that political officials and candidates could not successfully sue media defendants for libel unless they could establish by "clear and convincing" evidence that defamatory falsehoods had been published with "actual malice." (376 U.S. 254, 279-80 [1964]).

As the Supreme Court tried to explain it, "actual malice" was a highly technical, often confusing legal term; in a practical sense, the "actual malice" test meant that any libel plaintiff who had to satisfy its requirements would find it extremely difficult to win a lawsuit against the American news and entertainment industries.[8] The crucial question, then, for those interested in non-political expression, including works of popular culture, became how far would the Supreme Court extend the "actual malice" test?

The rhetoric and rationale of *Times v. Sullivan* suggested one answer. According to Justice William Brennan, the "actual malice" rule carried out "the central meaning" of the First Amendment: "a profound and national commitment to the principle that debate on *public* issues should be uninhibited, robust and wide open . . . ." The results Justice Brennan conceded, might sometimes include "vehement, caustic, and unpleasantly sharp attacks" on individual reputations, but these departures from elite standards of linguistic propriety represented part of the price to be paid for faithful obedience to the "central meaning" of the First Amendment. (376 U.S. at 270, 271). Using the same basic line of argument that Lewis Powell would adopt in his *Zacchini* dissent, Justice Brennan insisted that any less-libertarian standard would "chill the kind of free, vigorous discussion that the First Amendment was intended to protect.

Taken together, the "chilling" effect and "central meaning" rationales pointed toward application of the *Sullivan* principle to more than purely "political" expression. And in a series of post-*Sullivan* decisions, the Supreme Court gradually broadened the "categories" of cases to which the constitutional, "actual malice" test applied. In a 1967 decision arising out of a *Saturday Evening Post* story alleging corruption in big-time college football, a majority of Justices held that, in any defamation suit brought by a "public figure," the *Sullivan* standard would have to be satisfied. (*Curtis Publishing Co. v. Butts*, 388 U.S. 130 [1967]). A badly-split Supreme Court later announced that the same test would be constitutionally required in all defamation cases where the matter under discussion was "a subject of public or general interest." *Rosenbloom* v. Metromedia, Inc. 403 V.S. 29 [1971].

According to most observers, "*Sullivan*'s travels" left the American popular media largely exempt from liability for libel when it discussed any "newsworthy" subjects or persons. And as specialists in First-Amendment law noted, the logic of the dominant "marketplace of ideas" metaphor could place courts in the position of being forced to hold that whatever the media chose to carry over the airwaves or put into print seemed, almost by definition, something that would be a subject of "public or general interest."[9]

But the 1971 *Rosenbloom* holding proved the apogee of this approach to libel law. In fact, it rested on a strange coalition of Justices, with Chief Justice Burger and his "Minnesota Twin," Harry Blackmun, providing crucial votes for extending the *Sullivan* ruling. Only three years later, with the composition of the Court changed and with Justice Blackmun reversing field, *Gertz v. Robert Welch Inc.* (418 U.S. 323 [1974]) tried to bury any "newsworthy" or "public interest" approaches as the universal constitutional standards for libel cases. Although *Gertz* retained the "actual malice" hurdle for libel plaintiffs who were political officials and for legitimate "public figures," it held that states need not, as a matter of constitutional law, use this very stringent standard in cases brought by purely "private" individuals. Thus, the focus of legal inquiry would supposedly center not, as under the *Rosenbloom* test, on the subject matter of the allegedly libelous material but on the status—"public" or "private"—of individual plaintiffs. At the same time, *Gertz* also narrowed the legal definition of a "public figure," establishing a complex, two-tier legal theory, the intricacies of which are of secondary importance here. In fact, the alleged shift in inquiry was largely a legal fiction since determination of the "public/private" status of libel plaintiffs invariably reverted to an evaluation of the subject matter to which their name had been linked.[10]

The crucial point, once again, transcended narrow and technical legal holdings: Supreme-Court watchers generally interpreted *Gertz* as a strong signal that a majority of the Supreme Court wanted to discourage what it considered "irresponsible" pandering to popular tastes by the mass media. Similarly, *Gertz* professed to stand up for people who found their reputations and other personal interests cavalierly invaded, especially by pop culture entrepreneurs.[11] Ironically, it was Lewis Powell, the staunch advocate of a "newsworthy" approach in his *Zacchini* dissent, who wrote the opinion in *Gertz*.

The clash between the underlying principle of Powell's dissent in the case of the human cannonball and his approach to the First Amendment and popular culture in *Gertz* becomes apparent when the intervening libel case of *Time, Inc. v. Firestone* is considered (424 U.S. 448 [1976]). Unlike *Sullivan*, the *Firestone* case, though it involved social mores in the Deep South, raised no grave political issues. Instead, to critics of the popular media this well-publicized lawsuit became another symbol of the media's penchant for seizing upon trivial items and marketing them in the form of "celebrity journalism." To a majority of the Supreme Court, the fact that this brand of popular journalism undoubtedly commanded the interest of the American public—witness the success of tabloids such as the *National Enquirer* and magazines such as *People*—did not give it the highest possible status in constitutional law.

Actually, *Firestone* itself presented a rather tame and innocent example of "sensationalized" celebrity journalism. In its "Milestones" section, *Time* magazine reported that an heir to the Firestone Tire fortune had been granted a divorce from his third wife, a prominent Palm Beach socialite who employed a clipping service to keep track of her appearances in the mass media, on "grounds of extreme cruelty and adultery." This characterization of the case turned out, despite *Time*'s efforts to interpret a very muddled divorce decree, to be false. Mary Alice Firestone successfully sued *Time* for libel.

When the case reached the Supreme Court on appeal, a majority of the Justices took a very hard line, rejecting *Time*'s claims that the Firestones' well-publicized trial was a "public controversy" and that the celebrity-conscious Mrs. Firestone was herself a "public figure." Instead, the Court held that *Time* must defend itself without benefit of the very favorable "actual malice" test, on the theory that Mary Alice Firestone was a purely "private" person, whose problems that magazine had dragged into public view and whom it had then libeled.

Time v. Firestone, of course, was a very complex case, and different lawyers can read it in various ways; but close students of the popular media saw the majority opinion as another clear statement that guarantees of free speech would apply differently when the Supreme Court was dealing with popular journalism considered merely "of public interest" rather than with expression deemed by judges to be "in the public interest." The obfuscatory discussion of Ms. Firestone's status, as to whether she was a "private" or a "public" person, could not hide the fact that the basic distinctions in this case turned on the subject matter of *Time*'s story.[12]

Again, it should be stressed that the subject-matter distinction, lurking in the background of *Zacchini* and libel cases such as *Firestone*, is not the sole property of card-carrying "conservatives" like Byron White and William Rehnquist, the Justice who authored the opinion in *Firestone*. Indeed, support for legal doctrines that will relegate popular journalism—and presumably popular culture in general—to the fringes of the First Amendment's protective umbrella comes from one of the country's most outspoken free-speech libertarians, the political columnist Anthony Lewis.

Reflecting upon the twenty-year odyssey of *Sullivan*, Lewis condemned extension of its "actual malice" protection out of its original "political" context. Although Lewis did allow that the First Amendment should, in some way, protect "not only political but artistic expression . . . its primary concern must be political speech, because in some measure the 'core purpose' of the amendment relates to self government." Lewis argued that the *Rosenbloom* "public interest" approach "went too far" and that even *Gertz*'s "public figure" test can produce undesirable results. "The best-known public figures in this country," people whom courts were most likely to view as required to meet the stringent "actual malice" test in libel suits, "are movie stars—and what do they have to do with 'the central meaning' of the First Amendment?" There is little doubt that Lewis would also argue that libelous stories about "human cannonballs" should also land outside the center of the First Amendment's zone of protection. Thus, Lewis forthrightly follows the same approach used, though more covertly, in Supreme Court cases such as *Firestone* and *Zacchini*.[13]

Libel cases involving publications such as the *National Enquirer* have also endorsed giving the avowedly popular media a lesser amount of First-Amendment protection than extended to purely "political" cultural products. In the celebrated Carol Burnett libel case, for example, Judge Smith of the Los Angeles County Superior Court explicitly employed his own evaluation of the cultural worth of the *Enquirer* in determining the level of First-Amendment protection the publication should enjoy. According to Judge Smith, the paper engaged "in a form of legalized pandering designed to appeal to the readers' morbid sense of curiosity." This kind of journalism, the judge conceded, had proved of great interest to the American public; and, he complained, it "has been enormously profitable" to the *National Enquirer*. "While the First Amendment . . . permits such journalistic endeavor, it does not immunize the defendant from accountability" for "flagrant" violations of "the rules" of defamation law. Thus, Judge Smith, like Anthony Lewis, had no doubts that the Burnett libel suit "was unrelated to public affairs." Taking his cue from Supreme Court decisions such as *Firestone* and *Zacchini*, Judge Smith had no difficulty assigning popular journalism a lesser status than "political speech" or other expression considered to be in the public's "real" interest to hear and see.[14]

In the specialized language used for First-Amendment discourse, the approach favored by a current majority of the Supreme Court—and even by some of its "liberal" critics such as Lewis—raises the complex problem of "content neutrality." Despite the apparently unequivocal language of "libertarian" decisions such as *Police Dept. v. Mosely* which reject "content" distinctions, the fundamental issues here are difficult to unravel. Does, for example, the First Amendment require that "the law" adopt an agnostic position toward the type of expression at issue—as the Supreme Court has held that it does in purely "political" expression—or does both logic and sensitive social policy demand that courts make certain types of content distinctions?[14]a

There are a number of difficulties with the kind of content analysis urged by Anthony Lewis and used in the *Zacchini* and *Burnett* cases. Most obviously, there is the question of how judges can draw sensible, workable and defensible boundaries between different kinds of expression. Although Lewis does concede the difficulty of line-drawing, he still confidently proposes that in libel cases judges can—and should—make judgments about the degree of constitutional protection based upon "the reality of influence in public affairs" of the expression being challenged.[15]

The issue of boundary-drawing, however, is far more complex than this. Consider, once again, the problem of the flying Zacchini. Justice White, who was familiar with the problems of drawing lines for both first downs and for legal principles, tried to move the yardsticks in *Zacchini* according to a hard-headed view of the "facts," not simply according to some illusive legal ideas. Yet, as Justice Powell pointed out, White's "factual" statement that WEWS-TV had "appropriated" Zacchini's "entire act" was open to easy challenge. As Powell accurately observed, the "entire act" formula was a highly arbitrary, totally abstract concept, in both culture and in law. Surely, he suggested, the Great Zacchini actually "performed"—by warming up the crowd, for example—for much longer than fifteen seconds; Justice White's view of popular culture simply ignored this reality.

Indeed, one could extend Justice Powell's point. How, for instance, did Justice White expect future courts to determine, under his new legal yardstick, when a cultural performance actually began and ended? Were judges supposed to become cultural critics, deciding at least for legal purposes when particular acts had become complete enough to satisfy Justice White's rule? More important, why are judges—people who are rarely elected by popular vote and who are selected almost entirely from elite segments of society—to be empowered to make decisions?

But Justice Powell's dissent, like most other examples of conventional legal discourse, stopped short of asking such troubling questions. Indeed, it also employed the same general brand of First-Amendment line-drawing as Justice White's majority opinion. Claiming to be developing clearer lines of distinction than Justice White, Powell argued that the media should be privileged to broadcast footage, such as that of the human cannonball, so long as it did so as "a routine part of a regular news program" rather than as "a subterfuge or cover for private or commercial exploitation." (433 U.S. at 581) Thus Powell tried to separate "public" edification from "private" and "commercial" (i.e. pop cultural) expression. Such a categorical distinction, quite obviously, ignored the fact that "the news" itself had long since become a hybrid cultural product conveying a good deal of entertainment and possessing considerable commercial value for the private corporations that created and marketed it.[16] Although Justice Powell's dissent used different terms and reached a different result, it ultimately relied on the same types of abstract categorical rationales, especially the categories of "in" versus "of" public interest, as used in White's majority opinion, in the *Burnett* libel case, and in Anthony Lewis's formulation of defamation law.

Thus, Justice Powell's dissent displays the same problem as Justice White's majority opinion: critics can easily show that its attempt to draw hard and fast bounds, in either law or culture, between "information" and commercial "entertainment" must, of necessity, be a very subjective enterprise.

Such problems, as the case of the human cannonball demonstrates, are not hypothetical or even minor ones, especially in an age when critics have targeted the popular media's coverage of both individuals and controversial issues for special legal attention. Obviously, the issue of "content" discrimination becomes exceedingly complex when courts confront materials challenged as "pornographic"; indeed, emergence of a radical, feminist approach to both legal theory and rulemaking has made the issue of "pornography"—with the controversial question of the relationship between this type of pop cultural product and violence against women—one of the most vigorously contested areas of First-Amendment consciousness.[17] And even when cases do not raise the question of pornography, legal issues related to the popular media's handling of the reputations, privacy, and other interests of the people whom it features in its pages and programs has already come to bedevil both the courts and the purveyors of popular culture.[18]

Apparently clear-cut, categorical formulae, such as that suggested by Justice Powell in his *Zacchini* dissent, can quickly break down. In *Stephano v. News Group Publications, Inc.* (470 N.Y.S. 377 [A.D., 1984]), for example, a trial court granted *New York* magazine summary judgment against a professional model whose picture had been used, without his permission, in the popular publication's "Best Bets" section. The trial court, following a categorical rule similar to the one suggested by Powell, accepted the claim of *New York*'s editors that a picture of Stephano modeling a "bomber jacket" was simply a "newsworthy" matter of general interest, a service to the many readers who need to keep abreast of the latest pop cultural styles, and not an advertisement published for "commercial" purposes. Over a strongly-argued dissenting opinion, which insisted that the "Best Bets" column merely fulfilled *New York* readers' expectations of finding information on "what would become stylish and where it can be bought," the Appellate Division of the New York Supreme Court overturned the summary judgment and sent the case back for a trial. (470 N.Y.S at 383) The court's majority refused to accept *New York*'s own view of where the lines between the "newsworthy" and "editorial" pieces, as against "publications for the purposes of trade" and "advertisements in disguise," were to be drawn (470 N.Y.S. at 380).

The validity of legal-cultural boundary-drawing is particularly suspect when courts purport to draw objective lines between popular expressions "of public interest" and those about "public affairs," which are "in the public's interest to know." Richard Nixon and his loyal defenders, it might be recalled, always argued that the "Watergate episode" raised no "real" questions of public affairs; in this view "Watergate" became a subject of "public affairs" only after items of political "gossip," appropriate to the pages and the journalistic style of the *National Enquirer*, distorted popular political culture. In other words, some people's stories of fundamental political importance appear to others as "legalized pandering designed to appeal to the readers' morbid sense or curiosity." Thus, categories such as "newsworthy" are never (to use a technical legal word) "vaccuum-bounded."[19] The idea that someone can, or ever could, magically separate the complex reality of human communication into such neat, artificial categories has been ridiculed by numerous legal and media critics.

Similarly, First-Amendment commentators have used recent trends in popular literature to underscore the problems with such boundary-drawing in defamation law. Novels of "faction," such as Andrew Greeley's *The Cardinal Sins* and Robert Coover's *The Public Burning*, employ theories of knowledge that stress the impossibility of separating the "subjective" from the "objective," and they blend together fact and imagination. Yet, under conventional libel rules, Greeley's "factional" novel about the Catholic Church in Chicago would not qualify for certain defenses, such as the "actual malice" test, even though other works of non-fiction, including ones by the same author on the same subjects, would undoubtedly merit such protections. By what standards of law or of cultural criticism should "factional" works be given second-class constitutional status? Are unconventional popular authors to be treated more harshly by the courts than those who work in safe, orthodox cultural traditions? How can these types of "content distinctions" ever be applied fairly and rationally?[20]

Finally, the distinctions that many courts and even liberals such as Anthony Lewis would apparently like to make between the journalism of the *New York Times* and that of the *National Enquirer* carry their own elitist biases, ones that have come to be legitimized in legal decisions such as the *Burnett—National Enquirer* case. Yet, legal categories based solely on the content of different styles of popular journalism rest on shaky cultural ground. Such respected critics as Jacques Ellul, for example, have argued that the front pages of mainstream papers *really* take readers on excursions through the worlds of the trivial and nonsensical. To pretend that the complexities of political life, let alone of human existence, can be reduced to the neat patterns of supposed "facts" contained in mainstream journalism's pat formulae, according to Ellul, is to flee from reality into the realm of sheer "illusion."[21] Other media and legal commentators have forcefully argued that the pages of popular publications such as the *National Enquirer* feature stories "no more self-evidently absurd than the evening headlines of the *Washington Post* or lead story on *CBS Evening News*." Similarly, to millions of people, "the romantic life of Elizabeth Taylor or Michael Landon either reveals more of the human condition or provides more of a relief from the mundane routines of daily life than the statistical machinations of David Stockman."[22]

II

Hopefully, by this time, the moral of the human cannonball's flight has hit home: the traditional legal theories that have been used to deal with works of popular culture are difficult to defend in either legal or cultural terms. Legalists, for example, can offer principles that pretend to separate, on some *objective* basis, speech that is "of public interest" from trivia that merely "interests" the public, but no such effort has eliminated the element of subjectivity, the problem of personal values.[23]

Similarly, even the terms of legal argument employed in traditional First-Amendment adjudication, ones such as "newsworthy" or "of general or public interest," can be used to justify one particular course of legal action *and* precisely the opposite result, depending upon how particular judges come to frame the issues. As in other areas of law, arguments about the content of the First-Amendment status of various kinds of cultural expression can be seen as "a stylized form of rhetoric" that can be invoked either to protect or not to protect expression that is under some type of legal challenge. And as *Zacchini* demonstrates, any attempt to justify or determine a particular result by appealing to "the facts," immediately confronts the same conflict of objectivity and subjectivity embedded in First-Amendment theory itself. Such was the basic lesson taught by the "legal realists" of the 1920s and 1930s, and such is the equally disquieting message that has been revived by the "critical" legal scholars of the 1980s.[24]

Quite obviously not every legal analyst would accept this vision of the problem.[25] (Indeed, given the view of "the law" which this article employs, it would be totally inconsistent to expect universal agreement.) Yet, in recent years a new generation of First-Amendment scholars, many of whom still consider themselves "libertarians," especially when compared to positions taken by the Burger Court, has vigorously criticized earlier "libertarian" efforts to frame "general" theories and to map out "categorical" guides to First-Amendment adjudication. In a general sense, their "deconstruction" of First-Amendment paradigms first proposed in the 1950s parallels the dismantling, by recent scholars of American popular culture, of the general model of "mass culture." Just as the sweeping, abstract idea of "mass culture" has been undermined by specific studies on the *real* nature of popular culture, so have "general" First-Amendment theories and "categorical" approaches come under attack from a diverse collection of First-Amendment students, most of whom consider themselves, in one way or another, heirs of the "legal realist" tradition of the 1920s and 1930s.[26] Thus, many "realistic" and self-proclaimed "critical" legal scholars tend to agree that current First-Amendment doctrines, especially when they deal with issues involving popular culture, cannot be rationalized into clear, objective categorical principles. To continue traditional debates, making new distinctions that become more rarified and undoubtedly more artificial than the ones that preceded them, is only to travel further down a dead-end road.[27] The most pressing tasks for those interested in First-Amendment issues are the inter-related ones of "deconstructing" traditional approaches and figuring out how to construct new ones. This article, of course, has chosen the easier (and safer) task of deconstruction.

Not surprisingly, agreement between "realistic" and "critical" analysts generally ceases when the issue of "what should be done next" is asked. For most of the "radicals" the only way out of current dilemmas requires a complex process of first imagining and then experimenting with *both* new cultural and legal forms.[28] Dismissing such proposals at reconstruction as sheer "utopianism," the hard-headed realists insist that legal decision-makers must take the world essentially as it is but should openly acknowledge—as more traditional legal analysts refuse to do—the impossibility of ever drawing objective boundary lines. All First-Amendment adjudication, including that involving works of popular culture, these "realists" insist, cannot avoid difficult value decisions and case-by-case, ad hoc balancing. Moreover, they argue, judges should no longer be able to hide their value preferences behind deceptive legal formulae.[29]

For those concerned about the ambiguous and oftentimes second-class constitutional status of works of popular culture, either approach would represent an improvement over the circular and deceptive categorical paths that courts are now taking.

Notes

[1]Donald L. Gillmor and Jerome A. Barron, *Mass Communication Law*, 4th ed. (St. Paul: West Publishing, 1984), pp. 368-72.

[2]David Kairys, "Freedom of Speech," in Kairys, ed., *The Politics of Law* (New York: Pantheon, 1982), pp. 140-71, at 163.

[3]Thomas I. Emerson, "First Amendment Doctrine and the Burger Court," 68 *California Law Review* 422, at 423 (1980); Franklyn Haiman, "Comments on Martin Redish's The Warren Court, the Burger Court, and the First Amendment Overbreadth Doctrine," 78 *Northwestern University Law Review* 1071, at pp. 1071-72 (1983).

[4]For analyses that highlight the ways in which the Burger Court's free-expression decisions reflect its larger concern with property rights, see Norman Dorsen and Joel Gora, "Free Speech, Property, and the Burger Court: Old Values, New Balances," *Supreme Court Review* 195 (1982) and Mark Tushnet, "Corporations and Free Speech," in Kairys, ed., *Politics of Law*, pp. 253-61; for a critique of the "right to know" approach, see Gerald L. Baldasty and Roger A. Simpson, "The Deceptive 'Right to Know': How Pessimism Rewrote the First Amendment," 56 *Washington Law Review* 365 (1981).

[5]For an analysis of "cold-war libertarianism," see Norman L. Rosenberg, *Protecting the "Best Men": An Interpretive History of the Law of Libel* (Chapel Hill: Univ. of North Carolina Press); for a critique of "general theories" of the First Amendment, see Steven Shriffin, "The First Amendment and Economic Regulation: Away from a General Theory of the First Amendment," 78 *Northwestern University Law Review* 1212 (1983); and for a critical view of "categorical" approaches to First Amendment issues, see Pierre J. Schlag, "An Attack on Categorical Approaches of Freedom of Speech," 3 *U.C.L.A. Law Review* 671 (1983).

[6]The argument that even the "libertarian" decisions of the Warren Court ignored the power of the private mass media has been developed by a number of scholars. See, for example, Jerome A. Barron, *Public Rights and the Private Press* (Toronto: Butterworth, 1981) and David Anderson, "A Response to Professor Robertson: The Issue is Control of Press Power," 54 *Texas Law Review* 271 (1976). The Burger Court endorsed a broad view of "editorial discretion" in *Miami v. Tornillo* 418 U.S. 241 (1974).

[7]See, for example, Norman L. Rosenberg, "Thomas M. Cooley, the Law of Libel, and Liberal Jurisprudence," 4 *Puget Sound Law Review* 39 (1980) and Everette Dennis, "The Press and the Public Interest: A Definitional Dilemma," 23 *DePaul Law Review 937 (1974)*.

[8]On the inherent confusion in the idea of "actual malice," see Donald L. Gillmor, "Justice William Brennan and the Failed 'Theory' of Actual Malice," 59 *Journalism Quarterly* 249 (1982).

[9]William Cohen, "A New Niche for the Fault Principle: A Forthcoming Newsworthiness Privilege in Libel Cases," *U.C.L.A. Law Review* 371 (1970).

[10]Arthur Frakt, "Defamation Since *Gertz v. Robert Welch, Inc.*: The Emerging Common Law," 10 *Rutgers-Camden Law Journal* 471, at pp. 585-86.

[11]See Gerald Ashdown, "*Gertz* and *Firestone*: A Study in Constitutional Policy—Making," 61 *Minnesota Law Review* 645 (1977).

[12]See Ashdown, passim and Rosenberg, "Cooley," at p. 94 n. 202.

[13]Anthony Lewis, "*New York Times v. Sullivan* Reconsidered: Time to Return to 'The Central Meaning of the First Amendment'," 83 *Columbia Law Review* 603, at p. 623.

[14]*Burnett v. National Enquirer*, 7 *Media Law Reporter* 1321 (California Superior Court, Los Angeles County, 1981).

[14a]See, for example, Frederick Schauer, "Categories of the First Amendment: A Play in Three Acts," 34 *Vanderbilt Law Review* 265, at pp. 283-89 (1980) and Paul Stephen III, "The First Amendment and Content Discrimination," 68 *Virginia Law Review* 203 (1982).

[15]Lewis at p. 624.

[16]See, for example, Stanley Cohen and Jock Young, eds. *The Manufacture of News* (Beverly Hills: Sage, 1981) and Herbert I. Schiller, *Who Knows: Information in the Age of the Fortune 500* (Norwood, N.J.: Ablex Publishing, 1982).

[17]In contrast to the earlier attempts to use criminal ordinances to get at "obscenity," the newer jurisprudence aimed at "pornography" and "racial epithets" seeks to use civil lawsuits. See, for example, Ruth Colker, "Pornography and Privacy: Towards the Development of a Group Based Theory for Sex Based Intrusions of Privacy," 1 *Law and*

Inequality 191 (1983) and Richard Delgado, "Words That Wound: A Tort Action for Racial Insults, Epithets and Name-Calling," 17 *Harvard Civil Rights-Civil Liberties Law Review* 158 (1982). Thus, as in the *Zacchini* case, legal conflict pit the "right" of free speech against various "rights" asserted by individuals and groups who feel, much like libel plaintiffs, that the media has trampled their fundamental liberties.

[18]See, for example, Francis J. Flaherty, "The Law's Literary Life: Publishers Under Attack," 6 *National Law Journal* (April 2, 1984) 1.

[19]See Elizabeth Mensch, "The History of Mainstream Legal Thought," in Kairys, ed., *The Politics of Law*, pp. 23-29.

[20]See Isidore Silver, "Libel, the 'Higher Truths' of Art and the First Amendment," 126 *University of Pennsylvania Law Review* 1065 (1978) and Rodney A. Smolla, "Let the Author Beware: The Rejuvenation of the American Law of Libel," 132 *Ibid* 1 (1983), at 42-47.

[21]Jacques Ellul, *The Political Illusion* (New York: Knopf, 1967), pp. 49-67.

[22]Smolla, at 41, 41n. 193.

[23]See Gerald Frug, "The Ideology of Bureaucracy in American Law," 97 *Harvard Law Review* 1277 (1984).

[24]Frug at 1294.

[25]See, for example, Jennifer J. Martin, "What's Entertainment? An Inquiry into the Educational and Amusing Aspects of Educational Play Parks," 5 *Communication: Entertainment Law Journal* 795 (1983) (plea for "objective" standards to define "amusement" and "education")

[26]For a brief discussion of the theory of mass culture and its critics see Simon Frith, *Sound Effects: Youth, Leisure, and the Politics of Rock and Roll* (New York: Pantheon, 1982), pp. 41-48, 61-63; and for a similarly brief, but equally penetrating analysis of various periods in legal consciousness see Mensch, , pp. 18-39.

[27]For a thoughtful presentation of the neo-realist position, see Shiffrin; for a sample of more "critical" legal perspectives, see C. Edwin Baker, "The Process of Change and the Liberty Theory of the First Amendment," 55 *Southern California Law Review* 293 (1982) and Staughton Lynd, "Communal Rights," in *Information Packet and Readings, Eighth National Conference of Critical Legal Studies* (mimeo, 1984).

[28]See, for example, Frug; Lynd; and Robert Gordon, "New Developments in Legal Theory," in Kairys, ed., pp. 281-93. It should be emphasized that "critical" legal scholars are not, as their own critics sometimes charge, "nihilists." A "critical" approach requires neither the jetisoning of the idea of "law" nor of the use of legal "rules"; critical analysts insist, however, that both law and rules should be conceived and applied differently than they would be by "mainstream" liberal legalists. See, for example, Warren Lehman, "Rules in Law," 72 *Georgetown Law Journal* 1517 (1984).

[29]Steven Shiffrin, "Liberalism, Radicalism, and Legal Scholarship," 30 *U.C.L.A. Law Review* 1103 (1983). Shiffrin's thoughtful and major essay proposes an "eclectic liberalism" as the best approach to legal issues; on First-Amendment issues, he offers what might be called, in contrast to the "categorical libertarianism" of the 1940s-1960s, an "eclectic, ad hoc libertarianism." See Shiffrin, "Away from a Central Theory."

A Voyage to the Roots of the Republic

David Broder*

Imagine yourself in a school multipurpose room. It is 9:30 on a Saturday morning, with an autumn drizzle outside. About 120 men and women are sitting in a semi-circle of folding chairs. All live in northern Virginia, but their ages and occupations are as diverse as the mixture you would find in any nearby suburban shopping mall.

One man takes the podium and argues in a three-minute speech that the members of the convention which wrote the original Constitution fully intended that the people themselves would change that Constitution, as needed, by the same mechanism—a constitutional convention. "To deny that option," he says, "is to distrust the people."

The following speaker says that, of course, that method of amendment is available, but it should not be used "to deal with transient policy issues ... but only in times of supreme national catharsis." The debate swings back and forth between proponents and critics of amendments by constitutional convention, until the presiding officer opens the floor to all the "delegates." Their comments and arguments fill the air, much as they did in Philadelphia when Article V—the amendment clause—was first debated.

What is going on here? It is the Jefferson Meeting—a citizens' forum that takes the Constitution of the United States off the library shelf and makes it, once again, the center of attention for Americans concerned about the health of their Republic. They have come together for a day of intense debate, designed to stimulate their thinking on the question whether the Constitution, in these altered times, is well-adapted to serve its original ideals.

I was asked to preside at part of the Jefferson Meeting in Arlington, and I have rarely been part of a more stimulating and enjoyable gathering. It's my hope that many more communities and schools can discover the excitement of this experience.

The project was launched two years ago by a fine retired journalist, Charles Bartlett. Its aim, says Alice O'Connor, the first director, is simply to "promote discussion of the first principles of our government and

*Reprinted from *The Washington Post*, Dec. 1, 1985. Used by permission.

provide a more critical appreciation of the Constitution." It is not an advocacy group nor a forum for debating school prayer, abortion, or balanced-budget amendments.

One important ground rule is that everybody is a "delegate" and no one is introduced by reference to title or occupation. The sponsors don't want assertive experts making others behave deferentially. The rule works so well that in Williamsburg one sales-woman delegate did not discover until the end of the day that her opponent in debate, delegate Jerry Baliles, was the state attorney general—and now governor-elect.

The topics for the daylong debates are chosen from a list of six issues currently in controversy. In addition to the possibility of a new consitutional convention (to write a balanced-budget amendment or make broader changes), the topics included term limits for members of Congress and federal judges, changes in the method of electing the president and his tenure in office, the line-item veto, and the legislative veto.

Delegates are recruited from churches, clubs, civic associations, business and labor groups. They meet one evening to divide themselves into teams focusing on particular topics. The next morning those selected by their fellow delegates open the debate on each issue, and then everyone may join in. At the Arlington session we found that passions were still rising and positions were still being clarified when the 90 minutes for each topic came to a close.

We also found (and Richard Lawrence of the Virginia Jefferson Foundation says this is typical) that the debate quickly came to focus not on legalisms or mechanistic arguments but on the fundamental values embedded in the Constitution.

"Do you trust the people or not?" speakers would demand. "Our government was designed to resist the tyranny of the majority," others would reply. What some saw as elitism others saw as true republicanism. What appeared to some a radical experiment looked to others like a needed tune-up on an overworked engine.

With mounting excitement we discovered what we had forgotten: that debating the Constitution quickly leads you to think hard about the nature of society, of justice, freedom, and law. Whether one finds himself thinking, as I do on most issues, that we cannot improve on the original, or asserting, as others did so well, that reverence for the real Constitution requires revision and adaptation of its provisions, the Jefferson Meeting turns into a voyage of discovery to the roots of this Republic.

It is a trip thousands of Americans of all ages should make in the next few years. I know of no better way to celebrate—and revitalize—our magnificent two-century-old experiment in self-government.